CAMBRIDGE LIBRARY COLLECTION

Books of enduring scholarly value

British and Irish History, General

The books in this series are key examples of eighteenth- and nineteenth-century historiography which show how centuries of political, social and economic change were interpreted during the height of Britain's power. They shed light on the understanding of dynasty, religion and culture that shaped the domestic, foreign and colonial policy of the British empire.

Catalogue of the Anglo-Jewish Historical Exhibition, Royal Albert Hall, London, 1887

The pogroms in Russia following the assassination of Alexander II led many Jewish scholars in Europe to examine closely the history and culture of their people. Over three months in 1887 the Anglo-Jewish Historical Exhibition in London aimed 'to promote knowledge of Anglo-Jewish History; to create a deeper interest in its records and relics, and to aid in their preservation', while also determining 'the extent of the materials which exist for the compilation of a History of the Jews in England'. Artefacts illuminating this history, together with religious art and miscellaneous antiquities, were placed on public display and a series of lectures was given. Various academic enterprises, including the *Bibliotheca Anglo-Judaica* – also edited by Joseph Jacobs (1854–1916) and Lucien Wolf (1857–1930) and reissued in this series – were undertaken as a direct result of this important event. The descriptive catalogue of exhibits, first published in 1888, is also well illustrated with a number of full-page photographs.

Cambridge University Press has long been a pioneer in the reissuing of out-of-print titles from its own backlist, producing digital reprints of books that are still sought after by scholars and students but could not be reprinted economically using traditional technology. The Cambridge Library Collection extends this activity to a wider range of books which are still of importance to researchers and professionals, either for the source material they contain, or as landmarks in the history of their academic discipline.

Drawing from the world-renowned collections in the Cambridge University Library and other partner libraries, and guided by the advice of experts in each subject area, Cambridge University Press is using state-of-the-art scanning machines in its own Printing House to capture the content of each book selected for inclusion. The files are processed to give a consistently clear, crisp image, and the books finished to the high quality standard for which the Press is recognised around the world. The latest print-on-demand technology ensures that the books will remain available indefinitely, and that orders for single or multiple copies can quickly be supplied.

The Cambridge Library Collection brings back to life books of enduring scholarly value (including out-of-copyright works originally issued by other publishers) across a wide range of disciplines in the humanities and social sciences and in science and technology.

Catalogue of the Anglo-Jewish Historical Exhibition, Royal Albert Hall, London, 1887

COMPILED BY
JOSEPH JACOBS AND LUCIEN WOLF

CAMBRIDGE
UNIVERSITY PRESS

CAMBRIDGE UNIVERSITY PRESS

Cambridge, New York, Melbourne, Madrid, Cape Town,
Singapore, São Paolo, Delhi, Mexico City

Published in the United States of America by Cambridge University Press, New York

www.cambridge.org
Information on this title: www.cambridge.org/9781108055048

© in this compilation Cambridge University Press 2012

This edition first published 1888
This digitally printed version 2012

ISBN 978-1-108-05504-8 Paperback

It is strongly recommended to use a large reading-glass when examining the photographs in this Catalogue, as it is very difficult for the unaided eye to see the details or many of the inscriptions.

CATALOGUE

OF THE

ANGLO-JEWISH

HISTORICAL EXHIBITION

ROYAL ALBERT HALL, LONDON, 1887

COMPILED BY

JOSEPH JACOBS AND LUCIEN WOLF

ILLUSTRATED BY

FRANK HAES

PUBLICATIONS OF THE EXHIBITION COMMITTEE
No. IV.

LONDON

F. HAES, 28, BASSETT ROAD, W.

1888

NOTE.

This Illustrated Edition of the Catalogue of the Anglo-Jewish Historical Exhibition has been prepared in response to a wish generally expressed for a permanent record of the exhibits most noteworthy for their artistic value or historical associations. It has been thought desirable to add at the end a copy of the Report, which contains a short history of the Exhibition.

The negatives were taken by Mr. Frank Haes (a member of the Executive Committee) on the Eastman negative paper in McKellan's roller slide; the prints have been printed in Collotype by the Autotype Company, and are the first from such negatives which have been published in England. Some idea of the scale may be given by the labels, which were almost exactly one inch in length. The coins are of the actual size.

No. *138*

TABLE OF CONTENTS.

	PAGE
HONORARY OFFICERS AND COMMITTEES	vii
LIST OF EXHIBITORS	xiii
PREFACE	xxv

I. HISTORIC RELICS AND RECORDS.

INTRODUCTION	1
(a) Pre-Expulsion Period	7
(b) Title deeds, &c.	13
(c) Pictures, &c., of Jewish buildings.	14
(d) Trowels, &c.	18
(e) Synagogue Documents, &c.	19
(f) Personal Relics	20
(g) Montefioriana	23
(h) Autographs and Family Documents	26
(i) MSS. and Books of Historic Interest	31
(j) Beni-Israel	44
(k) Portraits	47
(l) Newman Collection.	68
(m) Miscellaneous Prints, &c.	78

II. JEWISH ECCLESIASTICAL ART.

INTRODUCTION	83

Synagogue :—

(a) Ark and Curtain	85
(b) Perpetual Lamp	86
(c) Lavers for Priests	86
(d) Scrolls of the Law, &c.	87
(e) Synagogue Decoration	96
(f) Synagogue Music	97

Home :—

(g) Mezuzoth and Misrachs	99
(h) Sabbath Requisites	100
(i) Festival Requisites	106
(j) Shekhita	114

II. Jewish Ecclesiastical Art—*continued.*

Personal :— PAGE

(*k*) Weddings 115

(*l*) Circumcision 116

(*m*) Tephillin and Talith 117

(*n*) Charms 118

(*o*) Miscellaneous 119

(*p*) Straus Collection 120

(*q*) Sassoon Collection 128

III. Antiquities.

Introduction. 133

(*a*) Manuscripts— 134

Crawford Collection 140

(*b*) Books 143

(*c*) Inscriptions, &c. 145

(*d*) Temple 146

(*e*) Palestine Exploration Fund 147

(*f*) Sandeman Collection 148

(*g*) Seals and Rings 149

IV. Coins and Medals.

Introduction, by H. Montagu, F.S.A. 151

Detailed Descriptions 158

Supplementary Exhibitions :—

(i.) Public Record Office 175

(ii.) South Kensington Museum 181

(iii.) British Museum 183

LIST OF ILLUSTRATIONS.

1. MENASSEH BEN ISRAEL (mezzotint after Rembrandt) . . *Frontispiece.*

2. BODLEIAN EWER AND ANCIENT SHOFAR . . . *Opp. page* 7

3. "AARON, SON OF THE DEVIL". . . . . „ 9

4. TWO HEBREW SHETAROTH AND LATIN STARRUM WITH JEWISH SEALS „ 11

5. CHARTER OF EDWARD I. TO CANTERBURY CATHEDRAL . . „ 12

6. OLIVER CROMWELL'S SALVER. LAVER OF GREAT SYNAGOGUE,
   AND WINE CUPS . . . . „ 20

7. MONTEFIORE TESTIMONIAL . . . . . . „ 24

8. SIGNATURES TO PETITION TO PARLIAMENT . . . „ 33

9. SMALL ARKS FOR SCROLLS OF THE LAW . . . . „ 85

10. HAMBRO' SYNAGOGUE CURTAIN . . . . . „ 86

11. SCROLL OF LAW WITH BREASTPLATE AND POINTER (belonging
    to Lord Zouch) . . . . „ 87

12. SMALL SCROLLS OF THE LAW . . . . . „ 88

13. MANTLES AND BELLS } . . . . . . „ 89

14. MANTLES AND BELLS } FOR SCROLLS OF THE LAW . „ 90

15. BREASTPLATES . } . . . . . „ 91

16. SHOFAROTH AND SABBATH LAMPS . . . . „ 97

17. KIDDUSH CUPS, SPICE BOXES, &C. . . . . „ 101

18. PASSOVER DISHES, HANUCA LAMPS, SABBATH CANDLESTICKS
    AND SHEKEL PLATE . . . . . . „ 106

19. HANUCA LAMPS . . . . „ 108

20. MEGILLOTH (Scrolls of Esther) . . . . „ 112

21. POINTERS, RINGS AND CHARMS . . . . . „ 115

22. ARK FROM MODENA FOR SCROLL OF THE LAW (Strauss Collection) „ 120

23. MARRIAGE CONTRACT (Strauss Collection) . . . „ 125

24. ILLUMINATED HAGADA (F. D. Mocatta) . . . „ 138

25. ILLUMINATED HAGADA (Lord Crawford) . . . „ 142

26. EARLY JEWISH COINS . . . . . . „ 158

27. JEWISH COINS . . . . „ 164

28. CARICATURE ON ISSUE ROLL . . . . . „ 176

CORRIGENDA.

Page	10	*for*	"temperatorum"	*read*	"dampnatorum"	(*No.* 19)
,,	20	,,	"border and handles"	,,	"handles"	(,, 616)
,,	32	,,	"No. 1030"	,,	"967 a"	(,, 788)
,,	47	,,	"chalk drawing"	,,	"mezzotint"	(,, 947)
,,	48	,,	"Studium"	,,	"Stadium"	(,, 953)
,,	60	,, .	"No. 1125"	,,	"1225"	(,, 1057)
,,	68	,,	"Wixill"	,,	"Wivell"	(,, 1131)
,,	70	,,	"McArdale"	,,	"McArdell"	(,, 1153)
,,	127	,,	"Archangel"	,,	"holy ark"	(,, 2019)
,,	141	,,	"SAMARITAN"	,,	"ARABIC"	(,, 2166)
,,	153	,,	"trouville"	,,	"*trouvaille*"	
,,	154	,,	"ωHP"	,,	"HPΩ"	
,,	156	,,	"Jews under"	,,	"Jews. Under"	
,,	161	,,	"ΕΑΛΥΚΥΙΑΣ"	,,	"ΕΑΛΩΚΥΙΑΣ"	(,, 2347)

ADDENDA.

[Received during the course of the Exhibition.]

THREE SCROLLS OF LAW.   *Count Camondo, Paris.*
Written in India. Mounted in Ivory.

ANCIENT SCROLL OF LAW.   *Lord Zouch.*
With quaint bells and appurtenances. [See Illustration 11.]

AUTOGRAPH LETTER OF CHARLES II. AS PRINCE OF WALES.   *E. Lucas.*
Dated 1648. From the Hague, acknowledging receipt of loan of £300 from
Jewish merchants.

HEBREW BIBLE.   *A. Mocatta.*
On which Jewish Lord Mayors of London were sworn in. With Inscriptions.

SCROLL OF THE LAW.   *Dr. Goldschmidt, Leipzic.*
Written on deerskin by order of Rev. Solomon Hirschell, who employed ten
Rabbis to study the Talmud while it was being written.

MINIATURE PORTRAIT OF ABRAHAM LUMBROSO DE MATTOS MOCATTA.
                                                              F. D. Mocatta.
Philanthropist and Communal worker, 1730–1800.

MINIATURE PORTRAIT OF ESTHER MOCATTA.   *F. D. Mocatta.*
Wife of preceding, daughter of Isaac Lamego, 1737–1799.

ANGLO-JEWISH HISTORICAL EXHIBITION.

An Exhibition illustrating Anglo-Jewish History and Jewish
Ecclesiastical Art, at the Royal Albert Hall, Kensington,
with the following objects:—

1. To promote a knowledge of Anglo-Jewish History; to create a
   deeper interest in its records and relics, and to aid in their
   preservation.
2. To determine the extent of the materials which exist for the
   compilation of a History of the Jews in England.

Chairman.
F. D. MOCATTA, Esq.

Vice-Chairman.
JOHN EVANS, Esq., D.C.L., F.R.S.,
President Society of Antiquaries, Treasurer Royal Society.

Chairman Literary and Art Sub-Committee.
CHARLES TRICE MARTIN, Esq., B.A., F.S.A.

Treasurer.
J. N. CASTELLO, Esq., B.A.

Hon. Secretaries.
Rev. MORRIS JOSEPH.
I. SPIELMAN, Esq., Assoc. M.I.C.E.

Hon. Sec. Literary and Art Sub-Committee.
JOSEPH JACOBS, Esq., B.A.

Assistant Secretary.
P. ORNSTIEN.

General Committee.

Rev. Dr. ADLER, Chief Rabbi.

Rev. Dr. H. ADLER.

MARCUS N. ADLER, Esq., M.A.

A. ASHER, Esq., M.D.

Rev. S. A. BARNETT, M.A.

ALFRED H. BEDDINGTON, Esq.

H. BEHREND, Esq., M.D.

WALTER BESANT, Esq., M.A., Sec. Pal. Ex. Fund.

S. R. SCARGILL - BIRD, Esq., F.S.A.

Rev. Canon BOGER.

ROBERT BROWNING, Esq., LL.D.

ERNEST DE BUNSEN, Esq., Ph.D.

M. CASTELLO, Esq.

J. DE CASTRO, Esq.

Rev. Canon CHEYNE.

THOMAS CHRISTY, Esq., F.L.S.

HYDE CLARKE, Esq., V.P., R. HIST. SOC.

ALFRED L. COHEN, Esq.

Rev. FRANCIS L. COHEN.

LIONEL L. COHEN, Esq., M.P.

H. H. COLLINS, Esq., F.R.I.B.A.

FREDERIC H. COWEN, Esq.

Professor CREIGHTON.

CHARLES DAVIS, Esq.

FREDK. DAVIS, Esq.

ISRAEL DAVIS, Esq., M.A.

MAURICE DAVIS, Esq., M.D.

M. D. DAVIS, Esq.

Lord DENMAN.

Rev. Canon DRIVER.

Sir BARROW ELLIS, K.C.S.I.

LEWIS EMANUEL, Esq.

Rev. J. T. FOWLER, M.A., F.S.A.

ELLIS A. FRANKLIN, Esq.

M. FRIEDLANDER, Esq., Ph.D.

FRANCIS GALTON, Esq., M.A., F.R.S., President Anthropological Institute.

Rev. Dr. M. GASTER,

JAMES GLAISHER, Esq., Chairman Pal. Ex. Fund.

Sir JULIAN GOLDSMID, Bart., M.A. M.P.

Major GOLDSMID, D.A.Q.M.G.

FREDK. GOODALL, Esq., R.A.

H. GUEDALLA, Esq.

FRANK HAES, Esq.

Rev. M. HAINES.

A. HARTSHORNE, Esq., F.S.A.

Rev. H. R. HAWEIS, M.A.

J. R. HERBERT, Esq., R.A.

W. HOLMAN HUNT, Esq.

A. H. JESSEL, Esq.

EDWARD JOSEPH, Esq.

GEORGE JOSEPH, Esq., B.A.

WALTER JOSEPHS, Esq.

M. ZADAC KAHN, Grand Rabbin de Paris.

Rev. BROOKE LAMBERT, M.A.

Sir E. LECHMERE, Bart., M.P., M.A., F.S.A.

S. LEVY, Esq.

Rev. S. S. LEWIS, M.A., F.S.A.

W. S. LILLY, Esq.

J. M. LISSACK, Esq., Jun.

ISIDORE LOEB, Esq., Paris.

Dr. L. LOEWE, M.R.A.S.

Rev. W. H. LOWE, M.A.

Rev. A. LÖWY.

HENRY LUCAS, Esq.

SEYMOUR LUCAS, Esq., A.R.A.

JOHN MACGREGOR, Esq., M.A.

F. W. MADDEN, Esq. M.R.A.S.

Sir PHILIP MAGNUS, B.A., B.Sc.

Rev. Professor MARKS.

H. J. MATHEWS, Esq., M.A.

Professor MELDOLA, F.R.S.

HORATIO LUCAS MICHOLLS, Esq.

H. MONTAGU, Esq., F.S.A.,
V.P. Numismatic Soc.

SAMUEL MONTAGU, Esq., M.P.

CLAUDE G. MONTEFIORE, Esq.,
M.A.

A. SEBAG-MONTEFIORE, Esq.

J. SEBAG-MONTEFIORE, Esq.

LESLIE MONTEFIORE, Esq.

WALTER MORRISON, Esq., M.P.

ASSUR H. MOSES, Esq.

A. MYERS, Esq.

ASHER I. MYERS, Esq.

BENJAMIN NEWGASS, Esq.

LAURENCE OLIPHANT, Esq.

W. H. OVERALL, Esq.

Earl PERCY, Pres. Royal Archæological Inst.

JAMES PICCIOTTO, Esq.

REGINALD STUART POOLE, Esq.,
British Museum.

F. G. HILTON PRICE, Esq., F.S.A.

M. ERNST RENAN.

P. LE PAGE RENOUF, Esq., Pres.
Soc. Bib. Archæology.

B. W. RICHARDSON, Esq., M.D.,
F.R.S.

Rev. WILLIAM ROGERS, M.A.

Lord ROTHSCHILD.

Baron FERDINAND DE ROTHSCHILD,
M.P.

LEOPOLD DE ROTHSCHILD, Esq.

WALTER RYE, Esq.

W. H. RYLANDS, Esq., F.S.A.,
Sec. Soc. Bib. Archæology.

CHAS. K. SALAMAN, Esq., Hon.
Mem. Acad. St. Cecilia, Rome,
Vice-Pres. Mus. Assoc. Lond.,
&c., &c.

JOHN SAMUEL, Esq.

STUART M. SAMUEL, Esq.

Sir SAUL SAMUEL, K.C.M.G., C.B.

ARTHUR D. SASSOON, Esq.

Sir ALBERT SASSOON, K.C.S.I.

J. BRIGSTOCKE SHEPPARD, Esq.,
LL.D.

Sir JOHN SIMON, M.P.

Rev. S. SINGER.

HENRY SOLOMON, Esq.

I. SOLOMONS, Esq.

M. H. SPIELMANN, Esq.

Viscountess STRANGFORD.

Miss ANNA SWANWICK.

Professor SYLVESTER, F.R.S.

Archdeacon WATKIN.

A. WERTHEIMER, Esq.

The Very Rev. The DEAN OF
WESTMINSTER.

LUCIEN WOLF, Esq.

Rev. CHAS. H. H. WRIGHT, D.D.,
M.A., Ph.D.

Rev. W. WRIGHT, D.D., Brit.
For. Bible Soc.

Lord WYNFORD.

Lady WYNFORD.

Executive Committee.

Rev. Dr. H. Adler.
J. N. Castello, Esq., B.A.
John Evans, Esq., D.C.L., F.R.S.
Charles Davis, Esq.
Israel Davis, Esq., M.A.
Major Goldsmid, D.A.Q.M.G.
Frank Haes, Esq.
Joseph Jacobs, Esq., B.A.
Edward Joseph, Esq.
Rev. M. Joseph.
Rev. A Löwy.

F. W. Madden, Esq., M.R.A.S.
Charles Trice Martin, Esq., B.A., F.S.A.
F. D. Mocatta, Esq.
J. Sebag-Montifiore, Esq.
Asher I. Myers, Esq.
James Picciotto, Esq.
W. H. Rylands, Esq.
I. Spielman, Esq., Assoc. M.I.C.E.
Lucien Wolf, Esq.

Literary and Art Sub-Committee.

J. M. Castello, Esq., B.A.
Rev. F. L. Cohen.
Charles Davis, Esq.
M. D. Davis, Esq.
John Evans, Esq., D.C.L., F.R.S.
Rev. Dr. M. Gaster.
J. Jacobs, Esq., B.A., Hon. Sec.
Rev. Morris Joseph.
Rev. A. Löwy.

Charles Trice Martin, Esq., B.A., F.S.A., Chairman.
F. D. Mocatta, Esq.
Asher J. Myers, Esq.
J. Picciotto, Esq.
W. H. Rylands, Esq.
I. Spielman, Esq., Assoc. M.I.C.E.
Lucien Wolf, Esq.

Music Committee.

D. Barathy, Esq.
Rev. F. L. Cohen.
F. H. Cowen, Esq.
D. M. Davis, Esq.
Rev. M. Hast.

Rev. H. R. Haweis.
B. L. Mosely, Esq.
J. Oppenheimer, Esq.
Henri de Sola, Esq.
Dr. C. G. Verrinder.

List of Guarantors.

A. H. Beddington, Esq.

Dr. H. Behrend.

J. N. Castello, Esq., B.A.

M. Castello, Esq.

Lionel L. Cohen, Esq., M.P.

Charles Davis, Esq.

Ellis A. Franklin, Esq.

Sir Julian Goldsmid, Bart., M.P.

Edward Joseph, Esq.

Henry Lucas, Esq.

F. D. Mocatta, Esq.

Hyman Montagu, Esq.

Samuel Montagu, Esq., M.P.

A. Sebag-Montefiore, Esq.

J. Sebag-Montefiore, Esq., J.P.

Benjamin Newgass, Esq.

The Rt. Hon. Lord Rothschild.

Baron F. de Rothschild.

John Samuel, Esq.

Stuart M. Samuel, Esq.

Sir Albert Sassoon, K.C.S.I.

Henry Solomon, Esq.

I. Spielman, Esq.

Asher Wertheimer, Esq.

LIST OF EXHIBITORS.

ABECASIS, Mrs. J. S., 53, Sutherland Avenue, 1715.

ABRAHAM & SONS, Commercial Street, Whitechapel, 1643.

ADLER, Rev. Dr. H., Delegate Chief Rabbi, 5, Queensborough Terrace, 637, 813, 828–831, 854, 860, 869, 874, 894, 895, 898, 899, 905, 941, 942, 952, 962, 987, 1685, 1757, 2086, 2087, 2093–2096, 2107, 2108, 2240, 2241, 2291.

ADLER, M. N., M.A., 21, Queensborough Terrace, 759, 1649, 1650, 1855, 2191, 2204, 2601–2605.

ADLER, Rev. Dr. N. M., Chief Rabbi, 36, First Avenue, Brighton, 523, 524, 583, 585, 586, 625, 628, 776, 777, 791, 811, 861, 862, 783, 1450, 1460, 1515, 2116, 2135, 2205.

AGUILAR, The Misses, 91, Maryland Road, W., 532, 764, 972, 1686.

ALMOSNINO, Mrs., 1, Hawley Place, W., 1394, 2625.

ALLIANCE ASSURANCE COMPANY, St. Bartholomew Lane, E.C., 646, 1047

ARTOM, Mrs., 43, Fisbury Road, West Brighton, 1716.

ASCHER, Rev. B. H., 97, Highbury New Park, 549, 863, 1617, 1717.

ASHER, A., M.D., 18, Endsleigh Street, W.C., 619.

ASSOCIATION FOR RELIGIOUS KNOWLEDGE, 812.

D'AVIGDOR, E. H., Manor House, Bushey, Herts, 1723.

D'AZEVEDO, Miss, Portuguese Buildings, Heneage Lane, 974, 1255

BABINGTON, Rev. C. C., M.A., 2556–2598.

BACH & Co., Norwich, 7, 8.

BALLIOL COLLEGE, Oxford, 511, 2082, 2088.

BARNED, J. L., 10, Cambridge Square, W., 569, 590.

BARNED, H., 10, Cambridge Square, W., 560, 573, 633, 590, 997, 1000a, 1000b, 1109a, 1635, 1651.

BARNETT, Miss REIKA, 26, Marquess Road, N., 1101.

BARTLETT, Messrs., 18, Blenheim Street, Great Marlborough Street, 2151–2253.

BENAS, B. L., 5, Princes Avenue, Liverpool, 807, 1364, 1652, 1653, 1719, 1758, 2599, 2600.

BENI ISRAEL, 906–939.

BENJAMIN, D., 86, Westbourne Terrace, 540, 551, 594, 588, 1618, 1640.

BENRIMO, Miss, 28, Formosa Street, W., 1720.

BERLIN, N. I., 1593a.

BERLIN, Rev. B., 1535, 1759.

BERLIN, Rev. Dr. M., 15, Upper Alma Street, Newport, Mon., 1552.

BERLIN, N. T., 4, Oakley Crescent, City Road, 630–632, 638, 794–796, 1073, 1554, 1837, 1842, 1867.

BERLINER, Dr. A., 516.

BERLINER, Rev. B., 6, Marlborough Place, 1535.

BERLYN, W. A., N. Kaizersgracht, Amsterdam, 1553.

BERNAYS, L., 1709a.

BETH HAMIDRASH, St. James' Place, Aldgate, 779–782, 786–789, 792, 798, 876
    893, 897, 940, 1007, 1080, 1718, 2127, 2128.
BLOK, Dr. M., 1845.
BOARD OF DEPUTIES, BRITISH JEWS, 615.
BOARD OF GUARDIANS (Jewish), Devonshire Square, E.C., 1100.
BODLEIAN LIBRARY, Oxford, 1.
BRANDON, Miss, J. R., 53, Sutherland Avenue, 2192–2194.
BRESLAU SEMINARY, 774, 2133, 2134.
BROMLEY, Mrs. E., 12 Eccleston Square, 1841, 1892.
BROWNING, R., 19, Warwick Crescent, 2206, 2207.

CANTERBURY CATHEDRAL, DEAN AND CHAPTER OF, 508, 509.
CARVALHO, Mrs. S. N., 8, Inverness Terrace, 1555.
CASTELLO, J. N., The Roccles, West Hill, Sydenham, 1610.
CASTELLO, MANUEL, 979.
CASTELLO, Mrs. D., 960, 986, 1760.
CASTRO, J. DE, 12, Leinster Square, 627, 627a, 1044, 1721, 1761, 1868, 2195, 2208,
CITY OF LONDON SCHOOL, 1066.
COHEN, Dr. A., 10, Stranraer Place, W., 742, 743, 1654.
COHEN, A., 10, Maida Vale, 1462, 1611.
COHEN, A. L., 106, Westbourne Terrace, 1071, 1536.
COHEN, B. and A., 92, High Street, E., 1463–1465, 1495, 1655, 1722.
COHEN, B. L., 30, Hyde Park Gardens, 980, 1036, 1054, 1070, 1386, 2115, 2196,
    2197.
COHEN, Rev. F. L., Synagogue Chrs., Vowler Street, Walworth, 1537, 1538, 1556,
    1557.
COHEN, H. L., 2, Cleveland Terrace, 1057, 1634.
COHEN, I. M., 6, Wharf Road, Stockton-on-Tees,
COHEN, L. A., 49, Vyse Street, Birmingham, 1264, 1461, 1539, 1656, 1762, 1763,
    1897.
COHEN, Mrs. LIONEL L., 9, Hyde Park Terrace, 1657.
COHEN, Miss L., 5, Great Stanhope Street, 1634, 1822.
COHEN, SAMUEL I., Great St. Helens, E.C., 1001.
COHEN, Mrs. S., 5, Clanricarde Gardens, 624.
COHEN, W. H., 21, Hamilton Terrace, 1644, 1687, 1850, 2284–2286.
COHEN, WOOLF H., 82, Strand, 1316, 1599.
COHEN, L., Chichester Place, Harrow Road, 1109, 1762, 1763, 1822, 1897.
COLLINS, H. H., 534, 542a, 542b, 548a, 553, 554.
COLLINS, Rev. G. W., M.A., Corpus Christi College, Cambridge, 515.
CORTISSOS, Miss C., Jews' Infant School, Heneage Lane, 955, 2141.
CRAWFORD, Right Hon. the Earl of, 2, Cavendish Square, 2155–2190.

DAVIDS, Master SL., 41, Hanway Street, 857.
DAVIDSON, Rev. E. A., 1540.
DAVIDSON, STRACHAN J. L., Balliol College, Oxford, 2606–2608.
DAVIS, C. S., 27, Wallace Road, N., 1081.
DAVIS, D. M., R.A.M., 36, Walterton Road, 1558–1565.
DAVIS, F., 24, Park Crescent, 1724–1726, 1869–1871.
DAVIS, J., 35, Compton Terrace, 1496.
DAVIS, M., M.D., 11, Brunswick Square, 653, 705, 707, 710, 712, 717, 725, 730,
    731, 737, 741, 747–751, 752–755.
DAVIS, EMANUEL, Messrs., 2, Finsbury Circus, 541, 541a, 543b, 563, 566, 567, 568,
    570.

DIRECTOR OF JEWISH MEAT MARKET, Vienna, 1818.
DURLACHER, A., **1286, 1566.**

ELLIS, C. J., **1872.**
ELLIS, GEORGE, 8, Bolton Road, St. John's Wood, 678, 1084, 1265.
ELLIS, Sir J. WHITTAKER, Bart., 801.
EMANUEL, EMANUEL, J.P., Grove House, Southsea, 832.
EMANUEL, LEWIS, 91, Gloucester Terrace, W., 651, 679, 713–715, 721, 724, 726,
    727, 740, 873, 1078, 1113, 1764, 1765.
EMANUEL, LEWIS, High Holborn, 1315
EMANUEL, P. H., 12, Ordnance Row, Portsea, 1266.
EVANS, Dr. JOHN, F.R.S., Nash Mills, Hemel Hempstead, 1414, 1823, 1824,
    1828, 1873, 1874, 2287, 2288, 2469 2517.

FALK, P., 23, Kensington Palace Gardens, W., **1658, 1712, 2209.**
FINZI, S. L., 94, Oxford Gardens, West Kensington, W., 1016.
FONSECA, Mrs. R. H., 49, Westbourne Park Crescent, W., 1079.
FOWLER, Rev. J. T., M.A., F.S.A., Durham, 1688, 1755, 1875, 2244–2247, 2624.
FRANKENSTEIN, S., 19, Tenter Street, E., 1727.
FRANKLIN, A. E., 28, Pembridge Villas, W., 1782.
FRANKLIN, Mrs., **1646.**
FRANKLIN, E. A., 35, Porchester Terrace, Hyde Park, W., 1876, 1877.
FRANKLIN, E. G., **1395, 1689, 1728, 1729.**
FRANKLIN, E. L., 9, Pembridge Gardens, W., 1619, 1645, 1766, 1862.
FRANKS, A., 4, Hutchinson Street, E., 1267.
FRAZER, Dr. W., 20, Harcourt Street, Dublin, 959, 964.
FRIEDLANDER, ARTHUR M., 21, Sutherland Gardens, W., 1567.
FRY, THEODORE, M.P., Woodbourne, near Darlington, 1396, 1777.
FUNKENSTEIN, S., 105, Praed Street, W., 2248.

GALTON, F., F.R.S., 42, Rutland Gate, S.W., 1280.
GINSBURG, Rev. C. D., **2119–2123.**
GOLDBERG, H., **1642a.**
GOLDSCHMIDT, Messrs., care of Mr. Edward Joseph, 158, New Bond Street, W.,
    2083.
GOLDSMID, Major A., Hartley Villa, Holland Street, Kensington, 744, 992, 1659,
    1730, 1783, 1784, 1863.
GOLDSMID, Sir J., M.P., St. John's Lodge, Regent's Park, N.W., 775, 799, 820,
    1017, 1028, 1042, 1056, 2070–2080.
GOLDSMID, Lady LOUISA, St. John's Lodge, Regent's Park, N.W., 1089.
GOLDSMID, Miss, 26, Cambridge Square, W., 948, 994, 1043.
GOLDSMID, Mrs. Y., 31, Lexham Gardens, W., 990, 991, 1000.
GOLDSTEIN, Miss SOPHIA, 5, London Road, Southwark, 1856.
GOLDSTONE, JOSEPH, 5, Artillery Street, E., 2626.
GOLLANCZ, Rev. S. M., 154, Houndsditch, E., 1365, 1405, 1451, 1525, 1541, 1785,
    2114, 2210.
GOODMAN, Mrs., 21, Blenheim Crescent, Notting Hill, 1091.
GROENWOOD, H., 86, Newington Green Road, N., 1786.
GUEDALLA, H., 30 Connaught Square, W., 842, 847, 852, 870, 989a, 998a, 1018a,
    **1397, 1517, 1568–1571, 1713, 1731, 2092, 2105, 2106, 2126, 2136, 2138,
    2139a, 2211.**

HAËS, F., 28, Bassett Road, W., 15, 17, 513, 514, 634, 837, 1005, 1542.
HANRECK, G., 117, Bethnal Green Road, 1467, 1591.

HAMBURGER, LEOPOLD, Frankfurt-am-Main, 2301-2468.

HARRIS, HENRY, 22, Great Prescott Street, 1398.

HARRIS, H. S., 63, Coleman Street, E.C., 719.

HARRIS, M., 38, Warrington Crescent, 858, 1015.

HARRIS, Rev. R., 77, Sutherland Gardens, 956, 1732.

HARRIS, Rev. S. H., Jews' Hospital and Orphan Asylum, 790.

HARRIS, S., C.C., 38, Pembridge Villas, 733, 735, 736.

HART, J. L., 20, Pembridge Square, W., 1812, 2619.

HART, S., 8, Jewry Street, Aldgate, 1594.

HARTOG, Madame, 5, Portsdown Road, W., 1120, 1692, 1733.

HAST, Rev. M., 21, Great Prescott Street, E., 1572-1574, 1690, 1734.

HAWEIS, Rev. H. R., Cheyne Walk, Chelsea, 1112.

HAYMAN, S., 61, Cable Street, St. George's, E., 1261.

HEAL, AMBROSE, Amidia, Crouch End, N., 1293-1304.

HENRIQUES, Mrs. D., 2, Chester Place, Hyde Park, 650, 1053a.

HENRIQUES, J. A., 1041a.

HERBERT, M. H., 73, Gunterstone Road, West Kensington, 853.

HEYMANN, B., Hamburg House, Percival Road, Clifton, near Bristol, 693, 2609.

HOFFNUNG, S., 3, Hyde Park Gate, S.W., 1399.

HORN, Mrs., 1452, 1466, 1660, 1691.

HUNT, W. HOLMAN, 1754, 1849a.

HYAM, H. L., 57, Mildmay Grove, 552.

HYAM, P., Chatham Synagogue, 1595.

ISAAC, R. C., 94, Belsize, Road, N.W., 1278a.

ISAACS, LEWIS, 3, Victoria Chambers, Aldgate, 1291, 1292, 2110.

JACOBS, A. M., 18, Cross Street, Hatton Garden, 1661.

JACOBS, Mrs. G., 2, Portsdown Road, 1878.

JACOBS, JOSEPH, B.A., 88, Shirland Gardens, 517-520, 530, 531, 564, 835, 871, 872, 896, 900, 1334-1360.

JACOBS, MARK, 8, Grafton Street, Mile End Road, 1620, 1662.

JACOBS, SAMUEL, 4, Victoria Square, Temple Street, Bristol, 521a.

JACOBS, Mrs. R., 123, Highbury New Park, 1290.

JAMES, EDMUND, 3, Temple Gardens, Temple, E.C., 1613, 1614, 1621, 1663, 1664.

JESSEL, A. H., 1787.

JEWS' COLLEGE, Tavistock House, Tavistock Square, 808, 821-827, 836, 839, 2146-2148.

JEWS' FREE SCHOOL, Bell Lane, Spitalfields, 522, 626a, 1022, 1055, 1068, 1090, 1105, 1115, 1116.

JEWS' HOSPITAL AND ORPHAN ASYLUM, West Norwood, 557, 561, 993, 996, 1021, 1026, 1097, 1497.

JONES, D., 1864.

JOSEPH EDWARD, 138, New Bond Street, 1252, 1387, 1468, 1543, 1665, 1693, 1694, 1788-1790, 1825, 1829, 1848, 1857, 2101, 2102.

JOSEPH, Mrs. HENRY, 1622.

JOSEPH, Mrs. H., 636.

JOSEPH, ISAAC, Buscot Lodge, Warwick Road, 1666.

JOSEPH, Rev. M., 9, Carfield Gardens, N.W., 545, 574, 804-806, 868, 1575, 1596, 1894.

JOSEPH, N. S., 34, Inverness Terrace, 562, 976, 1735.

JOSEPH, Mrs. S., 38, Queenborough Terrace, W., 623, 1695.

JOSEPHS, WALTER, 751a, 757, 809, 810, 1020.

KEIZER, Rev. M., 17, Brondesbury Road, Kilburn, **1576.**
KEYSER, Mrs. E., 25, Craven Hill Gardens, **1778.**
KING, Rev. C. W., Trinity College, Cambridge, **12.**
KISCH, HENRY, 4 Brick Court, Temple, **1638.**
KOHN, ZEDEK, 61, Mildmay Road, N., **840, 856, 2129.**
KRAILSHEIMER, JULIUS, 10, Throgmorton Avenue, E.C., **1454, 1469.**

LAMBERT, Rev. BROOKE, M.A., The Vicarage, Greenwich Park, **1380, 1609.**
LAMBERT & Co., Coventry Street, W., **1455, 1667, 1791–1793.**
LAWTON, EPHRAIM, Southend-on-Sea, Essex, **542.**
LAZARUS, JACOB, 10, Hove Street, Bedford Square, **1014.**
LEVI, Mrs. A., Kilburn Priory, 2, **761, 1010, 1257, 1269, 1668.**
LEVIN, LEWIN, 1, Bevis Marks, E.C., **1633.**
LEVY, AUGUSTUS SAMUEL, 3, Windermere Terrace, Princes Park, Liverpool, **1779.**
LEVY, B., **966.**
LEVY, D. A., 43, Lanark Villas, Maida Vale, W., **978, 998, 1597.**
LEVY, HENRY, Gertrude House, St. Mark Street, E., **841.**
LEVY, Rev. H. P., 10, Gloucester Street, Middlesborough, **526.**
LEVY, Miss KATE, 481, Caledonian Road, **1794, 1879.**
LEVY, LEWIS, York House, Bow Road, E., **1600.**
LEVY, SOLOMON, 4, Edith Road, West Kensington, **1415, 1648, 2139.**
LEWIS, Mrs. DAVID, Devonshire House, Princes Park, Liverpool, **845, 1013, 1470, 1623–1625, 1647, 1669, 1696, 1736, 2139.**
LEWIS, LEWIS, 4, The Drive, West Brighton, **619, 1636, 2113.**
LEWIS, Rev. S. S., Corpus Christi College, Cambridge, **11, 2541–2555.**
LINDO, ARTHUR, 71, Shooter's Hill Road, Blackheath, **1737.**
LINDO, E. A., 20, Woburn Place, W.C., **1781.**
LINDO, E. H., Spanish and Portuguese Synagogue, Bevis Marks, E.C., **533.**
LINDO, Miss, 12, St. Petersburgh Place, Bayswater Road, W., **2142–2145.**
LINDO, Miss, 20, Warwick Road, W., **802, 803, 953.**
LINZBERG, M., 113, Sandringham Road, West Hackney, **556, 1626, 2291.**
LION, EMANUEL, 65, Marquess Road, N., **1895.**
LIPMAN, Rev. N., 53, Great Prescott Street, **1400.**
LIVERPOOL NEW SYNAGOGUE, **546.**
LOCKETT, A., **525.**
LOEB, ISIDORE, Paris, **2217–2239.**
LOEWE, Dr. L., Oscar Villas, Broadstairs, Kent, **2610–2618.**
LOWENTHAL, LEOPOLD, 78, Elgin Avenue, St. Peter's Park, **2293.**
LÖWY, Rev. A., 100, Sutherland Gardens, W., **1061.**
LUBLIN, Miss JOSEPHINE, 1, Stanhope Terrace, Regent's Park, N.W. **666.**
LYON, G. L., 8, South Street, E.C., **739, 1008, 1260, 1598, 1780, 2289**
LYON, Messrs. M. and S., 135, High Holborn, **1627, 1851.**
LYONS, Rev. S., 4, Charlotte Street, Portland Place, **1268.**

MACKINNON, W., per Mr. Bartlett, 18, Blenheim Street, Great Marlborough Street, **2249, 2250, 2254.**
MAGDALEN COLLEGE, Oxford, **510.**
MARIANS, M., 50, Bassett Road, Notting Hill, **1589.**
MARKS, Rev. Professor, 34, Upper Berkeley Street, W., **620, 1795.**
MARKS, EMANUEL, 16, Marlborough Hill, N.W., **1305–1312.**
MARTIN, CHARLES TRICE, B.A., F.S.A., Public Record Office, **3, 16.**
MELDOLA, Professor R., 6, Brunswick Square, W.C., **760, 760a, 760b, 989, 1064, 2212.**

b

MENDELSSOHN, H. S., 14, Pembridge Crescent, W., 1117.
MERTON, Mrs. B., 77, Westbourne Terrace, W., 1046.
MERTON, J. S., 10, Kilburn Priory, N.W., 1390.
MOCATTA, A. DE MATTOS, 47, Gloucester Square, W., 655, 716, 800, 951.
MOCATTA, F. D., 9, Connaught Place, W., 655, 1263, 1697, 1738, 1796, 1797,
    2103, 2104, 2112, 2117, 2118, 2140, 2199, 2200.
MONTAGU, HYMAN, F.S.A., 34, Queen's Gardens, Hyde Park, W., 692, 696,
    1798, 1852, 2518-2538.
MONTAGU, SAMUEL, M.P., 12, Kensington Palace Gardens, W., 591, 616, 580, 587,
    1279, 1471, 1495, 1615, 1670, 1799, 1800, 1826, 2089, 2623, 2623a.
MONTEFIORE, A. M. SEBAG, 13, Westbourne Terrace, W., 685.
MONTEFIORE, CECIL SEBAG, 1842a.
MONTEFIORE, JACOB, 35, Hyde Park Square, W., 971, 1043a.
MONTEFIORE, Mrs. J. M., 4, Great Stanhope Street, Mayfair, 1102.
MONTEFIORE, J. SEBAG, 40, Westbourne Terrace, W., 657-659, 667, 686, 1052a.
MORO, G. DI R., West View, Goldsmith's Gardens, Acton, 1072, 1592, 1712a, 1739,
    1817, 1817a, 1838, 1846, 1880, 1881, 2201.
MORJOSEPH, A., St. Mary's Chambers, St. Mary Axe, E.C., 635.
MORRIS, N., 1453.
MOSELEY, A., 998a.
MOSELEY, H. P., 2116a.
MOSES, A. H., 33, Devonshire Place, Portland Place, W., 1628.
MOSS, MAURICE, 76, Ladbroke Grove Road, W., 1009, 1601.
MOSTYN, A., 13 Randolph Gardens, Maida Vale, N.W., 600.
MYERS, ASHER I., 42, Oxford Road, Kilburn, N.W., 13, 642, 718, 865, 875, 1037,
    758.
MYERS, BARNETT, 9, Chester Terrace, Regents Park, N.W., 1629.
MEYERS, Mrs. HANNAH, 11, Randolph Gardens, W., 1289.
MYER, SYDNEY, 21, Sutherland Avenue, W., 1059, 2620.

NAHON, JUDAH, 74, Queensborough Terrace, W., 1085, 1593, 1602, 1671, 1858,
    1882-1884, 1899, 2091a.
NAHON, Rev. S., Chief Rabbi, Tetwan, 1418.
NATHAN, MICHALL, S., 21, Bedford Square, W.C., 647.
NELSON BARNET, 63, Corporation Street, Middlesborough, 640.
NEUMEGEN, Mrs., Gloucester House, Kew, 1063, 1363, 1366, 1401, 1472, 1544,
    1672, 1801.
NEWMAN, the late A. A., 36, Westbourne Park Villas, 1121a-1250, 1673
NEWMAN, Mrs. A., 848, 849, 1121.
NEWMAN, S., 1, Woodsom Villas, Westbourne Road, Forest Hill, 2294.

OLIPHANT LAURENCE, Haifa, 2150.
OVEN, L. VAN, 954a.
OPPENHEIM, SAMUEL S., 27, Cleveland Gardens, W., 621.

PALESTINE EXPLORATION FUND, 1, Adam Street, Adelphi, W.C., 2256-2270.
PARIENTE, S., 2137.
PASS, Mrs. M. DE, 23, Norfolk Square, W., 1802.
PHILLIPS, H., 11, Commercial Street, Whitechapel, 1417.
PHILLIPS, Rev. ISAAC, Synagogue Chambers, Portsea,
PHILLIPS, S. J., 113, New Bond Street, W., 1702, 1853, 1885, 2202, 2295.
PLATNAUER BROS. Bristol, 548b.

PLYMOUTH HEBREW CONGREGATION, Catherine Street, Plymouth, 524, 614, 1041*b*.
POLACK, Rev. L., 20, Portland Street, Finsbury Park, 547.
PRAAG, W. VAN, 107, Sutherland Gardens, W., 591.
PRICE, J., 20, Catherine Wheel Alley, E.C., 1391, 1402.
PYKE, JOSEPH, Devonshire Place House, Devonshire Place, 1499, 1886.

QUARITCH BERNARD, 15, Piccadilly, W., 2084, 2085, 2091, 2098, 2099, 2111, 2149, 2213-2215.

RAALTE B. VAN, 19, Lisle Street, Leicester Square, W., 1523, 1524.
RAPHAEL, M. N., 12, Little St. Andrew St., Upper St. Martin's Lane, W.C., 593.
RASSAM, H., 10, Rochester Gardens, Brighton, 2282, 2283.
RHEINBERG, N., 64, Pryland Road, N., 1698, 1833.
ROCO, Rev. S. J., 1, Heneage Lane, Bevis Marks, E.C., 1674, 1866.
ROSEBERY, Earl and Countess of, 1103, 1103*a*.
ROTHSCHILD, L., 5, Hamilton Place, W., 594, 1361, 1630, 1675, 1676, 1703, 1849, 2203, 2255.
RUBENSTEIN, S. J., 57, Oxford Gardens, Notting Hill, 844, 850, 1313, 1314.
RYLANDS, W. H., 11, Hart Street, Bloomsbury, W.C., 618.

ST. PAULS CATHEDRAL, DEAN AND CHAPTER, 500-507.
SALAMAN, C. K., 24, Sutherland Gardens, W., 654, 720, 728, 734.
SALOMON, P. J., 1473.
SALOMONS, Mrs. R., 1077.
SAMSON, D. N., 72, Grosvenor Road, Canonbury, N., 723, 793, 797, 1803.
SAMSON, E., 136, Houndsditch, E., 1631, 1704.
SAMSON, S. A., 76, Shirland Gardens, W., 1740, 2290.
SAMUEL, STUART M., 3, Kensington Palace Gardens, W., 1632, 1741, 1804, 1805.
SANDEMAN, Mrs. G. G., 15, Hyde Park Gardens, W., 2271-2281.
SARPHATI, I. M., 65, Ely Terrace, Mile End, 1707.
SASSOON, I. S., Ashley Park, Walton-on-Thames, Surrey, 1392, 1416*a*, 1546, 1616, 1806-1808, 1830, 1831, 1843, 1844, 1888, 1893, 2100, 2124, 2125, 2130, 2131.
SASSOON, R. D., 1, Belgrave Square, S.W., 2031-2065.
SAMUELS, E. T., Venner Lodge, Sydenham, 1887.
SCHAAP, L., 9, Ferntower Road, Canonbury, 1367, 1545, 1845, 1865.
SCHIFF, HERMANN M., 18, Pembridge Gardens, W., 2216.
SCHLOSS, Mrs. D. F., 2, Portugal Street, W., 1093.
SCHLOSS, SIGISMUND, Osborne Villa, St. Mary's Road, Bowdon, 1278.
SCHLOSS, SOLOMON, 30, Leinster Square, W., 1677, 1742.
SECKEL, Mrs., 20, Portland Road, Finsbury, N., 650.
SEYMOUR, Mrs., 5, Chesterfield Gardens, W., 1362, 1403.
SILVERTON, JOHN NORTHERNHAY, Rotton Park Road, Edgbaston, Birmingham,
SINGER, Miss S., 1679.
SINGER, Mrs. SIMEON, 12, St. Petersburg Place, W., 1678.
SOCIETY OF ANTIQUARIES, 5.
SOCIETY OF BIBLICAL ARCHÆOLOGY, 11, Hart Street, W.C., 2090.
SODEN-SMITH, R. H., Science and Art Department, S.W., 1827.
SOLA, Rev. CLARENCE DE, 652, 671, 706, 711, 745, 746, 756, 784, 785, 833, 859, 867.
SOLA, Miss DE, 93, Marylands Road, 963, 970, 988, 1003, 1062, 1065, 1111, 1118, 1580.
SOLA, Rev. M. DE, Canada, 778.

SOLOMON, AARON, 158, Alexandra Road, St. John's Wood, N.W., 1283.

SOLOMON, ADOLPHE, 18, Wallace Road, Canonbury, 1288.

SOLOMON, Miss, Edmonton House, Edmonton, 838, 1708, 1745.

SOLOMON, HENRY, 25, Inverness Terrace, W., 1254, 1259, 1284, 1680, 1709, 1743, 1744, 1809.

SOLOMON, LEWIS, 55, New Broad Street, E.C., 539, 544, 561, 565.

SOLOMON, MICHAEL, 28, Oxford Road, Kilburn, 622.

SOLOMON, PHILIP, 113, Sutherland Gardens, W., 1810.

SOLOMONS, ISRAEL, 108, Belgrave Road, Birmingham, 536-7, 555, 558-560, 573, 576-578, 581-583, 834, 843, 846, 851, 855, 864, 866, 961, 967, 969, 981, 984, 1011, 1012, 1024, 1032, 1034, 1039, 1041, 1044a, 1051, 1058, 1069, 1074a, 1088, 1092, 1256, 1258, 1270-1272, 1275-1277, 1282, 1317-1319, 1368, 1603, 1839, 1847.

SPIELMAN, I., 3, Westbourne Crescent, Hyde Park, W., 5a, 6, 10, 656, 660-664, 668-677, 680-684, 687, 689, 691, 1038, 1273, 1274, 1281, 1746, 1840, 1860, 1889.

SPIELMAN, Mrs. M. A., 23, Oxford Square, W., 5a, 732.

STRAUSS, Mrs. R. S., The Holme, Prestwich, Manchester, 1681, 1714, 1834.

STRAUSS, M., 44, Chaussée d'Antin, Paris, 1901-2030.

STRAUSS, Mrs., 100, Lancaster Gate, W., 1699, 1747, 1748.

SYNAGOGUE, BAYSWATER, Chichester Place, Harrow Road, 1107, 1404, 1419, 1474-1477, 1479-1481, 1516.

SYNAGOGUE, CENTRAL. Great Portland Street, 1369, 1428, 1483, 1504-1507, 1527.

SYNAGOGUE, BEVIS MARKS, 521, 592, 599, 607-613, 613a, 648, 665, 680-684, 698, 983, 985, 1048, 1053. 1104, 1114, 1427a, 1420-1427, 1482, 1500-1503, 1521, 1522, 1526, 1682. 1752, 1753.

SYNAGOGUE, CHATHAM, 548, 1371, 1484, 1485, 1551, 1754, 1835.

SYNAGOGUE, DALSTON. Poets' Road, Dalston, 1372, 1751.

SYNAGOGUE, GREAT, St. James's Place, Aldgate, 604, 605, 626, 639, 957, 958, 968, 975, 1006, 1076, 1086, 1373-1376, 1388, 1393, 1406-1408, 1429-1434, 1456-1458, 1486-1494, 1508-1511, 1547-1550, 1750, 1836, 1896.

SYNAGOGUE, HAMBRO', Church Row, Fenchurch Street, 601-603, 1409-1412, 1435-1442, 1749.

SYNAGOGUE, NEW, Great St. Helens, E.C., 596, 589, 1002, 1060, 1067, 1377, 1378, 1512-1514.

SYNAGOGUE, NEW WEST END, 10, St. Petersburg Place, Bayswater Road, W., 1413, 1443-1445.

SYNAGOGUE, Ramsgate, 664a, 1389, 1446-1448, 1683, 1706.

SYNAGOGUE, SPANISH AND PORTUGUESE, Ramsgate, 579, 590, 947, 1018.

SYNAGOGUE, UNITED, 4, Charlotte Street, W., 1075, 1087, 1098, 1108, 1119.

SYNAGOGUE, WESTERN, St. Alban's Place, Haymarket, 1045, 1381, 1382, 1449.

SYNAGOGUE, WEST LONDON, 34, Upper Berkeley Street, W., 1090, 1092.

TODROS, BARONESS MADELINA DE, 641.

TOLANO, ABRAHAM, 9, Howley Place, W., 606.

TWYMAN, Miss M., 1049.

ULLMANN, ELIAS, Secretary Jews' Congregation, 16, Blaichstrasse, Frankfort-on-Maine, 629.

VAN PRAAG, William, 591, 598, 1027, 1285.

VAN THAL, 9, Great Alie Street, E., 1815, 1816.

VALLENTINE, P., 9, Huntley Street, Bedford Square, W.C., 1004, 1700, 1813, 1898.
VERRINDER, Dr. C. G., 1, Finborough Road, South Kensington, 1581.

WALEY, Mrs. S., 22, Devonshire Place, Portland Place, W., 1094.
WALFORD, LIONEL D., 19, York Terrace, Regent's Park, 1890.
WASSERZUG, H., 33, Thornhill Road, Barnsbury, N., 1582.
WERTHEIMER, ASHER, 8, Connaught Place, W., 1891.
WESTMINSTER, DEAN OF, Westminster Abbey, 19–499.
WILLIAMS, Rev. J. DE K., The Paragon, Hackney, 950.
WILLIAMSON, GEORGE, Dunstanbeorh, Church Hill, Guildford, Surrey, 1590.
WOHLE, S., 113, Euston Road, King's Cross, 1701, 1705.
WOLF, LUCIEN, 49, Lanark Villas, Maida Vale, W., 18, 512, 550, 553, 538, 575, 694, 695, 761, 763, 949, 954, 965, 967a, 971a, 973, 977, 982, 995, 999, 999a, 1019, 1023, 1025, 1029, 1031, 1033, 1035, 1035a 1040, 1050, 1052, 1074, 1074b 1082, 1083, 1095, 1106, 1110, 1251, 1253, 1262, 1320-1343, 2621, 2622.
WOOLF, SIDNEY, 101, Lexham Gardens, 1710.
WRIGHT, WILLIAM, D.D., Woolsthorpe, The Avenue, Upper Norwood, 2536-2540.

ZOUCH, Lord, 2132.

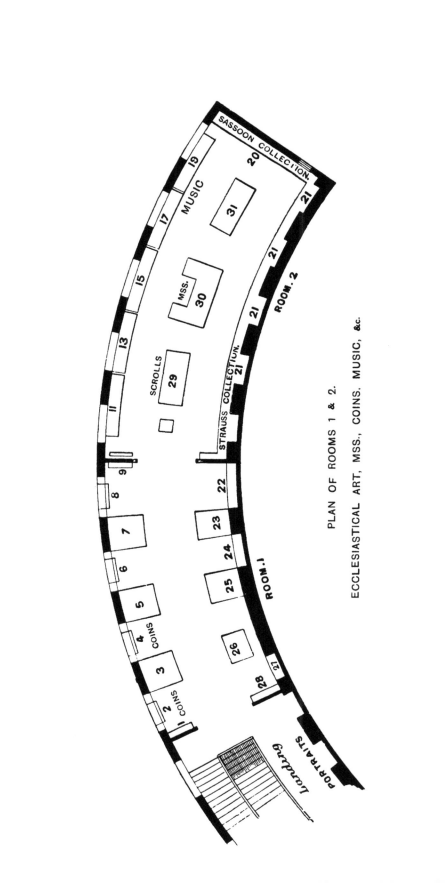

PLAN OF ROOMS 1 & 2.

ECCLESIASTICAL ART, MSS., COINS. MUSIC, &c.

PLAN OF ROOMS 3 & 4.

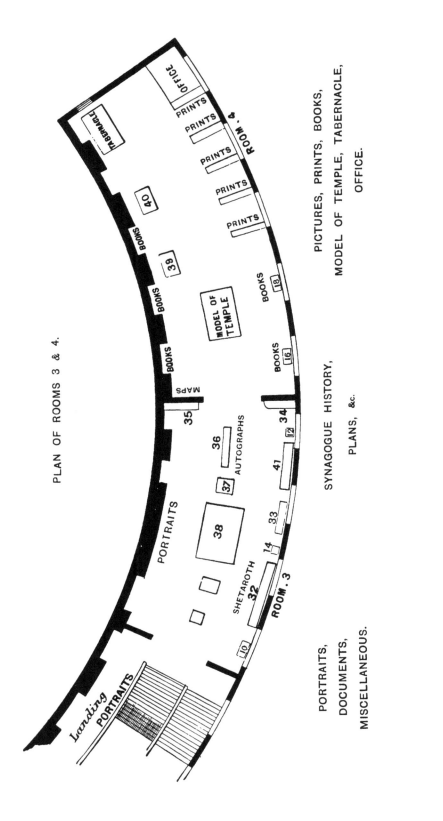

PICTURES, PRINTS, BOOKS,
MODEL OF TEMPLE, TABERNACLE,
OFFICE.

SYNAGOGUE HISTORY,
PLANS, &c.

PORTRAITS,
DOCUMENTS,
MISCELLANEOUS.

PREFACE.

——◆◇◆——

THE original plan of the Anglo-Jewish Historical Exhibition (the idea of which was started by Mr. I. Spielman, the Hon. Secretary) was to bring together all objects illustrating the history of the Jews in England. It was however soon determined to add to this illustrations of Jewish ecclesiastical art, both in this country and abroad. And when the offers of exhibits came in, so many interesting objects were offered illustrating Jewish antiquities of nearly all times and countries, that the scope of the Exhibition was further extended to include these. Thus the following Catalogue of objects is divided into three parts, dealing respectively with exhibits illustrating Anglo-Jewish history, objects used in Jewish culture, and MSS. and other antiquities throwing light on Jewish life and thought generally.

This extension of the scope of the Exhibition has prevented the full display of all the objects sent in; these, however, have been entered in the Catalogue, so that it should preserve within its covers a record of all the objects illustrating Anglo-Jewish history to be found in this country. By the kindness of the Deputy Keeper of the Record Office, and of the Trustees of the British Museum, and of the South Kensington Museum, supplementary exhibitions are being held at those buildings; catalogues of these are appended to the present one.

In one direction it was found impossible to catalogue all the objects sent in. The number of books submitted was so large and yet, from the bibliographical point of view, so incomplete, that it was decided to display only a selection, and only to catalogue those specially exhibited. At the same time, the Executive Committee has entrusted to the editors of the present Catalogue the task of compiling a complete bibliography of Anglo-Jewish history and literature. This is now ready for the press, and will shortly be published under the title of *Bibliotheca Anglo-Judaica.* It is contemplated adding to this the names of those who have kindly forwarded books to be exhibited, and to indicate by numbers the books thus forwarded. The Catalogue and Bibliography will thus, between them, contain as full an account as possible of all the materials for Anglo-Jewish history.

In the compilation of the present Catalogue we have to acknowledge the assistance of Mr. W. Chaffers, F.S.A., in the technical description of the gold and silver plate, and of Mr. H. Montagu, F.S.A, Vice-President Numismatic Society, for the Catalogue of Coins for which he has kindly made himself responsible. Mr. C. Trice Martin has been good enough to draw up the Catalogue of the Documents at the Record Office selected for exhibition, and Mr. E. Maunde Thompson has superintended the description of the Charters and MSS. shown by the Manuscript Department of the British Museum. We have to express our cordial acknowledgment for aid which has materially lightened the task of describing so many objects appealing to such varied tastes and requiring such a wide range of technical knowledge. The shortness of time which an exhibition affords for the compilation of a catalogue must be our excuse for any errors into which we have fallen. We would add that, with regard to the transliteration of Hebrew words, we have, for the convenience of the ordinary visitor, retained the system, or want of system, current among English Jews.

JOSEPH JACOBS.
LUCIEN WOLF.

I.—HISTORIC RELICS AND RECORDS.

THE history of the Jews in England is divided into two marked sections by the dates 1290 and 1656; at the former they were expelled, at the latter they began to be readmitted. Their connection with the general history was entirely different in the two periods. In the Norman and Angevin periods they formed a body closely connected with the government of the country and constituting an integral part of its financial system. Since the re-admission they have been one among various bodies of Dissenters from the National Church, and as such their political history has been closely connected with that of Dissent in general. In both periods, however, their religious views have been a determining factor as regards their social position, and, as will be seen, it was entirely their creed that determined their anomalous position in mediæval England.

The history of the English Jews before the Expulsion may be shortly summarised as a financial experiment of the Norman kings, which was rendered necessary by the policy of the Church towards "usury," but which was ultimately rendered impossible by its costly character and by the rise of popular religious feeling due to the Crusades and the Friars. Before the Conquest there is no trace of Jews in England beyond a few clauses in Church documents which might easily have been copied from similar ones in Continental deeds. But when England was added to those countries of the European littoral which were being organised by the Normans, it was by special invitation of William that the Jews came from Rouen. The function they had to play was a double one. On the one hand, the contact of England with the Continent brought about a change in the economic system from one of barter to one in which large amounts of capital were needed, especially for the change in architecture from wood to stone buildings. This capital could not be forthcoming from any but Jews, owing to the principle of the Canon Law which forbade the loan of money on interest by any one under its ecclesiastical jurisdiction. On the other hand, the king was the largest capitalist in the country, and though it is a moot point how far the money lent by the Jews was actually the king's in the first instance, there is no doubt that the Exchequer treated the money of the Jews as held at the pleasure of the king. There was a special "Exchequer of the Jews," presided over by special " Justices of the Jews," and all the deeds of the Jews had to be placed in charge of exchequer officers, or else they ceased to be legal documents. They thus formed a kind of sponge which first drained the country dry owing to the monopoly of capitalist transactions given them by the Canon Law, and then could be squeezed into the Royal Treasury. How important their contributions to this were may be judged from the fact that on one occasion the tallage of the Jews reached 60,000 marks against 70,000 supplied by the rest of the country. There was scarcely an important building in the country which was not raised by means of Jewish capital. Their operations were not confined to the large towns, as has been usually supposed. One of the facts brought out in investigations undertaken in connection with the present Exhibition has been their wide-spread dispersion throughout all the settled parts of England. (*See* Map, No. 519, to which some twenty further places could be added if they did not elude identification.)

Such a system of indirect taxation could not fail to be enormously expensive. In order that Jews should lend money, they had to possess it, and this involved keeping a large number of persons (amounting at the Expulsion to nearly one per cent. of the population) in affluence. But there was another influence which prevented the Jews from assimilating with the people of a country established on the feudal principle, that citizenship involved spiritual communion. They could not enter the guilds which were founded on a religious basis, and their possession of land was expressly opposed by the monks on the ground that this would put into their hands spiritual benefices. Their social isolation was intensified by the hatred with which they were regarded as the arch-enemies of the Church, the sole exception to the consensus of Europe in favour of Christian doctrine. It is characteristic that the chief outbreak of popular fury against them—the heroic episode of York Castle—took place when the Crusading fever reached its height in England, and that the Expulsion took place under the king who, after Richard I., was most imbued with the Crusading spirit. Nor were the Jews uninfluenced by the same spirit; it is recorded that in 1211 no less than three hundred Rabbis of France and England started for a pilgrimage to the Holy Land.

The worsening of the condition of the Jews can be distinctly traced to the religious revival in England due to the Franciscans. The Lateran Council of 1215 accentuated the isolation of the Jews by ordering them to wear a distinctive mark, which in England took the characteristic form of a piece of cloth attached to the upper garment, in the shape of the two tablets of the Law as seen in the synagogues to the present day (see No. 14). Synagogues in many instances were handed over to the Church on trivial pretexts. There is some indication that the enmity of the Church was embittered by the spread of Judaism among certain classes. One Jewish list of martyrs includes twenty-two proselytes burnt in England, and even if the number be exaggerated, there is other evidence of Jewish proselytism in England. The Church met the movement by establishing a conversionist establishment in "New Street," on the site of the present Record Office (*see* No. 11), where converts were supported for life; this building was used for the purpose down to the time of Charles II. (*see* Public Record Exhibits, No. 50), and thus gave evidence of Jews in England at all periods from the Expulsion to the re-admission.

The time came when the need of a special class of capitalists and of the special kind of taxation was no longer felt. From that moment the fate of the Jews in England was fixed, and it came significantly enough in the extension of the Canon Law about usury to the Jews, in the first Parliament of Edward I., immediately after his return from the Holy Land (*see* Brit-

Mus. Exhibits, No. 33). When usury was denied to the Jews, they ceased to have a *locus standi* in the country. They could not hold land, nor enter any trade, owing to their religion; and to have rescinded these restrictions argued an amount of toleration impossible to expect in a European country in the Middle Ages. The Expulsion of 1290 followed logically on the anti-usury enactment of 1275, and we can only conjecture that the intermediate period was filled with the necessary rearrangement of the national finances, which chiefly took the form of substituting for the Jews, Cahorsins, and Italians, who had not the religious difficulties. It is right to add that as far as their anomalous position admitted of it, scrupulous justice was done to Jews in their negotiations; and that the ordinary idea of their general ill-treatment is based on a few popular outbreaks uncontrollable by the authorities. Their position, as unofficial tax-gatherers, ensured their general good treatment on the part of the kings, except in the case of John. The inherent difficulty of the Jewish position in England during this period was the difference of creed, which prevented their belonging to the nation unless they belonged to the National Church. To expect the Church to have contravened this funda-mental principle would be to anticipate history by six centuries. To expect the Jews to renounce their creed would be to neglect the experience of twenty centuries. The two positions were irreconcilable, and the Jews had to leave England when the law of the Church was extended to them.

The relics of their stay, collected in the present Exhibition, are exceedingly scanty, as is natural when we reflect how few remains there are prior to the fourteenth century. A few stone dwelling-houses (Nos. 5 to 9), which the Jews were about the first to build, a few local names, a couple of cari-catures in which Jews are characteristically enough represented as " sons of the devil" (Nos. 14, 15), and a bronze ewer (No. 1), almost exhaust the list. A grammatical work (No. 515), some Hebrew poems, by Meir of Norwich, now in the Vatican, and a couple of works of an eminent Spanish Jew, Abraham ibn Ezra, written while in the "island of the corner of the earth " (= Angleterre), are the sole records of their literary activity. But from their quasi-official position, it is natural that the chief records should be in the public documents of the time. There is scarcely a single one of these before 1290 that has not some reference to Jews; and there were also whole series of rolls devoted exclusively to the pleadings and tallages of the Jews (Record Office Exhibits, No. 3). Besides these there are still extant more than two hundred Hebrew documents termed Shetaroth,* which are nearly all shown in the present Exhibition. As these form our only guide to the inner life of the Jewish communities at the time, albeit mainly confined to their legal relations, the Committee of the Exhibition has entrusted their publication, together with English abstracts, to Mr. M. D. Davis, who has made the subject a life-long study.

---

* Hebrew שטר, " contract," Latinised as *starrum* and *starra*. It used to be said that the Star Chamber received its name from having been the receptacle of these documents, and it is difficult to see how such a tradition could have arisen without foundation in fact, whereas the *camera stellata* can be easily enough explained as a folk-etymology of this.

Before leaving this section of Anglo-Jewish history, we may refer to the impression left on the popular mind by the peculiar position of the Jews. Religious opposition fixed upon the Jews crimes which the same principle had attributed to the early Christians; and the crime of child murder for ritual purposes was first brought against the Jews in England. The charge was undoubtedly believed in, and many Jews suffered for it; but modern cases have shown its utter baselessness, which also comes out on careful examination of the original records. But the combined ideas of cruelty and usury become connoted with the name of Jew in the popular mind, and have been made a part of English literature by Marlowe and Shakespeare. Strangely enough, perhaps the most enduring survival of the pre-Expulsion period is the popular impression that all Jews are rich usurers—a proposition roughly true of that period, but ludicrously beside the fact at the present day, in a community which unfortunately has a larger proportion of poor than any other in England.

Though the Jews were thus expelled the realm, we have traces of them in England in one form or another during the interim. We find in the fourteenth century the Commons complaining that many professing to be Italians were in reality Jews. In the fifteenth the Spanish ambassador complains to Henry VII. of the asylum afforded the expelled Spanish Jews in England, and in the sixteenth Elizabeth's physician, Rodrigo Lopez, and P. Ferdinandus, teacher of Hebrew at Cambridge, were among Jews known to be in this country. And throughout, the "House of Converts" found a supply of men and women ready to forswear their faith for the material comforts it offered them. But no return of the Jews as a body could become possible till the State recognised the legality of difference of creed. Cromwell first did this as an Independent, and it is to Cromwell that the Jews owe their readmission to England.

The date of the return is fixed approximately by the lease of the Spanish and Portuguese burial-ground at Stepney, dated February 1657 (see No. 52). Except with regard to the specific nature of the assurances given to the Jews by Cromwell, the events which led up to the resettlement are tolerably clear. The motives of the Dutch supporters of Menasseh ben Israel were mainly commercial. The agitation against the monopoly of the companies of Eastern merchants in England, and the attempts of Cromwell to render the trade free, had stimulated a new activity on the part of English shippers, and, in the middle of the seventeenth century, the Dutch were feeling acutely the commercial competition of the English in the East Indies. None were more deeply interested in that branch of trade than the Jews of Amsterdam, and hence it became desirable for them to be able to establish correspondents and agencies in England without hindrances or risk. At the same time events had been preparing the English people to consider the question of the return in a favourable spirit. The Puritans had given an Old Testament bias to Christian thought, and the Messianic pretensions of Sabbathai Zevi had helped to strengthen the conviction that some kind of fulfilment of prophecy by means of the Jews was at hand. The question how to propitiate the Jews exercised men's minds, and in 1649 culminated in a formal petition to Lord Fairfax and the General Council of Officers for their recall. It is stated that this petition was "favourably received" (*see* No. 820). No action resulted from it, however, but during the next few years the question seems to have been continuously before the public. Towards the end of 1655 Menasseh ben Israel (*see* No. 947), who, from his home in Amsterdam, had sent more than one communication to the Protector and other leading men in England, personally visited London with a view to obtaining an authoritative permission for his co-religionists to dwell again in that country. The course of his mission is marked in the State papers and other documents shown in the supplementary exhibitions held at the Record Office and the British Museum (*see* R. O. Nos. 37 to 43; B. M. No. 36). Notwithstanding the personal interest of Cromwell, no formal permission was granted by the Council of State for the Jews to take up their abode in England; but some unofficial authorisation was obtained from the Protector by which Menasseh's followers were enabled to meet privately for prayer (*see* R. O. No. 43), and to acquire a burial-place. Without such a licence it is obvious that they would not have purchased the Stepney graveyard, to which reference has been made.

The history from this date divides itself into two parts—an external and and an internal history; the former recording the successive stages in the struggle for emancipation, the latter tracing the gradual growth, organisation, and development of the community. From the nature of the connivance by which the Jews had settled in the country their position was at first equivocal and precarious. They were both aliens and dissenters, and, as such, liable to all kinds of petty persecution at the hands of common informers. Their individual denization was opposed by the mercantile public; they were indicted for worshipping in the synagogue, and on one occasion (1685) a crowd of them were arrested at the Royal Exchange for not attending church. As late as 1835, not only could no Jew sit in Parliament, but he was prevented from holding any civil or military office under the Crown or any situation in corporate bodies. He might be excluded from practising at the bar, or as an attorney or notary, from voting at elections, and from taking degrees at the Universities.

The first legislative attempts at partial emancipation were made outside England—in the American colonies and Ireland. In 1740 an Act of Parliament was passed providing for the naturalisation of foreigners and others, including Jews, after seven years' residence in British colonies. This measure was hampered by so many restrictions and conditions that it was almost useless. The second attempt (1745) was a Platonic demonstration on behalf of religious liberty by the Irish House of Commons—there being scarcely any Jews in Ireland at the time,—but it also proved abortive, in consequence of the hostility of the Peers. One result of the Irish Bill was the establishment of the Board of Deputies (*see* No. 614), which was formed to watch the progress of the measure, and which has continued its existence to the present time. In 1753 the first serious effort to place the Jews on an equality with their fellow-countrymen was made by the famous "Jew Bill." This measure, which was initiated in the Lords, and received the assent of both the Commons and the Crown, provoked an unexampled outburst of intolerance in the country. Partisans of the Bill were mobbed, and the country was flooded with ribald broadsheets and caricatures, in which every species of

obloquy was heaped ·on the unoffending Hebrews. The Ministry became
alarmed, and quickly introduced and passed another Bill to repeal the
obnoxious measure. By this display of intolerance the progress of Jewish
emancipation was seriously retarded, and it was not until 1830 that the
question was again brought before the public.

In the meantime the Jews had prospered, and many ·of them had
achieved high social position. They acutely felt ·their exclusion from
civil and political rights, and sought the first favourable opportunity of
bringing their claims before Parliament. This was afforded by. the distinctly
liberal tendency of public feeling manifested in the repeal of the Test and
Corporation Act in 1828. Sir Isaac Lyon Goldsmid, Mr. N. M. Rothschild,
Sir David Salomons, and Sir Moses Montefiore, assisted by ·the Board of
Deputies, organised a small movement and enlisted the support of influential
friends. In 1830 the struggle commenced with the introduction of Mr.
Robert Grant's Bill for the Repeal of the Civil Disabilities of the Jews. The
measure was defeated on the second reading. Three years later another effort
was made and with better success. The Commons passed the Bill, but the
Lords threw it out. Year by year the campaign was now prosecuted with
unwearying zeal; but the obduracy of the Lords proved insurmountable.
New tactics were resolved upon. Leading Jews became candidates for public
officers, from which, in the then state of the law, they were excluded.
This at once changed the question from an academic to a practical one,
and also had the effect of enlisting as friends the large section of the upblic
who by their votes had committed themselves to the eligibility of Jews for
public employment. In this way municipal (1835) and corporate (1845)
offices were successively thrown open to Jews, and in 1847 an attack was
made on Parliament itself. Here however the resistance was most obstinate.
Even such friends of the Jews as the Duke of Sussex hesitated to regard
this phase of the question as an integral part of Jewish rights. To administer
the law was one thing; to be concerned in making it in a country which
was Christian by statute, was held to be both dangerous and anomalous. The
contest raged round the wording of the oath which the Jewish members
of Parliament—Baron Lionel de Rothschild and Sir David Salomons—refused
to take. For eleven years the question was debated; but in 1858, by the
good offices of Mr. Disraeli, a compromise was arranged with the Lords, by
which the whole of the Jewish claim was conceded. Two years later an Act
received the royal assent enabling Jews on all occasions whatsoever to omit
the words "on the true faith of a Christian," from the Oath of Allegiance.
Since that date Jews have been prominent among the members of the Lower
House. One, Sir George Jessel, afterwards Master of the Rolls (*see* No. 1110),
served as Solicitor-General, and Baron H. de Worms has twice filled the
Under-Secretaryship to the Board of Trade in a Conservative Ministry. What
lingering doubt there might have been as to the eligibility of Jews for
membership of the higher House was removed in 1885, when Mr. Gladstone
created Sir Nathaniel de Rothschild a peer (*see* No.·1119).

The internal history of the community follows a course very similar to that
of their political progress, with the exception that it has been continuous and
peaceful. The only disturbing feature was the Reform Movement of 1840—

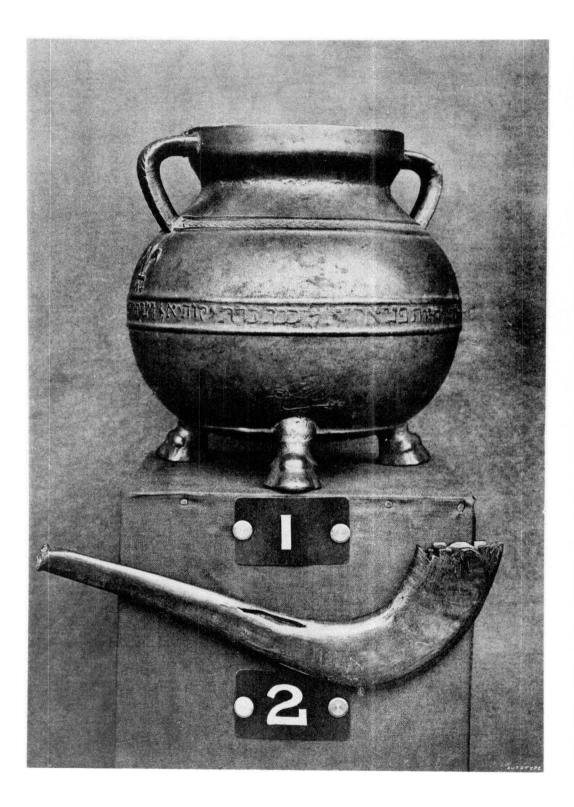

a movement the significance of which was much exaggerated at the time, and all the bitterness of which has long since passed away. Much of the history of this period may be read in the following pages, in the documents relating to public institutions, the relics of public men, and the notes appended to the entries of portraits of communal celebrities and other exhibits.

---

a.—PRE-EXPULSION PERIOD.

[*See also* RECORD OFFICE and BRITISH MUSEUM EXHIBITS.]

1. EWER. *Bodleian Library, Oxford*

    Bronze, 9¾ in. high, 30 in. round broadest circumference
    Two handles and three feet, above each an ornament (stag, bird, flower). Ornamented with two fleurs-de-lys, one on each side immediately under the junction of the handles. Inscription on the cincture read by Gagnier

הנדר יוסף בן הק״ר יחיאל זצ״קל המשיב ושואל. לקהל כהואל
כדי לחזות פני אריאל ככת בדת יקותיאל וצדקה תציל מנמותﬨ

    "The gift of Joseph, son of the Holy [= martyred] Rabbi Yechiel (may the memory of the holy and righteous be a blessing), who answered and directed the congregation as he desired, in order to see the face of Ariel [Jerusalem] as it is written in the law of Yekuthiel [? = Solomon] 'Righteousness (charity) delivereth from death'" (Prov. x. 2).

    Found by a fisherman in a brook in Suffolk about 1696, it passed into possession of Dr. Covel, whose executors sold it to the Earl of Oxford, from whom it passed to Dr. Rawlinson and thence into the Ashmolean Museum. The interpretation of the inscription, and the object for which the ewer was used, is still disputed among authorities, most being of opinion that it was a receptacle for the charitable funds of a congregation, Dr. Neubauer holding that it was a laver used for washing the dead. See Margoliouth, *Jews in East Anglia*, and Dr. Neubauer in *Academy*, 1870, p. 188.

2. SHOPHAR. *Mrs. Arabella Levi.*

    Carved horn used by Jews on high festivals, supposed to be of the pre-Expulsion period, discovered in the foundations on rebuilding premises in Leadenhall Street in 1855.

3. JEW'S TALLY—FACSIMILE. *C. T. Martin.*

    Receipts at the Exchequer were given in long pieces of wood called tallies which were notched to indicate the sums received and then split down in two, each part being a check on the other. The original in the Record Office (No. 8) is a tally of Josce of Kent.

4. JEWISH COIN—ENGRAVING.   *Joseph Jacobs.*
Given in Selden *De jure Naturali et gentium juxta disciplinam
Hebræorum,* p. 187, and stated by him to have been found
at Shene in Surrey.   Obverse, Head of Moses.   Reverse,
Hebrew - inscription : לא יהיה אלהים אחרים על פני (*see*
No. 2626).

5. JEW'S HOUSE, LINCOLN.   *Soc. of Antiquaries.*
Formerly the property of Bellaset of Wallingford—one of
the earliest stone dwelling-houses in existence.   Engraving in Pugin, specimens of Gothic architecture.   Pl. 2.

5a. JEWS' HOUSE, LINCOLN.   *I. Spielman.*
Photograph.

6. JEWISH HOUSE, BURY ST. EDMUNDS.   *I. Spielman.*
Photograph.   Said to have been originally a monastery
which came into the possession of Jews, who used it as a
synagogue.

7. VAULTS, NORWICH.   *Bach & Co.*
Photograph.   Supposed to be the synagogue of Jews of
Norwich before the expulsion.

8. VAULTS, NORWICH.   *Bach & Co.*
Photograph.   Another view of the same.

9. MUSIC HOUSE, NORWICH.   *Dr. M. Davis.*
Photo.   The name is said to be a corruption of " Moses'
house," and local tradition attributes it to the Jews.

10. TOMB OF ST. HUGH OF LINCOLN.   *I. Solomons.*
Engraving in Tovey's *Anglia Judaica,* p. 143.   St. Hugh
of Lincoln was the boy-martyr alleged to have been
murdered by Jews and referred to by Chaucer at the end
of the " Prioresse's Tale."

11. SKETCH OF "DOMUS CONVERSORUM"—FACSIMILE. *Rev. S. S. Lewis.*
From the Corpus Christi Coll. (Cambridge) MS. of Matthew
Paris, done by the historian's own hand.   The building,
for converted Jews, stood on the side of the present
Record Office.

12. SEAL OF A JEW.   *Rev. C. W. King.*
Found at Woodbridge, co. Suffolk.   Inscription : S. NATHI
ΓEDERICI ALEᴗИDRI IVD.   Device a wyvern, regardant,
and star.   Vide *Arch. Journ.* xli. 168–170.

13. SEAL OF JACOB OF LONDON—ENGRAVING.   *Asher I. Myers.*
In Tovey's *Anglia Judaica,* p. 183.   Oval, a gryphon rampant.   Inscription : S' IACOBI D' LVNDRES.

14. " AARON, SON OF THE DEVIL."   *Joseph Jacobs.*
Photograph of entry on Forest Roll of Essex, 5 Ed. I.
(1277) now at Record Office.   The portrait or caricature
is the earliest dated sketch of a mediæval Jew.   The badge
on the dress represents the Two Tables of the Law, which
all Jews were obliged to wear in saffron taffity.   The
subject of the sketch, written by the clerk who made the

entry, was probably Cok [? Isaac, Heb. *Yitzchak*] son of Aaron, mentioned in the accompanying entry, of which the following is a translation :—

COLCHESTER to wit : By the same it was brought forward that a certain doe was started in Wildenhaye Wood by the dogs of Sir John de Burgh, sen., which doe in her flight came by the top of the City of Colchester, crossing towards another wood on the other side of that city. And there issued forth Saunte son of Ursel, Jew of Colchester, Cok son of Aaron, and Samuel son of the same, Isaac the Jewish chaplain, Copin and Elias, Jews, and certain Christians of the said city, to wit: William Scott [2s.], Henry the Gutter [2s.], Henry the Toller [2s.], and others. And these with a mighty clamour chased the same doe through the south gate into the aforesaid city and they so worried her by their shouting that they forced her to jump over a wall and she thus brake her neck to wit, on Wednesday next after the feast of St. Nicholas in the fifty-second year of the reign of King Henry [7 Dec., 1267]. And there came upon them Walter the Goldsmith, Bailiff [half a mark] and Robert the Toller [2s.], beadle of the same city, and others that are dead, and carried thence the game and had their will of it. And these came not nor did their attorneys. Thereupon it was ordered to the Sheriff that he summon the aforesaid Jews from day to day, and a day was set to the Bailiffs of Colchester for producing the others mentioned, within three weeks from Easter Day. And the aforesaid Saunte and Isaac put in an appearance and being convicted were cast into prison. And the aforesaid Cok stayeth at Lincoln, therefore was it ordered to the Sheriff of Lincoln to produce him within one month from Easter. And the aforesaid Saunte being led forth from prison was fined forty shillings on the surety of Vives of Gipewis [Ipswich], Vives of Clare and Mosse Panel of Haverhulle, Jews. And the aforesaid Elias came not nor was he to be found. Therefore let him be driven forth, &c. And the aforesaid Isaac being led forth from prison was fined in four marks on the surety of Joce of Cantuar [Canterbury] Jew, Abraham son of Aaron, Isaac son of Chera, Jew, Saer son of Radulph of Colchester, and Richard Pruet of the same. And later came forward the aforesaid Copin and Samuel and are committed to prison, and being led forth were fined, that is to say, Copin in two marks on the surety of Vives son of Coperun, and Aaron son of Leo, Jews. And the aforesaid Samuel in one mark on the surety of Jacob of London and Saunte son of Ursel of Colchester, Jews. And the Sheriff Lincoln answereth nought concerning the aforesaid Cok the Jew but contemned the mandate of the Justiciars, &c. Wherefore he is at mercy one hundred shillings. And the said Cok who came not ten marks by taxation of the Justiciars.

15. CARICATURE OF JEWS.   *F. Haes.*
> Photograph of a drawing at the top of an Issue Roll of the
> Exchequer (engraved in Devon's *Issues of Exchequer,* in
> Wright's *History of Caricature,* and in Pike's *History of
> Crime*).   The figures represent Isaac of Norwich with
> three faces (probably to show his wide dealings), Mosse
> Mok with scales and clipped coin seized by the demon
> Colbif, and Avegay, a Jewess near " Dagon."   No text
> accompanies the drawing, the exact import of which is
> uncertain.

16. DOMESDAY, OXFORDSHIRE—FACSIMILE.   *C. T. Martin.*
> Containing an entry of land held by " Fil' Manasse," sup-
> posed to be the first Jew referred to in English history,
> as, later on, it is recorded that he was fined for holding
> land without king's permission.

17. CHARTER OF KING JOHN—PHOTOGRAPH.   *F. Haes.*
> Copy of charter entered on the charter Roll of 2 John at
> Record Office.   The text refers to previous charters, the
> originals of which are no longer extant.   This is there-
> fore the earliest extant State document relating to the
> Jews of England.

18. MAGNA CARTA—FACSIMILE.   *Lucien Wolf.*
> Sections 13 and 14 relating to the Jews, and the conditions
> under which debts due to them could be recovered.

19–35. JEW ROLLS.   *Dean of Westminster.*
> Relating to the affairs of the Jews in England in the reigns
> of Henry III. and Edward I. *inter alia* headed :—
> " Ista debita capta sunt pro debitis Domini Regis.   Hec
> sunt debita extracta ab Archa Cyrographaris Norwic per
> preceptum Domini Regis ad ferenda apud Westm."
> " Debita extracta ab archa Domini Regis."
> " Cyrographa extracta ab archa cyrographorum MS. Rotu-
> lus de debitis (Judeorum) solutis."
> " Rotulus de debitis Domini Regis occasione Judeorum
> temperatorum et fugitiorum.   Carte extracte ab archa
> cyrographaria Norviciensis."
> " Tallia et cyrographa extracta ab archa cyrographaria de
> Norwic."

36. WRIT (46 HENRY VI.)   *Dean of Westminster.*
> Addressed " Cyrographariis Christianis et Judeis Cantuar,"
> directing them to take out of the chest certain charters.

37–61. TITLE DEEDS.   *Dean of Westminster.*
> Twenty-five pieces of parchment, being deeds relating to
> " Terre tenementa redditus concesse Judeis," temp. Hen.
> III. and Edw. I., some with Hebrew attestations.

62–67. WRITS. *Dean of Westminster.*
Temp. Henry III. and Edward I. Relating to Jews.

68–78. DEEDS OF SALE. *Dean of Westminster.*
Eleven pieces of parchment, being sales to Jews of messuages
and tenements in various places. Temp. Hen. III. and
Edw. I.

79–89. HEBREW SHETAROTH. *Dean of Westminster.*

90–182. SHETAROTH. *Dean of Westminster.*
Ninety-three pieces of parchment, being Hebrew Shetaroth,
varying in size from a superficial inch to a foot. Some
with Latin.

183–220. SHETAROTH. *Dean of Westminster.*
Thirty-eight ditto.

221–345. WRITS. *Dean of Westminster.*
One hundred and twenty-five pieces of parchment, being
writs of various kinds relating to the Jews. Temp. Henry
III. and Edw. I.

346–394. BONDS. *Dean of Westminster.*
Forty-nine pieces of parchment, being bonds of private individuals to Jews. Temp. Henry III. and Edw. I.

395–404. QUITTANCES. *Dean of Westminster.*
Ten pieces of parchment labelled " acquetantiae spectantis
Judeis."

405–418. INSTRUCTIONS TO JUSTICES OF JEWS. *Dean of Westminster.*
Fourteen pieces of parchment labelled " Brevia Justiciari-
orum Judeorum."

419–433. BONDS. *Dean of Westminster.*
Fifteen pieces of parchment, being bonds of private individuals to Jews.

434–437. BONDS. *Dean of Westminster.*
Four similar to preceding.

438–452. BONDS. *Dean of Westminster.*
Fifteen similar to preceding.

453–499. BONDS. *Dean of Westminster.*
Forty-seven similar to preceding.

500–507. DEEDS. *St. Paul's Cathedral, Dean and Chapter.*
Eight deeds, pre-Expulsion period. Two of them have
Hebrew endorsements.

508. CHARTER. *Dean and Chapter of Canterbury Cathedral.*
Original Charter under the seal of Edward I., 1291, granting to Christ Church the houses of the Jews lately
banished.

509. CONVEYANCE.   *Dean and Chapter of Canterbury Cathedral.*
Conveyance of a messuage in Canterbury from Dom. Alan,
     of Christ Church, to Aron fil. Josse of Leicester, with
     Hebrew endorsement.

510. DEED AND SEAL.   *Magdalen College, Oxford.*
Relating to Mildegoda, a Jewess of Oxford, with her seal
     attached.

511. WRIT, DATED 1359.   *Balliol College, Oxford.*
Document in which Wyclif, the reformer, is declared to
     be unlawfully seised of a house in London, formerly
     belonging to Thippe, Jewess of Southwark.

512. HEBREW SHETAROTH—FACSIMILES.   *Lucien Wolf.*
Accompanying an article of the Rev. J. T. Fowler, M.A.,
     F.S.A., in *Yorkshire Archæological Journal,* III. pp. 55–63.
     The signature to No. 2 is that of the celebrated "Aaron
     of York," the prototype of Scott's "Isaac of York" in
     Ivanhoe.

513. SHETAR—PHOTOGRAPH.   *F. Haes.*
From original in Record Office.

514. WRIT WITH HEBREW ENDORSEMENT.   *F. Haes.*
Photograph. The Hebrew endorsement refers to the persons
     who gave bail for the several Jews imprisoned because
     they had not paid tollage. (*See* No. 11.)

515. THE SEPHER HASSOHAM.   *Rev. G. W. Collins.*
A Hebrew Grammar and Lexicon, by Rabbi Moseh ben
     Yishak, of England. Edited by George Wolseley Collins,
     M.A. Part I. London, 1883.

> This work, which exists in MS. in the Bodleian Library, is one of the few
> literary efforts which have been preserved of the English Jews of the
> pre-Expulsion period. The author, R. Moses Hanasiah, may be identified
> with Rabbi Moses Hanakdan, author of a treatise on points and accents,
> published in the Rabbinic Bibles. Lived in England about the middle
> of the thirteenth century (Neubauer, *Hist. Lit. de la France*).

516. POEMS OF MEIR BEN ELIAS OF NORWICH.   *Dr. A. Berliner.*
Copy of Vatican MS. The chief poem consists of a cento
     of Biblical verses.

517. IGGERETH HA-SHABBATH.   *Joseph Jacobs.*
By Abraham ibn Ezra. Written while in England, 1158.
     Personifies the Sabbath, in whose mouth is placed a
     poem reciting the beauties of the day.

518. YESOD MOREH.   *Joseph Jacobs.*
By Abraham ibn Ezra. A philosophical treatise, written
     while in England, 1158, by the celebrated commentator,
     grammarian, traveller, and wit.

Hardus dei gra Rex Augl Dominus Hibn z Dux Aquitan omnibz ad quos pfentes litte puenint salut
Sciatis qd concessimus pro nob z heredibz nris z dais nob nr ppto Priori z conuentui eccle xpi Cantuar
domos illas cum pan in Cantuar que fuerint Elye de London indee que ad viginti solidos ectenduntur et
domos illas cum pan in eadem Ciuitate que fuerunt Mossei le Peytr indee ipsd cambium nrm que ad duo
decim solidos ectenduntur et tenementum illud cum pan in eadem Ciuitate quos fuit Crampsonis le Chape
ppn indee quod ad duodecim denarios ectenditur et tenementum illud valuum cum pan in eadem Ciuita
te quos fuit Isaac ppn indee quod ad duos solidos ectenditur et tam illud cum pan in eadem Ciuitate quos
fuit Soye que fuit ippte vines Selyomon indee ippea Domu Cristine de Vedam quod ad sex solidos z octo de
narios ectenditur p gdium eopdem Judeg A regno nro vtinqm csteaend nia in manu nra Crystencia Ha
bend z tenend eadem Priori z conuentui z successoribz suis vel an illa semsu consuetudinem Ciuitatis
predce dare vel assignare voluint de nob z heredibz nris impperpm Reddend inde nob z heredibz nris
duos denarios p manus Ballivor nrop eiusdem Ciuitatis singulis annis ad scm nrm cd quibus et faci
endo aliis Dominis frodi illius servicia inde debita consueta In cui rei testimonium has litteras nras fieri
fecimus patentes Test ... ...

508

519. MAP. *Joseph Jacobs.*
Distribution of Jews in England prior to the Expulsion,
compiled from the records.

520. MAP OF LONDON—RALPH AGGAS, 1560. *Joseph Jacobs.*
Marking Old Jewry in 1290 and the places where Jews
dwelt on their return about 1650.

b.—TITLE DEEDS, ETC.

521. LEASE OF THE SPANISH AND PORTUGUESE BURIAL-GROUND AT
STEPNEY. *Bevis Marks Synagogue.*
Dated February, 1657.
> This document fixes the date of the re-settlement of the Jews in England.
> The burial-ground is that now known as the Beth Holim, and the first
> interment took place in Ellul 5417 (September, 1657), when one Isaac
> Brito was buried. The tomb is no longer recognisable as, in some re-
> arrangement of boundaries, a wall was built across it.

521a. TITLE DEEDS OF LONDON PROPERTY. *S. Jacobs.*
Dated 1773, and declared before the London Beth Din
(Ecclesiastical Tribunals).

522. COPY OF INSCRIPTION. *Jews' Free School.*
On brass plate placed under foundation stone of Original
Jews' Free School building and now deposited under the
memorial stone of the hall of the present building.
Founded 1817 for an unlimited number of children.
Rebuilt in 1883. Is the largest elementary school in the
world. Has nearly 3,500 children on its registers.

523. TITLE DEEDS, ETC. *Dr. N. M. Adler, Chief Rabbi.*
Relating to the Jews' Burial-Ground at Sheerness.

524. TITLE DEEDS. *Dr. N. M. Adler, Chief Rabbi.*
Of Jewish Burial-Ground at Lynn.

524a. TITLE DEEDS. *Plymouth Hebrew Conf.*
Of Burial-Ground of Plymouth Hebrew Congregation (1758).

525. SHORT HISTORY OF THE MIDDLESBOROUGH CONGREGATION.
A. Lockett.
Written by Town Clerk and accompanied by newspaper
extracts.

526. EXTRACTS FROM MINUTES *Middlesborough Town Council.*
Of Town Council, Middlesborough, relating to the Jewish
Burial-Ground.

c.—PICTURES, PLANS, ETC., OF JEWISH BUILDINGS.

530. MAP OF LONDON, 1720.   *Joseph Jacobs.*
  Indicating position of Jewish buildings and residences in
  middle of last century.

531.· MAP OF LONDON, 1887.   *Joseph Jacobs.*
  Indicating position of chief Jewish buildings and distribution of Jewish population of London.

532. BEVIS MARKS SYNAGOGUE.   *The Misses Aguilar.*
  By J. M. Belisario. Congregation first established in King
  Street, Aldgate, 1656; synagogue in Bevis Marks built in
  1701 and consecrated in 1702. Is the oldest Jewish synagogue in use in England. The lease was purchased and
  presented to the congregation in 1748 by Benjamin
  Mendes da Costa, Esq., F.R.S.

533. BEVIS MARKS SYNAGOGUE.   *E. H. Lindo.*
  Engraving.

534. BRYANSTONE STREET SYNAGOGUE.   *H. H. Collins.*
  Exterior.

535. GREAT SYNAGOGUE, DUKE'S PLACE, HOUNDSDITCH. *Lucien Wolf.*
  Pugin & Rowlandson del. et sculp., Sunderland Aquat.
  Congregation first established in Broad Court, Mitre
  Square, Aldgate, 1692. Duke's Place Synagogue built in
  1722, at the sole expense of Moses Hart, Esq., of Isleworth,
  brother of Rabbi Uri Phaibus Hamburger ben Hirz, the
  then Chief Rabbi. Taken down and rebuilt in 1790,
  partly at the expense of the congregation and partly
  (£4000) of Mrs. Judy Levy, of Albemarle Street, daughter
  of Moses Hart. One of the Constituent Synagogues of
  the United Synagogue.

536. GREAT SYNAGOGUE, DUKE'S PLACE, LONDON.   *I. Solomons.*
  Exterior. Eastgate, sculpt.

537. GREAT SYNAGOGUE, DUKE'S PLACE, LONDON.   *I. Solomons.*
  Smaller print.

538. SYNAGOGUE, GREAT ST. HELENS, LONDON.   *Lucien Wolf.*
  I. H. Shepherd, H. Melville. Congregation first established
  in Leadenhall Street, 1760. Removed to Great St. Helens,
  1837. Above building erected 1855. One of the Constituent Synagogues of the United Synagogue.

539. HAMBRO' SYNAGOGUE—VIEW OF THE ARK.   *L. Solomons.*
  The Hambro' Synagogue was founded in 1736, and bequeathed to the congregation by E. P. Salomon, Esq., in
  1805. Now one of the Constituent Synagogues of the
  United Synagogue.

539a. CENTRAL SYNAGOGUE.   *N. S. Joseph.*
  Elevation of the Porch. The Synagogue was founded as a
  branch of the Great Synagogue in 1855, and the present

building erected in 1870. One of the Constituent Synagogues of the United Synagogue, and the seat of government of that body.

540. DRAWING, BAYSWATER SYNAGOGUE. *D. Benjamin.*
In Chichester Place, Harrow Road. Erected 1863 ; en-
larged 1885. One of the Constituent Synagogues of the
United Synagogue.

540*a.* NEW WEST END SYNAGOGUE. *H. J. Phillips.*
Photo ; interior ; in St. Petersburg Place, W. One of
the Constituent Synagogues of the United Synagogue.

541. EAST LONDON SYNAGOGUE. *Messrs. Davis & Emanuel.*
Interior view, coloured.

541*a.* EAST LONDON SYNAGOGUE. *Messrs. Davis & Emanuel.*
Plan. Erected under the auspices of the United Synagogue,
and consecrated in 1877.

542. EAST END SYNAGOGUE, STEPNEY. *E. Lawton.*
Photos.

542*a.* BOROUGH SYNAGOGUE. *H. H. Collins.*
Interior.

542*b.* NORTH LONDON SYNAGOGUE. *H. H. Collins.*
Interior, coloured.

543. WEST LONDON SYNAGOGUE, UPPER BERKELEY STREET.
Messrs. Davis & Emanuel.
Two interior views, coloured. The congregation was
founded by seceders from the Orthodox Synagogue in
1841. First established in Burton Street, and afterwards
in Margaret Street, Cavendish Square. The above
building was erected in 1870.

543*a.* WEST LONDON SYNAGOGUE. *Messrs. Davis & Emanuel.*
Ground plan.

543*b.* WEST LONDON SYNAGOGUE. *Messrs. Davis & Emanuel.*
Outside view.

543*c.* WEST LONDON SYNAGOGUE. *West London Synagogue.*
Photo.

544. GERMAN SYNAGOGUE, SPITAL SQUARE. *L. Solomon.*
Exterior. Founded in New Broad Street, 1858. Present
building opened in 1886.

545. SYNAGOGUE, PRINCES ROAD, LIVERPOOL. *Rev. M. Joseph.*
Three photographic views.

546. NEW SYNAGOGUE, LIVERPOOL. *Liverpool New Synagogue.*
Founded 1842.

547. OLD CHATHAM SYNAGOGUE. *L. Polack.*
Lead pencil sketch of synagogue, supposed to have been
built about the year 1760 on part of the ground at
present occupied by the Chatham Memorial Synagogue,
demolished in 1869.

548. CHATHAM SYNAGOGUE.   *Chatham Synagogue.*
  Plan.   Erected in 1870 by Simon Magnus, in memory
  of his only son, Captain Lazarus Simon Magnus.

548a. CHATHAM SYNAGOGUE.   *H. H. Collins.*
  Interior.   Photo.

548b. SYNAGOGUE, BRISTOL.   *Platnauer Bros., Bristol.*
  Photograph of interior.   Founded 1835.   Present Synagogue
  built 1871.

549. SYNAGOGUE, SYDNEY, N.S.W., 1845.   *B. H. Ascher.*
  Wood engraving, accompanying laws.   First Synagogue
  established in Sydney.

550. GREAT SYNAGOGUE, SYDNEY, N.S.W.   *Lucien Wolf.*
  Wood engraving, accompanying report for 1878.

551. MELBOURNE SYNAGOGUE.   *D. Benjamin.*
  Drawings of interior and exterior.   Founded 1853.

552. KIMBERLEY DIAMOND-FIELDS SYNAGOGUE.   *H. L. Hyam.*
  During Day of Atonement, 1881.   Interior.   Rough wood
  engraving.

553–554. PLANS OF SYNAGOGUES.   *H. H. Collins.*

555. THE JEWISH SYNAGOGUE, 1752.   *I. Solomons.*

556. INTERIOR OF A SYNAGOGUE.   *M. Linsberg.*

557. OLD JEWS' HOSPITAL, MILE END.   *Jews' Hospital.*
  Founded in 1806, "for the support of the aged, and for
  the [education and employment of youths," by Benjamin and Abraham Goldsmid, who collected a fund of
  £10,000 for that purpose.   Removed in 1861 to Norwood.
  Amalgamated with the Jews' Orphan Asylum in 1876.

558. JEWS' HOSPITAL, MILE END ROAD.   *I. Solomons.*
  T. Prallert del. et sculpt., 1819.

559. JEWS' HOSPITAL, MILE END ROAD.   *I. Solomons.*
  Smaller print.

560. JEWS' HOSPITAL—TECHNICAL SCHOOL.   *L. Solomon.*

561. JEWS' HOSPITAL AND ORPHAN ASYLUM, NORWOOD—PRESENT
  BUILDING.   *Jews' Hospital.*
  Water-colour drawing.   The Orphan Asylum was established in 1831, and enlarged in 1866.   On its amalga-
  mation with the Jews' Hospital (*see* No. 557) in 1876, it
  was removed from St. Mark Street, Goodman's Fields, to
  Norwood.

562. JEWS' FREE SCHOOL.   *N. S. Joseph.*
  Drawings and Plans.   (*See* No. 522.)

563. JEWS' INFANT SCHOOL, COMMERCIAL STREET.
                        Messrs. Davis & Emanuel.
  Three sheet plans.   Founded (Gravel Lane, Houndsditch)
  in 1841.   The school now possesses two large establish-
  ments, one in Commercial Street, the other in Tenter
  Street, and has accommodation for 1500 children.

564. TAVISTOCK HOUSE, NOW JEWS' COLLEGE. *Joseph Jacobs.*
Engraving in Forster's "Life of Dickens." Jews' College
was founded 1852, for educating and training students
for the Jewish ministry. Removed from 10, Finsbury
Square, to Tavistock House in 1881.

565. BOROUGH JEWISH SCHOOLS. *L. Solomon.*
After the enlargement; exterior. Founded 1807.

566. JEWISH HIGH SCHOOL FOR GIRLS, CHENIES STREET.
Messrs. Davis & Emanuel.
Plan, lithographed.

567. MONTEFIORE COLLEGE, RAMSGATE. *Messrs. Davis & Emanuel.*
Plan. Established and endowed by the late Sir Moses
Montefiore, Bart., in 1866: "As a memorial of his sincere
devotion to the law of God as revealed on Sinai and
expounded by the revered sages of the Mishna and the
Talmud; as a token of his love and pure affection to
his departed consort, Judith, Lady Montefiore, of blessed
memory, whose zeal and ardent attachment to the religion
of her forefathers adorned all her actions in life."

567a. MONTEFIORE COLLEGE, RAMSGATE.
Perspective view, coloured.

567b. MONTEFIORE COLLEGE, RAMSGATE.
Two photographs.

568. ARIA COLLEGE, PORTSEA. *Messrs. Davis & Emanuel.*
Two sheets of plans. Founded in accordance with the
directions of the will of the late Lewis Aria, Esq., who
bequeathed upwards of £20,000 for its endowment. Its
object is the training of Jewish divines.

569. JEWISH SCHOOL IN LIVERPOOL. *L. Barned.*
Model. Founded 1840; present building erected 1852.

570. JEWISH HOME, STEPNEY GREEN. *Messrs. Davis & Emanuel.*
Three sheets of drawings.

571. JEWISH SCHOOLS, STEPNEY GREEN.
Three sheets of drawings. Founded 1865; present building
erected 1872.

572. JEWISH WORKING MEN'S CLUB, ALIE STREET.
One sheet of drawings.

573. JEWISH TOMBS, WHITECHAPEL. *I. Solomons.*
Engraving, containing copies of necrographic emblems.

574. GRACE AGUILAR'S HOUSE AT TEIGNMOUTH. *Rev. M. Joseph.*
Pencil sketch.

575. MERTON, SURREY. *Lucien Wolf.*
Seat of the late Asher Goldsmid, Esq. Engraving from the
Lady's Magazine.

576. MORDEN, SURREY.   *I. Solomons.*
Seat of the late Abraham Goldsmid, Esq.

577. BELVEDERE HOUSE, KENT.   *I. Solomons.*
Seat of the late Sampson Gideon, Esq.

578. PROSPECT PLACE, SURREY.   *I. Solomons.*
Seat of M. J. Levy, Esq. (*See* also Newman Collection,
Nos. 1191–1217.)

d.—TROWELS, ETC.

579. TROWEL, SILVER.   *Span. and Port. Synagogue.*
Used by M. D. Lindo, Esq., acting on behalf of Mrs. Sarah
Lara, on laying the corner stone of the Spanish and Por-
tuguese Jews' Infant School, 18th Aug. 1843:

580. TROWEL, SILVER.   *S. Montagu, M.P.*
Used by S. Montagu, Esq., M.P., on laying the memorial
stone of Dalston Synagogue, 8th July, 1885.

581. TROWEL, SILVER.
Used by S. Montagu, Esq., M.P., on laying the crowning
stone of the German Synagogue, Spital Square, 17th
January, 1886. (*See* No. 544.)

582. TROWEL, SILVER.
Used by S. Montagu, Esq., M.P., on laying the memorial
stone of Swimming Baths of Jewish Working Lads'
Institute, June 23, 1886.

583. TROWEL, SILVER.   *Rev. Dr. Adler, Chief Rabbi.*
Used at laying corner stone of Bayswater Synagogue,
July 10th, 1862. (*See* No. 540.)

584. TROWEL, SILVER.   *L. de Rothschild.*
Used by Leopold de Rothschild, Esq., on laying the
foundation stone of the West End Synagogue, June 7th,
1877. Handle represents one of the miharets of the
Synagogue, and back engraved with façade. (*See*
No. 540a.)

585. TROWEL, SILVER.   *Rev. Dr. Adler, Chief Rabbi.*
Used by the Chief Rabbi on laying the foundation stone
Manchester Great Synagogue, April 29th, 1857.

586. TROWEL, SILVER.   *Rev. Dr. Adler, Chief Rabbi.*
Used by the Chief Rabbi on laying foundation stone of the
Jews' Orphan Asylum, March 10th, 1846.

587. GOLD KEY.   *S. Montagu, M.P.*
Used at reconsecration of Sandy's Row Synagogue, June 6,
1886.

588. TROWEL, SILVER.   *D. Benjamin.*
Used by D. Benjamin, Esq., on laying the foundation stone
of the New Synagogue, Melbourne, December 1, 1853.
(*See* No. 551.)

589. TROWEL, SILVER. *New Synagogue.*
　　Presented to Rev. Solomon Herschell in commemoration of
　　　laying the first stone of the New Synagogue, Great
　　　St. Helens, 10th May, 1837. Returned to the New
　　　Synagogue, after the death of the Rev. Solomon Herschell
　　　by L. Lucas, Esq. (*See* No. 538.)

590. TROWEL. *L. Barned.*
　　Used in laying stone of Jewish School at Liverpool. (*See*
　　　No. 569.)

591. PAPIER MACHE TABLE. *William Van Praag.*
　　Presented to the late Morris Van Praag, Esq., Warden of
　　　the Hambro' Synagogue. Has a pictorial representation
　　　of the interior of the Hambro' Synagogue. (*See* No. 539.)

592. BEADLE'S STAFF. *Bevis Marks Synagogue.*
　　Used in the Bevis Marks Synagogue for many years.

593. BEADLE'S STAFF *M. N. Raphael.*
　　Of Western Synagogue ; silver gilt (1816).

e.—SYNAGOGUE DOCUMENTS, ETC.

600. REGISTER BOOK FOR OFFERINGS OF THE CHELTENHAM CONGRE-
　　GATION. *A. Mostyn.*
　　Containing list of the congregation, and laces for registering
　　　offerings without writing, on Sabbaths and Festivals.

601. MINUTE BOOK OF HAMBRO' SYNAGOGUE. *Hambro' Synagogue.*
　　Containing entry relating to Lord George Gordon. (*See*
　　　No. 984.)

602. MINUTE BOOK AND LAWS OF THE HAMBRO' SYNAGOGUE, 5525 =
　　1765. *Hambro' Synagogue.*

603. MS. BOOK OF LAWS OF HAMBRO' SYNAGOGUE, 5555 = 1795.
　　　　　　Hambro' Synagogue.

604. MINUTE BOOK OF GREAT SYNAGOGUE. *Great Synagogue.*

605. LAW BOOK OF GREAT SYNAGOGUE, 1790. *Great Synagogue.*

606. DOCUMENT *A. Tolano.*
　　Relating to origin of the Society Queheloth de Israel.
　　　London, 5438 = 1678.

607. REGISTERS OF BIRTHS. *Bevis Marks Synagogue.*

608. REGISTERS OF BURIALS. *Bevis Marks Synagogue.*

609. MINUTE BOOKS. *Bevis Marks Synagogue.*

610. ASCAMOT. *Bevis Marks Synagogue.*
　　MS. Book of Laws of the Spanish and Portuguese Jews'
　　　Congregation, London. Spanish and Portuguese, 5424 =
　　　1664. Among the signatures in this book are those of
　　　Sir Solomon de Medina, Sampson Gideon (p. 15), Moses
　　　Mendes (p. 22), &c.

611. Ascamot.   *Bevis Marks Synagogue.*
     MSS. Book of Laws and Regulations of the Congregation
     of Spanish and Portuguese Jews, London. Revised and
     amended, 1850 = 5610

612–613. Two Legacy Boards.   *Bevis Marks Synagogue.*
     " Pauta dos que deixarao Legados," &c. Containing records,
     among others, of legacy of £1,000 by " Simson Abu-
     diente" (Sampson Gideon), father of the first Lord
     Eardley, the condition attached to the bequest being that,
     although he had left the Synagogue, he should be buried
     in the cemetery of the congregation; also legacy of £20
     by Benjamin d'Israeli (grandfather of Lord Beaconsfield).

613a Panta dos Senhores Parnassim, &c. (5566).

                               Bevis Marks Synagogue.
     List of Officers of Bevis Marks Synagogue. Contains
     record of the election of Isaac Disraeli (father of Lord
     Beaconsfield) to the office of Parnas. It was in conse-
     quence of the disagreements which arose from his refusal
     to serve this office that he and his family seceded from the
     Synagogue.

614. Minute Book of Plymouth Synagogue.   *Plymouth Heb. Cong.*
     Date 5539 [= 1779].

     First Minute Book of the Board of Deputies.
                     Board of Deputies of British Jews.
     From 1760 to 1828. The Board was first established in
     1745 as a Committee of Diligence to watch the progress
     of the Jewish Naturalization Bill introduced, in that
     year, into the Irish House of Commons. In 1760 the
     Committee was transformed into the " Deputies of the
     Portuguese Nation." In 1812 the German Congregations
     became represented on the Board, which from that date
     became the principal political organization of the English
     Jews under the title of London Committee of Deputies of
     British Jews.

f.—PERSONAL RELICS.

616. Silver Salver.   *S. Montagu, M.P.*
     Presented by Menasseh ben Israel to Oliver Cromwell,
     whence it came into the possession of the first Earl of
     Argyll. The main body is Dutch work of about the
     middle of the XVII. Cent. The border and handles have
     been added later, and bear the Queen Anne mark.

617. Hanuca Lamp.   *Dr. A. Asher, M.D.*
     Dutch manufacture; dated A.M. 5418 [=A.D. 1657]. Said to
     have been the property of the Haham who accompanied
     the Jews to England on their return—Jacob Sasportas.
     (*See* No. 953.)

618. Masonic Arms.   *W. H. Rylands.*
     Designed by Jacob Jehuda Leon, surnamed Templo, who
     visited London in 1678 with a model of the Temple,

which he was permitted to exhibit to Charles II. and his Court. Templo was an ingenious draughtsman, and designed vignettes for the illustration of the Talmud, some of which were afterwards published by Surenhusius. The present exhibit consists of a painted mahogany panel, with arms in gold and colour, crest, supporters and masonic emblems. It was engraved by Laurence Dermott in his "Ahimon Rezon" (2nd edit., London, 1764), and described as from the "collection of the famous and learned Hebrewist, architect, and brother Rabi Jacob Jehuda Leon." In the original the motto was in Hebrew.

619. PAINTING ON LINEN.   *Lewis Lewis.*
    Illumination displayed in the window of a house in King's Road, Brighton, by the late Chief Rabbi, the Rev. Solomon Herschell, on the proclamation of peace in 1808. Design: a large tree with four branches, representing respectively, Austria, Prussia, France and Russia, united together at the root by England, surrounded by Hebrew and English Scriptural quotations.

620. GOLD SEAL.   *Rev. Prof. Marks.*
    Belonging to the late Chief Rabbi, Rev. Solomon Herschell; with impression of seal on sealing wax.

621. WOODEN SNUFF-BOX.   *S. S. Oppenheim.*
    With Hebrew Inscriptions, presented by Rev. Solomon Herschell to Mr. Simeon Oppenheim.

622. CHINA CUP.   *M. Solomon.*
    With portrait of Rev. Solomon Herschell, the late Chief Rabbi.

623. PASSOVER DISH.   *Mrs. S. Joseph.*
    For the Seder ceremony, used by the late Chief Rabbi, Rev. Solomon Herschell.

624. SABBATH LAMP.   *Mrs. S. Cohen.*
    Silver; seven burners, with perforated borders masks and scroll and curled edges, five pieces, hook and chains. London Hall Mark 1767. Belonged to the late Chief Rabbi, Rev. Solomon Herschell.

625. SILVER TUREEN.   *Dr. N. M. Adler, Chief Rabbi.*
    Presented as a Testimonial to the late Chief Rabbi, Rev. S. Herschell, by the Committee of the Jews' Free School.

626. ADDRESS OF CONGRATULATION.   *Great Synagogue.*
    Written by Rev. S. Herschell on the union of the Great, Hambro', and New Synagogues.

626a. ADDRESS.   *Jews' Free School.*
    Presented to Rev. Solomon Herschell on laying foundation stone of Free School, 1821.

627. ENAMEL MASONIC JEWEL.   *J. de Castro.*
    Presented to exhibitor's grandfather in 1785. Inscription.

627a. Dagger.   *J. de Castro.*
   Presented to exhibitor's father for having headed a volun-
      teer band of white citizens against a negro riot in
      Barbados (1820).

628. Cup—Australian Gold.   *Dr. N. M. Adler, Chief Rabbi.*
   Presented to the Chief Rabbi by the Melbourne Hebrew
      Congregation, shortly after the discovery of gold in
      Australia.   Exhibited at the Exhibition of 1851.

629. Invitation to Wedding of N. M. de Rothschild, 1812.
                                                              E. Ullman.
   With autograph of the bridegroom.

630. Certificate of Admission to Dublin University of Nathan
      Lazarus Benmohel.   *N. I. Berlin.*
   Parchment, Latin, February 6, 1832.   Said to be first Jew
      admitted to an English University.   (*See* No. 1073.)

631. Two Letters of Nathan L. Benmohel,   *N. I. Berlin.*
   On his admission at Dublin as M.A., and on XXXIX
      Articles being dispensed with.

632. Diploma of M.A., T.C.D.   *N. I. Berlin.*
   Taken by Nathan L. Benmohel, June 1846, the first Jew to
      obtain a University degree in the United Kingdom.   A
      native of Hamburg, came to Dublin 1829, taught German,
      French and Hebrew.   Took his B.A. in 1836.   Died
      1869.

633. Diploma to A. de Symons.   *H. Barned.*
   By Royal Jenneriam Society, 1803.

634. Stars of Order of Tower and Sword and of the Knights
      of Christ.   *F. Haes.*
   Presented by Portuguese Government to David Haes, late
      Vice-President of the London Jews' Free School.

635. Gold Medal.   *A. Morjoseph.*
   Presented to Haham Meldola (*see* No. 985) by the Emperor
      of Germany.

636. Silver Jug.   *Mrs. H. Joseph.*
   Inscription : מתנה לשרה קילה ביום חתנתי " Presented to
      בשנת נעת חיה ולשרה בן משה עזריאל לוי Sarah on the day
      of my wedding in the year 1695.   Israel Levi."

637. Testimonial.   *Rev. Dr. H. Adler, Delegate Chief Rabbi.*
   From the Hamburg Hebrew Congregation to Rev. Dr. H.
      Adler, with silver relief of façade of new synagogue in
      Hamburg.

638. Testimonial.   *N. I. Berlin.*
   In *repoussé* silver; to R. A. L. Benmohel by Portsmouth Con-
      gregation, 1824.

639. Letter.   *Great Synagogue.*
   Relating to visit of three Royal Dukes to the Synagogue,
      dated 1809.

640. PATENT OF NATURALIZATION OF MR. NELSON AND FIVE OTHERS.
B. Nelson.
Each person had to pay a fee of £50. Mr. Nelson was warden of the Hope Place Synagogue, Liverpool.

641. MS. PENTATEUCH. *Baroness Madelina de Todros.*
Brought from Spain by the Todros family when expelled by Ferdinand and Isabella.

642. STATUETTE OF JEWISH OLD CLOTHESMAN. *A. I. Myers.*
In eighteenth century costume. Metal.

g.—MONTEFIORIANA.

SIR MOSES MONTEFIORE.
For portraits, *see* Nos. 1047–1053.

650. AUDIENCE *Miss Seckel.*
Of Sir M. Montefiore and M. Adolphe Cremieux with Mehemet Ali (1840).

651. AUTOGRAPH LETTER *L. Emanuel.*
From Sir Moses Montefiore to Mr. Lewis Emanuel, written in the Holy City of Jerusalem, July 28, 1875.

652. AUTOGRAPH LETTER *C. I. de Sola.*
From Sir Moses Montefiore to Rev. D. A. de Sola (1836), acknowledging receipt of the first volume of the latter's translation of the Forms of Prayer.

653. AUTOGRAPH LETTER *Dr. M. Davis.*
From Sir Moses Montefiore, Bart.

654. AUTOGRAPH LETTER *C. K. Salaman.*
From Sir Moses Montefiore to Mr. C. K. Salaman, relative to his journey to the Holy Land. Date, March 1849.

655. AUTOGRAPH LETTER *A. de Mattos Mocatta.*
Of introduction by Sir Moses Montefiore in Hebrew and English to the Haham Bashi of Constantinople.

656. TWO LETTERS, *Per I. Spielman.*
Each three pages long, written by Sir Moses Montefiore in his 95th year.

657. LETTER FROM PRINCE CHARLES OF ROUMANIA
J. Sebag Montefiore.
To Sir Moses Montefiore, stating that the Jews of Roumania are well cared for by the Government, and that religious persecution does not exist in the country.

658. LETTER FROM THE EMPEROR OF MOROCCO *J. Sebag Montefiore.*
To Sir Moses Montefiore.

659. ORIGINAL FIRMAN OF SULTAN OF TURKEY GRANTING EQUAL RIGHTS TO JEWS. *J. Sebag Montefiore.*
Obtained by Sir Moses Montefiore, through his mission to the East in 1840.

660. LETTER FROM CHIEF RABBI   *Per I. Spielman.*
To Sir Moses Montefiore.

661. LETTER FROM MRS. GARFIELD.   *Per I. Spielman.*
Of congratulation to Sir Moses Montefiore in 1881.

662. TWO ROUGH NOTE BOOKS.   *Per I. Spielman.*
Containing notes written by Sir Moses Montefiore during
his travels to the East.

663. LITHOGRAPHED COPY OF SIR MOSES MONTEFIORE'S WILL.
Per I. Spielman.

664. CENTENNIAL CONGRATULATIONS.   *Per I. Spielman.*
Telegrams of congratulation upon Sir M. Montefiore's
hundredth birthday, bound into a volume.

664a. CENTENNIAL ADDRESSES   *Ramsgate Synagogue.*
From various public bodies, on Sir Moses Montefiore's
hundredth birthday.

665. TESTIMONIAL   *Bevis Marks Synagogue.*
To Sir M. Montefiore, with copy of Firman.

666. SMALL ENGLISH BIBLE.   *Josephine H. Lublin.*
Formerly belonging to Sir Moses Montefiore. Contains
notes in the handwriting of Sir Moses.

667. PRAYER BOOK.   *J. Sebag Montefiore.*
Bound in silver; with miniature of Sir Moses Montefiore.

668. ACCOUNT OF SIR MOSES MONTEFIORE'S GOLDEN WEDDING.
On satin.   *Per I. Spielman.*

669–676. REPORTS   *Per I. Spielman.*
Of Sir Moses Montefiore to the Board of Deputies, 1872, and
other Reports and Pamphlets (8).

677. PROSPECTUS   *Per I. Spielman.*
Of the sale of East Cliff Lodge, Ramsgate, in 1832, when
it was purchased by Sir Moses Montefiore.

678. HEBREW ALMANACK PROOF (5606).   *G. Ellis.*
By De Lara. Dedicated to Sir Moses Montefiore.

679. PLAN OF TABLE   *Lewis Emanuel.*
At the inauguration dinner given by Sir Moses Montefiore
(then Moses Montefiore, Esq.) on 4th Oct. 1837, as
Sheriff of London and Middlesex.

680. SILVER TROPHY.   *Bevis Marks Synagogue.*
Presented to Sir Moses Montefiore in acknowledgment of
his mission to the East in 1840, on behalf of his persecuted
co-religionists.

681. JUG AND BASIN.   *Bevis Marks Synagogue.*
Presented by the late N. M. Rothschild, Esq., to Sir Moses
Montefiore, at the opening of the Ramsgate synagogue.

AUTOTYPE

682. SMALL SCROLL OF THE LAW. *Bevis Marks Synagogue.*
Used by Sir M. Montefiore on his travels.

683. " JEWS' WALK." *Bevis Marks Synagogue.*
Board formerly on wall at Guildhall. Removed at the
instance of Sir M. Montefiore (1838).

684. GILT CUP PRESENTATION. *Bevis Marks Synagogue.*

685. SILVER CUP PRESENTATION (FRANKFORT).

685*a*. GOLD WATCH REPEATER. *A. M. Sebag-Montefiore.*
In *repoussé* case. Formerly the property of Mrs. Rachael
Montefiore (mother of Sir M. Montefiore).

686. TALITH (PRAYING SCARF). *J. Sebag Montefiore.*
Used by Sir Moses Montefiore. Embroidered corners.

687. BREAD TICKETS. *Per I. Spielman.*
Given away by Sir Moses Montefiore on Saturday instead of
money.

688. PHOTOGRAPH OF A CHEQUE FOR £100
Presented by Sir Moses Montefiore to the Board of Guardians
on his hundredth birthday. It was the custom of Sir
Moses, on his birthdays, to give to public institutions
sums of money corresponding with the number of years
of his age.

689. PASSPORTS OF SIR MOSES MONTEFIORE. *Per I. Spielman.*
For the years 1816, 1823, 1836, 1846, 1857, 1859, 1862,
1863, 1867, 1868, 1870, 1871, 1872, 1875.

690. VISITING CARD OF " MR. SHERIFF MONTEFIORE."

691. INVITATION CARD *Per I. Spielman.*
Of Messrs. George Carroll and M. Montefiore, Sheriffs elect,
1837, to a banquet at Merchant Taylors' Hall.

692. CITY OF LONDON BROKER'S MEDAL. *Hyman Montagu.*
Lately belonging to and inscribed with the name of the
late Sir Moses Montefiore, Bart. Only twelve such
medals were issued to Jews, the object being to limit the
number of Jewish brokers.

693. MEDAL. *B. Heymann.*
Struck by Gebrüder Nathan at Hamburg (1841), in commemoration of Sir Moses and Lady Montefiore's journey
to Egypt. Silver gilt. *Obv.* Arms and Hebrew inscription. *Rev.* Inscriptions in German.

694. MEDAL. *Lucien Wolf.*
Struck in London in honour of Sir Moses Montefiore's
hundredth birthday. *Obv.* Bust; &c., כל אשרי *Rev.* A
UNIVERSAL TRIBVTE, &c. Issued by Loewenstark &
Sons.

695. MEDAL.   *Lucien Wolf.*
  Struck at Corfu in honour of Sir Moses Montefiore's hun-
    dredth birthday.   *Obv.* Bust.   *Rev.* A MOSE MONTE-
    FIORE SINTESI PERFETTA DEL GIVDAISMO NEL SVO
    CENTENARIO VIII KESVAN.   5645.

696. MONTEFIORE MEDAL.   *Hyman Montagu.*

698. TESTIMONIALS.   *Bevis Marks Synagogue.*
  Presented to Sir Moses Montefiore on various public occa-
    sions.   Nos. 4, 8, 14, 16, 21, 27, 29, 31, 33, 34, 35, 36,
    43, 44, 45, 53.

MONTEFIORE COLLEGE, RAMSGATE; *see* No. 567.

h.—AUTOGRAPHS AND FAMILY DOCUMENTS.

705. AUTOGRAPH LETTER.   *Dr. Maurice Davis.*
  From Grace Aguilar, novelist and writer on Jewish history
    and religion, author of "Spirit of Judaism," "Women of
    Israel," and a large number of popular works ("Vale of
    Cedars," &c.); 1816–1847.

706. AUTOGRAPH LETTER.   *C. I. de Sola.*
  From Grace Aguilar to Rev. D. A. de Sola. Refers to some
    friendly criticisms by Miss Charlotte Montefiore on one
    of her early tales, "The Perez Family."

707. AUTOGRAPH LETTER.   *Dr. M. Davis.*
  From John Barnett (composer).

708. AUTOGRAPH LETTER.   *Dr. M. Davis.*
  From Morris Barnett to Charles Matthews, and signed
    Moses ben Methusaleh. Barnett was a well-known
    dramatist and actor, author of "The Serious Family,"
    "Monsieur Jacques," "The Bold Dragoons," &c.; b. 1800,
    d. 1850.

709. AUTOGRAPH LETTER.   *Dr. M. Davis.*
  From Sir Julius Benedict, composer, son of Jewish banker
    at Stuttgart, author of several English operas ("Lily of
    Killarney," &c.); b. 1804, d. 1886.

710. AUTOGRAPH LETTER.   *Dr. M. Davis.*
  From J. P. Benjamin, Q.C.   (*See* No. 1113.)

711. AUTOGRAPH LETTER.   *C. I. de Sola.*
  Italian. From Michael Bolaffey to Haham Raphael Meldola
    (1817). Bolaffey was musical director to Duke of Cam-
    bridge, and descendant of an ancient Jewish family, the
    Abulafias.

712 AUTOGRAPH LETTER.   *Dr. M. Davis.*
  From John Braham to Miss Lewis (1853).   (*See* No. 1035.)

713. AUTOGRAPH LETTER. *Lewis Emanuel.*
From Coleridge to Professor Hurwitz referring to the latter's "Hebrew Tales," about to be published at the date of the letter, 1826. (*See* No. 1077.)

714. AUTOGRAPH LETTER. *Lewis Emanuel.*
From Coleridge to Professor Hurwitz, complimenting him on a Jewish dirge composed on the death of the Princess Charlotte.

715. AUTOGRAPH LETTER. *Lewis Emanuel.*
From Emanuel Deutsch. *See* No. 1112.

716. AUTOGRAPH LETTER. *A. de Mattos Mocatta.*
From I. D'Israeli to I. Mocatta. Referring to the address by the latter to the Spanish and Portuguese Jews. (*See* No. 1031.)

717. AUTOGRAPH LETTER. *Dr. M. Davis.*
From B. Disraeli (Lord Beaconsfield) to Charles Matthews. (*See* No. 1082.)

718. AUTOGRAPH LETTERS. *Asher I. Myers.*
From George Eliot, the celebrated novelist, interesting in the present connection as the author of "Daniel Deronda." One letter refers to a remarkable Jew in whom the writer was interested, and was penned immediately after the death of Mr. G. H. Lewes, at a date when she is said in her biography not to have written letters. The other refers to her motives in writing "Daniel Deronda."

719. LETTER OF FREDERICK VII. OF DENMARK. *H. S. Harris.*
To grandfather of exhibitor, on his surrendering to the State certain church lands and benefices which would belong to him on his purchase of the Barony of Ringstadt, 1810.

720. AUTOGRAPH LETTER. *C. K. Salaman.*
From Baron de Goldsmid to Mr. C. K. Salaman. Dated 3rd Dec., 1849. (*See* No. 1042.)

721. AUTOGRAPH LETTER. *Lewis Emanuel.*
From the late Benjamin Gompertz, F.R.S., dated 22nd Sept. 1857. (*See* No. 1043a.)

722. AUTOGRAPH LETTER. *D. N. Samson.*
From Rebecca Gratz to Mrs. M. N. Nathan, dated Philadelphia, Aug. 19th, 1840. Miss Gratz was the original of Rebecca in Scott's "Ivanhoe." An earnest worker for philanthropic movements. Scott heard of her through Washington Irving. b. 1782, d. 1869.

723. AUTOGRAPH LETTER. *D. N. Samson*
From Rebecca Gratz to the late Rev. M. N. Nathan.

724. AUTOGRAPH LETTER.   *Lewis Emanuel.*
From the late S. A. Hart, R.A.   (*See* No. 1084.)

725. AUTOGRAPH LETTER.   *Dr. M. Davis.*
From S. A. Hart, R.A.

726. AUTOGRAPH LETTER.   *Lewis Emanuel.*
From Numa Hartog, B.A.   Letter dated 1871.   (*See*
No. 1120.)

727. AUTOGRAPH LETTER.   *Lewis Emanuel.*
From the late Michael Henry.   Dated 1874.   Writer was
editor of *Jewish Chronicle.*

728. AUTOGRAPH LETTER.   *C. K. Salaman.*
From Rev. S. Herschell to Mr. Isaac Cowen.   Dated 1817.
(*See* No. 1004.)

729. AUTOGRAPH LETTER.   *Lewis Emanuel.*
From the late Rt. Hon. Sir George Jessel, Master of the
Rolls.   (*See* No. 1010.)

730. AUTOGRAPH   *Dr. M. Davis.*
Of Alexander Lee (composer).

731. AUTOGRAPH LETTER.   *Dr. M. Davis.*
From Nelson Lee (dramatist).

732. AUTOGRAPH LETTER.   *Mrs. A. M. Spielman.*
From N. M. Rothschild, dated Manchester, 1807, returning
thanks for order of £72 6*s.*   (*See* No. 1036.)

733. AUTOGRAPH LETTER.   *S. Harris.*
From Baron Lionel de Rothschild to H. Harris.   Dated
11th Aug. 1847.   (*See* No. 1086.)

734. AUTOGRAPH LETTER.   *C. K. Salaman.*
From Sir D. Salomons, Bart., M.P., to Mr. C. K. Salaman.
(*See* No. 1066.)

735. AUTOGRAPH LETTER.   *S. Harris.*
From Mr. David Salomons.   Dated 1841.

736. SIGNATURE OF SAMPSON SAMUEL.   *S. Harris.*
Acknowledgment from Jewish Board of Deputies.   Dated
1857.   Mr. Samuel was for many years Secretary of
Board of Deputies, and accompanied Sir M. Montefiore
on his mission to Morocco.   b. 1804, d. 1868.

737. LETTER AND SKETCH.   *Dr. M. Davis.*
From Abraham Solomon, artist, painted, "Waiting for the
Verdict," and other popular works.   b. 1824, d. 1862.

739. AUTOGRAPH LETTER. *G. L. Lyon.*
From W. M. Thackeray to the Secretary of the Jews and
General Literary and Scientific Institute, Sussex Hall,
Leadenhall Street. Refers to a lecture he had delivered
at the Institute.

740. AUTOGRAPH LETTER. *Lewis Emanuel.*
From Professor Waley, in reply to one asking him to allow
himself to be nominated as a candidate for the London
School Board, 1879. (*See* No. 1093.)

741. AUTOGRAPH LETTER. *Dr. M. Davis.*
From Dr. Joseph Wolff, the celebrated traveller and
enthusiast. b. 1795, d. 1862.

742–743. AUTOGRAPH LETTERS. *Dr. A. Cohen.*
From Joseph Zedner. (*See* No. 1085.)

744. MARRIAGE SETTLEMENT. *Major A. Goldsmid.*
With autographs of Benjamin and Abraham and Asher
Goldsmid. Dated 1804. (*See* Nos. 990 and 993.)

745. AUTOGRAPH LETTER. *C. I. de Sola.*
From Dr. Delitzsch to Rev. D. A. de Sola. Dated 1837.
German. Dr. D. is the celebrated Biblical scholar, author
of "History of Jewish Poetry," &c.; b. 1813.

746. AUTOGRAPH LETTER. *C. I. de Sola.*
From Dr. Fürst to Rev. D. A. de Sola. Dated 1842.
German. Fürst was an eminent Jewish scholar and
bibliographer; author of Hebrew and Chaldic Lexicon
(translated into English), and of the most complete
Biblical Concordance. b. 1805, d. 1873.

747. AUTOGRAPH LETTER. *Dr. M. Davis.*
From Abraham Geiger, the eminent Jewish reformer.
b. 1810, d. 1874.

747a. AUTOGRAPH LETTER. *Dr. M. Davis.*
From F. Halevy, the composer. b. 1799, d. 1862.

748. AUTOGRAPH LETTER. *Dr. M. Davis.*
From F. Mendelssohn-Bartholdy, the celebrated composer.
b. 1803, d. 1847.

749. AUTOGRAPH LETTER. *Dr. M. Davis.*
From Meyerbeer, the celebrated composer. b. 1794, d. 1864.

750. AUTOGRAPH LETTER. *Dr. M. Davis.*
From Heinrich Heine, the celebrated poet, b. 1799, d. 1852.
Heine visited England, and has recorded his impressions
in his "Englische Fragmente."

751. AUTOGRAPH LETTER. *Dr. M. Davis.*
From B. Moscheles, musician. b. 1794, d. 1870.

751a. Autograph Letter.   *W. Josephs.*
Hebrew.   From Solomon Munk to Michael Josephs.
Munk (b. 1805, d. 1867) was a celebrated Hebraist.
Translated the "Guide of the Perplexed" of Maimonides.

752. Autograph Letter.   *Dr. M. Davis.*
From Rachel, celebrated tragedienne. b. 1820, d. 1858.

753. Autograph Letter.   *Dr. M. Davis.*
From R. Solomon Rapaport, of Prague. Talmudic scholar :
author of "Erech Millin," and other works. b. 1790,
d. 1867.

754. Autograph Letter.   *Dr. M. Davis.*
From Dr. Salaman, of Hamburg, a celebrated Jewish
preacher. A volume of his Sermons has been translated
by Miss Anna Maria Goldsmid. (*See* No. 758.)

755. Autograph Letter.   *Dr. M. Davis.*
From Leopold Zunz, the greatest Jewish scholar of the
nineteenth century. Author of "Gottesdientsliche Vort-
raege," &c., b. 1794, d. 1886. Zunz visited England to
consult Hebrew MSS. of Bodleian.

756. Autograph Letter.   *C. I. de Sola.*
From Dr. Zunz to Rev. D. A. de Sola. Dated 1841. In
German.

Autograph Letters.
From Sir Moses Montefiore ; *see* Montefioriana, Nos. 651–656.

757. Autograph Letter.   *W. Josephs.*
From I. M. Jost to Michael Josephs. English. Jost was a
distinguished Jewish historian, b. 1793, d. 1860.

758. Solomon's Sermons.   *A. I. Myers.*
Translated by A. M. Goldsmid. With autograph notes of
the Duke of Sussex.

759. Hebrew Pentateuch.   *M. N. Adler, M.A.*
Curiously bound. Autograph of Rev. David Schiff, Chief
Rabbi (1752.)

760. Pedigree of Meldola Family.   *Prof. R. Meldola, F.R.S.*
Biography in verse of Rev. Dr. Meldola. With pedigree of
Meldola family going back to A.D. 1340. (*See* No. 985.)

760a. Letter.   *Prof. Meldola.*
From Duke of Sussex, acknowledging receipt of a copy of a
sermon by Haham Meldola (1818).

760b. Letter.   *Prof. Meldola.*
From Prince Regent, acknowledging copy of sermon by
Haham Meldola (1818).

761. Pedigree.   *Mrs. Arabella Levi.*
Descriptive family pedigree, illustrated with signs of the
Zodiac, written and painted by Moses Mordccai, 1799.

762. COLLECTION OF JEWISH PEDIGREES. *Lucien Wolf.*
  Printed, and in MS.

Abarbanel.	De Sola.	Mocatta.
Abendana.	De Stern.	Montefiore.
Aboab.	De Vahl (Samuel).	Nieto.
Abudiente (Gideon).	De Worms.	Phillips.
Adler.	Duran.	Ricardo.
Aguilar.	Franco.	Rothschild.
Almosnino.	Goldsmid.	Salomons.
Azulay.	Gompertz.	Samuda.
Belinfante.	Guedalla.	Sasportas.
Benas.	Henriques.	Sassoon.
Benedict.	Herschell.	Schwarzschild.
Bing.	Kimchi.	Simon.
Bolaffey.	Levy.	Suasso.
Brandon.	Lindo.	Van Oven.
Castello.	Lopes.	Wagg.
Cohen.	Lousada.	Waley.
Cortissos.	Luzzatto.	Wilner.
D'Avigdor.	Meldola.	Ximenes.
Disraeli.	Mendes da Costa.	Yulee.
De Pass.		

763. JEWISH COATS OF ARMS. *Lucien Wolf.*
  Collection of coloured sketches of coats of arms of the
  following Anglo-Jewish families :— Mendes da Costa,
  Rothschild, Goldsmid, Montefiore, De Worms, Salomons,
  Mocatta, Castello, Waley, Cohen, Villareal, De Vahl,
  Lopes, Gideon, Herschell, Lara, Lousada, Medina,
  Phillips, Ricardo, Sassoon, Suasso, Ximenes, &c.

764. COATS OF ARMS *Misses Aguilar.*
  Of Belisario and Aguilar families.

i.—MSS. AND BOOKS OF HISTORIC INTEREST.

MANUSCRIPTS.

774. LOS HUMILDES SUPPLICACIONES DE MENASSE BEN ISRAEL
  MEDICINA. *Breslau Seminary.*
  En nombre de La Nacion de los Judios a Sa Alteza el Señor
  Protector Oliver Cromwell de la Republica de Inglaterra,
  Scocia y Yrlanda en Londres Traduzido de l'original
  Ingles. 12°. pp. 30.

775. " RESEARCHES OF ABRAHAM," BY CARDOSO.
  Sir Julian Goldsmid, Bart., M.P.
  " The book 'Bekur Abraham' (the Researches of Abraham)
  on Cabbala, by the physician Abraham Cardoso, translated
  into Hebrew and revised by Solomon da Costa Athias."
  London, 5476=1716.

776. COLLECTANEA. *Dr. N. M. Adler, Chief Rabbi.*
  By Solomon da Costa Athias (1717), containing מנחת יהודה
  by R. Perez Ha-Cohen ; Odes by R. Moses Abudiente, &c.

777. COLLECTANEA.   *Dr. N. M. Adler, Chief Rabbi.*
Written by Solomon da Costa Athias. Dated London, 5477
= 1717.   London.   [Contains אור הדרשנים (Light of
Preachers), by Isaac Sahalon; Hebrew Elegy on the
death of William, Duke of Gloucester; Hebrew Elegy on
death of William III., by R. Joseph ben Danim; Piz-
monim, by R. Israel Nagara ; Riddles, Epitaphs, &c.]

778. MANUSCRIPT.   *Rev. M. de Sola, Canada.*
English version of Portuguese Prayer-Book : *temp.* George I.

779. HEBREW RESPONSES OF R. HIRSCH.   *Beth Hamidrash.*
Between 1728 and 1744. For R. Hirsch, *see* No. 968.

780. HEBREW RESPONSES.   *Beth Hamidrash.*
By R. Hirsch. At end others by R. Löb Nordon of London.

781. HEBREW CASUISTICAL NOTES, &c.   *Beth Hamidrash.*
By R. Zebi Hirsch.

782. HEBREW NOTES ON THE MISHNA, &c.   *Beth Hamidrash.*
Copied from the margins of books belonging to Zebi
Hirsch, Rabbi of London. At end appears the following
entry: "I Thom. Benyon, jun., Hereby Maketh oath that
the Thread manefactury by us is all made from pure flax
withouth anny Mixture of anny other matirual, נעשה בפני,
Lord Myer." [Probably in reference to the prohibition
against wearing clothes made of wool and linen together.
Deut. xxii. 11.]

783. אמונת אומן   *Dr. N. M. Adler, Chief Rabbi.*
By the Physician, Meyer Schomberg. Dated 5506 A.M.
= 1746. London.

784. SERMON.   *Clarence de Sola.*
Original MS. of a sermon preached in Spanish, by a member
of the De Sola family on Shabbat Nachmu 5517 = 1757.
[Supposed to be by Abraham de Isaac de Sola.]

785. SERMON.   *C. de Sola.*
Original MS. of a sermon preached in Spanish, by a member
of the De Sola family, in the year 5521 = 1761. [Supposed
to be by Abraham de Isaac de Sola.]

786. TALMUDIC TREATISE.   *Beth Hamidrash.*
By Naphtali ben Abraham. Written in London, 1772.
Hebrew.

787. SCRAPBOOK OF R. DE FALK.   *Beth Hamidrash.*
Mostly mystical, about 1773. Mentions incidentally that
he received letters from R. Simeon Boaz through Prince
Chartorisky.

788. NOTARIKON OF R. DE FALK.   *Beth Hamidrash.*
For account of R. Falk, *see* No. 1030.

your Petitioners as in duty bound will ever pray.—

Lionel de Rothschild

N M Rothschild

Otto E Nichols

Philip Salomons

John Helbert & Israels

Levi Salomons

David Brandon

M Montefiore Jr.

Joseph Cohen

Samuel Samuel

Joseph S Brenton

Silva & San Queen

H Isaac

Isaac L Goldsmid

789. ס' השמות   *Beth Hamidrash.*
By R. de Falk. Cabbalistical notes on Divine names.

790. PAPERS.   *Rev. S. H. Harris.*
Written by Rabbi de Falk.

791. MS. SERMONS IN HEBREW.   *Dr. N. M. Adler, Chief Rabbi.*
By R. David Tebele Schiff, Chief Rabbi of London, preached by him on London; also Novellæ on Talmud. (*See* No. 996.)

792. MANUSCRIPT.   *Beth Hamidrash.*
One volume containing תפוחי זהב במשכיות כסף two mystical commentaries on Ecclesiastes, by Abraham ben Rabbi Naphtali טנג [Taussig Neun Gerschel] written in London 1773. Fol. 111. צפנת פענח the author quotes Latin texts, among others Virgil with Dryden's translations, of which he gives Hebrew translations.

793. AUTOGRAPH SERMON.   *D. N. Samson.*
By Mr. Solomon Nathan, in the Liverpool Synagogue, Seel Street, in the year 1824 or 1825.

794. ORTHOGRAPHIA HEBRÆO-ANGLICANA;   *N. I. Berlin.*
Or new system of Writing English in Hebrew, current hand-writing after the usage prevailing in Germany, by N. L. Benmohel (1830).

795. AN ESSAY IN VERSE.   *N. I. Berlin.*
Towards a comparison between the history of the Children of Israel during their journey from Egypt to the Promised Land, and that of the Reformation, by N. L. Benmohel, M.A., T.C.D.

796. "PRIMITIVE ETHNOLOGY."   *N. I. Berlin.*
A Normal Onomasticon, tending to be a Guide, Basis, and Tribute to Sammlung Altdeutscher Eigennamen, by N. L. Benmohel [incomplete].

797. AUTOGRAPH SERMON   *D. N. Samson.*
Of Rev. M. N. Nathan, delivered at Old Liverpool Synagogue, Seel Street, in 1832, on behalf of the Liverpool Dispensaries.

798. MANUSCRIPT.   *Beth Hamidrash.*
Menachem Meiri's קרית ספר. At end are some letters signed Sol. Hirschel [1837].

799. TWO VOLUMES OF CORRESPONDENCE.   *Sir Julian Goldsmid.*
With leading Statesmen on Jewish Disabilities. 1828–58.

800. PETITION   *A. de Mattos Mocatta.*
To the House of Commons to abolish the words, "On the faith of a Christian," from the Parliamentary Oath, signed by Sir Moses Montefiore, Baron Lionel de Rothschild, Sir Isaac Goldsmid, Moses Mocatta, Esq.

D

801. Testimonial.   *Sir J. Whittaker Ellis, Bart.*
    Presented to Sir J. W. Ellis, at the conclusion of his
    Mayoralty, 1882, by the Executive Committee of the
    Mansion House Fund for the Relief of Russian Jews, in
    recognition of the Mansion House Meeting of Feb. 1, 1882,
    which resulted in the collection of over £100,000 for the
    relief of Jewish victims of Russian persecution.

802. "A Treatise on Jewish Customs."   *Miss Lindo.*
    By the late E. H. Lindo.

803. "Sacred Instructions, a Dialogue."   *Miss Lindo.*
    By the late E. H. Lindo.

804. Diary of Grace Aguilar.   *Rev. M. Joseph.*

805. Poems, 1833.   *Rev. M. Joseph.*
    By Grace Aguilar.

806. MSS. Stories, etc.   *Rev. M. Joseph.*
    By Grace Aguilar:—"Adah, a Simple Story;" "Home
    Scenes;" "Val des Ravages;" "Sabbath Thoughts."

807. Commonplace Book of R. Azariah Benas.   *B. L. Benas, J.P.*
    Medical prescriptions in Hebrew and Latin, mathematicæ
    formulæ. Paper read thereon before Historic Society of
    Lancashire, Feb. 10, 1876.

808. "Mourning Bride," in Hebrew.   *Jews' College.*
    Congreve's well-known play, translated, with Hebrew, by
    Abraham Tung, 1756.

809. Manuscript Writings,   *Walter Josephs.*
    In Hebrew and English, of the late Michael Josephs.
    (*See* No. 1020).

810. English and Hebrew Dictionary and Rabbinical Dictionary
    (MSS.) By the late Michael Josephs.   *Walter Josephs.*

811. Translation   *Dr. N. M. Adler, Chief Rabbi.*
    Of Haham D. Nieto's work on Nature and Divine Providence.
    Dated 1853.

812. Lectures on Jehuda Halevi's "Cuzari."
                                 Association for Religious Knowledge.
    By the late Rev. Barnett Abrahams, B.A., founder of the
    Jewish Association for the Diffusion of Religious Know-
    ledge.

813. Manuscript Scrap Book.   *Rev. Dr. H. Adler.*
    Of the late Emanuel Deutsch. (*See* No. 1112.)

BOOKS.

For other books not bearing directly on Anglo-Jewish History, see Section III.,
p. 196, and British Museum Exhibits.

820. Volume of Tracts, 1649–1834.   *Sir J. Goldsmid.*
    From the Duke of Sussex's Library. The first is exceedingly
    rare, containing "The petition of the Jewes for the

Repealing of the Act of Parliament for their banishment out of England, presented to his Excellency [Lord Fairfax] and the generall Councell of Officers on Fryday, Jan. 5, 1648," London, 1649, the first tract relating to the return of the Jews to England. The petitioners are Mrs. Cartwright and her son Ebenezer, residing in Amsterdam.

821–824. Four Convolutes of Tracts on Anglo-Jewish History.
Jews' College.

Collection of the late Rev. A. L. Green.

[This Collection is the most complete one in the country. The late Rev. A. L. Green (*see* No. 1109) was the pioneer in the study of Anglo-Jewish history and of the literature connected with it. The following list of short titles of the pamphlets has been kindly prepared by Dr. M. Friedländer, Principal of Jews' College. For fuller details of pamphlets, &c., see *Bibliotheca Anglo-Judaica.*]

I.—Pamphlets referring to the Political State of the Jews in England.

1. Address of 'Manasseh b. Israel to the Lord Protector in behalf of the Jewish nation. 1655. Reprint, London, 1868.
2. A short demurrer to the Jewes long discontinued remitter into England, by W. Prynne. London, 1656.
3. Vindiciae Judaeorum, by Manasseh b. Israel. 1656.
4. Petition against the Jewes, by Thos. Violet. London, 1661.
5. A Historical and Law treatise against the Jews and Judaism. London, 1703.
6. The complaint of the children of Israel in a letter to a Reverend High Priest of the church by law established, by Solomon Abrabanel of the house of David. Second edition. London, 1736.
6a. Reprint of the same under the title: An epistle from a High Priest of the Jews to the Chief Priest of Canterbury, on the extension of the Catholic Emancipation to the Jews. London, 1821.
7. Reasons offered to the consideration of Parliament, for preventing the growth of Judaism. Republished, London, 1738.
8. Consideration on the Bill for a general Naturalization. London, 1748.
9. The Expediency of a general Naturalization of foreign Protestants and others. London, 1751.
10. An Epistle to the Freeholders of Great Britain, containing some observations upon the Bill for Naturalizing foreign Jews. London, 1753.
11. The Case of the Jews considered, by a Christian. London, 1753.
12. The rejection and restoration of the Jews according to Scripture, by Archaicus. London, 1753.
13. A review of the proposed Naturalization of the Jews, by a Merchant (Hanway). London, 1753.
14. Admonitions relating to the Jews, by Archaicus. London, 1753.
15. Some considerations on the Naturalization of the Jews, by J. E. Gent. London, 1753.

16. Considerations on the Bill to permit persons professing the Jewish Religion to be naturalized by Parliament. London, 1753.
17. Further Considerations on the Act to permit, etc. London, 1753.
18. An answer to a Pamphlet, entitled Considerations on the Bill to permit, etc., by Romanie. London, 1753.
19. Letters admonitory and argumentative, from J. H—y, Merchant to J. S—r, Merchant (Hanway). London, 1753.
20. Apology for the Naturalization of the Jews, by a True Believer. London, 1753.
21. A full answer to a fallacious Apology artfully circulated through the kingdom, by a Christian. London, 1753.
22. A modest Apology for the citizens and merchants of London who petitioned against the Naturalization of the Jews, by Romanie. London, 1753.
23. A letter to a friend concerning Naturalizations, by Josiah Tucker. London, 1753.
24. Remarks on the Reverend Mr. Tucker's Letter on Naturalizations, in two letters to a friend. London, 1753.
25. A letter to the Publick on the Act for Naturalizing the Jews, by A. Z. London, 1753.
26. The Jew's Advocate. London, 1753.
27. A letter to the worshipful Sir John Barnard, Knt,, on the Act of Parl. for Naturalizing the Jews. London, 1753.
28. A sermon preached at the Parish church of St. George, Hanover Sq., on occasion of the clamours against the Act for Natur. the Jews, by Revd. Mr. Winstanley. London, 1753.
29. An earnest and serious Address to the Freeholders and Electors of Great Britain on occasion of the clamour, etc., wherein the Act is defended upon Christian principles, by An Orthodox Member of the Church of England. London, 1753.
30. The other side of the question, being a collection of what has appeared in defence of the late Act. London, 1753.

Collection of late Rev. A. L. Green—*continued.*

31. The que-tion whether a Jew born within the British Dominions was, before the making of the late Act of Parl., a person capable, by law, to purchase and hold lands to him and to his heirs, by a Gentleman of Lincoln's Inn. London, 1753.
32. A reply to the famous Jew Question, in a letter to the Gentleman of Lincoln's Inn, by a Freeholder of the County of Surrey. London, 1754.
33. Remarks upon some passages in a dedication to the Jews, by W. Warburton, Dean of Bristol. London, 1759.
34. A Letter to the Right Honorable Sir Thomas Chitty, with Appendix on the Natural. of the J. London, 1760.
35. Religious intolerance no part of the general plan either of the Mosaic or Christian dispensation, by Jos. Tucker. London, 1774.
36. A collection of Testimonies in favour of religious liberty. London, 1790.
37. An attempt to remove prejudices against the Jews, by Th. Withbury. London, 1804.
38. Vindication of the Jews, by Th. Withbury. London, 1809.
38a. Copy of correspondence between the Chief Rabbi, Dr. Solomon Herschel and J. J. Lockhart of Oxford, on the validity of oaths taken by Jews. Copied from *Morning Chronicle,* June 26, 1817.
39. Brief Memoir of the Jews in relation to their civil disabilities. London, 1829.
40. Jewish Emancipation. A poem, by Levite. London, 1829.
   History of the Jews in England. Enquiry into their civil disabilities, by J. Blunt. London, 1830.
42. Remarks on the civil disabilities of British Jews, by Francis Henry Goldsmid. London, 1830.
43. Extracts from the public journals, on the disabilities of the Jews. London, 1830.
44. The arguments advanced against the enfranchisement of the Jews, considered, by Francis Henry Goldsmid. London, 1831.
45. The British Jew to his fellow countrymen. London, 1833.
46. A speech in the House of Lords on the removal of certain disabilities of the Jews, by R. Whately. London, 1833.
47. A letter to Isaac L. Goldsmid on certain misstatements concerning the Jewish religion, by Hyman Hurwitz. London, 1833.
48. An appea' to the Public in behalf of the Jews. London, 1834.
49. Observations on the civil disabilities of British Jews, by John Coles. London, 1834.
50. Debate in the House of Commons and in the House of Lords on the Bill for removing the civil disabilities of the Jews. London, 1834.
51. A letter to the Right Reverend the Lord Bishop of Chichester, upon the Emancipation of the Jews, by Basil Montagu. London, 1834.
52. A short statement in behalf of the Jews with an Appendix containing The Jews' Relief Bill, etc. London, 1835.
53 A sermon on the occasion of the death of the Chief Rabbi, 27, 11, 1842, by Henry Hawkes. Position of the Jews. London, 1843.
54. A plea for the Jews, by S. A. Bradshaw. London, 1844.
55. Jewish Emancipation, by an Israelite. London, 1845.
55a. Address of the Jewish Association for the Removal of Civil and Religious disabilities, to the Electors of the City of London. Extracted from the *Jewish Chronicle,* July 16th, 1847.
56. The position of the Jews as indicated and affected by the return to Parliament of Baron Lionel de Rothschild, by Matthew P. Haynes. London, 1847.
57. The Emancipation of the Jews, by G. Gawler. London, 1847.
58. An Appeal to the British nation on behalf of the Jews, by Barnard Von Oven. London, 1847.
59. Ought Baron de Rothschild to sit in Parliament? by Barnard von Oven. London, 1847.
60. A word with the Earl of Winchelsea, by "One of the People." London, 1847.
61. Progress of Jewish Emancipation since 1829.
62. Jewish Legislators and Israel's conversion. A Scriptural enquiry, by the Rev. L. Clotworthy Gillmor. London, 1848.
63. Remarks deprecating the proposed admission of H r Majesty's Jewish subjects to seats in the House of Commons, by John Travers Robinson. London, 1848.
64. A few words on the Jewish disabilities, by Henry Faudel. London, 1848.
65. Advocacy of Jewish Freedom, by W. Thornborrow. London, 1848.
66. On the Proscriptions and Persecutions of the Jews, by M. Bignon, translated from the French by a Lady. London, 1848.
67. Forty reasons for resisting the removal of the Jewish disability. London, 1848.
68. Reply to the arguments advanced against the removal of the disabilities of the Jews, by Francis Henry Goldsmid. London, 1848.
69. Substance of a speech on the motion of Lord John Russell for a Committee of the whole House, with a view to the removal of Jewish disabilities, by W. E. Gladstone. London, 1848.
70. Speech of Sir Robert Peel in the House of Commons, on the 2nd reading of the J. Disabilities Bill. London, 1848.
71. Speech of Richard Whately in the House of Lords, Aug. 1, 1833, on J. disabilities, with additional remarks. London, 1848.
72. The Status of the Jews in England from the time of the Normans to the reign of H. M. Queen Victoria, by Charles Egan. London, 1848.
73. Substance of a speech on the Jewish question, by W. F. Campbell, May 4, 1848. London, 1849.
74. Jewish dogmas. A correspondence between Dr. Raphall and C. N. Newdegate. London, 1849.
75. Dr. Croly versus civil and religious liberty. Letter by Aaron Levy Green. London, 1850.
76. Parliamentary Oaths, by Mr. Alderman Salomons. London, 1850.
77. The Jew question considered in a letter to Sir Robert H. Inglis by Veritas. London, 1851.
78. The Claims of the Jews on a Christian state, by Rev. D. McGill. London, 1851.
79. Report of the case Miller versus Salomons, by Augustus Goldsmid. London, 1852.

Collection of late Rev. A. L. Green—*continued.*

80. Some arguments against the admission of Jews into Parliament, by a Protectionist. London, 1852.
81. The Jew our Lawgiver. London, 1853.
82. Jewish Emancipation, by a country vicar. London, 1853.
83. Justice to all men; the Jew at home the safety of civilisation, by John H. L. Christien. London, 1854.
84. Can a Jew sit in Parliament, and why not? by Rev. J. C. Edwards. London, 1855.
85. The Anglo-Hebrews, their past Wrongs and present Grievances, by a clergyman of the Church of England. London, 1856.

86. The admission of the Jews into Parliament, by the author of the phrase "Un-Christianize the Legislature." London, 1857.
87. Barons of Parliament, a song.
88. Resolutions of the Court of Common Council of the City of London, March 4, 1858, concerning the removal of Jewish dis abilities.
89. The Oaths Bill; extracted from the *Times,* April 28, 1858.
90. The Jews in England, their History and Wrongs, by Th. Slingsby Duncombe. London, 1861. [Privately printed.]

825–827. THREE VOLUMES OF ORDERS OF SERVICE. *Jews' College.*

ORDER OF DIVINE SERVICE ON SPECIAL OCCASIONS.

A.—*Laying the Foundation, Consecration, Re-op ning of Synagogues, Schools, Hospitals.*

1. Brighton New Central Synagogue, Laying the foundation stone, 10 Kislev, 5635.
1a. Brighton New Central Synagogue, Consecration, 23 Ellul, 5635.
2. Bristol Synagogue, Consecration, 22 Ellul, 5546.
2a. Dover Synagogue, Consecration, 25 Ab, 5623.
3. Glasgow New Synagogue, Consecration, 28 Ellul, 5618.
4. Kingston, Jamaica, Synag. of the Portug. Jews' Congregation, Renewal of the Dedication, 5602.
5. Liverpool New Hebr. Congreg. Synagogue. Consecration, 5 Nisan, 5604.

LONDON.

6. Bayswater Synagogue, Laying the foundation stone, 5622.
7. Bayswater Synagogue. Consecration, 14 Ab, 5623.
8. Bevis Marks Portug. Synagogue, Commemoration of the Dedication, 5575.
9. Bevis Marks Portug. Synagogue, Renewal of Dedication, 27 Ellul, 5603.
10. Bevis Marks Portug. Synagogue, Reopening, 23 Ellul, 5619.
10a. Bevis Marks Portug. Synagogue, Installation of Prof. Artom as Haham, 8 Tebet, 5627.
11. Borough New Synagogue. Consecration. 2 Nisan, 5627.
11a. Borough New Synagogue, Reopening, 21 Ellul, 5636.
11b. Broad Street Synagogue, Consecration, 28 Iyar, 5627.
12. Bryanstone Street Portug. Synagogue, Laying the foundation stone, 11 Nisan, 5620.
13. Bryanstone Street Portug. Synagogue, Dedication, 8 Nisan, 5621.
14. Central Branch Synagogue, Laying the foundation stone, 6 Nisan, 5629.
15. Central Branch Synagogue, Consecration, 6 Nisan, 5630.
16. Cutler Street Polish Synagogue, Consecration, 15 Ellul, 5627.
16a. Dalston Synagogue, Consecration, 22 Tamuz, 5645.
17. East London Synagogue, Laying the foundation stone, 23 Nisan, 5636.
18. East London Synagogue, Consecration, 5637.
19. Great Synagogue, Consecration, 24 Ellul, 5526.

20. Great Synagogue, Consecration, 11 Nisan, 5550
21. Great Synagogue, Consecration, 24 Ellul, 5595.
22. Great Synagogue, Re-opening, 18 Ellul, 5612.
23. Great Synagogue, Installation of Chief Rabbi, the Rev. Dr. Nathan Marcus Adler, 4 Tamuz, 5605.
24. Maiden Lane Synagogue, Consecration, 19 Ellul, 5618.
25. Maiden Lane Synagogue, Re-opening, 14 Adar, 5611.
26. New Synagogue, Laying the foundation stone, 5 Iyar, 5597.
27. New Synagogue, Re-opening, 21 Ellul, 5607.
28. New Synagogue, Re-opening, 23 Ellul, 5615.
29. New West End Synagogue, Consecration, 6 Nisan, 5639.
30. North London Synagogue, Laying the foundation stone, 27 Kislev, 5628.
31. North London Synagogue, Consecration, 6 Nisan, 5628.
32. North London Synagogue, Re-opening, 15 Ellul, 5633.
33. Portland Street Synagogue, Consecration, 10 Nisan, 5615.
34. St. John's Wood Synagogue, Consecration, 28 Ellul, 5636.
35. St. John's Wood Synagogue, Laying the foundation stone, 15 Adar, 5642.
36. St. John's Wood Synagogue, Consecration, 14 Ab, 5642.
37. West London Synagogue of British Jews, Laying the foundation stone, 4 Sivan, 5608.
38. West London Synagogue of British Jews, Consecration, 26 Ellul, 5630.
39. Western Synagogue, Consecration, 24 Ellul, 5617.
40. Western Synagogue, Re-opening, 26 Ellul, 5625.
41. Western Synagogue, Re-opening, 22 Ellul, 5630.
42. Wigmore Street Synagogue of the Portug. Jews, Consecration, 27 Ellul, 5613.

43. Melbourne Hebrew Congregation, Consecration of Synagogue, 5637.
43a. Manchester Hebrew Congregation, Consecration of Synagogue, 11th March, 5618.
44. Merthyr Tydvil Synagogue, Consecration, 10 Tamuz, 5637.

Collection of late Rev. A. L. GREEN—*continued*.

45. Ramsgate Synagogue, Re-opening and 50th anniversary of the wedding of Sir M. Montefiore and Lady Judith Montefiore, 30 Sivan, 5622.
46. Sunderland Synagogue, Laying the foundation stone, 3 Tamuz, 5621.
47. Wolverhampton Synagogue, Consecration, 14 Ellul, 5619.
48. MS. notes in reference to Great Synagogue.
49. Installation of Honorary officers in Great Synagogue. MS.
50. Public religious examination of children, Bayswater Synagogue, 13 Sivan, 5626.
51. Prayer for the Ceremony of Religious majority, by Dr. Artom, 5627.
52. Service on Presentation of a Sefer-torah, Great Synagogue, 5579.
53. Service on Presentation of a Sefer-torah, Bevis Marks Synagogue, 19 Iyar, 5620.
53a. Service on Presentation of a Sefar-torah, Bevis Marks Synagogue, 11 Nisan, 5611.
54. Service on Presentation of a Sefer-torah, Bryanstone Synagogue, 23 Ellul, 5625.
55. Order of Service on the occasion of making collections for the "Metropolitan Hospital Sunday Fund."
56. Prayer in the Spanish and Portug. Synagogue on behalf of the oppressed Jews of Russia, 29 Shebet, 5642.
57. Service on the occasion of the visit of Royal Princes, MS., April 14, 1809.

1. Psalms and Ode, at the re-opening of the Gates of Hope School.
2. Opening of the new premises of Jews' College, June 27, 1881.
3. Jews' Convalescent Home, Opening, Heshvan 1, 5630.
4. Jews' Convalescent Home, Consecration of the New Wing for Children, May 16,5635.
5. Jews' Hospital, Consecration of Synagogue, 23 Adar, 5578.
6. Jews' Hospital, Prayer on the Anniversary.
7. Jews' Hospital, Laying the foundation stone, 28 Sivan, 5621.
8. Jews' Deaf and Dumb Home, Consecration, 22 Tebet, 5627.
9. Jews' Free School, Consecration and Examination, Jan. 13, 5582.
10. Jews' Free School, Consecration, 28 Iyar, 5626.
11. Westminster Jews' Free School, Consecration, June 20, 5618.
12. Jews' Infant School, Consecration, 14 Sept. 5601.
12a. Jews' Infant School, opening of the New School, July 23, 5618.
13. Jews' Orphan Asylum, opening of the New School, April 15, 5626.
14. Prayer for the use of Jewish patients. Supplied by the United Synagogue.
15. Great Ealing School, Consecration, Iyar 14, 5640.

B.—*On occasions of general Distress and of general Rejoicing.*

1. Prayer in the Synagogue at Barbados, on the Anniversary of the great calamity, 2 Ellul, 5591.
2. Prayer on the day of general humiliation and thanksgiving for protection during the earthquake, 29 Adar, 5603.
3. Prayer during the Severe Visitation raging in Europe; to be used in German Synag., 5592.
4. Prayer during the Severe Visitation raging in Europe; to be used in Sp. and Port. Jews' Syn., 5592.
4a. Thanksgiving for abundant Harvest, West London Syn., 5603.
5. Prayer to avert the consequences of the famine, Oct. 17, 5607.
6. Service, on day of humiliation, on account of famine, March 24, 5607.
7. Service, Thanksgiving for abundant harvest, Oct. 17, 5608.
7a. Prayer, on account of the prevailing Cholera.
8. Service, Thanksgiving, for the cessation of the Cholera, in Duke's Pl. Syn. and Bevis Marks Syn., Nov. 15, 5610.
9. Service, Thanksgiving, for the cessation of the Cholera in other synagogues, Nov. 15, 5610.
11. Thanksgiving for abundant harvest, Sp. and Port. Syn., Oct. 7, 5615.
12. Thanksgiving for abundant harvest, Ashkenazim, Oct. 7, 5615.
14. Prayer for relief from the cattle plague, 5626.
15. Thanksgiving for relief from the cattle plague, Nov. 24, 5627.
16. Order of Service, in reference to the American War, Dec. 13, 5537.
17. Order of Service, on Fast Day, on account of the French Revolution, April 19, 1793.
18. Order of Service, Thanksgiving for victory, 5559.
19. Order of Service, on Fast day, on account of the war, 15 Sivan, 5564.

20. Order of Service, Thanksgiving for victory, 14 Kislev, 5566.
21. Order of Service, Thanksgiving for victory in India, 15 Nisan, 5606.
22. Prayer for the continuance of Peace, 5608.
23. Prayer for victory, Ashkenazim, 26 April, 5614.
24. Prayer for victory, Sephardim, 26 April, 5614.
25. Prayer for victory, Sephardim, March 21, 5615.
26. Thanksgiving for victory, Ashkenazim, Oct. 4, 5616.
27. Thanksgiving for the restoration of peace, Ashkenazim, May 4, 5616.
28. Prayer for the restoration of peace, Sephardim, May 4, 5616.
29. Prayer for victory, Sephardim, Oct. 7, 5618.
30. " " " West London Syn. of British Jews, Oct. 7, 5618.
31. Prayer for victory, Ashkenazim, Oct. 7, 5618.
32. Thanksgiving for victory, Ashkenazim, April 30, 5619.
33. Thanksgiving for success in Abyssinia, in German and Portug. Synag., July 4, 5628.
34. Order of Service on the occasion of the Jubilee of George III., Oct. 25, 1809.
34a. Order of Service on the occasion of the Funeral of Princess Charlotte, 1817.
35. A dirge chaunted in the Great Synagogue on the day of the funeral of Princess Charlotte, Kislev 10, 1817.
36. The same MS.
37. Prayer and Psalms, on the day of the funeral of Queen Charlotte, Kislev 4, 1818.
38. Prayer and Psalms, on the day of the funeral of King George III., Adar, 5580.
38a. A dirge chaunted in the Great Synagogue on the day of the funeral of George III., 5580.
39. Prayer for the recovery of King George IV., Sivan 14, 1830.

Collection of late Rev. A. L. GREEN—*continued.*

40. Order of Service for the day of burial of King William IV., January 5, 5597.
41. Thanksgiving for the birth of a Prince, 29 Heshvan, 5602, and of a Princess, 3 Kislev, 5601.
42. Order of Service for the day of burial of the Duke of Sussex, 4 Iyar, 5603.
42*a*. Masonic form of Service at the lodges of Joppa and Israel, 4 May, 1843, on the day of burial of the Duke of Sussex.
43. Thanksgiving for the birth of a Princess, 25 March, 5608.
44. Thanksgiving for the birth of a prince, 16 April, 5613.
45. Form of Service for the day of burial of the Prince Consort, Ashkenazim, 23 Dec., 5622.
46. Form of Service for the day of burial of the Prince Consort, Sephardim, 23 Dec., 5622.
47. Thanksgiving for the birth of a Prince, Jan. 16, 5624.
48. Prayer for the recovery of the Prince of Wales, Tebeth, 5632.
49. Thanksgiving for the recovery of the Prince of Wales, Jan. 27, 5632.
50. Prayer for the safety of Sir Moses Montefiore on his journey to the East, 22 Sivan, 5600.
51. Thanksgiving for the success of Sir Moses Montefiore on his journey to the East, Adar 15, 5581.
52. Prayer for the success of Sir Moses Montefiore's mission to Rome, 5619.
53. Prayer for the success of Sir Moses Montefiore's mission to Morocco, Kislev 10, 5624.
54. Thanksgiving in the Sephardim Synagogue for the success of Sir Moses Montefiore's mission to Morocco, Nisan 5, 5624.
55. Thanksgiving in the Ashkenazim Synagogue for the success of Sir Moses Montefiore's mission to Morocco, Nisan 5, 5624.
56. Prayer for the safety of Sir Moses Montefiore on his journey to Palestine, 5626.
57. Prayer for the success of Sir Moses Montefiore's mission to Roumania, 24 Tamuz, 5627.
58. Thanksgiving on the return of Sir Moses Montefiore from Roumania, Ashkenazim, 21 Elul, 5627.
59. Thanksgiving on the return of Sir Moses Montefiore from Roumania, Sephardim, 21 Elul, 5627.
60. Prayer for the safety of Sir Moses Montefiore on his journey to Russia, July 18, 5632.
61. Service in memory of Sir Moses Montefiore, 4 Ab, 5645.
62. Prayer and Thanksgiving on Sir Moses Montefiore completing his hundredth year, 26 Oct. 5645.
63. The Montefiore Centenary. Account of the Doings at Bevis Marks Synagogue, and at East Cliff Lodge, and the Guedalla College, Jerusalem. London, 1885.

828. TRACTS. *Rev. Dr. H. Adler, Delegate Chief Rabbi.*
Relating to Anglo-Jewish History.

829–831. COLLECTION *Rev. Dr. H. Adler.*
Of orders of Service, Prayers and Thanksgivings on various occasions of national and communal interest. 3 vols.

832. BILL. *E. Emanuel.*
"Jewish Disabilities Removal," 7 & 8 Vict. 1845. An Act for the Relief of Persons of the Jewish Religion elected to Municipal Offices. In frame.

833. SONG. *C. I. de Sola.*
"Rothschild and Victory." [A relic of the emancipation struggle.]

834. ANGLIA JUDAICA. *I. Solomons.*
By d'Blossiers Tovey. Oxford, 1738. This is the first history of the English Jews, and still remains the standard authority on the early period.

835. SKETCHES OF ANGLO-JEWISH HISTORY. *Joseph Jacobs.*
By James Picciotto. London, 1875. The standard authority on the modern history of the English Jews. Mr. Picciotto was the first to give documents relating to the secession of the Disraelis from the synagogue.

836. JEWISH CALENDAR. *Jews' College.*
By I. Abendana. Oxford, 1692. First Anglo-Jewish Almanack issued by a Jew.

837. JEWISH COOKERY BOOK.   *F. Haes.*
   Published 1846.

838. ALEXANDER'S ALMANACK FOR 1791.   *Miss Solomon.*
   For use of commercial travellers, containing list of market
   towns, their distance from London, and the days of the
   coaches starting and the places of departure, all in
   Jewish, German, and Hebrew characters.

839. "THE HEBREW INTELLIGENCER," JAN. 1, 1823.   *Jews' College.*
   Earliest Anglo-Jewish Newspaper.

840. "JEDIDJAH."   *Rev. J. Kohn-Zedek.*
   A Hebrew periodical (1818) published in Berlin, containing
   Poem in Hebrew and English on the Anniversary Meeting
   of the Jews' Hospital, March 26, 1817.

841. COPY OF "LONDONER ISRAELIT."   *Henry Levy.*
   Published 1878, and edited by the Rev. Naphtali Levy.
   Earliest Judeo-German newspaper published in London.

842. "DE RESURRECTIONE MORTUORUM" (Spanish).   *H. Guedalla.*
   By Menasseh ben Israel.   Amsterdam, 1637.

843. "DE CREATIONE."   *I. Solomons.*
   By Menasseh ben Israel, Amstel., 1635.

844. BIBLIA HEBRAICA CUM PUNCTIS.   *S. J. Rubenstein.*
   Typis Menasseh ben Israel, 1639. (From the Duke of
   Sussex's Library.)

845. A HEBREW PSALTER OF MENASSEH BEN ISRAEL, 1646.
                                              Mrs. David Lewis.

846. מקוה ישראל   "ESPERANCA DE ISRAEL."   *I. Solomons.*
   By Menasseh ben Israel.   Amsterdam, 5410=1650.   With
   autograph date and remarks by Robert Southey.

847. "HOPE OF ISRAEL."   *H. Guedalla.*
   By Menasseh ben Israel.

848. "THE COUNTERFEIT JEW." LOND., 1653.   *Mrs. A. Newman.*
   Refers to a person named "Josephus ben Israel," who came
   to Newcastle under name of Horseley.

849. "THE CASE OF THE JEWES STATED";   *Mrs. A. Newman.*
   Or the Jewes Synagogue opened with their preparations on
   the morning before they go thither, and their doings at
   night when they come home: their practices in their
   Synagogues, and some select actings of theirs in England,
   upon Record.   London, 1656.

850. "CONCILIADOR"   *S. J. Rubenstein.*
   Of Menasseh ben Israel, with portrait by Rembrandt.
   Translated by E. H. Lindo, 1856.

851. שלחן טהור *I. Solomons.*
By Joseph Pardo, edited by his son David Pardo. London, 1686. Both Joseph Pardo and his son were readers at the first Synagogue of the Portuguese Jewish Congregation of London.

852. COMPENDIUM OF DINIM *H. Guedalla.*
For Spanish and Portuguese Jews. Amsterdam, 1690. By David Pardo, Hazan at Bevis Marks Synagogue.

853. "MATTEH DAN." *M. H. Herbert.*
By David Nieto. 1714. Hebrew and Spanish. A philosophical dialogue dealing with the Karaite heresy: termed by its author "the Second Kusari."

854. "EXEMPLAR DE PENITENCIA."
Dr. H. Adler, Delegate Chief Rabbi.
Sermons by Jacob de Castro Sarmento. 1724.

855. RELIGION, CEREMONIES AND PRAYERS OF THE JEWS. *I. Solomons.*
By Gamaliel ben Pedahzur. London, 1738.

856. BENE HANE'ARIM. *Rev. J. Kohn-Zedek.*
Poems by Ephraim Luzzato. London, 1768. Contains Hebrew poem on bringing Charlotte of Mecklenburg to England for her marriage with Geo. III.

857. "TEPHILLOTH." *Samuel Davids.*
Printed by W. Tooke, A.M. 5530. First Translation of Daily Prayers into English. Translated by B. Meyers and A. Alexander.

858. "KEHILATH JAHACOB." *M. Harris.*
Being a vocabulary of words in the Hebrew language, arranged in 58 chapters, on various subjects. Hebrew, English and Spanish. 1773.

859. "ORDEN DE LA ORACION, &c., &c." *C. de Sola.*
Order of Service held in Bevis Marks Synagogue on 13 Dec. 1776 (3 Tebet 5537 = 1776) upon the day appointed as a day of humiliation and prayer for the success of the Royal arms, and restoration of peace, at the time of the revolt of the American Colonies, including the sermon of Rabbi Moseh Cohen d'Azevedo. Hebr. and Span.

860. פרקי אבות. *Dr. H. Adler, Delegate Chief Rabbi.*
Ethics of the Fathers, with Commentary by Rabbi Hirsch Loebel of Berlin, Chief Rabbi of London, with Portrait of the author.

861. RABBINICAL DECISIONS. *Dr. N. M. Adler, Chief Rabbi.*
By R. David Schiff, Chief Rabbi of London.

862. יסוד הלחות.   *Dr. N. M. Adler, Chief Rabbi.*
Tables of Sunrise and Sunset, to determine beginning and
end of Sabbath and Festivals. By R. Raphael Hanover,
with marginal notes by R. Hirsch, Berlin, and Rev. Solomon
Herschell.

863. "HAMEASSEF."   *Rev. B. H. Ascher.*
Hebrew Periodical published at Königsberg, by the School
of Mendelssohn, containing prayer recited by Jews of
Great Britain for speedy recovery of George III. and
thanksgiving on His Majesty's restoration to health. The
latter written by Naphtali Hartwig Wessely (1789).

864. "THE JEW, A COMEDY."   *I. Solomons.*
By Richard Cumberland. Lond., 1794. In its humble way
this drama is an English parallel to Lessing's *Nathan der
Weise.* It advocated on the stage tolerant views with
regard to the Jews, in face of much popular prejudice.

865. ALEXANDER'S COVERS.   *Asher I. Myers.*
Issued with his edition of the Machzor, and conveying his
views on the topics of the day in very pungent terms.
Some numbers are illustrated. Only one complete set is
known to exist.

866. BIOGRAPHY OF B. GOLDSMID.   *I. Solomons.*
Memoirs of the life and commercial connections of Benjamin
Goldsmid, Esq., of Roehampton, by L. Alexander.
London, 1808. Portrait of Mrs. B. Goldsmid.

867. DECLARATION OF REPENTANCE FOR APOSTASY.   *C. I. de Sola.*
Entitled: "Judah Catarivas, native of the Holy Land,
penitent, to his Israelite brethren" (5570 = 1810).

868. FIRST ENGLISH SERMON.   *Rev. M. Joseph.*
"The Faith of Israel." A discourse delivered at the Jews'
Synagogue, Seel Street, Liverpool, on 2nd May, 1819, by
Rabbi Tobias Goodman, Liverpool, n. d. [The first sermon
delivered in English at an English Synagogue.]

869. לשון זהב.   *Dr. H. Adler, Delegate Chief Rabbi.*
Novellæ on Talmud and Decisions by R. David Teble Schiff,
Chief Rabbi of London, and edited by Rabbis Mordecai,
Gabriel, Beer and Nathan Adler. Offenbach, 1822.

870. "HEBREW MELODIES."   *H. Guedalla.*
Words by Lord Byron. Music by Braham & Nathan. [This
copy belonged to John Braham.]

871. "GENIUS OF JUDAISM."   *Joseph Jacobs.*
By Isaac D'Israeli. (*See* No. 1031.)

872. DAILY PRAYERS. *Joseph Jacobs.*
Used by the West London Synagogue of British Jews. The West London Synagogue was founded by seceders from the orthodox congregations in 1840, and the above revised Prayer Book was compiled on " Reform " lines by the Rev. Prof. Marks and Rev. A. Löwy. In the excommunication hastily issued by the orthodox Ecclesiastical authorities, and subsequently withdrawn, the Prayer Book was specifically referred to. The whole controversy is now happily a matter of history.

873. DEUTSCH'S ARTICLE ON THE TALMUD. *Lewis Emanuel.*
Copy of the *Quarterly Review*, containing Emanuel Deutsch's article on " The Talmud," Oct. 1867. Created greatest literary sensation of recent periodical articles.

874. CODE *Dr. H. Adler, Delegate Chief Rabbi.*
Of Standards of Examination in Hebrew Religion issued by the Chief Rabbi, 1886.

875. EDUCATIONAL STATISTICS. *Asher I. Myers.*
List of Jewish schools of London, with number of scholars, amount of grant, percentage of passes.

876–893. HEBREW WORKS. *Beth Hamidrash.*
Eighteen Hebrew Works printed in London.

  1. אורים ותומים (on a divorce case). R. Uri P. Hamburger, 1707.
  2. אש דת (controversy). R. David Nieto. 1715.
  3. אזהרות (on 613 Precepts). R. Jacob Chagiz. 1719.
  4. תולדות יעקב (Exegesis). R. Jacob b. Eliezer. 1770.
  5. הדרת מלך (on Zohar). RR. Isaac Loria and Chajim Vital. 1770.
  6. התורה והחכמה (Essays). M. Gumpel. 1771.
  7. אבן שהם (Exegesis). R. Moses ben Judah. 1772.
  8. דרך איש ישר (translated from an Indian MS.). Abraham van Oven. 1778.
  9. לחם עוני (on Hagada). R. Raphael Chasan. 1784.
  10. פרסומי ניסא (on Hanuca). R. Raphael Chasan. 1784.
  11. עלה תרופה (on Vaccination). R. Abraham Nonski. 1785.
  12. מורה באצבע (on Ritual). R. Chajim Joseph. 1791
  13. תורת חיים (Ritual). Moses Edrehi. 1792.
  14. עשרה מאמרות (Cabbala). R. Eliakim b. Abraham. 1794.
  15. מדרש פנחס (Talmudic Exegesis). R. Phineas b. Patta. 1795.
  16. צוף נובלות (Theology). R. Eliakim b. Abraham. 1799.
  17. מנחת קנאות (Controversy). R. Meir Rintil. 1817.
  18. נתיבות אמת (against McCaul) R. Judah Middleman. 1847.

894. "CATALOGUE OF HEBREW MSS. IN BODLEIAN LIBRARY."
Dr. H. Adler, Delegate Chief Rabbi.

By Dr. A. Neubauer, M.A. The Bodleian has the largest collection of Hebrew MSS. in the world.

895. FACSIMILES OF HEBREW MSS. IN BODLEIAN LIBRARY.
Dr. H. Adler, Delegate Chief Rabbi.
By Dr. A. Neubauer, M.A. The facsimiles include one of an autograph of Moses Maimonides.

896. " CATALOGUS LIBRORUM HEBRÆORUM IN BIBLIOTHECA BODLEIANA.
                                        Joseph Jacobs.
By M. Steinschneider, the celebrated Jewish bibliographer.
The Bodleian has the largest collection of Hebrew works
of any library in the world.   The nucleus was formed by
the celebrated Oppenheimer collection.   The catalogue is
the most important bibliographical work produced by a
Jew.

897. " CATALOGUE OF MSS. IN UNIVERSITY LIBRARY, CAMBRIDGE."
     PT. I.   *Beth Hamidrash.*
     By Dr. S. M. Schiller-Szinessy, M.A.

898. " CATALOGUE OF HEBREW BOOKS IN BRITISH MUSEUM."
                          Dr. H. Adler, Delegate Chief Rabbi.
     By J. Zedner.   1867.

899. " CATALOGUE OF MSS. IN THE JEWS' COLLEGE [BETH HAMI-
     DRASH], LONDON."   *Dr. H. Adler, Delegate Chief Rabbi.*
     By Dr. A. Neubauer, M.A. [privately printed].   1886.

900. MAP OF BRITISH EMPIRE.   *Joseph Jacobs.*
     Showing past and present congregations of the British
     Empire.

k.—BENI ISRAEL.

[A remarkable colony of Jews in India, said to have been established since
490 A.D., when one Joseph Rabban conducted a band of refugees from
Persia to Cranganor.   They are now settled, to the number of 7000, in
Bombay and neighbourhood.   They are divided into two classes or castes
that never intermarry : the white Jews and the black, who are descendants
of former proselytes.   Closely connected with them are the Jews of Cochin,
who claim to have settled even earlier in India, and are likewise divided
into two castes, white and black.   The present collection has been forwarded by the Beni Israel as a fraternal recognition to the Jews of Great
Britain, and was collected by Messrs. S. SOLOMON and J. EZEKIEL.]

905. TAMIL INSCRIPTION.   *Rev. Dr. H. Adler.*
     Copy of the celebrated inscription in which the Brahmin
     Airvi grants to Joseph Rabban and his companions
     certain privileges.   A Hebrew translation and English
     version is given in Brit. Mus. Exhibits, No. 41.

906. GOLD MEDAL.   *Beni Israel.*
     Presented in 1830 to Subedar Damiljie Israel, of the 16th
     Regiment Native Infantry, by the Hon. East India
     Company.

907. GOLD WATCH.   *Beni Israel.*
     Presented in 1862 to the late Subedar Major Ezekiel Bapujee
     Israel, of the 12th Regiment of Native Infantry, by the
     Colonel and officers of the Regiment.

908. GOLD STAR   *Beni Israel.*
     Of the first class Order of British India, conferred in
     1882 on Subedar Major Moses Bapujee Malaker of the
     12th Regiment Native Infantry.

909. SILVER MEDAL AND CLASP. *Beni Israel.*
For Kirkir and Poona. Given to Subedar Major Ellojee Dawoodje Israel, 7th Regiment Native Infantry, for distinguished service from 1799 to 1826.

910. BRONZE MEDAL. *Beni Israel.*
For distinguished service at the taking of Seringapatam. Given to Samuel Ezekiel Kharcelkar. Obverse, a British lion subduing the Indian tiger, with Arabic inscription, and English date 4th May, 1799. Reverse, entry of British army into Seringapatam, with Persian inscription and Mohammedan date 27th, Zilkad, A.H. 1213.

911. TALISMAN. *Beni Israel.*
With Hebrew inscription, worn by Beni Israel girls on the head.

912. HANUCA LAMP. *Beni Israel.*
Marble; as used by the Beni Israel.

913. SABBATH LAMP. *Beni Israel.*
Brass; used by Bombay Jews. Tumblers with ordinary oil lights are placed in the brass rings.

914. INSTRUMENT USED IN CIRCUMCISION. *Beni Israel.*

915. WEDDING RING. *Beni Israel.*
Worn by Beni Israel ladies. Silver.

916. BETROTHAL RING. *Beni Israel.*
Silver; worn by Beni Israel girls.

917. "MUNNY" TALISMAN. *Beni Israel.*
For married women. Gold bead with string of small black glass beads. Not worn by unmarried girls or widows.

918. "MUNNY" TALISMAN. *Beni Israel.*
Of Jewesses of Cochin. Gold necklace worn both by black and white Jewesses when married. Usually buried with wearer or presented to synagogue after her death.

919. WEDDING RING. *Beni Israel.*
Silver; worn by black Jewesses of Cochin. Generally buried with the wearer.

920. SHOPHAR. *Beni Israel.*
Brought from Aden : said to be the horn of an animal called "Cudoo."

921. HANUCA LAMP. *Beni Israel.*
Brass; used by Arabic Jews in Bombay.

922. SHOPHAR. *Beni Israel.*
Used by Arabic Jews in Bombay. Ram's horn.

923. PORTRAIT OF SUBEDAR MAJOR MUSAJEE BELAJEE.   *Beni Israel.*
Behadur of the 19th Regiment Native Infantry and Native
Commandant of the Tanna Police. A native painting.

924. PORTRAIT OF SUBEDAR MAJOR EZEKIEL BAPUJEE.   *Beni Israel.*
Sirdar Bahadur of the 12th Regiment Native Infantry.
Died 14th Feb., 1878. Served with distinction throughout
the Mutiny.

925. PORTRAIT OF ELIJAH JOSEPH.   *Beni Israel.*
Hazan of the first Beni-Israel Synagogue in Bombay for 36
years, from 1835 to 1871.

926. PORTRAIT OF JOSEPH EZEKIEL.   *Beni Israel.*
Head Master of David Sassoon Benevolent Institution,
Bombay, Fellow and Hebrew Examiner of the University
of Bombay.

927. PHOTOGRAPH OF SOLOMON ABRAHAM ERULKAR.   *Beni Israel.*
M. B. Durham, a Beni Israel practitioner at Bombay.

928. PHOTOGRAPH OF SYNAGOGUE, BOMBAY.   *Beni Israel.*
The first built for Beni Israel in 1796 by Samuel Ezekiel
Dewarker, Native Commandant of the 6th Battalion, who
died in Cochin in 1797.

929. PHOTOGRAPH OF SYNAGOGUE, BOMBAY.   *Beni Israel.*
The second, built in 1843.

930. PHOTOGRAPH OF THE SYNAGOGUE, BYCULLA.   *Beni Israel.*
Built in 1864 by David Sassoon, Esq.

931. PHOTOGRAPH OF THE SYNAGOGUE IN THE FORT.   *Beni Israel.*
Erected by Messrs. Sassoon in 1880 in memory of the late
E. D. Sassoon, Esq.

932. PHOTOGRAPH OF BENI ISRAEL FAMILY.   *Beni Israel.*
Showing characteristic costume.

933. PHOTOGRAPH OF BLACK JEWS OF COCHIN.   *Beni Israel.*
Showing characteristic costume.

934. PHOTOGRAPH OF ARABIC JEWS AT BOMBAY.   *Beni Israel.*
Showing characteristic costume.

935. MARATHI NEWSPAPER.   *Beni Israel.*
Entitled *Or Emeth,* "the Light of Truth," the Organ of the
Beni Israel. In progress.

936. PRAYER BOOKS IN MARATHI.   *Beni Israel.*
Eight vols. giving Propitiary prayers (Selicoth), Marriage
Ceremony, New Year, Hanuka, Day of Atonement (two
vols.), the Ethics of the Fathers and the remission of vows
and prayers offered at the sea shore.

937. DOCTRINAL WORKS IN MARATHI. *Beni Israel.*
"Scripture proofs of the Jewish doctrine." "The true aspect of Judaism."

938. EDUCATIONAL WORKS IN MARATHI. *Beni Israel.*
Hebrew Primer, Elementary Hebrew Grammar, Chronological Outlines of Ancient Jewish History.

939. THE TRAVELS OF RABBI DAVID D'BETH HILLEL. *Beni Israel.*
Madras, 1832. First Jewish book published in India.

940. RELIGIOUS CEREMONIES OF JEWS OF MALABAR.
Beth Hamidrash.
Hebrew treatise on, with calendar 1768–1795. MS.

941. THANKSGIVING SERVICE, JUBILEE CEREMONY, FEB. 16, 1887.
In Hebrew, Marathi, and English. *Rev. Dr. H. Adler.*

942. SERMONS IN MAHRATI. *Rev. Dr. H. Adler.*
Translated from the English of Dr. H. Adler, and published by the Society for the Diffusion of Religious Knowledge among the Israelites.

k.—PORTRAITS.
[Arranged chronologically in order of birth]

947. MENASSEH BEN ISRAEL. *Spanish and Portuguese Synagogue.*
Chalk Drawing after etching by Rembrandt.

[The chief instrument in securing the return of the Jews to England (see Introduction, pp. 4, 5). Born in Lisbon *circa* 1604. Settled in Amsterdam. Rabbi of the local New Synagogue 1622. Established a Hebrew printing press 1627. (*See* Brit. Mus. Exhibits, Nos. 126–153.) Proceeded to England 1652 to plead with Cromwell for the readmission of his co-religionists into England; and obtained the unofficial consent of the Protector to the return. Menasseh read and understood ten languages, and was a voluminous writer. Friend of Caspar Barlæus, Vossius, Grotius, and Huet. Queen Christina of Sweden was among his many readers and admirers. Died at Middleburg 1657.]

948. MENASSEH BEN ISRAEL. *Miss Goldsmid.*
Etching by Rembrandt.

949. MENASSEH BEN ISRAEL, æt. xxxviii. *Lucien Wolf.*
Salom Italia sculp. 1642.

950. MENASSEH BEN ISRAEL BEFORE CROMWELL AND HIS COUNCIL.
Rev. J. de K. Williams.
Oil, by S. A. Hart, R.A.

The last of the four meetings of the Council, convened by Cromwell, to consider the petition of Menasseh Ben Israel for the re-admission of the Jews to England. Menasseh was summoned by the Protector to appear before the Council, to rebut certain arguments that had been urged against his proposals. The meeting took place on the 14th December, 1655, and ended in a decision adverse to the Jews. (*See* Introduction, p. 5.)

951. MENASSEH BEN ISRAEL BEFORE CROMWELL AND HIS COUNCIL.
By S. A. Hart, R.A. *F. D. Mocatta.*

952. YAHACOB SAPORTAS.   *Rev. Dr. H. Adler.*
P. van Gunst sculp.

First Chief Rabbi of the Jews of England after their return. Born at Oran
in North Africa, 1618. Was successively Rabbi of Tlemcen and Salé in
Morocco; and in 1649 was sent by the Moorish Government on a
diplomatic mission to Spain. He subsequently settled in Amsterdam,
whence he accompanied Menasseh ben Israel to England in 1656. On the
formation of a Jewish congregation in London he was appointed Chief
Rabbi. On the outbreak of the Plague in 1666 he returned to Amsterdam, and in 1681 became Chief Rabbi in that city. Died 1698.

953. FERDINANDO MENDEZ, M.D.   *Miss Lindo.*
Water-colour by his daughter Catherine da Costa, Aug. 7,
1721.

Distinguished physician. Born in Portugal, a crypto-Jew. Physician to
King John IV. of Portugal. Accompanied Catherine of Braganza, bride
of Charles II., to England, where he openly joined the synagogue.
Created a fellow of the College of Physicians, 1687. Was one of the
physicians who attended Charles II. in his last illness. Author of
"Studium Apollinare." Died 1725.

954. RABBI SOLOMON AELYON.   *Lucien Wolf.*
J. Houbraken sculp.

Chief Rabbi of the Spanish and Portuguese congregations of England. Born
at Safed in Palestine, 1664. Settled in Salonica, and became a prominent agitator on behalf of the pseudo-Messiah, Sabbethai Zevi. In
1696 was appointed Haham of the Portuguese Jews of England in succession to Jacob Abendana. Resigned 1701, and became a member of the
Rabbinate of Amsterdam. Died 1728.

954a. DAVID NIETO.   *L. van Oven.*
J. McArdell sculp.

Chief Rabbi of the Spanish and Portuguese Congregations of England. Born
at Venice 1654. Practised as a physician and Jewish preacher at
Leghorn. Succeeded Solomon Aeylon (*see* No. 954) as Ecclesiastical
Chief of the London Portuguese Jews, 1702. Author of "Pascologia,"
"Matteh Dan," &c. Haham Nieto was one of the most accomplished
Jews of his time, and was equally famous as philosopher, physician,
poet. mathematician, astronomer, and theologian. Died 1728.

955. DON JOSÉ CORTISSOS.   *Miss C. Cortissas.*
Oil Portrait in Court dress of reign of Queen Anne.

Contractor-General for the allied forces of Great Britain, Portugal, and
Holland in the war against Spain in 1706. Rendered important services
to the army of the Earl of Peterborough on its retreat from Barcelona.
Settled in England 1712. Born 1656. Died 1742.

956. HAHAM ZEVI.   *Rev. R. Harris.*
Grandfather of the late Chief Rabbi, Dr. Herschell, in
whose possession the portrait formerly was. Oil.

One of the most distinguished Rabbis of his time. Born 1656. Ecclesiastical
Judge at Amsterdam. His interest for English Jews arises from the fact
that he was grandfather of Dr. Solomon Hirschel (*see* No. 1004), and
that, in 1705, the question of the orthodoxy of Haham Nieto's (*see*
No. 954a) sermons was referred to him by the Elders of the Bevis Marks
synagogue. His judgment was in favour of Nieto. Died 1718.

957. MOSES HART. *Great Synagogue.*
Oil.

> Founder of the Great Synagogue, Duke's Place, London, the first building of which he erected entirely at his own cost in 1722. Native of Breslau, and brother of Rabbi Uri Phaibus (see No. 958), Chief Rabbi of the German Jews of England.

958. RABBI URI PHAIBUS. *Great Synagogue.*
Oil.

> First Chief Rabbi of the German Jews in England, and brother of the founder of the synagogue in Duke's Place. Born at Breslau in 1670. Officiated as Rabbi in the first German synagogue in Broad Court, Mitre Square. Died 1756. Sometimes called Rabbi Philip Hart, also Aaron Hart.

959. RABBI AARON HART. *William Frazer, F.R.C.S.I., M.R.I.A.*
Mezzotint engraving by James McArdell   First state.
Only one other example in this condition is known.

960. RABBI AARON HART. 1751. *Mrs. D. Castello.*
McArdell sculp.

961. RABBI AARON HART. *I. Solomons.*
McArdell sculp.

962. RABBI MOSES GOMEZ DE MESQUITA.
Rev. Dr. H. Adler, Delegate Chief Rabbi.

> Chief Rabbi of the Portuguese-Jewish Congregations of England. Born 1688. Appointed Haham on the resignation of Isaac Nieto. Died 1751.

963. RABBI MOSES GOMEZ DE MESQUITA. 1751. *Miss de Sola.*

964. RABBI MOSES GOMEZ DE MESQUITA. *William Frazer.*
By John Faber. Mezzotint. 1752.

JACOB DE CASTRO SARMENTO.

> Physician and author. Born at Braganza 1691, and graduated at the University of Coimbra 1710. Settled in London 1720. Author of "Exemplar de Penitencia" (Lond. 1724), and several other works in theology and medicine. Fellow of the Royal Society 1725. Died 1762.

See Newman Collection, No. 1185.

965. JONAS COHEN. *Lucien Wolf.*
Photo. of an oil painting by Van Heer, 1743.

> Member of a distinguished Jewish family. Born at Amersfoort in Holland 1698. Died 1780. Ancestor of the Cohen and Gompertz families in England, and of branches of the Goldsmid and Montefiore families.

966. MR. AND MRS. HENRY ISAACS. *B. Levy.*
Circa 1760.

> Mr. Isaacs was the son of the first Jew established in Oxford after the Return.

967. MRS. CATHARINE DA COSTA VILLAREALE. *I. Solomons.*
Engraving.

> Daughter of Anthony da Costa, an opulent London merchant and Director of the Bank of England. Born 1709. Became the wife of Joseph da Costa Villareal, 1727. On his death married William Mellish. Her daughter, Elizabeth, became Viscountess Galway.

E

967a. THE "BAAL SHEM."   *Lucien Wolf.*
Photograph from an oil painting by Copley.

Dr. Haim Samuel de Falk, a mysterious Rabbi, who resided in London about
the middle of the eighteenth century. Called "the Baal Shem" because
of his reputed Cabalistical powers. Gave a *Kemea* (charm) to Philip
Egalité, and was widely consulted on occult subjects. His MSS. are
preserved in the Beth Hamidrash. (*See* Nos. 787–790.) Born *circa*
1710. Died 1782.

968. RABBI HIRSCH.   *Great Synagogue.*
Oil.

Chief Rabbi of the German-Jewish congregations of Great Britain. Born in
Poland, 1721. Succeeded R. Uri Phaibus (see No. 958) as Chief Rabbi of
the Duke's Place Synagogue, London, 1757. Resigned 1764. Chief Rabbi
in Halberstadt (1764), Mannheim (1770), and Berlin (1772). Died 1800.
Sometimes called Rabbi Zevi ben Aryeh Hirsch Loebel (*see* No. 860), and
Hart Lyon.

969. RABBI HART LYON.   *I. Solomons.*
I. Turner pinxit; E. Fisher fecit.

970. DR. BENJAMIN DE SOLA.   *Miss de Sola.*
Photo of a painting.

Court physician to William V., Prince of Orange, and an ancestor of the
De Sola family. Born in Portugal, 1735. Settled in Holland, 1749.
Author of several medical works. Died at Curaçoa, 1815.

971. ESTER HANA MONTEFIORE.   *Jacob Montefiore.*
Oil.

Grandmother of Sir Moses Montefiore, and ancestress of the Montefiore
family in England. Daughter of Massaod Racab, a coral merchant of
Leghorn, and born in that city 1735. Became the wife of Moses Vita
Montefiore, the elder, in 1752, and settled in London shortly after that
date. Died at Stoke Newington 1812, having had eighteen children.

971a. ESTER HANA MONTEFIORE (ÆT. 17).   *Lucien Wolf.*
Engraving of a miniature in the possession of Mr. J. B.
Montefiore.

JOSEPH D'ALMEIDA.

An eminent stock-broker. Born 1716; died 1788.
See Newman Collection, No. 1139.

972. REV. ISAAC LOPEZ.   *The Misses Aguilar.*
I. M. Belisario del.

Cantor at Spanish and Portuguese Synagogue, Kingston, Jamaica.

973. MOSES MENDES.   *Lucien Wolf.*
European Magazine, plate, proof before letters.

Poet. Born in London. Honorary M.A. of Oxford, 1750. Author of several
musical comediettas produced at Drury Lane, of which "The Chaplet"
and "The Shepherd's Lottery" were the most successful. He also wrote
"The Seasons, in imitation of Spenser," being a lament on the death of
his friend Thomson, "The Battiad," "The Squire of Dames," and several
romances in prose. Died 1758.

974. MOSES COHEN D'AZEVEDO.   *Mrs. d'Azevedo.*
Oil.

Chief Rabbi of the Portuguese-Jewish congregations of England. Succeeded
Haham Mesquita in 1765. Died 1784.

975. RABBI DAVID TEBELE SCHIFF. *Great Synagogue.*
Oil.

> Chief Rabbi of the German-Jewish congregations of Great Britain. Born at Frankfort, and member of the Rabbinate of that city. Invited to England 1765, and appointed Chief Rabbi, in succession to Rabbi Hirsch (see No. 968). Author of זהב לשון זקן published posthumously. Died 1792.

976. RABBI DAVID TEBELE SCHIFF. *N. S. Joseph.*
Miniature.

977. BARON D'AGUILAR. *H. G. Lousada.*
Miniature.

> Ephraim Lopez Pereira, second Baron d'Aguilar. Born in Austria 1739. Settled in England with his father, and was naturalised 1757. Succeeded to his father's title and fortune, 1759. A miser and eccentric. His establishment at Colebrook Row, Islington, was known as Starvation Farm. Died 1802, leaving a large fortune hidden away in crevices and corners of his dwelling.

LEVY BARENT COHEN.

> Communal worker. Son of Bernard Cohen of Amsterdam. Born 1740. Warden of the Great Synagogue; President of *Meshibath Nephesh* charity.
> *See* Newman Collection, No. 1137.

978. HYMEN COHEN. *D. A. Levy.*
Miniature.

> Warden of the Great Synagogue, and an active worker in the Anglo-Jewish community.

979. MANUEL CASTELLO. *M. Castello.*
Miniature on ivory.

> An ancestor of the Castello family, and the first to settle in England. Born at Rotterdam, 1740. Died at London, 1818.

980. MOSES SAMUEL. *Benjamin L. Cohen.*
Oil.

> A prominent member of the Anglo-Jewish community. Born at Krotoschin, 1742; came to England and became wealthy. One of the founders of the Jews' Hospital. Contributed generously to the erection of the Bath Synagogue. Died 1839.

981. MR. LEONI AS ARBACES. *I. Solomons.*
Engraving.

> Opera singer and composer. Real name Myer Lyon. Was at first a chorister at the Great Synagogue, *circa* 1770. Obtained much success on the operatic stage, and as a composer of songs and sacred melodies. Braham was one of his pupils. Returned to the Synagogue and became a Jewish minister at Kingston, Jamaica.

MRS. JUDITH LEVY.

> Daughter of Moses Hart, founder of the Great Synagogue (*see* No. 957), and a generous benefactor of her co-religionists. Married Elias Levy, a wealthy financier and government contractor. Contributed £4000 towards the cost of re-building the Great Synagogue. Died 1803.
> *See* Newman Collection, No. 1161.

982. David Levi. *Lucien Wolf.*
Bromley sculp.; Drummond pinx.

Hebraist and Controversialist. Born 1742. Translated the Hebrew Prayer-book into English for the Bevis Marks Congregation, and published a Pentateuch in Hebrew and English, and "Lingua Sacra," a Hebrew Grammar, and Hebrew and English Dictionary. Wrote several odes for the Jewish community on occasions of public celebrations. Defended Judaism against the attacks of Dr. Priestley, and replied to Thomas Paine's onslaughts on the Old Testament. Died 1801.

983. Hazan Salom. *Bevis Marks Synagogue.*
Oil.

Cantor at the Bevis Marks Synagogue, 1779. Died 1818.

983a. Mrs. M. Samuel. *Mrs. B. Merton.*

Wife of Moses Samuel; born 1750; died 1833. (*See* No. 980.)

984. Lord George Gordon. *I. Solomons.*
I. de Fleur pinxt.

The famous agitator and hero of the "No Popery" riots of 1780. His interest for the Jewish community arises from the fact that he became a convert to Judaism. He was formally "called to the Law" in the Hambro' Synagogue, and made an offering of £100 (*see* No. 601). Born 1750; died 1793.

985. Rev. Raphael Meldola. *Bevis Marks Synagogue.*
Oil.

Chief Rabbi of the Spanish and Portuguese congregations in England. Born 1754, at Leghorn, and appointed to his spiritual office in 1805. He had previously acted as Dayan in his native city. Author of קרבן מנחה (Leghorn, 1791) חופת חתנים (Leghorn, 1797) דרך אמונה (London, 1848 posthumously), &c. Died 1828.

986. Rev. Raphael Meldola. *Mrs. D. Castello.*
Engraving, 1806.

987. Rev. Raphael Meldola. *Dr. H. Adler, Delegate Chief Rabbi.*
Engraving.

988. Rev. Raphael Meldola. *Miss de Sola.*
Photo.

989. Rev. Raphael Meldola. *Prof. R. Meldola, F.R.S.*
Outlined in minute Hebrew writing.

989a. David Montefiore. *H. Guedalla.*
Miniature.

Second surviving son of Moses Vita Montefiore (*see* No. 971), and uncle of Sir Moses Montefiore. Born 1755.

990. Benjamin Goldsmid. *Mrs. Y. Goldsmid.*
Oil.

Financier. Born in London, 1755. Head of the banking house of Benjamin and Abraham Goldsmid. Was almost exclusively employed by Mr. Pitt in connection with the negotiation of loans for the British Government during the war with France. A prominent worker in the Anglo-Jewish community. Founder of the Naval Asylum. Died 1808.

991. THE GOLDSMID FAMILY. *Mrs. Yeates-Goldsmid.*
Oil. Authorship uncertain; believed to be by Sir William Beechey.

> Children of Benjamin Goldsmid, of Roehampton (*see* preceding No.). The tall figure in the centre is John Louis Goldsmid, the eldest son; the one on the left is the second son Henry; the boy with hat in hand is the third son Albert, afterwards a major-general, who had two horses shot under him at Waterloo; the child stooping to hold the dog is the fourth son James, afterwards subaltern in the 53rd regiment, who was lost at sea when the troopship foundered; and the child in white is the fifth son, Lionel, late of the 19th Dragoons, and grandfather of Major A. Goldsmid.

992. EDWARD GOLDSMID, OF HARLEY STREET. *Major A. Goldsmid.*
Water-colour sketch.

> A noted beau in his day. Chairman of the Globe Company, and a familiar figure in City circles. Born 1763; died 1853.

993. ABRAHAM GOLDSMID. *Jews' Hospital.*
Bust.

> Financier. Born in London, 1756. Member of the banking firm of B. & A. Goldsmid. In conjunction with his brother, Benjamin Goldsmid (*see* No. 990), he collected a fund of £10,000 in 1799, for the establishment of the Jews' Hospital. Died 1810.

994. ABRAHAM GOLDSMID. *Miss Goldsmid.*
Engraving by Bartolozzi after portrait by Medley.

995. ABRAHAM GOLDSMID. *Lucien Wolf.*
Medley pinxt.; Ridley sculpt.

996. ABRAHAM GOLDSMID. *Jews' Hospital.*
Portrait (engraved).

997. ABRAHAM GOLDSMID. *H. Barned.*
Engraving, tinted.

998. ABRAHAM GOLDSMID. *D. A. Levy.*
Represented with cheques for £2000 in his hand, collected for a London charity. Deighton pinx.

998a. EZEKIEL, ABRAHAM EZEKIEL. *A. Moseley.*
Miniature.

> Engraver. Born at Exeter 1757. Engraved portraits by Opie, Sir Joshua Reynolds, and others. Also well known as a miniature painter and a scientific optician. Died 1806.

RICHARD BROTHERS.

> An English fanatic, who styled himself "nephew of the Almighty and Prince of the Hebrews;" born about 1758; quitted the Naval service to preach the approach of the Millennium, and "to lead the Hebrews to the land of Canaan." Jerusalem was to become the capital of the world, and the Jews to be restored in 1798. He does not appear to have excited any interest in the Jewish community, but obtained a considerable Gentile following. Author of several tracts on the subject of his mission. Died 1824.

See Newman Collection, No. 1135.

998b. SAMUEL MONTEFIORE. *H. Guedalla.*
Miniature.

> Third surviving son of Moses Vita Montefiore (*see* No. 971), and uncle of Sir Moses Montefiore. Grandfather of Exhibitor. Born 1759; died 1806.

999. COLONEL ISAAC FRANKS. *Lucien Wolf.*
Photograph from a miniature in the possession of Miss Sarah Joseph, Montreal.

Aide-de-Camp to General Washington. Born in New York, 1759. Joined the American revolutionary army 1776, and became confidential aide-de-camp to General Washington. After the peace of 1783 filled several civil commissions. Died 1822.

999a. JACOB KIMHI. *Lucien Wolf.*
Butterworth sculp.

Descendant of the ancient and distinguished family of Kimhi. Born at Constantinople *circa* 1760. Author of שושנת יעקב. Was a slipper seller at the Royal Exchange, and a noted London character. His picturesque appearance earned him the notice of Oseas Humphreys, who painted his portrait. Died 1820.

1000. MRS. JESSE GOLDSMID. *Mrs. Yeates-Goldsmid.*
Oil.

Daughter of Israel Levien Solomons, of Clapton. Became the wife of Mr. Benjamin Goldsmid 1783. Died 1836.

1000a. BARON LYON DE SYMONDS. *H. Barned.*

1000b. POLLY DE SYMONDS. *H. Barned.*
Miniature.

Daughter of Aaron Goldsmid, and wife of Baron Lyon de Symonds. Died 1841.

1001. MYER LEVY. *S. I. Cohen.*
S. Polack del.

Principal reader of the New Synagogue, Leadenhall Street, *circa* 1750.

1002. REV. MOSES MYERS. *New Synagogue.*
Oil.

Chief Rabbi of New Synagogue, *circa* 1750.

1003. DANIEL COHEN D'AZEVEDO. *Miss de Sola.*
Engraving, 1797.

Rabbi of the Portuguese community of Amsterdam. Died 1822.

1004. REV. SOLOMON HERSCHELL. *P. Vallentine.*
Bust.

Chief Rabbi of the German-Jewish congregations of the British Empire. Son of Rabbi Hirsch (*see* No. 968), and born in London 1762. For nine years Rabbi of Prenzlau, Prussia. Elected to succeed R. David Schiff (*see* No. 95) as Chief Rabbi of the Duke's Place Synagogue, London, in 1802. Died 1842.

1005. REV. SOLOMON HERSCHELL. *F. Haes.*
Portrait model, full length. Plaster coloured.

1006. REV. SOLOMON HERSCHELL. *Great Synagogue.*
Oil.

1007. REV. SOLOMON HERSCHELL. *Beth Hamidrash.*
Oil.

1008. REV. SOLOMON HERSCHELL. *G. L. Lyon.*
Tinted engraving. The Rabbi is represented in the white satin *sargenes* which he was in the habit of wearing at Synagogue on the High Festivals.

1009. Rev. Solomon Herschell. *M. Moss.*
Miniature on ivory.

1010. Rev. Solomon Herschell. *Mrs. Arabella Levi.*
Engraving.

1011. Rev. Solomon Herschell. *I. Solomons.*
Ridley sculpt.

1012. Rev. Solomon Herschell. *I. Solomons.*
Slater pinxt. ; Holl sculpt.

1013. Rev. Solomon Herschell. *Mrs. David Lewis.*
By W. Holl, after a portrait by F. B. Barlin (1803).
Mr. F. B. Barlin was the son of the reader of the Chatham Synagogue

1014. Rev. Solomon Herschell. *Jacob Lazarus.*
Needlework portrait.

1015. Rev. Solomon Herschell. *M. Harris.*
Portrait formed by words of the Hallel (Prayer of Thanksgiving) and of the Song of Songs, in Hebrew. Written
by Rev. A. Levy, Ecclesiastical Assessor. Dated 5589.

1016. Rev. Solomon Herschell. *Samuel Leon Finzi.*
Pen and ink sketch. With scrolls of the Law closely
written in Hebrew.

1017. Rev. Solomon Herschell. *Sir Julian Goldsmid.*
Written in minute Hebrew characters.

1018. Mrs. Rachael Montefiore.
Spanish & Portuguese Congregation, Ramsgate.
Oil.
Mother of Sir Moses Montefiore, daughter of Abraham Mocatta ; born 1762.
Married Joseph Elias Montefiore, 1783 ; died 1841.

1018a. Mrs. Rachael Montefiore. *H. Guedalla.*
Miniature.

1019. Daniel Mendoza. *Lucien Wolf.*
Robinson pinx. ; Gardiner etched.
Famous pugilist and champion of England. Born 1763. Founder of the
so-called elegant or scientific school of boxing. Established a Boxing
Academy on the site of the present Lyceum Theatre. Held the belt from
1792 to 1795. Died 1836.

1020. Michael Josephs. *Walter Josephs.*
Miniature.
Hebraist. Born at Königsberg, Prussia, 1763. Settled in England and
published miscellaneous works in Hebrew. Author of a " Hebrew and
English Lexicon," and editor of the Law Book of the Great Synagogue
(Hebr. and Eng.), 1810. His Hebrew compositions were much admired.
Died 1849.

DAVID ABARBANEL LINDO.
Engraving.

Prominent member of the Bevis Marks Congregation. Uncle to Lord
Beaconsfield, whom he initiated into the Abrahamic Covenant; born
1765.

See Newman Collection, No. 1162.

1021. DR. JOSHUA VAN OVEN.   *Jews' Hospital.*
S. Drummond pinx.; engraved by T. Blood.

An active worker in the Anglo-Jewish community. Born in London, 1766.
Assisted in the foundation of the Jews' Hospital, and the transformation
of the London Talmud Torah into the Jews' Free School. Was the first
Vice-President of the latter institution. Died 1838.

1022. DR. JOSHUA VAN OVEN.   *Free School.*
Engraving.

REV. ISAAC POLACK.

Reader of the Great Synagogue. On the reopening of that edifice in 1766
he led the chanting of the dedication service.

See Newman Collection, No. 1173.

1023. MRS. BLAND.   *Lucien Wolf.*
Condé sculp.

Popular actress and singer. Daughter of Italian-Jewish parents named
Romanzini. Born 1769. Performed at Theatre Royal, Dublin; Drury
Lane and Haymarket, London, &c. Died 1810.

1024. DAVID RICARDO.   *I. Solomons.*
Holl sculp.

One of the most eminent political economists of his time. His father was a
leading member of the Bevis Marks Synagogue. Born at London, 1772.
Studied mathematics, chemistry and mineralogy. One of the promoters
of the London Geological Society. M.P. for Portarlington, 1719. Author of
"Principles of Political Economy and Taxation," &c. His works have
been collected and edited by J. R. McCulloch (London, 1846). Died 1823.

1025. RALPH BERNAL.   *Lucien Wolf.*
Wivell del., Thomson sculpt. 1822.

Politician. M.P. for Waterford and J.P. for co. Tipperary. Father of
Bernal Osborne, and grandfather of the present Duchess of St. Albans.

1026. DUKE OF SUSSEX.   *Jews' Hospital.*
Oil.

Patron of the Jews' Hospital, and a warm friend of Hebrew literature and
Anglo-Jewish communal progress. Sixth son of King George III. Born
at Buckingham, 1773. Was intimately associated with leading English
Jews, and used his influence for the promotion of the emancipation
movement. Frequently presided at Jewish public dinners and meetings.
Collected a splendid Hebrew library, which was dispersed at his death,
but of which some relics are shown in the present Exhibition (*see*
Nos. 2070–2081). Died 1843. His demise was publicly mourned in the
Jewish community.

1027. DUKE OF SUSSEX.   *William Van Praag.*
The tracing of this portrait consists of the biography of
the Duke in minute characters.

1028. LEVY SALOMONS. *Sir Julian Goldsmid.*
Water colour sketch.
Father of the late Sir David Salomons, Warden of the New Synagogue.
Born 1774. Died 1843.

1029. DUTCH SAM. *Lucien Wolf.*
Full length, in fighting attitude. 1819.
Pugilist, and one of the hardest hitters of his day. Real name, Samuel
Elias. Born in London, 1775. Died 1816.

1030. SOLOMON COHEN. *Mrs. B. Merton.*
Prominent worker in the London Jewish community. Warden of the Great
Synagogue. Father-in-law of the late Sir David Salomons. Born 1776.
Died 1864.

1031. ISAAC D'ISRAELI. æt. 11. *Lucien Wolf.*
Robinson sculp., 1777.
Miscellaneous writer, and father of Lord Beaconsfield. Born in London,
1766. Author of "Curiosities of Literature," "Genius of Judaism," &c.
Seceded from the Synagogue in 1814, in consequence of a difference with
the Elders arising from his refusal to serve the post of Warden. His
views on Judaism are recorded in his "Genius of Judaism," and show the
workings of strong Mendelssohnian influences. Attended the consecration of the West London Synagogue of British Jews (Reform) in 1842.
Died 1848.

1032. ISAAC D'ISRAELI. *I. Solomons.*
R. Graves sculpt. Proof on India paper.

1033. MR. D'ISRAELI. *Lucien Wolf.*
Ridley sculp.; Drummond pinx.

1034. ISAAC D'ISRAELI. *I. Solomons.*
J. B. Hunt sculp.; Drummond pinx.

ISMAEL AGA.
Engraving.
A noted beggar and character who haunted the purlieus of the Stock Exchange
See Newman Collection, No. 1128.

1035. JOHN BRAHAM. *Lucien Wolf.*
Cardon sculp.; Wood pinx.
Greatest tenor singer of his day. Born in London, 1774. Real name
Abrahams. First appeared at Drury Lane in opera, 1796; Covent
Garden, 1801. Sung in Paris and the leading cities of Italy. Composed
numerous songs, which met with great popularity, and were noted for
the beauty of their melody. Died 1856. Father of the late Countess of
Waldegrave.

1035a. JOHN BRAHAM. *Lucien Wolfe.*
In the character of Orlando. Drawn, etched and published
by R. Deighton, 1802.

1036. N. M. ROTHSCHILD. *Benjamin L. Cohen.*
Private plate by Walker.
Famous financier. Born at Frankfort, 1777. Came to England in 1790, and
seven years later established himself in Manchester as a manufacturer of
cotton goods. In 1802 removed to London and founded the present well-
known banking business. During the Napoleonic wars he rendered
important financial service to the British Government. Received letters
of denization, 1804. Created a baron of the Austrian Empire, 1822.
Died 1836.

1037. N. M. ROTHSCHILD.   *A. I. Myers.*
Stone Cameo.

1038. N. M. ROTHSCHILD.   *I. Spielman.*
Sketch.

1039. N. M. ROTHSCHILD.   *I. Solomons.*
Litho. by G. E. Madeley presented with *Sunday Herald.*

1040. N. M. ROTHSCHILD.   *Lucien Wolf.*
" The Shadow of a great Man."   Silhouette by Edouart.

1041. N. M. ROTHSCHILD.   *I. Solomons.*
"A View from the Stock Exchange."   (Coloured etching
    by Dighton, 1817.)

1041a. REV. ISAAC LYON.   *J. A. Henriques.*

1041b. JOSEPH JOSEPHS.   *Plymouth Heb. Cong.*
Water colour.

1042. SIR ISAAC LYON GOLDSMID.   *Sir Julian Goldsmid.*
Oil.   By Faulkner.

> Philanthropist. Born in London, 1778. The most prominent worker for
> the political emancipation of the Jews in England.   Assisted very largely
> in the foundation of the London University, of which he was a munificent
> supporter.   Created a baronet, 1841, and made Baron de Goldsmid and de
> Palmeira by the Portuguese Government, 1846.   Died 1859.

1043. SIR ISAAC LYON GOLDSMID.   *Miss Goldsmid.*
Oil.   By Partridge.

1043a. BENJAMIN GOMPERTZ.   *J. Montefiore.*
Photograph.

> Distinguished mathematician and actuary to the Alliance Insurance Company.
> Author of "On the Theory of Astronomical Instruments," and other
> works.   Born 1779.   Died 1865.

1044. HANANEL DE CASTRO.   *Joseph de Castro.*
Oil.   By Abraham Solomon.

> Prominent worker in the Anglo-Jewish community.   President of the
> Jews and General Literary and Scientific Institute.   Born 1796 ; died 1849.

1044a. SAMUEL SOLOMON, M.D.   *I. Solomons.*
Engraving.

> Widely known as the inventor of a patent medicine called " Balm of Gilead."
> Maternal grandfather of Henry J. Byron, the dramatist.   Born 1780.

1045. MYER SOLOMON.   *Western Synagogue.*
Oil.

> Founder of St. Alban's Place Synagogue.

1046. LYON MOSES.   *Mrs. B. Merton.*
Oil.

> Founder of the Jews' Orphan Asylum, 1831, and of the Lyon Moses
> Almshouses. 1838.

1047. SIR MOSES MONTEFIORE, BART., F.R.S.
Alliance Assurance Company.
Oil. By J. Richmond, R.A.

Philanthropist. Born at Leghorn, 1784. Served as Sheriff of London and Middlesex in 1837, and was High Sheriff of Kent in 1845. Was knighted at Guildhall on the 9th of November, 1837, on the occasion of the Queen's visit to the City, and was created a baronet 1846. Sir Moses is principally remembered for his labours on behalf of his persecuted co-religionists in various parts of the world, and for his efforts for the amelioration of the condition of the Jews of Palestine. He visited Jerusalem seven times (1827, 1838, 1849, 1855, 1857, 1866, and 1875), and undertook missions of a semi-public character to Egypt (1840), Russia (1846 and 1872), Rome (1859), Morocco (1863), and Roumania (1867). He celebrated the completion of his hundredth year in 1884, and died in 1885.

1048. SIR MOSES MONTEFIORE. *Bevis Marks Synagogue.*
Oil. In uniform of Deputy Lieutenant, holding the Turkish firman in his hands.

1049. SIR MOSES MONTEFIORE IN HIS 100TH YEAR. *Miss M. Twyman.*
Painted in oil by Exhibitor.

1050. SIR MOSES MONTEFIORE IN HIS 100TH YEAR. *Lucien Wolf.*
Drawn from life. With autograph. Proof of engraving from *Graphic.*

1051. SIR MOSES MONTEFIORE. *I. Solomons.*
Oil. By Roland Knight.

1052. SIR MOSES MONTEFIORE. *Lucien Wolf.*
Etching by E. L. Montefiore, 1879.

1052a. SIR MOSES AND LADY MONTEFIORE. *J. Sebag Montefiore.*
Miniature, *circa* 1813.

1053. LADY MONTEFIORE. *Bevis Marks Synagogue.*
Oil.

Wife of Sir Moses Montefiore, and his companion on many of his foreign missions. Daughter of Mr. Levi Barent Cohen. (*See* No. 1137.) Born in London, 1784. Became the wife of Sir Moses Montefiore in 1812, and assisted him in all his communal labours. Author of " Private Journal of a Visit to Egypt and Palestine " (1836), and " Notes from a Private Journal of a Visit to Egypt and Palestine " (1864; 2nd edit. 1885). Died 1862.

1053a. GROUP OF MONTEFIORE FAMILY. *Mrs. D. Henriques.*
Water colour. Represents Mr. and Mrs. Joseph Montefiore and family. The tall child in red is the eldest son, afterwards Sir Moses Montefiore.

1054. HANNAH, BARONESS DE ROTHSCHILD. *Benjamin L. Cohen.*
Engraving.

Third daughter of Levi Barent Cohen. (*See* No. 1137.) Became the wife of Mr. N. M. Rothschild (*see* No. 1036) in 1806. An active worker in the Anglo-Jewish community, taking especial interest in the Jews' Free School. Died 1850.

1055. HANNAH, BARONESS DE ROTHSCHILD.   *Jews' Free School.*
Engraving.

1056. ISABELLA, LADY GOLDSMID.   *Sir Julian Goldsmid.*
Oil.

Second daughter of Abraham Goldsmid, of Morden, Surrey. Born c. 1786;
became the wife of Sir Isaac Lyon Goldsmid, Bart., 1804; died 1860.

1057. REV. S. ASCHER.   *H. L. Cohen.*
Photograph.

Principal reader at the Great Synagogue. Born 1789. Died 1872.

SOLOMON BENNETT.

Theological writer and Hebraist. Author of the "Temple of Ezekiel," &c.
His portrait is engraved by himself.

See Newman Collection, No. 1130.

ISAAC NATHAN.

Composer and song writer. Born 1792. Author of "On the Theory of
Music," and numerous songs. Friend of Lord Byron, whose "Hebrew
Melodies" he set to music. Settled in Australia and died at Sydney, 1864.

See Newman Collection, No. 1125.

1058. DAVID SASSOON.   *I. Solomons.*
Lithograph.

Philanthropist. Born at Bagdad, 1792. Settled in Bombay, 1832, and
became one of the leading merchants of British India. His charities were
princely. He built and endowed Synagogues at Bombay, Poona, and
Byculla; gave £6000 towards the Building Fund of the Mechanics'
Institution, Bombay; founded and endowed a Reformatory and Industrial
Institution, an Asylum for the aged, a Hospital, &c. Died 1864.

CHARLES SLOMAN.

Actor and improvisatore. Author of "Fitful Fancies." Born 1793.
Died 1873.

See Newman Collection, No. 1187.

1059. A. MYER.   *S. Myer.*
Oil.

Member of Hereford Town Council, 1850.

1060. LOUIS LUCAS.   *New Synagogue.*
Oil, painted 1839.

President of the Jews' Free School, and an active member of other communal
institutions. Head of the firm of Lucas and Micholls, West Indian
merchants, of London and Manchester. Died 1851.

1061. REV. I. L. LINDENTHAL.   *Rev. A. Löwy.*
Oil. By Abraham Solomon.

Minister of the New Synagogue. Co-translator with D. A. De Sola and
Raphall of the Book of Genesis. Born in Brighton, 1796. Died 1863.

1062. REV. D. A. DE SOLA.   *Miss de Sola.*
Photo.

Minister of the Bevis Marks Synagogue, London. Born at Amsterdam, 1796.
Appointed Second Reader of Bevis Marks, 1818, and Preacher 1831.
Was a voluminous writer in Hebrew, English, German, and Dutch. Author
of an English translation of the Mishna (conjointly with Dr. Raphall),
"Ancient Melodies of the Portuguese Jews," "Festival Prayers," in
Hebrew and English, &c. Died 1860.

1063. LEOPOLD NEUMEGEN. *Mrs. Neumegen.*
Oil. By V. Leoni.

Jewish school-master, first at Highgate and subsequently at Kew. His school had a high reputation in the community, and among his pupils were Sir George Jessel, Master of the Rolls, Sir Benjamin Phillips, Lord Mayor, &c.

1064. REV. DR. DAVID MELDOLA, OF AMSTERDAM.
Prof. R. Meldola, F.R.S.
Oil; with laudatory verse by his pupil, Right Hon. Lord Montelan.

1065. REV. DAVID MELDOLA. *Miss de Sola.*
Oil.

Dayan (Ecclesiastical Judge) and presiding Rabbi of the Portuguese Synagogue of London. Son of Haham Raphael Meldola. Born at Leghorn, 1797. On the death of his father appointed to the spiritual direction of the Portuguese Synagogue, but without the rank of Chief Rabbi. Author of several theological works. In conjunction with Mr. Moses Angel, founded the *Jewish Chronicle*, 1841. Died at London, 1853.

1066. SIR DAVID SALOMONS. *City of London School.*
Bust.

A leading worker for the civil and political emancipation of the Jews. Born in London, 1797. First Jewish Sheriff of London and Middlesex (1835), and Alderman (1835). Returned to Parliament in 1851; and, although declining to repeat the words "on the true faith of a Christian" in the oath of allegiance, took his seat and voted three times. He was compelled to withdraw, and sued for penalties. First Jewish Lord Mayor, 1855-56. The Parliamentary oath having been meanwhile modified, Mr. David Salomons re-entered the House of Commons in 1859. Called to the Bar, 1849. Created a Baronet, 1869. Author of several pamphlets on Jewish disabilities, &c. Died 1873.

1067. SIR D. SALOMONS. *New Synagogue.*
Oil.

1068. ALDERMAN SIR DAVID SALOMONS. *Free School.*
Smith pinx; Skelton sculp.

1069. DAVID SALOMONS. *I. Solomons.*
Mrs. C. Pearson pinxt.; C. Turner, A.R.A., sculpt.

1070. LOUIS COHEN. *B. L. Cohen.*
Oil.

A leading member of the Anglo-Jewish community. Born 1799. One of the founders of the enlarged constitution of the Board of Deputies. Served as President of the Great Synagogue, and Vice-President of the Free School. Head of the firm of Louis Cohen & Sons, and a member of the Stock Exchange. Died 1882.

1071. LOUIS COHEN. *A. L. Cohen.*
Miniature. *Circa* 1850-2.

1072. HORATIO JOSEPH MONTEFIORE. *G. di R. Moro.*
Photo.

One of the founders of the West London Congregation of British Jews. Born 1798. Died 1867.

1073. NATHAN LAZARUS BENMOHEL.   *N. I. Berlin.*
Miniature, ivory, 1836.

> First Jew M.A. of an English university. Born about 1800, at Hamburg.
> Settled in Dublin, 1829, as teacher of languages. Entered the University
> after a course of private study, 1832; B.A. 1836; M.A. 1846. Deputy
> Professor of German and French at the Dublin University, 1839-42.
> Died 1869.

1074. THREE JEWISH PRIZE-FIGHTERS (Engraved).   *Lucien Wolf.*
(1) Barney Aaron.

> Nicknamed "The Star of the East." Born 1800. Reputed to have been
> one of the best of light-weights. Died 1859.

(2) Young Dutch Sam.

> Son of Samuel Elias. Born 1801. Died 1843.

(3) Aby Belasco.

> Nicknamed "The Leary Israelite." Born 1797. Described by authorities
> as a master of the science of boxing. Died 1824.

1074a. I. ISAACS AS HAWTHORN.   *I. Solomons.*
Kinnerley sculpt.

> Popular actor and singer.

1074b. MR. ISAACS.   *Lucien Wolf.*
See preceding, No.

1075. REV. DR. ADLER, CHIEF RABBI.   *United Synagogue.*
Oil. By B. S. Marks.

> Present Chief Rabbi of Great Britain. Born at Hanover, 1802 (British
> subject). Ordained for the Jewish ministry, 1828. Chief Rabbi of
> Oldenburg (1829), and Hanover (1830). Succeeded Dr. Solomon
> Herschell (see No. 1004) as Chief Rabbi of the Jews of Great Britain in
> 1845. Author of נתינה לגר, &c.

1076. REV. DR. N. M. ADLER, CHIEF RABBI.   *Great Synagogue.*
Oil. By S. A Hart, R.A.

1077. PROFESSOR HYMAN HURWITZ.   *Mrs. Reuben Salomons.*
Oil.

> Hebraist. Professor of Hebrew at University College, London. Author of
> "Hebrew Tales," "Vindiciæ Hebraicæ," &c. Friend of Coleridge.

1078. PROFESSOR HYMAN HURWITZ.   *L. Emanuel.*
Oil.

1079. REV AARON LEVY.   *Mrs. R. H. Fonseca.*
Oil. By S. Hart, R.A.

> Late Dayan (Ecclesiastical Assessor) of the London Jewish community.

1080. REV AARON LEVY.   *Beth Hamidrash.*
Oil.

1081. REV. AARON LEVY.   *C. S. Davis.*
Oil.

1082. BENJAMIN DISRAELI, ESQ., M.P. *Lucien Wolf.*
Robinson sculpt. ; Chalon pinx.

> Prime Minister of England. Born 1805. Initiated into the Abrahamic Covenant. Seceded from the Synagogue. During his brilliant political and literary career he never ceased to evince a warm interest in the race from which he had sprung. Assisted in the abolition of Jewish Disabilities, and at the Berlin Congress seconded and strongly supported the emancipation of the Jews of the Danubian Principalities. Prime Minister 1868 and 1874. Raised to the Peerage as Earl of Beaconsfield, 1876. Died 1881.

1083. BENJAMIN DISRAELI. *Lucien Wolf.*
A Sketch in Park Lane in 1844, by C. M.

1084. SOLOMON ALEXANDER HART, R.A. *George Ellis.*
Oil, painted by himself.

> Distinguished artist. Born at Plymouth, 1806. Achieved a reputation by painting scenes from the Jewish ceremonial and other Jewish subjects. Academician, 1840. Professor of Painting in the Royal Academy, 1854. Librarian 1865. Died 1881.

1085. JOSEPH ZEDNER. *J. Nahon.*
Photo.

> Jewish bibliographer. Born 1804. Assistant in the Printed Books Department of the British Museum. Under his supervision the Hebrew collection of the Museum was raised to a rank almost equal to that of the Bodleian. Died 1871.

1086. BARON LIONEL DE ROTHSCHILD. *Great Synagogue.*
Oil.

> Eldest son of Nathan Meyer Rothschild (see No. 1036), whom he succeeded (1836) as head of the banking firm of N. M. Rothschild & Sons, London. Born in London, 1808. Was a leading worker for the political emancipation of the English Jews. Returned to Parliament as one of the members for the City of London in 1847, 1849, 1850 and 1852, but excluded on account of his refusal to take the oath "on the true faith of a Christian." Elected once again in 1857, he was permitted to take his seat under the provisions of Lord Lucan's Bill, permitting a modification of the oath. A munificent supporter of Jewish institutions and all movements of public utility. Died 1879.

1087. BARON LIONEL DE ROTHSCHILD. *United Synagogue.*
Oil.

1088. BARON LIONEL DE ROTHSCHILD. *I. Solomons.*
Litho. Published by Hartwig.

1089. SIR FRANCIS GOLDSMID. *Louisa, Lady Goldsmid.*
Oil, by Rudolf Lehmann.

> Philanthropist. Born in London, 1808. First Jew called to the Bar, 1833; Q.C. 1858. Succeeded to the Baronetcy, 1858, on the death of his father, Sir Isaac Lyon Goldsmid. (*See* No. 1042.) A leading worker for the civil and political emancipation of the Jews, and author of several powerful pamphlets on the subject. Entered Parliament 1860. One of the founders of the West London Synagogue of British Jews (1842), and of the Anglo-Jewish Association. Died 1878.

1090. SIR FRANCIS GOLDSMID. *West London Synagogue.*
Oil. By Mrs. Louis Goodman, 1878.

1091. Sir Francis Goldsmid.   *Mrs. Goodman.*
Oil. By Mrs. L. Goodman. May, 1879.

1092. Sir Francis Goldsmid.   *I. Solomons.*
Etching.

1093. Prof. J. Waley.   *Mrs. D. F. Schloss.*
Oil.

> Distinguished lawyer and economist. Senior Conveyancing Counsel to the Court of Chancery. Worker for undenominational education in connection with Sir Isaac L. Goldsmid. First President of the Anglo-Jewish Association, 1871. Died 1874.

1094. S. W. Waley.   *Mrs. S. J. Waley.*
H. Hartshorn pinxit. Crayon.

> Brother of the preceding. Composer and Pianist.

1095. J. Löwenthal.   *Lucien Wolf.*
Engraving.

> Distinguished chess-player. Born at Buda-Pesth, 1810. Settled in England, 1851. Secretary of the St. George's Chess Club, 1852, and President of the St. James's Club, 1862. Edited a new and critical edition of the games of Labourdonnais and McDonnell, and was author of several other important contributions to chess literature. Died 1876.

1096. Sir Anthony de Rothschild, Bart.   *Jews' Free School.*
Oil. By Rebecca Solomon, 5636 = 1876.

> Second son of Nathan Meyer Rothschild, and member of the banking firm of N. M. Rothschild & Sons, London. Born at London, 1810. Created a Baronet, 1847. President of the United Synagogue Council, and one of the promoters of that Corporation. President of the Jews' Free School, of which he was a munificent supporter. Died 1876.

1097. Sir Anthony de Rothschild.   *Jews' Hospital.*
Oil.

1098. Sir Anthony de Rothschild.   *United Synagogue.*
Chalk Drawing.

1099. Rev. Prof. D. W. Marks.   *West London Synagogue.*
Oil. By Mrs. Louis Goodman, and presented by her to the Synagogue, Nov. 1877.

> Present Chief Minister of the West London Synagogue of British Jews. Born in London, 1811. Assistant reader in the Duke's Place Synagogue, and subsequently Secretary of the Orthodox Congregation at Liverpool. In 1840, when the Reform movement took place, Mr. Marks was elected Minister of the new congregation. Has remained its spiritual Chief ever since. Succeeded Prof. Hyman Hurwitz as Professor of Hebrew in the University College, London, 1848. Author of three volumes of sermons and other publications.

Baron Nathan, of Rosherville.

> Master of the ceremonies at Rosherville Gardens, and a noted *entrepreneur* of public entertainments. Died 1856.

See Newman Collection. No. 1122.

1100. Ephraim Alex.   *Jewish Board of Guardians.*
Oil.

> Founder of the Jewish Board of Guardians. Died 1883.

1101. REV. A. BARNETT. *Miss R. Barnett.*
As a Jewish Minister in full canonicals in Synagogue
descending the steps of the Ark with the scrolls of the
Law. Oil. Dated June 1st, 1840.
Chief Reader of the New Synagogue. Died 1885.

SIR BENJAMIN PHILLIPS.
A leading worker for the civil emancipation of the Jews. Born at London,
1811. Head of the firm of Faudel, Phillips & Co.; Alderman of London,
1857; Sheriff 1859-60, and Lord Mayor 1865-66. Knighted 1866.
Commander of the Order of Leopold of Belgium. Sir Benjamin took a
prominent part in the struggle for Jewish emancipation.

See Newman Collection, No. 1172.

1102. J. M. MONTEFIORE. *Mrs. J. M. Montefiore.*
Oil.
President of the Board of Deputies, in succession to his uncle, Sir Moses
Montefiore (1874). Born 1816. Died 1880.

1103. BARON MEYER DE ROTHSCHILD. *Earl and Countess of Rosebery.*
Oil. By G. F. Watts.
Fourth son of Nathan Meyer Rothschild (*see* No. 1036), and member of the
banking firm of N. M. Rothschild & Sons, London. Born at London, 1818.
Conspicuous for his attachment to horse-racing and field-sports. Won
the Derby with Favonius in 1871, and twice ran second for it with King
Tom and King Alfred. Also owner of Hannah, Corisande, and other
famous thorough-breds. M.P. for Hythe. Died 1874.

1103a. BARONESS MEYER DE ROTHSCHILD.
Earl and Countess of Rosebery.
Oil. By Sir F. Leighton, P.R.A.
Wife of the preceding. Daughter of Isaac Cohen, Esq. Born in London
1831; married 1850; died 1877. The present Countess of Rosebery is
her daughter.

1104. NATHANIEL MONTEFIORE. *Bevis Marks Synagogue.*
Oil. 1872.
Leading member of the Anglo-Jewish community. Born 1819. Fellow
of the Royal College of Surgeons; President of the Jews and General
Literary and Scientific Institute, 1849; President of the Elders of the
Bevis Marks Synagogue, of the Gates of Hope Schools, and Jews'
Emigration Society. One of the founders of the Synagogue at
Southampton. Died 1883.

1105. CHARLOTTE, BARONESS DE ROTHSCHILD. *Jews' Free School.*
Oil. By B. S. Marks.
Wife of Baron Lionel de Rothschild (*see* No. 1086); born at Naples;
married 1836. Her whole life was devoted to charity. She regularly
visited the homes of the poor and the communal schools, and bequeathed
£100,000 for benevolent purposes. Died 1884.

1106. HENRY RUSSELL. *Lucien Wolf.*
Litho. By J. W. Gear.
One of the most popular of modern song writers. Born at Sheerness, 1813.
Has written music to seven hundred and sixty songs, the words of many
of them being by Thackery, Charles Dickens, Charles Mackay, Tennyson,
Longfellow, and Tupper. Among his most popular productions are
"The Ship on Fire," "The Gambler's Wife," "There's a Good Time
Coming, Boys," "Cheer, Boys, Cheer," "Woodman, Spare that Tree,"
"Buffaloe Girls." Mr. Russell, whose original family name was Levy,
is still living.

F

1107. Sampson Lucas. *Bayswater Synagogue.*
Photo.
Prominent communal worker. Born 1821. Vice-President of the Jews'
Free School, 1862. One of the promoters of the United Synagogue, and
its first Vice-President, 1870. President of the Council, 1874. Warden
of the Bayswater Synagogue. Died 1879.

1108. Sampson Lucas. *United Synagogue.*
Chalk Drawing.

1109. Rev. A. L. Green. *L. Cohen.*
Photo. By Barraud.
Popular Jewish minister and preacher. Born in London, 1821. Minister at
Bristol, 1837. Junior minister and assistant secretary of the Great
Synagogue, London, 1851. First reader and preacher of the Central
Synagogue, Great Portland Street, 1855. During nearly half a century
Mr. Green was among the most prominent workers in the community.
He collected the finest library of Anglo-Jewish literature in the country,
and wrote much for the Jewish newspapers. Died 1883.

1109a. Samuel Lyon de Symons. *H. Barned.*
Photo.
An active and generous supporter of Synagogues and Charities. Born 1824;
died 1870.

1110. Sir George Jessel. *Lucien Wolf.*
Engraving.
Master of the Rolls, and one of the most eminent lawyers of his time.
Born at London, 1824. Called to the bar at Lincoln's Inn, 1847; Queen's
Counsel, and a Bencher of his Inn, 1865. M.P. for Dover, 1868.
Solicitor-General, 1871, and knighted, 1872. On the death of Lord
Romilly, 1873, nominated Master of the Rolls by Mr. Gladstone. Vice-
Chancellor of the London University, 1880. Died, 1883. In recognition
of his distinguished services a baronetcy was conferred on his son.

1111. Rev. Dr. Abraham de Sola, LL.D. *Miss de Sola.*
Photo.
Minister of the Portuguese Synagogue at Montreal, Canada, 1847, and
Professor of Hebrew and Semitic literature at McGill College, 1848.
Born at London, 1825. Author of a revised translation of the Jewish
Forms of Prayer (6 vols.), and numerous miscellaneous works. Was
distinguished as a champion of Jewish orthodoxy on the American
continent. In 1872 was invited to open the United States Congress with
prayer. Died 1882.

1112. Emanuel Deutsch. *Rev. H. R. Haweis.*
Photo.
Orientalist. Born in Prussian Silesia, 1829. Entered the service of the
British Museum, 1855. Wrote very largely on Oriental subjects in
periodicals and serial publications, "Chamber's Encyclopædia," Smith's
"Dictionary of the Bible," Kitto's "Cyclopædia of Biblical Literature,"
etc. His article on the Talmud in the *Quarterly* ran through nine
editions, and was translated into nearly every European language. Died
at Alexandria, 1873.

1113. Judah Peter Benjamin, Q.C. *L. Emanuel.*
Engraving. Piercy pinx.
Statesman and lawyer. Born in San Domingo, 1812. Admitted to the
American Bar, 1834. United States senator, 1852. Joined the Southern
cause, 1860, and appointed Attorney-General of the Confederacy.
Secretary of War, 1861. Secretary of State, 1862. Settled in London,
and called to the English Bar. Rose to a high rank in the legal profession. Author of 'A Treatise on the Law of Sale of Personal Property.'
(1866). Died 1884.

1114. Dr. Benjamin Artom. *Bevis Marks Synagogue.*
Oil. Presented to the Bevis Marks Synagogue by his
widow and brothers, according to his own wish.

Chief Rabbi of the Spanish and Portuguese congregations in England. Born
at Asti in Piedmont, 1834. Officiated as Jewish minister at Salazzo, and
subsequently as Rabbi at Naples. Elected Chief Rabbi of the Portuguese
Jews of England, 1866. Author of a volume of sermons. Died 1879.
Has been succeeded by Dr. Moses Gaster, 1887.

1115. Leonora, Baroness de Rothschild. *Jews' Free School.*
Engraving.

Eldest daughter of Baron Lionel de Rothschild, M.P. (*see* No. 1086);
born 1837. Became the wife of her cousin, Baron Alphonse de Rothschild, of Paris, 1857.

1116. Evelina, Baroness de Rothschild. *Jews' Free School.*
Photo.

Second daughter of Baron Lionel de Rothschild (*see* No. 1086); born
1839. Became the wife of Baron Ferdinand de Rothschild, 1865. Died
1866. The Evelina Hospital in Southwark was founded in her memory.

1117. Rev. Dr. H. Adler. *H. S. and H. E. Mendelssohn.*
Photograph.

Present delegate Chief Rabbi and chief minister of the Bayswater Synagogue.
Born in Hanover, 1839. Principal of Jews' College, 1863; resigned
1865. Minister of the Bayswater Synagogue, 1864. Delegate Chief
Rabbi, 1879. Author of a large number of published sermons, lectures
and magazine articles, including an historical sketch of "The Jews in
England" (1870).

1118. Rev. Samuel de Sola. *Miss de Sola.*
Photo.

Minister of the Bevis Marks Synagogue, London, in succession to his father,
1863. Born in London, 1839. Died 1866. Composed some of the
melodies at present used by the choir of the Synagogue.

1119. Lord Rothschild. *United Synagogue.*
Oil. By B. S. Marks.

First Jewish peer. Eldest son of Baron Lionel de Rothschild (*see*
No. 1086); born 1840. Succeeded to the Baronetcy on the death of
his uncle, Sir Anthony de Rothschild, 1876. Raised to the peerage,
1885. The picture by Mr. B. S. Marks represents his Lordship, on his
introduction to the House of Peers, taking the oath in the Jewish fashion,
with head covered and on the Hebrew Bible. Lord Rothschild is President of the United Synagogue Council and of the Jews' Free School.

1120. Numa Edward Hartog. *Madame Hartog.*
Photo.

Born in London, 1846. Had a brilliant university career, and became
Senior Wrangler in 1869. Honorary Secretary of the Society of Hebrew
Literature. His early death in 1871 caused wide-spread sorrow.

1121. Alfred A. Newman. *Mrs. A. Newman.*

Born 1851; died 1887. An active member of the several Committees of
the present Exhibition. Deeply interested in Anglo-Jewish history, he
brought together a remarkable collection of books, pamphlets, and portraits bearing on the subject (*see* Nos. 1121a–1250). He started and
organised the movement against the demolition of the ancient synagogue
in Bevis Marks, 1885. Outside the Jewish community he is remembered
for his efforts to bring about a revival of the blacksmith's art in its
mediæval phases.

l.—THE COLLECTION OF PORTRAITS AND PRINTS OF THE LATE ALFRED NEWMAN.

[Arranged alphabetically, serving as key to preceding biographies.]

1121*a.* FRAME OF PORTRAITS.

1. Rev. Dr. N. M Adler, Chief Rabbi. (Wood, from newspaper.)
2. Jew Merchant (after Rembrandt).
3. A. Goldsmid. (From *European Magazine.*)
4. Rabbi A. J. Schwarzenberg.
5. Mr. [Isaac] D'Israeli. (From *European Magazine.*)
6. S. A. Hart, R.A. (Wood, from newspaper.)
7. Baron H. de Worms.

1122. FRAME OF PRINTS, &c.

1. Book Plate of Sir I. L. Goldsmid, Bart.
2. Mr. Simmonds as Beau Mordecai in Macklin's *Marriage à la Mode.* (De Wilde pinxt.; Scriven sculpt.)
3. Book Plate of I. L. Goldsmid.
4. Menasseh ben Israel. (Wood, after Rembrandt.)
5. Mr. Braham in 1800. (H. Allard sculpt.)
6. Mendoza. (From *Boxiana.*)
7. D. Ricardo. (W. Holl sculpt.)
8. Braham in character. (E. James del., 1804.)
9. Baron Nathan, of Rosherville, performing his celebrated *pas* among the eggs and tea things. *See* after No. 1099.

1123. BARNEY AARON.
"The Star of the East." Wood-Engraving from the *Sporting Life.* (*See* No. 1074.)

1124. BARNEY AARON.
Reprint from *Boxiana.*

1125. REV. DR. N. M. ADLER, CHIEF RABBI OF ENGLAND.
Private Plate. Hempf. pinxt.; G. Zobel sculpt. Published Feb. 1852. (*See* No. 1075.)

1126. DR. N. M. ADLER, OBER-RABBINER VON ENGLAND.
German print of the Chief Rabbi.

1127. JOHN ADOLPHUS, ESQ., F.S.A.
Allingham pinx.; Ridley sculp. Pub. by Vernet and Hood, 1803.

Advocate and Author. Said to have been of Jewish parentage. Born 1766. Died 1845.

1128. ISMAEL AGA.
Published by R. Wilkins in 1812. Called the Jew Pedlar in Catalogue. (*See* after No. 1034.)

1129. ABY BELASCO.
G. Sharpello pinx.; R. Cooper fecit. Same as in *Boxiana.* (*See* No. 1074.)

1130. S. BENNETT.
G. Frazer pinx. Engraved by himself. Published as a frontispiece to the "Temple of Ezekiel." (*See* after No. 1057.)

1131. RALPH BERNAL.
Wixill pinx.; Thompson sculpt. (*See* No. 1025.)

1132. DR. EPHRAIM BONUS, MEDICUS JUDÆUS.
J. Lyryus fecit.

1133. JOHN BRAHAM.
Published by Kelly. (*See* No. 1035.)

1134. MR. BRAHAM IN THE CHARACTER OF ORLANDO.
Drawn, etched, and published by R. Deighton, 1802.

1135. RICHARD BROTHERS, PRINCE OF THE HEBREWS.
" Fully believing this to be the Man whom God has appointed, I engrave his likeness, William Sharp." Published by W. Sharpe, 1795. (*See after* No. 998*a.*)

1136. CHAOU WAN-KWEI AND CHAOU KIN-CHING.
Two Chinese Jews of Kao-fung-foo.

1137. MR. COHEN [LEVY BARENT COHEN].
Drawn, etched, and published by R. Deighton, 1817. This
is a re-issue by McLean, 1824. (*See after* No. 977.)

1138. BARON D'AGUILAR.
Published by Kirby, 1802. (*See* No. 977.)

1139. JOSEPH D'ALMEIDA.
Lauranson pinx.; J. Jones sculpt., and published 1783.
(*See after* No. 971*a.*)

1140. DANIEL COHEN D'AZEVEDO, HEBRÆORUM AMSTELODAMENSIUM
LUSITANORUM SYNAGOGARCHA. *Ætat.* 46.
Dated in Hebrew, 1697. (*See* No. 1003.)

1141. BENJAMIN DISRAELI.
A. E. Chalon pinxit.; H. Robinson sculpt. (*See* No. 1082.)

1142. ISAAC DISRAELI. *Æt.* 11.
Engraved by H. Robinson from a picture by an Italian
artist, 1777. (*See* No. 1031.)

1143. MR. DISRAELI.
Original pencil sketch of Isaac D'Israeli by Count D'Orsay
(Inscrip. " A. D'Orsay fecit, 1848).

1144. I[SAAC] D'ISRAELI.
Alfred Croquis (Maclise) del. Published by J. Fraser.

1144*a.* ISAAC D'ISRAELI.
Denning pinx. Cook sculp.

1145. DUTCH SAM.
Coloured. In fighting attitude. Pub. by S. W. Fores,
1819. (*See* No. 1029.)

1146. DUTCH SAM.
From *Boxiana.*

1147. YOUNG DUTCH SAM.
Son of the late phenomenon of the P.R. J. Rogers sculpt.
Same as in *Boxiana.* (*See* No. 1074.)

1148. DR. SAMUEL DE FALK, THE " BAAL SHEM."
Engraved by Butterworth, after a painting in the possession
of W. H. Goldsmid, Esq. One of four artists' proofs.
(*See* No. 967*a.*)

1149. ABRAHAM GOLDSMID.
Medley pinxt.; F. Bartolozzi sculpt. (*See* No. 993.)

1150. LORD GEORGE GORDON, A PRISONER IN THE TOWER OF LONDON.
Wood Engraving. (*See* No. 984.)

1151. LORD GEORGE [GORDON] IN HIS CELL.
Wood Engraving. "G. G., &c."

1152. MOSES GORDON, OR THE WANDERING JEW.
Lord George Gordon. Published 1788 by A. Davis, Birmingham.

1153. THE MOST LEARNED AARON HART, RABBI. AGED 81.
B. Dandridge pinx.; J. McArdale sculp. (*See* No. 958.)

1154. MOZE HENRIQUES.
J. Greenwood del & fecit, 1761.

1155. REV. SOLOMON HERSCHELL.
Frederick Benjamin Barlin pinxt.; W. Holl sculpt. Dedicated by the painter to his friends and patrons, Benjamin and Abraham Goldsmid. Published by Barlin, 1803. Coat of arms: scroll with Hebrew inscription surmounted by crown, supporters lion and unicorn. (*See* No. 1004.)

1156. REV. SOLOMON HERSCHELL, CHIEF RABBI OF THE GERMAN JEWS IN LONDON.
Engraved by Ridley for the *European Magazine*, from the original Drawing by Drummond.

1157. MENASSEH BEN ISRAEL, THEOLOGUS ET PHILOSOPHUS HEBRÆUS.
Salom Italia sculpt., 1642. *Ætat.* 38. (*See* No. 947.)

1158. MENASSEH BEN ISRAEL.
After Rembrandt, 1636.

1159. JACOB KIMHI, A JEW BORN IN CONSTANTINOPLE.
Humphreys, R.A., pinxit.; Singleton sculpt. Published 1799 by Richardson. Represented selling slippers. (*See* No. 999a.)

1160. DAVID LEVI.
Drummond pinxt.; Bromley sculpt. From the *European Magazine*, 1799. (*See* No. 982.)

1161. MRS. JUDITH LEVY, THE RICH JEWESS.
Usually called the "Queen of Richmond Green." (*See* after No. 981.)

1162. DAVID ABARBANEL LINDO.
Drawn from a Daguerreotype by J. H. Lynch. Painted by M. and N. Hanhart. (*See* after No. 1020.)

1163. THE MOST LEARNED HIGH PRIEST HART LYON, RABBI.
I. Turner pinxt.; E. Fisher fecit. (*See* No. 968.)

1164. PROF. D. W. MARKS.
Private plate. A. Solomon pinxt.; S. Marks sculpt. (*See* No. 1099.)

1165. THE REV. RABBE RAPHAEL MELDOLA.
Chief Minister of the Synagogue of the Spanish and Portuguese Jews in the City of London, to his worthy and benevolent patron, David Abarbanel Lindo, Esq., this plate is by permission inscribed by his obedient humble servant, J. Lopez. F. B. Barlin pinxt.; Joshua Lopez sculpt. Published 1806. Coat of arms: shield with tree. (*See* No. 985.)

1166. MOSES MENDELSSOHN.
Prag, published by Hoffman.

1167. MOSES MENDEZ.
Bromley sculpt., for *European Magazine,* 1792. (*See* No. 973.)

1168. DANIEL MENDOZA.
Etched by W. N. Gardiner from Robinson's portrait. Published by J. Tagge, 1789. (*See* No. 1019.)

1169. HAHAM GOMEZ DE MESQUITA.
Printed for Dr. Belisario. S. Da Silva pinxt.; J. Faber fecit., 1752. Inscription in English, Hebrew, and Spanish. (*See* No. 962.)

1170. SIR MOSES MONTEFIORE.
From the *Illustrated London News.* C. Roberts del. et fec. (*See* No. 1047.)

1171. MRS. ESTER MONTEFIORE.
From a miniature in the possession of J. B. Montefiore, Esq. Private proof. One of four proofs. (*See* No. 871.)

1172. THE RIGHT HON. THE LORD MAYOR, 1865-6 [SIR B. S. PHILLIPS].
Photograph with memoir. (*See* after No. 1101.)

1173. REV. ISAAC POLACK, D.D.
P. Leslie pinx.; R. Newman sculpt. Published P. Leslie, 1799. (*See* after No. 1022.)

1174. DAVID RICARDO.
Phillips pinx.; Hodgetts sculpt. Published by Colnaghi, 1822. (*See* No. 1024.)

1175. JOSEPH DE MENDOZA RIOS.
Proof before letters.

1176. THE LATE BARON LIONEL DE ROTHSCHILD.
Wood engraving from Illustrated paper. (*See* No. 1086.)

1177. BARON ROTHSCHILD
Taking the oaths in the House of Commons. Wood engraving from *Illustrated London News,* Aug. 3, 1850. (*See* No. 1086.)

1178. BARON MEYER DE ROTHSCHILD.
Wood engraving from *Graphic*, Feb. 14, 1874. (*See* No. 1103.)

1179. THE LATE BARON MEYER DE ROTHSCHILD.
From a sketch by R. Deighton. Wood engraving from the
Illustrated Sporting and Dramatic News, June 20, 1874.
(*See* No. 1103.)

1180. N. M. ROTHSCHILD.
C. Penny pinxit. Published by Smith, Elder, 1827. (*See*
No. 1036.)

1181. HENRY RUSSELL.
(*See* No. 1106.)

1182. [SIR] DAVID SALOMONS [BART., M.P.].
Mrs. Pearson pinxt.; C. Turner, A.R.A., sculpt. Published
1837 by Moon. (*See* No. 1066.)

1183. DAVID SALOMONS, ESQ.
Wood Engraving from *Pictorial Times*, Oct. 19, 1844.
(*See* No. 1076.)

1184. MISS CLARA SAMUELL.
Wood Engraving from the *Illustrated Sporting and Dramatic
News*, March 19, 1881.

1185. J. DE CASTRO SARMENTO, M.D.
Pine pinx.; Houston fecit. (*See* after No. 964.)

1186. HENRY SIMONS, THE POLISH JEW. Hos. iv. 6.
From the Trial Report.

1187. MR. SLOMAN AS JEMMY AND MR. BEVERLY AS JERRY.
In "Greeks and Turks on the intrepidity of a British Tar,"
Royal Coburg Theatre (Victoria). November 29, 1821.
(*See* after No. 1058.)

1188. S. SOLOMON, M.D.
I. Steel pinxt.; Ridley, Holl and Blood sculpt. Coat of
arms. Also in same frame,—

1189. GILEAD HOUSE, NEAR LIVERPOOL.
The seat of Dr. Solomon.

1190. MR. JOSHUA VAN OVEN.
S. Drummond, A.R.A., pinxt.; T. Blood sculpt. Published
by J. Ashburn, 1815. Private re-issue of original plate,
1886. (*See* No. 1021.)

1191. "THE NEW JEWISH SYNAGOGUE IN DUKE STREET, LONDON."
Exterior view. Eastgate sculp. The earliest known
sketch of the Great Synagogue.

1192. SYNAGOGUE, DUKE'S PLACE, HOUNDSDITCH.

Aquatint; Pugin et Rowlandson del et sculp.; Sunderland Aquat. Published 1809 by R. Ackerman. The building by Pugin, the characteristic figures by Rowlandson. From the *Microcosm of London.*

1193. NEW SYNAGOGUE.

The entrance to a Jews' Synagogue, Leadenhall Street. From the *European Magazine,* 1812 (?)

This was the Synagogue in which the congregation of the New Synagogue Great St. Helens, originally worshipped. It was known as the "New" Synagogue, afterwards Sussex Hall, when it was occupied by the Jews' and General Literary Institute.

1194. NEW SYNAGOGUE.

The Great Jewish Synagogue. Celebration of the Feast of Tabernacles. T. H. Shepherd pinx.; Melville sculp. Interior view towards the Hechal. The New Synagogue, Great St. Helens.

1195. NEW SYNAGOGUE.

Exterior of the New Synagogue, Great St. Helens. Wood Engraving from *The Mirror,* January 12, 1839.

1196. NEW SYNAGOGUE.

Interior of the Jews' Synagogue, Great St. Helens. Wood Engraving.

1197. NEW SYNAGOGUE.

Interior of the New Synagogue, Great St. Helens. Wood Engraving from *The Mirror,* January 5, 1839.

1198. BERKELEY STREET SYNAGOGUE.

Interior view of the New West London Synagogue (Berkeley Street). With ground plan. Litho.

1199. BERKELEY STREET SYNAGOGUE.

The West London Jewish Synagogue (Berkeley Street). Wood Engraving from the *Illustrated London News.*

1200. CENTRAL SYNAGOGUE.

The Central Jewish Synagogue, Great Portland Street. Wood Engraving from the *Illustrated London News.*

1201. BAYSWATER SYNAGOGUE.

Interior of the New Synagogue at Chichester Road, Bayswater. Wood Engraving from *Illustrated London News,* February 21, 1863.

1201a. THE NORTH LONDON SYNAGOGUE.

Jewish Synagogue, Barnsbury. Wood engraving from the *Illustrated London News,* October 3, 1868.

1202. CHATHAM MEMORIAL SYNAGOGUE.

Wood engraving from *The Builder,* September 10, 1870. Ground plan of the same.

1203. JEWISH SYNAGOGUE, BOURKE ST., WEST [MELBOURNE].
Wood Engraving from "Australia Illustrated."

1204. GOLD EMBROIDERED VEIL.
For the Ark of the Jewish Synagogue, Liverpool. Wood
Engraving from *Graphic*.

1205. JEWS' HOSPITAL.
Mile End Road, Whitechapel. Wood Engraving from the
European Magazine.

1206. THE JEWS' HOUSE, LINCOLN.
Wood Engraving, apparently from the *Illustrated London
News*.

1207. BELVIDERE, KENT.
The seat of Sir Sampson Gideon, Bart. R. Godfrey del et
sculpt.; Coat of Arms of the Gideon (Abudiente) family.

1208. VIEW.
A Prospect of Coppied Hall at Tottridge in the County of
Hertford, the seat of Joseph da Costa, Esq. Coat of arms
of the Da Costa family.

1209. PROSPECT PLACE, WIMBLEDON, SURREY.
A Villa belonging to M. J. Levy, Esq. S. Harding pinxt.;
J. Roberts sculpt. Published by Edwards.

1210. PROSPECT PLACE IN SURREY.
The Seat of M. J. Levy, Esq. (Small print).

1211. THE SEAT OF ABRAHAM GOLDSMID, ESQ., MORDEN, SURREY.
Drawn by Gylford and engraved by Hawkins. Published
by Stratford, 1806.

1213. THE SEAT OF BENJAMIN GOLDSMID, ESQ., ROEHAMPTON, SURREY.
Drawn and engraved by J. Hassell.

1214. THE SEAT OF BENJAMIN GOLDSMID, ESQ., ROEHAMPTON.
With eight views of the neighbourhood.

1215. THE MANSION OF BARON ROTHSCHILD, M.P., PICCADILLY.
Wood engraving from the *Builder*, November 1, 1862.

1216. THE MANSION OF BARON ROTHSCHILD, M.P., PICCADILLY.
Small Wood Engraving from *Illustrated London News*.

1217. MENTMORE, THE SEAT OF THE ROTHSCHILDS.
Seat of the late Baron Meyer de Rothschild, now occupied
by Lord Rosebery. Wood Engraving from the *Graphic*.

1218. CARICATURE (POLITICAL).
By Woodward. "King Jeremy treating his Jewish subjects
with Westphalia Venison." Coloured. Published by
Teyz, September 15, 1807.

1219. THREE CARICATURES FROM *Punch*.
1. Jewish Disabilities Bill in the House of Lords
2. On the Oaths Bill, June 27, 1857.
3. Russia's Difficulty, November 22, 1856.

1220. MOSES IN THE BULL RUSHES (CARICATURE).
Published 1794 by Laurie and Whittell.

1221. PICKLED PORK (CARICATURE).
Coloured. G. Grinagan (pseud.) inv. and fec. Published
by S. W. Fores, 1804.

1222. ELEVEN COMIC SKETCHES.
From various illustrated papers, illustrating the old clo'
trade.

1223. THREE CARICATURES.
By Rowlandson. (Coloured.)
1. "A Jew Broker," pub. by Fores, Jan. 1, 1801.
2. { "Get money, money still,
And then let Virtue follow if she will."

3. "Raising the Wind."
"When nobleman have lost racehorse and all their Rino spent,
Then little Isaac draws the bond and lends for cent per cent."

1224. CARICATURE.
"Jew purchasing old clothes." xviii cent. Pub. by
W. Davison, Alnwick. Coloured.

1225. CARICATURE.
"The Black Joke; or the Jew Harper and Demirep
Countess, *alias*, the Amorous Chambermaid, in her cabin
on board the Polacre." Pub. by J. Fairburn, Sept. 1820.
Coloured. [The "Jew-harper" is Isaac Nathan, the
musician.] (*See* before 1058.)

1226. CARICATURE.
Dealer in old clothes. Coloured.

1227. VALENTINES.
Three coloured valentines; Jewish subjects.

1228. CARICATURES.
Collection of 64 miscellaneous sketches from *Punch* and
other comic journals.

1229. CARICATURE.
Coffee's the Thing! Go it, ye Tigers. [Andrew Cohen.]
R. Deighton, 1823. Drawn, etched, and published by
R. D.

1230. CARICATURE.
"Will you let me a Loan?" [I. L. Goldsmid.] Drawn and
etched by Deighton. Published by McLean, 1824.

1231. CARICATURE.
A Pillar of the Exchange [N. M. Rothschild]. Published
by W. Clarke, probably by R. Deighton. Coloured.

1232. CARICATURE.

Mr. Montefiore. Drawn and etched .by Deighton, 1818.
Published by McLean, 1824. Coloured.

1232a. TWO CARICATURES.

"Jew-dish-us cakeman" [N. M. Rothschild].   Coloured.
No. 2 City Politics Series.

"The Modern Crœsus; Baron de Rothschild.   From No.
101 of *The Period*, July 9, 1870. Coloured.

1233. TWO CARICATURES.

From the *Sydney Punch*.

 1. " One of the right sort " [Mr. J. Josephson].
 2. " A most learned Rabbi " [Rev. A. B. Davis].

1234. THREE CARICATURES.

From the *Entr'acte*.

 1. The late Mr. Lionel Lawson. By A[lfred] B[ryan].
 2. Mr. Abrahams (Solicitor). By A[lfred] B[ryan].
 3. Mr. Morris Abrahams (Theatre Manager). By A[lfred]
    B[ryan].

1235. NINE CARICATURES—MISCELLANEOUS.

Six plain and three coloured.

1236. CARICATURE.

Jews receiving stolen goods.   Printed for R. Sayer and
J. Bennett, October, 1777.

1237. JEWISH CEREMONIES.

Book of Plates, published by Monath, of Nuremburg, apparently of the xvii cent.

1. Phylacteries and Praying Scarf.	16. Slaughtering Meat.
2. Prayer for New Moon.	17. Childbirth.
3. Sabbath Ceremonial (Synagogue at Rome).	18. Circumcision.
4. Baking Passover Cakes.	19. Redemption of Firstborn.
5. Passover.	20. Betrothal.
6. Pentecost.	21. Marriage Procession.
7. Ninth of Ab.	22. Marriage Ceremony.
8. New Year.	23. Marriage Ceremony (conclusion).
9. Atonement.	24. Baths of Purification.
10. Tabernacles.	25. Divorce.
11, 12. Purim.	26. Halitza.
13. Deathbed Ceremonies.	27. Customs, Implements, and Symbols.
14. Burial.	28. Wieselbinden.
15. Vows.	

1238. JEWISH CEREMONIES.

Seventeen Plates by Bernard Picart (1724).

1. Phylacteries and Praying Scarf, with Jew in same.	9. The Passover meal.
2. New Year.	10. Benediction of the Coharim (Priests).
3. The Day of Atonement.	11. Elevation of the Law.
4. Feast of Tabernacles (in the Synagogue).	12. Circumcision.
5. Feast of Tabernacles (at home).	13. Redemption of the Firstborn.
6. Rejoicing of the Law.	14. Marriage among the Portuguese Jews.
7. Escorting home the Bridegroom of the Law.	15. Marriage among the German Jews.
8. Searching for Leaven (Passover).	16. Circuit round the coffin.
	17. Jewish Interment.

These are the original plates as they appeared in the
" Coutumes Religieuses," &c.

1238a. JEWISH CEREMONIES.
Engravings. Wood.

1. The Feast of Tabernacles at the North London Synagogue. The reader shaking the Palm branch. *Graphic.*
2. A Jewish Wedding: a Sketch at the Synagogue, Duke's Place, Aldgate. *Illustrated London News*, April 15, 1876.
4. Election of Rabbi at the Synagogue, Great St. Helens. *Illustrated London News*; Dec. 21, 1844.

1239. JEWISH CEREMONIES.
Two etchings on India paper by Simeon Solomon. 1. Circumcision. 2. Passover Eve service.

1240. EIGHT WOOD ENGRAVINGS.
From various illustrated papers.

1. The Jews' Infant School Ball at Willis's Rooms.
2. At a Pawnbroker's.
3. Rag Fair.
4. Watch Fair at Houndsditch.
5. The Sunday Trading Question—a Sketch in Petticoat Lane.
6. Houndsditch Sunday Fair. Sketched by McConnell.
7. Petticoat Lane.
8. Scene in Petticoat Lane.

1241. TRAUER UM JERUSALEM. Horovitz pinxt.; Doby sculpt.
[Fast of Ninth of Ab.] A number of Polish Jews in a small synagogue bewailing the loss of Jerusalem on the traditional anniversary.

1242. LA CIRCONCISIONE.
By Novelli after Picart, engraved by Baratti. Letterpress in Italian and French.

1243. LA FESTA DI PASQUA.
Novelli after Picart. Published at Venice. Letterpress in Italian and French.

1244. JEW RABBI.
By Rembrandt. From the painting in the Devonshire collection. Pether sculpt. Published 1764.

1245. RANDALL THE IRISH LAD, AND BELASCO THE JEW CHAMPION.
Prize fight. Drawn and etched by Williams. Published by S. W. Fores, 1817.

1246. AMSTERDAM SYNAGOGUES.
The two great Synagogues of the German Jews in Amsterdam, together with the Jews' Hospital. J. de Beyer del.

1247. SONGS.
Forty-five from song books, &c., mostly humorous, chiefly by E. T. B. Box and Miss Bryant.

1248. MANUSCRIPT.
Providençia de Dios. Libro compuesto por el muy docto Sor. H. H. Saul Levi Morteira. MS. copied by Shelomoh Selivanani, fol. sh. 210 = 420 pp.

1249. MEGILLAH (ROLL OF ESTHER).
Illuminated.

1250. GERMAN PIPE, WITH HEAD OF RABBI.
Lid engraved with arms of the Duke of Sussex.

m.—MISCELLANEOUS PRINTS, PHOTOGRAPHS, DRAWINGS. ETC.

1251. THE STORY OF THE ROTHSCHILD FAMILY.   *Lucien Wolf.*
Two photos from paintings by Moritz Oppenheim.

> In 1806 Napoleon I. invaded Hesse Cassel. The Elector William, previous
> to his flight, deposited his fortune, with his Court Agent Maier Amschel
> Rothschild of Frankfort. The use of this large sum of money is said to
> have founded the fortunes of the Rothschild family, which were still
> further secured when, at the end of the Napoleonic wars, the sons
> of Maier Rothschild returned the money with interest.

1252. THE ROTHSCHILD HOUSE—FRANKFORT-ON-MAIN.   *E. Joseph.*
Photo.

> In this house (known as "Zum Grünen Schild") in the old Ghetto or Juden-
> gasse, of Frankfort, dwelt Maier Amschel Rothschild (b. 1743, d. 1802),
> the great-grandfather of Lord Rothschild, and the founder of the family.
> It dates from 1711 when, in consequence of the destruction of the
> quarter by fire, the Judengasse was rebuilt. Maier Rothschild purchased
> it in 1780, and all his nineteen children were born and reared within its
> walls. When last year the Judengasse was demolished, the heirs of
> Maier Rothschild caused the stones to be carefully preserved and num-
> bered, and the building has lately been re-erected in Frankfort. It serves
> as the head-quarters of the Rothschild charities in that city.

1253. A POLISH JEW.   *Lucien Wolf.*
Pencil sketch by R. Westall, R.A.

1254. JEWISH RABBI.   *H. Solomon.*
Appearing before the Sanhedrin at Paris, 1807.

1255. HAHAM DANIEL D'AZEVEDO.   *Miss d'Azeveda.*
Son of Haham M. C. d'Azevedo. About 1774. Miniature.

1256. RABBI WEARING A TURBAN.   *I. Solomons.*
Selomoh Salem of Adrianople, Rabbi at Portuguese Synagogue, Amsterdam, 1762.

1257. RABBI MEYER SIMON WEIL, POLISH RABBI.
                                                     Mrs. Arabella Levi.
Photograph from a painting.

1258. DR. EPHRAIM BONUS.   *I. Solomons.*
Joannes Lynyus fecit. Original unknown.

1259. R. AKIBA LEHERN.   *H. Solomon.*
Embroidered.

1260. A DRAUGHT OF THE CITY OF JERUSALEM ... TAKEN FROM THE
SOUTH EAST BY CORNEILLE LE BRUYN.   *G. L. Lyon.*
The explanatory letterpress is very curious, *e.g.* "The
Borough of Siloam," &c. (*circa* 1698).

1261. DUTCH SYNAGOGUE (ROTTERDAM).   *S. Hayman.*
Picture by Jeremiah Snook.

1262. PLAN OF THE ROYAL EXCHANGE, LONDON. *Lucien Wolf.*
Donowell del, Walker sculp.

Shows the several walks frequented by different classes of merchants. The south-east corner is allotted to Jews.

1263. EXPULSION OF JEWS FROM SPAIN. *F. D. Mocatta.*
Oil. S. A. Hart, R.A. Torquemada exhorting Ferdinand and Isabella to reject the 30,000 ducats offered by the Jews to remain in Spain.

1264. JEWS' WAILING PLACE. *L. Cohen.*
Western Wall, Jerusalem.

1265. GRAND SANHEDRIN DES ISRAELITES DE L'EMPIRE FRANCOIS ET DU ROYAUME D'ITALIE. *G. Ellis.*

1266. CEREMONIES ET COUTUMES RELIGIEUSES DE TOUT LES PEUPLES DU MONDE. *P. H. Emanuel.*
Amsterdam, 1783.

1267. CIRCUMCISION IN A SYNAGOGUE. *Abraham Franks.*
With key.

1268. SKETCHES OF ANCIENT JEWISH MUSICAL INSTRUMENTS.
Rev. S. Lyons.

1269. AN AGED JEW. *Mrs. Arabella Levi.*
Photograph from a painting.

1270. "A BILL OF EXCHANGE." *I. Solomons.*
Williams sculpt.

1271. JEW PURCHASING OLD CLOTHES. *I. Solomons.*

1272. CARICATURE. *I. Solomons.*
With dialogue in verse between R. Abraham ben Mordecai, Jeremiah van Husen, Simeon ben Bull, and Ephraim ben Bear.

1273. A JEWISH WOMAN GOING TO THE SYNAGOGUE. *I. Spielman.*

1274. A JEWESS WITH VEIL AND ORNAMENTS. *I. Spielman.*

1275. "AN ISRAELITE." *I. Solomons.*
Engraved by R. H. Dyer. India paper.

1276. "PORTRAIT OF A JEW." *I. Solomons.*
Rembrandt pinxt.; John Barnet sculpt.

1277. "A JEWESS." *I. Solomons.*
Rembrandt pinxt.; C. Corbutt fecit.

1278. THE TALMUD TEST. *S. Schloss.*
Rabbi examining a Jewish lad in Talmud. Oil. By Professor Oppenheim.

1278a. INAUGURATION OF THE SABBATH *R. C. Isaac.*
Oil. By Professor Oppenheim.

1279. "Jewish old Clothesman."   *S. Montagu, M.P.*
Oil.   By Meissonier.

1280. Jewish Composite Photographs.   *F. Galton, F.R.S.*
A number of photographs of Jewish lads being taken;
these were imposed one on another on the same sensitive
plate, which gave ultimately only the common features of
the various faces, and thus gives the nearest approach to
the Jewish type that science can afford.   Cf. *Journ. An-
throp. Instit.* Nov. 1885.

1281. Ceremony of *Halitza.*   *I. Spielman.*
Unloosing the shoe.   (Cf. Deut. xxv. 9, and Ruth. iv. 17.)

1282. The Jewish Synagogue, 1752.   *I. Solomons.*

1283. Jewish Life.   *A. Solomon.*
By S. Solomon.   Ten Photographs from Drawings of Simeon
Solomon, illustrating Jewish Ceremonials.

1. Circumcision.	6. Eve of Passover.
2. Marriage.	7. Fast for Destruction of Temple.
3. Mourning.	8. Day of Atonement.
4. Carrying the Scroll of the Law in Synagogue.	9. Feast of Tabernacles.
5. Sabbath Eve.	10. Feast of Dedication of the Temple.

1284. Etchings.   *H. Solomon.*
Jewish life.

1285. Twelve Engravings of Jewish Ceremonies.
William Van Praag.

1286. "Scènes de la vie Juive."   *A. Durlacher.*
Seventeen Heliographic reproductions of B. Picart's engravings of Jewish ceremonies in a portfolio.

1287. Circumcision.   *E. I. Samuels.*

1288. Eighteen Engravings.   *Adolphe Solomon.*

1289. Book of Engravings of Jewish Forms and Ceremonies.
Mrs. Meyers.

1290. Illustrations of Jewish Family Life and Ceremonies.
Mrs. Jacobs.

1291. The Washing of the Dead.   *L. Isaacs.*
Dated A.M. 5465.

1292. Jewish Funeral.   *L. Isaacs.*
Dated 5465.

1293–1304. Jewish Ceremonies.   *A. Heal.*
Twelve wood engravings printed by John Bowles, Cornhill.

1305–1312. Engravings.   *E. Marks.*
By B. Picart, 1721.

1313. PORTRAIT DU ROI DAVID.   *S. J. Rubinstein.*
Contenant le cinquième livre des Psaumes.   Hillel Brovermann.

1314. PORTRAIT DU ROI SALOMON CONTENANT LE CANTIQUE DES
CANTIQUES ET L'ECCLESIASTIQUE.   *S. J. Rubinstein.*
Hillel Brovermann.

1315. HANDKERCHIEF PRINT.   *Lewis Emanuel.*
"Divine Service on the Day of Atonement at Metz during
the Franco-German War."

1316. PORTRAIT OF MOSES.   *W. H. Cohen.*
Lines composed of the whole book of Deuteronomy.

1317–1319. BOOK PLATES.   *I. Solomons.*
Sir Moses Montefiore, four.
Sir Isaac Goldsmid, two.
Abraham Goldsmid.

1320. DANIEL MENDOZA (*see* No. 1019) AND RICHARD HUMPHREYS.
Prize fight.   Ryley pinx.; Grozer sculp.   *Lucien Wolf.*

1321. DAN BEATING THE PHILISTINES.   *Lucien Wolf.*
Prize fight between Mendoza and Ward.   Wood engraving,
published 1792.

1322. RANDALL THE IRISH LAD, AND BELASCO THE JEW CHAMPION.
                                                        Lucien Wolf.
Prize fight.   (*See* No. 1074.)   Coloured etching.   By
Williams.

1323. "THE BAKER KNEADING SAMMY'S DOUGH."   *Lucien Wolf.*
Prize fight between Baker and Dutch Sam.   (*See* No. 1029.)
Wood engraving, coloured by G. Cruikshank.

1324–1343. CARICATURES OF MODERN HEBREWS.   *Lucien Wolf.*
From *Vanity Fair.*   Chromo-litho.

1. Baron Lionel de Rothschild.
2. Baron Meyer de Rothschild.
3. Mr. Alfred de Rothschild.
4. Mr. Leopold de Rothschild.
5. Right Hon. Sir George Jessel.
6. Sir Francis H. Goldsmid, Bart., M.P.
7. Sir Albert Sassoon.
8. Mr. Lionel Cohen, M.P.
9. Mr. S. Montagu, M.P.
10. Sir John Simon, M.P.
11. Baron Henry de Worms.
12. Mr. H. L. Bischoffsheim.
13. Mr. Lionel Lawson.
14. Mr. Edward Levy Lawson.
15. Earl of Beaconsfield.
16. Mr. Bernal Osborne, M.P.
17. Sir Julius Benedict.
18. Mr. Joseph d'Aguilar Samuda.
19. Baron Paul Reuter.
20. Mr. Albert Grant.

1344–1360. JEWISH CEREMONIES.   *Joseph Jacobs.*
Italian issue of Picart's plates.

G

II.—JEWISH ECCLESIASTICAL ART.

THE historic origin and uses of the principal objects represented in this section are described under their respective heads; but as they all partake of an artistic character, it has been judged desirable to introduce them with some general observations on Jewish Ecclesiastical Art. Unfortunately this branch of study has no very distinct existence, and it would be extremely difficult to trace its history in any detail. It is more correct to speak of a geography than of a history of Jewish Ecclesiastical Art; for like the jargons of the Hebrew people, their manners and customs, their superstitions and other phenomena of their social life, their art is little more than a composite deposit of the contrastful impressions of a wide geographical dispersion, and of a varied and chequered history. Whether the Hebrew consciousness is normally deficient of artistic sympathies, or whether it has been dulled in this respect by the Biblical command anent graven images, are interesting questions upon which we need not dilate. Their discussion in these pages would not assist the reader to a better comprehension or appreciation of the exhibits to which we are referring. Our historic survey must be limited to the remark that, whatever the normal artistic capacities of the Hebrew people, they must have been strongly affected, if not altogether transformed, by the stupendous catastrophe of the Dispersion, and the career of ceaseless wandering and misery which subjected them to the perplexing influences of ever-changing surroundings.

In short, the peculiar nature of Jewish history left the Jews little leisure for the cultivation of art as art; and their efforts in this respect were less directed to the production of things of beauty, for the sake of their beauty, than to the illustration of the affection or reverence in which they held particular persons or things. For this purpose the mere richness of the gift was sufficient, and, design being to a certain extent a minor consideration, they borrowed freely from the art types of the nations among whom they dwelt, or from the more obvious methods of costly decoration. Their betrothal rings, for example, were frequently of immense size, but, except that they bore a Hebrew inscription signifying "Good Luck," they rarely differed from the similar rings in vogue among the Gentiles. A curious example of the indication of reverence for ritual paraphernalia by the mere costliness of the ornamentation is afforded by No. 1854 in the present exhibition, in which a pair of phylactery sheaths are encased in stout plates of gold set with large diamonds.

Throughout his history, the Jew has prized nothing more highly than that portion of the Scriptures which records the earliest traditions of his race, and contains his Sacred Law; and he has marked his reverence for it by a lavish ornamentation of the Scrolls from which it is read during Divine

G 2

service. Mantles of costly stuffs and rich embroidery are partially covered
with breastplates of silver or gold, and surmounted by elaborate crowns or bells.
Even the pointer with which the reader follows the text is frequently a
marvel of goldsmithery, and more often than not the index finger will be
found tipped with a jewel. Thus costumed, the scroll is enshrined in an
ark which, in the synagogue, is generally a fine piece of joinery or ironwork,
and in the home—being of smaller size—is more elaborate, sometimes even of
silver studded with precious stones. Two splendid examples of the latter
kind of arks are shown in the present Exhibition. (*See* Nos. 1361 and 1903.)
And then, finally, a velvet or satin curtain is hung before the ark, on which
figure suitable inscriptions and designs in bullion embroidery. It is curious to
notice that in their anxiety to bring the richest tributes to their Holy Law,
the Jews have not scrupled to evade the strict letter of the law with regard to
graven images. Heraldic representations of animals, and sometimes even
figures of the Law-giver and the High Priest occur on mantles and breastplates; and it was held that such representations, being only in partial
relief, did not constitute complete images. Of course the scope of ornamentation would have been much restricted without them.

After the Law, the home is perhaps the most precious thing in the eyes
of the Jew. As the former was the fountain-head of his spiritual consolation
in the evil days of his outlawry, so the latter was the source of all the
human comfort with which his sorrows were soothed. The domestic
religious exercises prescribed by his religion afforded many opportunities
for enhancing the sacred character of his home, and enabled him to
illustrate both his affection for the domestic hearth, and his reverence for
his faith, by a numerous ritual paraphernalia, in the design and con-
struction of which the ornamental arts were largely employed. For the
inauguration and termination of the Sabbath he used and still uses
candelabra, spice boxes and sanctification cups. Special dishes and goblets
were employed in the Passover meal; and the citron, used during the Feast of
Tabernacles, was enclosed in a case. The Feast of Dedication was honoured
with elaborate candlesticks; and the roll of Esther read on the Feast of
Purim was the object of specially magnificent ornamentation. The
illuminated *Megilloth*, as these rolls are called, with their varied but always
elaborate cases, are among the most remarkable objects displayed in the
Ecclesiastical Art Section of the present Exhibition. It is needless to pursue
the enumeration of the ritual utensils which Jews love to honour by means
of the decorative arts. Religious ceremonies compass the whole life of the
observant Jew, and hence the list of objects susceptible of artistic present-
ment is very long. We should add in conclusion that, while the designs
affected by Jewish ecclesiastical art are of the most cosmopolitan character,
some distinctive feature, common to the race and its history, generally appears
on each object. Sometimes it is a Hebrew inscription, sometimes such
traditional emblems as the seven-branched candlestick, the tablets of the
Law, or the interlaced triangle known as "the Shield of David." But
except in some form of charms these characteristic symbols are only incidental
and subordinate to a main design which has not the remotest connection with
the history of the Hebrew people.

SYNAGOGUE.

a.—ARK AND CURTAIN.

[The receptacle for the Scroll of the Law is termed the **Ark** (ארון הקדש),
which has usually two doors opening outwards. It is usually covered
by a **curtain** sliding on a rail. In the arrangement of the ark and the
curtain covering it, reminiscences of the Temple with its Holy of Holies
concealed by a curtain, has doubtless had an influence. In Spanish
synagogues the curtain is inside the doors, a relic of the times when such
a receptacle had to be concealed from the officers of the Inquisition. The
ark is sometimes portable, being used in domestic worship, or in travelling, and under those cases is without a curtain, and is termed a **case**.
See Nos. 1391–93.].

1361. ARK. *L. de Rothschild.*
Small, silver gilt, studded with stones. Russian. Early
XVII. Cent. Pierced and chased with uniforms, stags,
birds, and other devices.

1362. ARK. *Mrs. Seymour.*
Small, wood.

1363. ARK. *Mrs. Neumegen.*
Mahogany.

1364. CURTAIN FOR ARK. *B. L. Benas, J.P.*
From private Synagogue of Mr. P. Philips. XVIII. Cent.

1365. CURTAIN FOR ARK. *Rev. S. M. Gollancz.*

1366. CURTAIN FOR ARK. *Mrs. Neumegen.*
Presented to Mr. Neumegen by his pupils.

1367. CURTAIN FOR ARK. *L. Schaap.*
Gold embroidered velvet.

1368. CURTAIN FOR ARK. *I. Spielman.*
Fragment. Gold embroidered. XVIII. Cent.

1369. CURTAIN FOR ARK. *Central Synagogue.*
Centre piece. Presented to the Central Synagogue by Mr.
Wertheimer, and embroidered by R. Abraham and Sons.

1371. CURTAIN FOR ARK. *Chatham Hebrew Congregation.*
Embroidered.

1372. CURTAIN FOR ARK. *Dalston Synagogue.*
Embroidered velvet. Presented to the Dalston Synagogue
by Mr. I. Bernstein.

1373. CURTAIN FOR ARK. *Great Synagogue.*
White satin.

1374. CURTAIN FOR ARK. *Great Synagogue.*
Crimson velvet. Presented to the Great Synagogue by Mr.
Louis Nathan.

1375. CURTAIN FOR ARK.   *Great Synagogue.*
Blue and gold damask.   Presented to the Great Synagogue
by Mr. I. M. Marks.

1376. CURTAIN FOR ARK.   *Great Synagogue.*
Presented to the Great Synagogue by Mr. Solomon Keyser,
circa 1785.

1377. CURTAIN FOR ARK.   *New Synagogue.*
Crimson velvet, with gold fringe.   Crown in centre, decorated with coloured stones.

1378. CURTAIN FOR ARK.   *New Synagogue.*
Violet velvet, silver embroideries.

1379. CURTAIN AND VALANCE FOR ARK.   *Hambro' Synagogue.*
Red velvet centre, blue with silver embroidery, diaper
pattern.

b.—PERPETUAL LAMPS.

[In every synagogue a lamp (נר תמיד) is kept burning perpetually. It is
usually a swinging lamp, immediately in front of the Ark. Here again
there is a reference to the Temple service, where a perpetual lamp
was kept burning, as is known from the Maccabean legend of the Feast
of Dedication.]

1380. PERPETUAL LAMP.

1381, 1382. LAMP STANDS.   *Western Synagogue.*
Silver gilt.

c.—LAVERS FOR PRIESTS.

[Jews, being a nation of priests, the existence of a special class of priests
(*Cohanim*) was only rendered necessary by the Temple service, and the
" Sons of Aaron " have only one priestly function remaining to them at
the present day, the benediction mentioned in the Law. This is given with
hands upraised with a division between the middle and ring finger, a
position of the fingers which has become a characteristic of the Cohanim.
Before the solemn act the priests must ensure ritual purity by laving
the hands, which thus becomes part of the service and necessitates a
laver.]

1386. EWER AND BASIN.   *Benjamin L. Cohen.*
Stone.   Hebrew inscription.

1387. SILVER PLATE.   *E. Joseph.*
Probably stand of Laver.   Has bas-relief of Aaron the
High Priest.

1388. EWER AND SALVER.   *Great Synagogue.*
Ewer, silver, and handsomely *repoussé*.   In the centre the
priest's device of two hands in the act of benediction, surrounded by flowers and foliage.   Round the laver the
same device and ornamentation, and a Hebrew inscription.
Presented by the late N. M. Rothschild, escalloped border.
Hall Mark 1779.

1389. EWER AND SALVER. *Ramsgate Synagogue.*

Silver, *repoussé.* with leaves and scrolls, and border of grapes and fruit. Presented by the late N. M. Rothschild. Hall mark 1785.

d.—SCROLLS OF THE LAW AND APPURTENANCES.

[The reading of the Law being the central function of Jewish public worship, everything connected with it is decorated as sumptuously as possible. The **scroll** itself (ספר תורה) must be written, not printed or litho-graphed, nor must it be in book form, the ancient form of scroll being retained. The parchment (or leather) is attached to rollers with handles, termed "tree of life" (עץ חיים), by which the scroll is unrolled from right to left. When closed and about to be returned to the ark, it is tied securely by a **band**, which is often elaborately worked, and then is enclosed in a **mantle** to keep it free from dust. Attached to the top handles by chains is a **breastplate** (טס), on which is inscribed the name of the festival. Then comes the **pointer** (יד), by which the reader follows the text without touching the scroll. This is invariably in the shape of a hand with outstretched finger. On the two tops of the handles are placed **bells** to recall those attached to the high priest's dress in the Temple. Sometimes these are replaced by a **crown**. The function of carrying the scroll, thus adorned, to and fro from the Ark is an honour accorded to privileged persons on the chief holidays.]

1390. A SCROLL OF THE LAW. *J. S. Merton*

In silver-gilt case ornamented with *repoussé* scrolls and flowers, set with turquoise, garnets, &c.. and two small rosettes of rose diamonds and rubies. In the centre of the case a recess with the Commandments, enclosed by folding doors and nielloed Hebrew characters. A pair of gilt mounts to scrolls, and a pointer set with precious stones; columns at the angles.

1391. SCROLL OF THE LAW. *J. Price.*

In case. Ebony ark, gilt ornaments; a pair of silver-gilt bells, filigree, and six small bells on each; a silver breastplate with gilt Decalogue surmounted by two lions and crown, and an enamel star of pearls and dia-monds, and a silver pointer with chain.

1392. SCROLL OF THE LAW. *J. S. Sassoon*

In case. Silver cylindrical case. Pair of silver bells and pointer of Bombay work.

1393. SCROLLS OF THE LAW. *Great Synagogue.*

In silver case. Presented by Dr. Falck.

1394. SCROLL OF THE LAW. *Mrs. Almosnino.*

Small. With mantles and set of bells, *circa* 1770.

1395. SCROLL OF THE LAW. *E. A. Franklin.*

Miniature. Silver mounted. Purchased from the Execu-tors of the late S. M. Samuel. Esq.

1396. Scroll of the Law.   *Theodore Fry, M.P.*
Circa xvii. Cent.

1397. Scroll of the Law.   *H. Guedalla.*

1398. Scroll of the Law.   *Henry Harris.*

1399. Scroll of the Law.   *S. Hoffnung.*
Miniature.

1400. Scroll of the Law.   *Rev. N. Lipman.*
Small. Minute writing.

1401. Scroll of the Law.   *Mrs. Neumegen.*

1402. Scroll of the Law.   *J. Price.*

1403. Scroll of the Law.   *Mrs. Seymour.*
With Mantle.

1404. Scroll of the Law.   *Bayswater Synagogue.*

1405. Scroll of the Law.   *Rev. S. M. Gollancz.*

1406. Scroll of the Law.   *Great Synagogue.*
Silver handles. Presented by Mr. Samuel Joseph.

1407. Scroll of the Law.   *Great Synagogue.*
Written on leather.

1408. Scroll of the Prophets.   *Great Synagogue.*
The Portions read on Sabbaths.

1409. Scroll of the Law.   *Hambro' Synagogue.*

1410. Scroll of the Law.   *Hambro' Synagogue.*

1411. Scroll of the Law.   *Hambro' Synagogue.*

1412. Scroll of the Law.   *Hambro' Synagogue.*

1413. Scroll of the Law.   *New Synagogue.*
With gold handles.

1414. Band for Scroll of the Law.   *Dr. John Evans, F.R.S.*

1415. Band for Scroll of the Law.   *S. Levy.*

1416. Band for Scroll of the Law.   *A. Wertheimer.*
Embroidered.

1416a. Binders for Scroll of the Law.   *J. Sassoon.*

1417. Mantle for Scroll of the Law.   *H. Phillips.*
Velvet, with altar and seven-branched candelabrum.

1418. Mantle for Scroll of the Law.   *Rev. S. Nahon.*
Silk embroidery. Dated 1626.

1419. Mantle for Scroll of the Law.   *Bayswater Synagogue.*
Embroidered.

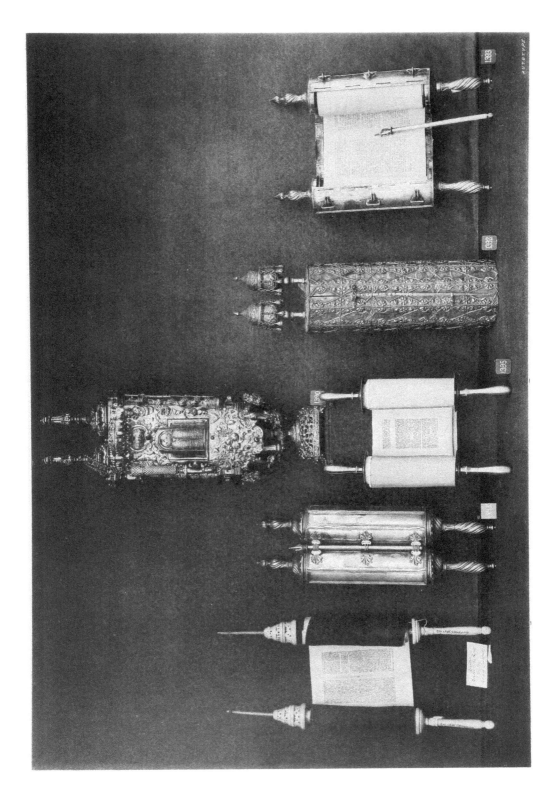

1420. MANTLE FOR SCROLL OF THE LAW. *Bevis Marks Synagogue.*
Alternate strips of red velvet and gold groundwork. A crown in centre. Probably English.

1421. MANTLE FOR SCROLL OF THE LAW. *Bevis Marks Synagogue.*
Embroidered silk and gold, designed in scrolls and leaves. Old Italian. Coronet in centre.

1422. MANTLE FOR SCROLL OF LAW. *Bevis Marks Synagogue.*
Embroidered on silk and blue velvet, and containing two in a circular monogram, surmounted by crown. Probably Dutch, *circa* 1740–60.

1423. MANTLE FOR SCROLL OF LAW. *Bevis Marks Synagogue.*
Gold brocade, with interlaced monogram M.D.C.

1424. MANTLE FOR SCROLL OF THE LAW. *Bevis Marks Synagogue.*
Gold brocade, with interlaced monogram M.L.B.

1425. MANTLE FOR SCROLL OF THE LAW. *Bevis Marks Synagogue.*
Velvet; floral designs.

1426. MANTLE FOR SCROLL OF LAW. *Bevis Marks Synagogue.*
Presented to the Bevis Marks Synagogue by Sir Moses Montefiore.

1427. MANTLE FOR SCROLL OF THE LAW. *Bevis Marks Synagogue.*
Presented to the Bevis Marks Synagogue by Sir Moses Montefiore.

1427a. MANTLE FOR SCROLL OF THE LAW. *Bevis Marks Synagogue.*
Old gold brocade.

1428. MANTLE FOR SCROLL OF THE LAW. *Central Synagogue.*
Embroidered by R. Abraham & Sons, with gold design in scrolls and wreaths.

1429. MANTLE FOR SCROLL OF LAW. *Great Synagogue.*
Circa 1760.

1429a. MANTLE FOR SCROLL OF THE LAW. *Great Synagogue.*
Circa 1760.

1430. MANTLE FOR SCROLL OF LAW. *Great Synagogue.*
White silk. Presented to the Great Synagogue by Mr. L. L. Cohen, M.P.

1431. MANTLE FOR SCROLL OF LAW. *Great Synagogue.*
Presented to the Great Synagogue by Mr. L. L. Cohen, M.P.

1432. MANTLE FOR SCROLL OF THE LAW. *Great Synagogue.*
Presented to the Great Synagogue by Mr. Eliason.

1433. MANTLE FOR SCROLL OF THE LAW. *Great Synagogue.*
Presented to the Great Synagogue by Samuel Joseph about 1820.

1434. MANTLE FOR SCROLL OF LAW. *Great Synagogue.*
Blue velvet. Presented to Great Synagogue by S. de Symon, Esq.

1435. MANTLE FOR SCROLL OF THE LAW. *Hambro' Synagogue.*
Gold brocade and velvet, covered with gold embroidery. In the centre in relief small ark with movable door displaying a miniature scroll. At sides ornamented door surmounted by crown and Hanuca lamp.

1436. MANTLE FOR SCROLL OF THE LAW. *Hambro' Synagogue.*
Gold dyed embroidered brocade, lined red silk.

1437. MANTLE FOR SCROLL OF THE LAW. *Hambro' Synagogue.*
Design, Moses and Aaron.

1438. MANTLE FOR SCROLL OF THE LAW. *Hambro' Synagogue.*
White and gold shells, presented to the Hambro' Synagogue by Mrs. Lazarus.

1439. MANTLE FOR SCROLL OF THE LAW. *Hambro' Synagogue.*
Dwarf; silver and blue velvet.

1440. MANTLE FOR SCROLL OF THE LAW. *Hambro' Synagogue.*
Presented to the Hambro' Synagogue by Lady Salomons.

1441. MANTLE FOR SCROLL OF THE LAW. *Hambro' Synagogue.*
Presented to the Hambro' Synagogue by Miss Levien.

1442. MANTLE FOR SCROLL OF THE LAW. *Hambro' Synagogue.*
Gold and red brocade.

1443. MANTLE FOR SCROLL OF THE LAW. *New Synagogue.*
Bullion embroidered velvet. Heraldic design, with priest's breastplate, studded with twelve stones (Exod. xxviii.) in the centre ; supporters, antelopes.

1444. MANTLE FOR SCROLL OF THE LAW. *New Synagogue.*
Bullion embroidered velvet. Tablets of the Law surmounted by crown studded with stones and supported by lions.

1445. MANTLE FOR SCROLL OF THE LAW. *New Synagogue.*
Bullion embroidered velvet. Floral design.

1446. MANTLE FOR SCROLL OF THE LAW. *Ramsgate Synagogue.*
Red silk, embroidered with gold and designed in bands and foliated scrolls.

1447. MANTLE FOR SCROLL OF THE LAW. *Ramsgate Synagogue.*
Blue velvet, with scrolls and leaves, and in centre arms of Sir Moses Montefiore, embroidered in gold and silk.

1448. MANTLE FOR SCROLL OF THE LAW. *Ramsgate Synagogue.*
Italian brocade in red and gold with blue leaves, designed in foliated scrolls.

1449. MANTLE FOR SCROLL OF THE LAW. *˙Western Synagogue.*
Bullion on green velvet. Heraldic design, with tablets of
the Law in the centre. Bequeathed by Mr. Leon Solomon
to the Western Synagogue. Exhibited at the Exhibition
of 1851.

1450. BREASTPLATE FOR SCROLL OF THE LAW.
Dr. N. M. Adler, Chief Rabbi.
For small Scroll: filigree silver with flowers, set with
stones. Hebrew inscription.

1451. BREASTPLATE FOR SCROLL OF THE LAW. *Rev. S. M. Gollancz.*
Silver. In the centre the seven-branched candlesticks and
tables of the Ten Commandments and movable feasts,
enclosed by columns and lions supporting a crown; three
bells on the base. XVII. Cent.

1452. BREASTPLATE FOR SCROLL OF THE LAW. *Mrs. Horn.*
Silver. In the centre a receptacle for movable feasts, bold
scroll border, Hebrew inscription, and three bells
suspended. Dated 5462 (1702).

1453. BREASTPLATE FOR SCROLL OF THE LAW. *N. Morris.*
Silver parcel gilt. In centre two lions supporting the
Commandments, a crown above, flanked by wheat sheaves,
surmounted by cornucopiæ, receptacle for movable feasts
beneath, with *appliqué* coral ornaments. Early XVII.
Cent.

1454. BREASTPLATE FOR SCROLL OF THE LAW. *Julius Krailsheimer.*
Silver gilt *repoussé*, with two columns on which are lions
rampant supporting a crown and ewer; below the
movable feasts and Austrian eagle; three bells suspended from the base. XVIII. Cent.

1455. BREASTPLATE FOR SCROLL OF THE LAW. *Lambert & Co.*
Silver. Engraved with the Ten Commandments between
twisted columns, crown above set with stones, and
beneath is a large piece of amber engraved with Hebrew
inscription. XVII. Cent.

1456. BREASTPLATE FOR SCROLL OF THE LAW. *Great Synagogue.*
Silver gilt *repoussé*, with diaper and scroll. A crown set
with stones *appliqué*, and two lions supporting Ten
Commandments. Movable plaques for festivals. Three
pendants on base. Dutch, XVIII. Cent.

1457. BREASTPLATE FOR SCROLL OF THE LAW. *Great Synagogue.*
Silver, scroll borders. Between two columns are slides for
festivals, chain at top and three pendants. XVIII.
Cent.

1458. BREASTPLATE FOR SCROLL OF THE LAW. *Great Synagogue.*
Silver, chased with diaper work and bold scroll borders,
movable slides. Two lions supporting three bells on base.
Temp. Louis XIV.

1459. BREASTPLATE FOR SCROLL OF THE LAW.
New West End Synagogue.
Silver gilt filigree, pierced border. Three bells and chain with pear-shaped ornament. Old Danish workmanship of the XVII. Cent.

1460. POINTER FOR SCROLL OF THE LAW.
Rev. Dr. N. M. Adler, Chief Rabbi.
Silver.

1461. POINTER FOR SCROLL OF THE LAW.   *L. Cohen.*
Silver gilt twisted stem.

1462. POINTER FOR SCROLL OF THE LAW.   *D. A. Cohen.*
Ivory handle, silver hand and gauntlet.

1463. POINTER FOR SCROLL OF THE LAW.   *B. & A. Cohen.*
Coral and ivory stem, silver hand.

1464. POINTER FOR SCROLL OF THE LAW.   *B. & A. Cohen.*
Silver, with bulbs.

465. POINTER FOR SCROLL OF THE LAW.   *B. & A. Cohen.*
Silver, with two gilt bulbs on the stem.

1466. POINTER FOR SCROLL OF THE LAW.   *Mrs Horn.*
Silver.

1467. POINTER FOR SCROLL OF THE LAW.   *George Hanrick.*
Ivory, with six figures. Hebrew inscription.

1468. POINTER FOR SCROLL OF THE LAW.   *Edward Joseph.*
Silver. XVII. Cent.

1469. POINTER FOR SCROLL OF THE LAW.   *J. Krailsheimer.*
Silver, octagonal, with chain. Nuremberg, XVII. Cent.

1470. POINTER FOR SCROLL OF THE LAW.   *Mrs. David Lewis.*
Ivory. Engraved R. I. C. Over 200 years old.

1471. POINTER FOR SCROLL OF THE LAW.   *S. Montagu, M.P.*
Silver. English workmanship. With hook at end.

1472. POINTER FOR SCROLL OF THE LAW.   *Mrs. Neumegen.*
Whalebone and silver, with ivory hand.

1473. POINTER FOR SCROLL OF THE LAW.   *B. J. Salomons.*
Silver chased.

1474. POINTER FOR SCROLL OF THE LAW.   *Bayswater Synagogue.*
Silver gilt, hexagonal stem, rose diamond in hand-chain.

1475. POINTER FOR SCROLL OF THE LAW.   *Bayswater Synagogue.*
Filigree silver, quadrangular handle, gilt hand, and emerald ring dated 5626 (1866).

1476. POINTER FOR SCROLL OF THE LAW. *New Synagogue.*
Silver gilt, spiral ribbon round stem, two diamond rings on
hand. XVII. Cent.

1477. POINTER FOR SCROLL OF THE LAW. *Bayswater Synagogue.*
Silver gilt, jewelled stem and boss, chased, and with two
chains. XVIII. Cent.

1479. POINTER FOR SCROLL OF THE LAW. *Bayswater Synagogue.*
Presented to the Bayswater Synagogue by Morris Van
Praag.

1480. POINTER FOR SCROLL OF THE LAW. *Bayswater Synagogue.*
Presented to the Bayswater Synagogue by Mr. Aguilar.

1481. POINTER FOR SCROLL OF THE LAW. *Bayswater Synagogue.*
Presented to the Bayswater Synagogue by Abraham Levien

1482. POINTER FOR SCROLL OF THE LAW. *Bevis Marks Synagogue.*
Coral. Presented to the Bevis Marks Synagogue by Mr.
Mendez da Costa.

1483. POINTER FOR SCROLL OF THE LAW. *Central Synagogue.*
Silver parcel gilt, set with stones.

1484. POINTER FOR SCROLL OF THE LAW. *Chatham Synagogue.*
Silver.

1485. POINTER FOR SCROLL OF THE LAW. *Chatham Synagogue.*
Ivory.

1486. POINTER FOR SCROLL OF THE LAW. *Great Synagogue.*
Agate handle and silver hand.

1486*a***.** POINTER FOR SCROLL OF THE LAW. *Great Synagogue.*
Silver, twisted stem, Hebrew inscription. XVIII. Cent.

1487. POINTER FOR SCROLL OF THE LAW. *Great Synagogue.*
Silver, plain stem, with three engraved bosses and a diamond
ring on finger. XVII. Cent.

1488. POINTER FOR SCROLL OF THE LAW. *Great Synagogue.*
Silver gilt, square handle, set with rubies and other stones.

1489. POINTER FOR SCROLL OF THE LAW. *Great Synagogue.*
Coral handle and gold mounts.

1490. POINTER FOR SCROLL OF THE LAW. *Great Synagogue.*
Silver gilt, chased triangular stem, jewelled, and diamond
ring on finger, Hebrew inscription, sapphire clasp and
chain set with garnets and agates. XVII. Cent.

1491. POINTER FOR SCROLL OF THE LAW.   *Great Synagogue.*
Silver, chased stem, square handle, set with rubies and
diamonds, finger ring and gilt chain.

1492. POINTER FOR SCROLL OF THE LAW.   *Great Synagogue.*
Silver, with chased belt set with stones, finger ring and
silver chain. XVII. Cent.

1493. POINTER FOR SCROLL OF THE LAW.   *Great Synagogue.*
Silver gilt, hand set with ruby and diamonds. XVII. Cent.

1494. POINTER FOR SCROLL OF THE LAW.   *Great Synagogue.*
Silver, chased stem, square handle set with rubies and
diamonds, finger ring and gilt chain. XVIII. Cent.

1495. BELLS FOR SCROLL OF THE LAW.   *B. A. Cohen.*
Silver, of three tiers and small bells on each, surmounted
by a fir cone.

1496. BELLS FOR SCROLL OF THE LAW.   *Isaac Davis.*
A pair of silver-gilt bells, elaborately ornamented with
repoussé and chased work, circular, of three tiers, enclosed
by six columns and three bands separating them, to which
are affixed trophies of musical instruments and shields,
surmounted by a rosette; bells at base hanging on
chains on a twisted column. XVII. Cent. Formerly in
the possession of a distinguished Hispano-Jewish family.

1497. BELLS FOR SCROLL OF THE LAW.   *Jews' Hospital.*
Silver gilt, of hexagonal shape, and three spheres of open
work filigree, and four rows of small bells, surmounted
by a crown, plain stem, Hebrew inscription " Crown of
the Law," XVII. Cent.

1498. BELLS FOR SCROLL OF THE LAW.   *S. Montagu, M.P.*
Parcel gilt small silver, with one row of gilt bells on scroll,
brackets surmounted by a closed crown. Modern.

1499. BELLS FOR SCROLL OF THE LAW.   *Joseph Pyke.*
Silver gilt, of three tiers of quadrangular temples enclosed
with galleries enclosing bells surmounted by a crown,
supported by brackets on a fluted columnar base. Temp.
Louis XV.

1500. BELLS FOR SCROLL OF THE LAW.   *Bevis Marks Synagogue.*
A pair of silver bells, three rows of small bells, of pierced
open work, showing on the interior a pineapple surmounted by a crown. Hall Mark of 1802.

1501. BELLS FOR SCROLL OF THE LAW.   *Bevis Marks Synagogue.*
Silver gilt, hollow, hexagonal, of two tiers of arcades of
twisted columns set with coloured stones, and three rows
of bells, surmounted by a crown on a twisted column.
Temp. Louis XIV.

1502. BELLS FOR SCROLL OF THE LAW.   *Bevis Marks Synagogue.*
Silver, hexagonal, with four arcades enclosed by galleries
containing as many bells, surmounted by a crown, the
base *repoussé* with scrolls.   XVII. Cent.

1503. BELLS FOR SCROLL OF THE LAW.   *Bevis Marks Synagogue.*
Silver, formed of two hollow spheres, hexagonal, with pro-
jecting brackets and bells, surmounted by a closed crown.
Early XVII. Cent.

1504. BELLS FOR SCROLL OF THE LAW.   *Central Synagogue.*
Silver, in three tiers of hexagonal form, pierced filigree,
gilt bells suspended from every angle, surmounted by a
coronet.   XVII. Cent.

1505. BELLS FOR SCROLL OF THE LAW.   *Central Synagogue.*
Silver, of four canopies, ribbed and nurled edges, to which
are suspended numerous gilt bells, surmounted by a pine-
apple.   English work, XVIII. Cent.   Adam's pattern.

1506. BELLS FOR SCROLL OF THE LAW.   *Central Synagogue.*
Silver, of four tiers of pierced scrolls, hexagonal, with
brackets supporting numerous bells, surmounted by a
crown.   Hall Mark of 1764.

1507. BELLS FOR SCROLL OF THE LAW.   *Central Synagogue.*
Silver, of two tiers, supported by eight columns, scroll
canopy top and three rows of bells ; on the upper tier are
two hands in benediction.   XVIII. Cent.

1508. BELLS FOR SCROLL OF THE LAW.   *Great Synagogue.*
Silver; formed of three hollow balls, the two lower ones
pierced and chased with eight brackets on each, supporting bells, surmounted by a crown.   Presented to the
Great Synagogue by Lord Rothschild, 5633.   XVIII. Cent.

1509. BELLS FOR SCROLL OF THE LAW.   *Great Synagogue.*
Silver; formed of four hexagonal galleries surrounding
arcades from which hang numerous bells, surmounted by
a crown, chased, the base *repoussé* with floriated scrolls.
XVIII. Cent., and Hebrew inscription at bottom.   Presented to the Great Synagogue by H. H. Cohen.

1510. BELLS FOR SCROLL OF THE LAW.   *Great Synagogue.*
Silver; formed of two hollow compartments, hexagonal,
with solid gilt bells hanging from the angle, surmounted
by a crown.   Early XVII. Cent.

1511. BELLS FOR SCROLL OF THE LAW.   *Great Synagogue.*
Silver, small ; of two rows of brackets holding bells, pierced
and chased with vases and festoons, surmounted by a
crown.   Adam's period.

1512. BELLS FOR SCROLL OF THE LAW.   *New Synagogue.*
Silver gilt.

1513. BELLS FOR SCROLL OF THE LAW. *New Synagogue.*
Silver; of four tiers, the two lower ones pierced, the upper two chased, and four rows of gilt bells, surmounted by a crown. Hall Mark of 1803.

1514. BELLS FOR SCROLL OF THE LAW. *New Synagogue.*
Silver gilt; formed of four hollow compartments of delicate filigree work, and as many rows of bells. French hall mark. Hebrew inscription "Crown of the Law." XVII. Cent.

1515. CROWN FOR SCROLL OF THE LAW. *Dr. N. M. Adler, Chief Rabbi.*
Silver; ornamented with filigree and set with stones and six bells. XVII. Cent.

1516. CROWN FOR SCROLL OF THE LAW. *Bayswater Synagogue.*
Oviform, *repoussé* with floriated scrolls, and set with stones, surmounted by the tables of the Decalogue; round the base a Hebrew inscription. XVIII. Cent.

1517. CROWN FOR SCROLL OF THE LAW. *H. Guedalla.*
Silver parcel gilt, of *appliqué* chased flowers and scroll belt, five bells suspended from the inside. XVII. Cent.

e.—SYNAGOGUE DECORATION.

[As is well known, the interior decoration of synagogues is very simple. There is always however included the **Tablets of the Law** with the initial words of the Ten Commandments, generally placed above the Ark. In English Synagogues the **Prayer for the Royal Family** is generally placed so that it can be read by the congregation. The **Reading Desk** on which the Scroll of the Law is placed is covered with a decorated cover.]

1521. TABLETS OF THE LAW. *Bevis Marks Synagogue.*
Painting, in Hebrew and Spanish, supported by figures of Lawgiver and High Priest.

1522. TEN COMMANDMENTS. *Bevis Marks Synagogue.*
Crimson and gold.

1523. FRAMED WRITTEN COPY OF HEBREW PRAYER FOR THE ROYAL FAMILY. *Bernard Van Raalte.*

1524. FRAMED WRITTEN COPY OF THE HEBREW VERSION OF "GOD SAVE THE QUEEN." *Bernard Van Raalte.*

1525. COVER FOR READING DESK. *Rev. S. M. Gollancz.*

1526. COVERING FOR READING DESK. *Bevis Marks Synagogue.*
Green and gold.

1527. COVER FOR READING DESK. *Central Synagogue.*
Embroidered by R. Abrahams & Sons. Presented to Central Synagogue by Mr. A. Wertheimer.

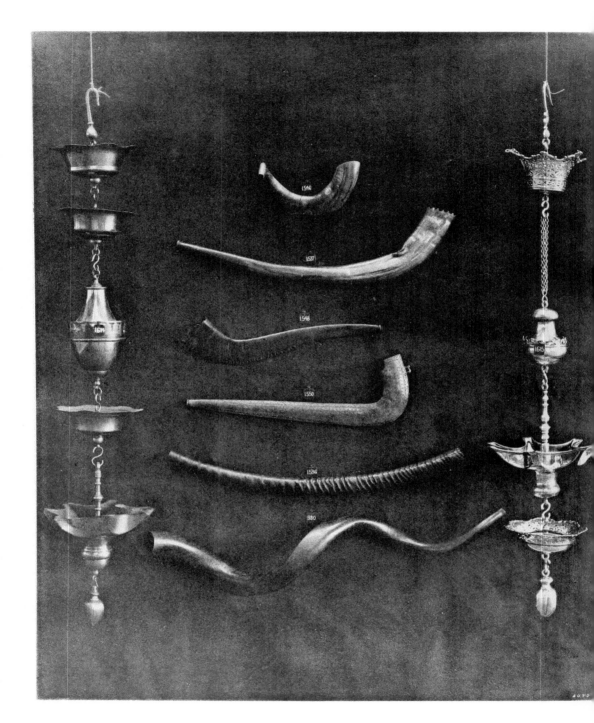

1528.	COVER FOR DESK.	*Dalston Synagogue.*
1529.	COVER FOR READING DESK.	*Hambro' Synagogue*

f.—SYNAGOGUE MUSIC—SHOPHAROTH.

[Music has always been the Jewish art *par excellence*, though the earliest forms seem to have the peculiar intervals so distressing to Western ears. Very little of contemporary Jewish music can be traced very far back, Arabic, French and German folk songs being discernible in the music of the Synagogue. The peculiar cantillation with which the Law is read has better claims to antiquity. And at least the **Shophar,** or ram's-horn trumpet, used on the New Year and the Fast of Atonement, is the same instrument as that referred to by the same name in the Bible.]

1535. SHOPHAR. *Rev. B. Berliner.*
Ram's-horn used in Synagogue on New Year. Quaint and old.

1536. SHOPHAR. *A. L. Cohen.*

1537. SHOPHAR. *Rev. F. L. Cohen.*

1538. SHOPHAR. *Rev. F. L. Cohen.*
Large.

1539. SHOPHAR. *L. Cohen.*

1540. SHOPHAR. *Rev. Ellis A. Davidson.*
Very old.

1541. SHOPHAR. *Rev. S. M. Gollancz.*

1542. SHOPHAR. *F. Haes.*
Straight and dark from age. Formerly belonging to Lyon Samuel, Esq., grandfather of Exhibitor, and used in Great Synagogue about 100 years ago.

1543. SHOPHAR. *E. Joseph.*
Ram's-horn trumpet used in New Year's service.

1544. SHOPHAR. *Mrs. Neumegen.*

1545. SHOPHAR. *L. Schaap.*

1546. TWO SHOPHAROTH. *J. S. Sassoon.*
From Bagdad. XVIII. Cent.

1547. SHOPHAR. *Great Synagogue.*
Belonged to the late Chief Rabbi.

1548. SHOPHAR. *Great Synagogue.*
Black from age.

1549. SHOPHAR. *Great Synagogue.*

1550. SHOPHAR. *Great Synagogue.*

1551. SHOPHAR. *Chatham Synagogue.*

1552. "Synagogale Melodien für Pianoforte." *Rev. Dr. M. Berlin.*
By A. Marksohn and W. Wolf.

1553. Pamphlets on Music.   *W. A. Berlyn.*
Eight. Dutch.

1554. Synagogue Music.   *N. I. Berlin.*
The Ancient Melodies of the Liturgy of the Spanish and
Portuguese Jews. By Emanuel Aguilar, with Preface by
Rev. Dr. A. Sola. 1857.

1555. Hebrew Melodies, Ancient and Modern. *H. E. N. Carvalho.*
Words by Byron, music by J. Braham and I. Nathan.

1556. Baal Tefillah, oder der Praktische Vorbeter.
     Rev. F. L. Cohen.
By A. Baer, Gothenburg, 1883.

1557. "The Tonic Accents of the Hebrew Pentateuch."
     Rev. F. L. Cohen.
Arranged by David Lewis, Liverpool [1884].

1558. Musical MS.   *D. M. Davis.*
"Yigdal," for four voices, by J. L. Mombach.

1559. Musical MS.   *D. M. Davis.*
Ancient Hebrew Melodies, by D. M. Davis.

1560. Musical MS.   *D. M. Davis.*
Chazanuth, modern Hebrew Melodies, by D. M. Davis.

1561. "God Save the Queen," in Hebrew.   *D. M. Davis.*
"El Shemor Hamolko," by D. M. Davis.

1562. Psalm xv. for Montefiore Centenary.   *D. M. Davis.*
By D. M. Davis.

1563. "El Norah Alilah."   *D. M. Davis.*
Portuguese ritual, by D. M. Davis.

1564. Shire Zion, "Songs of Zion."   *D. M. Davis.*
By G. Sulzer.

1565. "The Divine Service."   *D. M. Davis.*
By Rev. M. Hast.

1566. "Chants Hebraiques."   *A. Durlacher.*
By E. Jonas. Paris, 1887.

1567. Sixty-first Psalm.   *A. M. Friedländer.*
Set to music by A. M. Friedländer for Jubilee celebration.

1568. "Baal Tephillah."   *H. Guedalla.*
By A. Baer, 1883.

1569. Synagogue Music.   *H. Guedalla.*
By H. Weintraub

1570. SYNAGOGUE MUSIC.   *H. Guedalla.*
Liebling and Jacobson.

1571. "KOL RINA U' TEPHILLA."   *H. Guedalla.*
By Lewandowski, Berlin.

1572. "CHANTS RELIGIEUSES DES ISRAÉLITES."   *Rev. M. Hast.*
With introductory essay on Synagogue music by S. Naum-
burg, Paris, 1874.

1573. COMPOSITIONS.   *Rev. M. Hast.*
For (1) Weddings, (2) Hanuca Service, (3) Sabbath Service,
(4) Occasional.

1574. TRANSCRIPTIONS OF ANCIENT HEBREW MUSIC.   *Rev. M. Hast.*

1575. HEBREW MELODIES.   *Rev. M. Joseph.*
By A. Saqui.

1576. SWEET SONGS OF ISRAEL.   *Rev. M. Keizer.*
Mombach's musical compositions.

1578. HEBREW LOVE SONG.   *C. K. Salaman.*
Hebrew text by Jehuda Halevi; music by Charles Salaman.

1580. SYNAGOGUE MUSIC.   *Miss de Sola.*
Compositions by the Revs. D. A. de Sola and S. de Sola.
London.

1581. SYNAGOGUE MUSIC.   *Dr. C. G. Verinder.*
Four volumes as used in the Services of the West London
Synagogue. Composed and adapted by Charles Salaman.
Edited by C. G. Verinder.

1582. SYNAGOGUE MUSIC.   *H. Wasserzug.*
Shire Mikdash (Songs of the Temple). By the late H.
Wasserzug.

HOME.

g.—MEZUZAH AND MIZRACH.

[In fulfilment of the command "Thou shalt write them on the door posts of
thy house" (Deut. vi. 60), there is affixed to the right post of each
inhabited room a case containing parchment on which is written Deut.
vi. 4 *seq.*; it must be placed slanting, and the word שדי Almighty, must
be seen written on the roll of parchment. This is the **Mezuza.** A
Mizrach is a piece of ornamental writing containing some portion of
Scripture written in shape of some architectural figure, and placed on
the east wall, whence the name.]

1589. MEZUZAH.   *M. Marians.*
From China. With the verses written on an ear of wheat.

1590. MEZUZAH.   *G. Williamson.*

1591. MEZUZAH.   *George Hanreck.*
Doorpost ornament; gold case; shape of a dial. The
Holy Name is seen through a microscopic glass.

1592. MEZUZAH. *G. de R. Moro.*

1593. MEZUZAH. *J. Nahon.*
In silver case.

1593a. THREE OLD MEZZUGOTH. *N. I. Berlin.*

1594. MIZRACH *Solomon Hart.*
Parchment. Date 5157.

1595. MIZRACH. *P. Hyman.*
Parchment containing Ps. lxvii.

1596. MIZRACH. *Rev. M. Joseph.*
Figures formed in minute Hebrew lettering from the Bible.
Awarded a prize at the Louisiana State Exhibition, 1879.

1597. MIZRACH. *D. A. Levy.*
Composed of Pss. xxx. and civ., written in minute characters
in the form of a basket of flowers.

1598. MIZRACH. *G. L. Lyon.*
Chromo-lithograph, designed by D. Lara; published by
Moon. Dedicated to Hananel de Castro, Esq.

1599. MIZRACH. *W. H. Cohen.*
Written by T. Stibbe, of Amsterdam, containing Pentateuch
tablets, Prayer for British Royal Family, Benediction of
Priests, and a "Sephiroth" table.

1600. MIZRACH. *Lewis Levy.*
Written in 1738 by Aaron Hisq[uiahu] Mendoza.

1601. MIZRACH. *M. Moss.*
Inlaid wood.

1602. MIZRACH. *J. Nahon.*
Written.

1603. MIZRACH. *I. Solomons.*
Parchment.

h.—SABBATH REQUISITES.

[The Sabbath is welcomed "as a bride," by the devout Jew. According to
the Jewish proverb, " where there's light there's joy," the Sabbath Eve
is ushered in by the lighting of the **Lamp**, the form of which is not fixed,
but is usually of seven burners. A cup of wine, the **Kiddush Cup**, or
cup of sanctification, is tasted. The bread at the evening meal is of
special form (**Halla**), and before use is covered with the **Halla Cloth**.
The close of the Sabbath has also its own ceremonial, in which the
Kiddush Cup is again used, and the senses are gratified by the sweet
savour of the **Spice-box**, doubtless a reminiscence of the East.]

1609. SABBATH LAMP. *Rev. Brooke Lambert.*
Brass; six burners, three bulbs on stem, coronet above.
XVIII. Cent.

1610. SABBATH LAMP. *J. N. Castello.*
Silver; with seven burners, surmounted by coronet and
pendants. Dutch. XVIII. Cent.

1611. SABBATH LAMP. *Abraham Cohen.*
Brass.

1613. SABBATH LAMP. *Edmund James.*
Brass. Five pieces.

1614. SABBATH LAMP. *Edmund James.*
Brass. Six pieces.

1615. SABBATH LAMP. *S. Montagu, M.P.*
Silver; seven burners, coronet, pressed borders. Dutch.
XVIII. Cent. Formerly property of the late Louis Cohen.

1616. PAIR OF SABBATH CANDLESTICKS. *J. S. Sassoon.*
Silver; with lion rampant stem, *repoussé*, with medallions
of Biblical illustrations. German. XVII. Cent.

1617. KIDDUSH CUP. *Rev. B. H. Ascher.*
Silver; with Hebrew inscription. Early XVI. Cent. Presented by Rev. Solomon Herschell to members of his
family.

1618. KIDDUSH CUP. *D. Benjamin.*
Made of Australian gold, 1852, and presented to Mr. D.
Benjamin by the members of the Melbourne congregation
on his leaving that city.

1619. KIDDUSH CUP. *E. L. Franklin.*
Silver gilt; octagonal. Augsburg, *circa* 1700.

1620. KIDDUSH CUP. *M. Jacobs.*
Silver; with Hebrew inscription.

1621. KIDDUSH CUP. *Edmund James.*
Silver gilt; engraved designs and Hebrew inscription.
German. XVIII. Cent.

1622. KIDDUSH CUP. *Mrs. Henry Joseph.*
Old wine glass with Hebrew inscription in gold letters.
One of a quantity used ordinarily by exhibitor's grand-
father.

1623. CUP OF SANCTIFICATION. *Mrs. David Lewis.*
In case, for use while travelling. Silver-gilt tumbler,
repoussé with flowers. Nuremberg. XVII. Cent.

1624. KIDDUSH CUP.   *Mrs. David Lewis.*
Cup of Sanctification. Used in Habdala ceremony. Silver
filigree. Made by a Jewish artizan in Dover, 1853.

1625. KIDDUSH CUP.   *Mrs. David Lewis.*
Small Jug, in imitation of the ewer used by the Levites in
the Temple. Made from the egg of an Emu, mounted in
silver, chased terminal figure handle.

1626. ANTIQUE SILVER MUG.   *M. Linzburg.*
Hebrew inscription.

1627. KIDDUSH CUP.   *Messrs. M. & S. Lyon.*
Silver; engraved with Moses and Aaron, and Hebrew
inscription. Hall Mark 1785.

1628. KIDDUSH CUP.   *A. H. Moses.*
Silver; engraved with a portrait, and Hebrew inscription;
chased stem and foot. Hall Mark 1842.

1629. KIDDUSH CUPS.   *B. Meyers.*
Silver. Set of seven, one with a cover, with inscriptions.
Nuremberg. 1709.

1630. KIDDUSH CUP.   *L. de Rothschild.*
Silver; hexagonal, engraved with Moses, Aaron, and other
figures; Hebrew inscription above. German. XVII.
Cent.

1631. KIDDUSH CUP.   *E. Samson.*
Glass Goblet with Hebrew engraving, presented 100 years
ago to Mr. E. Samson (grandfather of exhibitor) by the
" Hand and Heart " Society.

1632. KIDDUSH CUP.   *S. M. Samuel.*
Silver; chased scrolls. XVII. Cent.

1633. KIDDUSH CUP.   *L. Levin.*
Silver *repoussé*, with Moses and Aaron and the Ten Commandments. Hall Mark 1861.

1634. KIDDUSH CUP.   *H. L. Cohen.*
Silver; chased with flowers and scrolls, and Hebrew inscription. Hall Mark 1767.

1635. KIDDUSH CUP.   *H. Barned.*
Cup of Sanctification. Silver gilt. Hebrew inscription.

1636. KIDDUSH CUP.   *L. Lewis.*
Silver; octagonal fluted base, with Hebrew inscription.
German. XVIII. Cent.

1637. KIDDUSH CUP.   *Bevis Marks Synagogue.*
Silver, chased on a tripod bracket. XVII. Cent.

1638. KIDDUSH CUPS. *Henry Kisch.*
Two with Hebrew inscription. Silver. Hall Mark 1792.

1639. KIDDUSH CUP. *S. J. Phillips.*
Octagonal, with floral ornaments. German XVII. Cent.

1640. KIDDUSH CUP. *D. Benjamin.*
Silver; two-handled, *repoussé* with scroll and flowers.
Dated 1852. Presented to present owner.

1641. KIDDUSH CUP. *Mrs. David Lewis.*
Silver filigree, with gilt liner.

1642. KIDDUSH CUP. *G. Yates.*
Silver gilt; pine apple shape. German. XVII. Cent.

1642a. KIDDUSH CUP. *H. Goldberg.*
Silver. Inscribed with Hebrew verses by Rabbi Aaron Levy.

1643. HALLA CLOTH. *A. Abraham & Sons.*
For use on Sabbath evenings, to celebrate the hundredth
birthday of Sir Moses Montefiore.

1644. HALLA CLOTH. *W. H. Cohen.*
For sanctification of Sabbath, with the benediction printed
thereon.

1645. BREAD CLOTH. *E. A. Franklin.*
For use on Sabbaths and festivals; embroidered. Modern.

1646. HALLA CLOTH. *Mrs. Franklin.*
Used for covering bread at home services on Sabbaths and
festivals.

1647. BREAD CLOTH. *Mrs. David Lewis.*
Used on Sabbaths and festivals to cover the consecrated
bread.

1648. SILK TABLE COVER. *S. Levy.*
Embroidered, with Hebrew inscription.

1649. SPICE BOX. *M. N. Adler, M.A.*
Silver filigree; cylindrical. XIII. Cent.

1650. SPICE BOX. *M. N. Adler, M.A.*
Silver; square, with sliding covers resting on four lions.
XVII. Cent.

1651. SPICE BOX. *H. Barned.*
Silver gilt. Hebrew inscription.

1652. SPICE BOX. *B. L. Benas, J.P.*
Silver filigree. XVII. Cent. Cylindrical, of three stages, and
flags said to have been used by R. Benjamin David, of
Triesti, ancestor of Mr. Benas.

1653. SPICE BOX.   *B. L. Benas, J.P.*
Silver filigree; square, with primals and flag; said to have been used by Saul Wahl.

1654. SPICE BOX.   *Dr. A. Cohen.*
Silver filigree; quadrangular, two tiers and flags at the angles. Made by Jewish workmen. Modern.

1655. SPICE BOX.   *B. and A. Cohen.*
Silver filigree; quadrangular; gilt birds and bells at the angles.

1656. SPICE BOX.   *L. L. Cohen, M.P.*
Silver gilt, of two tiers and canopy surmounted by the Sun, pierced and chased, with terminal figures, boy holding a flower on the stem. German. XVII. Cent.

1657. AN ANCIENT PERFUME BOX.   *Mrs. L. L. Cohen.*

1658. SPICE BOX.   *Philip Falk.*
Silver; cylindrical, in the shape of a tower, with flag at pinnacle, and filigree openings. German. XVII. Cent.

1659. SPICE BOX.   *A. Goldman.*
Silver filigree; locomotive, with six wheels. Made in Poland by Jewish workmen.

1660. SPICE BOX.   *Mrs. Horn.*
Silver; hexagonal, pierced and engraved, flags at angles. XVII. Cent.

1661. SPICE BOX.   *A. M. Jacobs.*
Silver; oval.

1662. SPICE BOX.   *Mark Jacobs.*
Silver. English Hall Mark 1749.

1663. SPICE BOX.   *E. James.*
Silver; of three tiers, quadrangular, of filigree, and four flags at the angles, the upper one engraved with the Decalogue, ball and flag at top, and bell enclosed. German. XVII. Cent.

1664. SPICE BOX.   *E. James.*
Silver gilt; quadrangular, of pierced designs, *appliqué* masks and figures at the angles, and cut crystal pendants; projecting brackets on the stem, and set with cut crystals. German. XVI. Cent.

1665. SPICE BOX.   *E. Joseph.*
For Habdala (conclusion of Sabbath). Silver; surmounted by four statuettes of warriors; bracket, stem, and pinnacle with a warrior. German. *Circa* 1620.

1666. SPICE BOX.   *Isaac A. Joseph.*
Silver filigree; design, a turret surmounted by a flag.

1667. SPICE BOX. *Lambert & Co.*
Silver; square, with compartments, sliding cover. German.
XVIII. Cent.

1668. SPICE BOX. *Mrs. Arabella Levi.*
For Habdala service. Curious old silver, artistically chased.

1669. SPICE BOX. *Mrs. David Lewis.*
Silver filigree; of two tiers, square, with flags at the angles.

1670. SPICE BOX. *S. Montagu, M.P.*
Silver filigree; octagonal, of three tiers, with circlets of
bells, flags and eagles, surmounted by a bird and flag.
Modern.

1671. SPICE BOX. *J. Nahon.*
Silver filigree; pyramidical.

1672. SPICE BOX. *Mrs. Neumegen.*
Silver filigree; of three tiers.

1673. SPICE BOX. *Mrs. A. Newman.*
Silver; quadrangular, with two bells. Hebrew inscription
on three sides. German. XVII. Cent.

1674. SPICE BOX. *Rev. S. J. Roco.*
Silver filigree; with semi-circular cover.

1675. SPICE BOX. *L. de Rothschild.*
Silver; hexagonal, three tiers of filigree work, small
rosettes *appliqué*. German. XVII. Cent.

1676. SPICE BOX. *L. de Rothschild.*
Silver filigree; three tiers at top. XVII. Cent.

1677. SPICE BOX. *S. Schloss.*
With candle-holder. Spice box held by man on stem.
German. XVII. Cent.

1678. SPICE BOX. *Mrs. S. Singer.*
Silver. Design, grapes and pomegranates; cover and two
handles, *repoussé* flowers. German. XVII. Cent.

1679. SPICE BOX. *Miss S. Singer.*
From Jerusalem. Globular, or serpent stem, pierced and
chased. XVII. Cent.

1680. SPICE BOX. *H. Solomon.*
Silver; oval, with divisions, *repoussé* with agricultural
figures. XVIII. Cent.

1681. SPICE BOX AND TAPER. *Mrs. R. Strauss.*
Combined in one. Silver. Spice in drawer. German.
XVIII. Cent.

1682. Spice Box.   *Bevis Marks Synagogue.*
And wine cup in box. Silver, of two tiers, pierced and engraved scrolls. XVII. Cent.

1683. Spice Box.   *Ramsgate Synagogue.*
Silver; chased with flowers. Hall Mark 1711.

i.—FESTIVAL REQUISITES.

[The chief Jewish festivals that are celebrated in the home, and thus require special requisites are Passover, Tabernacles, Hanuca (Feast of Dedication of the Temple), and Purim, or the Feast of Esther. The chief service of the Passover is that of the Passover Eve (**Seder**), when the story of the Exodus is told to the children, with appropriate symbols. Four glasses of wine are emptied, bitter herbs are eaten, and the bread is unleavened (מצה). In the centre of the table is placed a cup for the use of the Prophet Elijah if he should come to announce the coming of the Messiah. The Feast of Tabernacles is celebrated by residence in a booth (סכה Succa), which is built with only leaves and boughs for a roof. There is used besides the **Ethrog**, or citron, and the **Lulab**, or palm-branch, round which is twined myrtle and willow, which have all their symbolic teaching. The Feast of Dedication of the Temple, when the **Lamp** was miraculously kept alight for eight days, has for an appropriate symbol a eight-branched candelabrum, to which is attached a master lamp (termed "the beadle"), making nine in all; as many lamps are each evening lighted as the days of the feast that have come. Lastly, the feast that celebrates the salvation of the Jews by Esther is appropriately celebrated by reading the record of her deeds in the **Megilla,** or scroll of Esther.]

1684. Matzoth.
Cakes of Unleavened Bread.

1685. Passover Dish.   *Dr. H. Adler, Delegate Chief Rabbi.*
Used in Passover Night service; with Hebrew inscription.

1686. Passover Dish.   *The Misses Aguilar.*
China Plates, &c., used for Passover. Inscription פסח Passover.

1687. Passover Dish.   *W. H. Cohen.*
Platter for holding bitter herbs at Passover Night service. Silver gilt. Dutch.

1688. Passover Dish.   *Rev. J. T. Fowler, M.A., F.S.A.*
Pewter. Inscribed and engraved in a suitable manner. In the margin figures of animals, referred to in the חד גדיא Date C.E. 1773. A full description appears in *Notes and Queries,* 5th Ser., I., 426 and 493.

1689. Passover Dish.   *E. A. Franklin.*
Metal. Modern. Constructed by David Cohen from the design of the owner.

1690. Passover Dish.   *Rev. M. Hast.*
For holding requisites for the Seder service. Three tiers. Metal.

1691. SEDER SERVICE. *Mrs. Horn.*
For Passover Night.

1692. PASSOVER DISH. *Madame Hartog.*
Hebrew inscription, engraved by donor, who presented it as a wedding gift to exhibitor's grandmother 120 years ago.

1693. PASSOVER DISH. *E. Joseph.*
Silver plate, with reliefs and inscription showing that it was used in the Passover Service.

1694. PASSOVER DISHES. *E. Joseph.*
Three. China, with Hebrew inscriptions and illustrations of Biblical subjects [? Majolica].

1695. PASSOVER DISH. *Mrs. S. Joseph.*
Silver tray, with two receptacles with glass dishes pierced and chased.

1696. PASSOVER DISH. *Mrs. David Lewis.*
For Seder Service. China. Emblematical paintings. Paris, 1850.

1697. PASSOVER DISH. *F. D. Mocatta.*
Hebrew inscription. *Faience* work.

1698. SEDER COVER. *N. Rheinberg.*
Two hundred years old. German.

1699. PASSOVER DISH. *Mrs. N. Strauss.*
Silver.

1700. SEDER DISH. *P. Vallentine.*
For Passover Night.

1701. PASSOVER SERVICE. *S. Wohle.*
Salver, cups and bottles. Moabite stone, used at Passover.

1702. PASSOVER CUPS. *S. J. Philips.*
Cup used on Passover night. Silver. Augsburg work. The cup is called "the cup of Elijah the Prophet," and is left filled with wine in the centre of the table.

1703. PASSOVER CUPS. *L. de Rothschild.*
Six.

1704. PASSOVER CUP. *E. Samson.*
Large plain goblet (1 foot high), 150 years old. Engraved with representation of Seder service, and inscription in Hebrew. Originally belonged to great-grandfather of exhibitor, the Rev. Moses Myers, of the New Synagogue.

1705. PASSOVER BOWL. *S. Wohle.*
Jerusalem black Moabite stone, used at Passover. This stone is black during the day, grey at night, and changes to blue with red spots during summer.

1706. PASSOVER CUP.   *Ramsgate Synagogue.*
Porcelain, with medallion representations of Jewish cere-
monials, and Hebrew inscription, made at Herend, 1864.

1707. SCROLL.   *J. M. Sarphati.*
For counting days between Passover and Pentecost.

1708. SCROLL.   *Miss Solomon.*
For counting the Omer (days between Passover and Pente-
cost). Vellum, illuminated, in old oak case.

1709. SCROLL.   *H. Solomon.*
For counting Omer.

1709a. TABERNACLE.   *L. Bernays.*
As used every autumn with roof of leaves and boughs. All
meals are taken therein for the eight days of the festival.

1710. MODEL OF A JEWISH TABERNACLE.   *S. Woolf.*

1711. LULAB.

1712. ETHROG BOX (CITRON CASE).   *Philip Falk.*
Silver; tower-shaped; *repoussé* with scrolls. Dutch. XVII.
Cent.

1712a. ETHROG BOX.   *G. di R. Moro.*

1713. ETHROG BOX.   *H. Guedalla.*
Silver gilt. Presented by Sir M. Montefiore.

1714. ETHROG BOX.   *Mrs. R. Strauss.*
Silver, embossed with scrolls. Dutch. XVII. Cent.

1715. HANUCA LAMP.   *Mrs. I. S. Abecasis.*
Silver Hanuca lamp, the back plate *repoussé* with bold
scrolls, and master wick; in front eight burners and
tray, and hanging receptacle for oil at bottom. XVIII.
Cent.

1716. HANUCA LAMP.   *Mrs. Artom.*
Silver; the back *repoussé* with cherubs under a canopy, and
Hebrew inscription of 30th Psalm of David, with usual
lamps and master wick. Hall Mark of 1711.

1717. HANUCA LAMP.   *Rev. B. W. Ascher.*
Brass; the back engraved and pierced with nondescript
animals and usual lamp in front. XVII. Cent. Marked
"David Lopez Pereira."

1718. HANUCA LAMP.   *Beth Hamidrash.*
Brass, with eight branches, the pillars surmounted by a
crowned eagle. XVIII. Cent.

1719. HANUCA LAMP.   *B. L. Benas, J.P.*
Filigree silver. Dated 1804. Hebrew blessing engraved at
back. [Presented to Mr. P. Philips by his brother-in-law
Mr. M. Samuel.]

1720. HANUCA LAMP. *Miss Benrimo.*
Silver; the back *repoussé* with the prophet Elijah, and the widow's cruise of oil; cherubs and flowers surmounted by pomegranates, scroll border with the usual burners. London Hall Mark 1712.

1721. HANUCA LAMP. *J. de Castro.*
Silver, with eight burners and master light, plate semi-circular, top *repoussé* with flowers, surmounted by a crown. Hall Mark of Amsterdam, *circa* 1680.

1722. HANUCA LAMP. *B. & A. Cohen.*
Silver filigree, with gilt receptacle for the Decalogue, surmounted by two birds and pine-apple, and eight gilt burners with master burner and can.

1723. HANUCA LAMP. *E. H. d'Avigdor.*
Ancient pattern.

1724. HANUCA LAMP. *Frederick Davis.*
French. Bronze, pierced and chased with cherubs, &c., usual lamps. XVII. Cent.

1725. HANUCA LAMP. *Frederick Davis.*
Bronze; on the back two cherubs, masks and vases, with eight lamps. XVII. Cent. Probably Venetian.

1726. HANUCA LAMP. *Frederick Davis.*
Bronze; the back chased with the seven-branch candlestick and usual burners. XVII. Cent. Probably Venetian.

1727. HANUCA LAMP. *S. Frankenstein.*
Silver filigree, of fine designs, two gilt columns and crown *appliqué*, eight lamps in front in form of lions, with master wick, chain and implements. *Circa* 1700.

1728. HANUCA LAMP. *Ellis A. Franklin.*
Brass; with branches for eight candles and master candle, on a tripod. Modern.

1729. HANUCA LAMP. *E. A. Franklin.*
Silver; elaborately ornamented back of lions, dragons and birds, fruit and flowers, and filigree portals set with pink amethysts and other stones; in front eight lamps in form of pomegranates, and a Latin proverb. Attributed to the XVI. Cent.

1730. HANUCA LAMP. *Major A. Goldsmid.*
Carved olive wood with branches, and candles made by the Jewish boys at the Rothschild Technical School at Jerusalem.

1731. HANUCA LAMP.   *H. Guedalla.*
Silver; the back *repoussé*, with a canopy, enclosing a crown, flowers and scrolls, a master lamp surmounted by a crown, and a projecting coronet supporting eight burners. Dutch. Date *circa* 1700, since when in possession of exhibitor's family.

1732. HANUCA LAMP.   *Rev. R. Harris.*
Silver; plain back engraved in festoons, and eight burners in front. xviii. Cent.

1733. HANUCA LAMP.   *Madame Hartog.*
Brass; perforated back. xviii. Cent.

1734. HANUCA LAMP.   *Rev. M. Hast.*
Electro-plate, branches and pillar.

1735. HANUCA LAMP.   *N. S. Joseph.*
Silver; the back *repoussé*, with Judith and Holofernes, surmounted by a warrior; in front two columns supporting lions, and eight projecting burners and tray. Nuremberg Hall Mark. xvii. Cent.

1736. HANUCA LAMP.   *Mrs. David Lewis.*
Silver; the back in form of three Gothic temples; engraved designs, surmounted by a cock and eight lamps projecting, supported on two columns, a cock between. Wurtzburg. Modern.

1737. HANUCA LAMP.   *Arthur Lindo.*
Silver; the back *repoussé*, with Elijah fed by ravens; scroll border and master lamp, eight burners in front. Hall Mark 1709.

1738. HANUCA LAMP.   *F. D. Mocatta.*
Brass; perforated back, with Hebrew inscription. Italian. xvii. Cent.

1739. HANUCA LAMP.   *G. di R. Moro.*
Brass.

1740. HANUCA LAMP.   *S. A. Samson.*
Silver; plain back, engraved with Samson and the lion, eight lamps and the master lamp in front. London Hall Mark 1786.

1741. HANUCA LAMP.   *S. M. Samuel.*
Silver; back *repoussé*, with case of flowers, &c. Dutch. xvii. Cent.

1742. HANUCA LAMP.   *S. Schloss.*
Silver; semicircular back plate *repoussé*, with the seven-branched candlestick, and crown supported by two lions, eight burners in front resting on four lions, master wick at the side. German. xvii. Cent.

1743. HANUCA LAMP. *H. Solomon.*
Silver; back plate *repoussé*, with Judith and Holofernes, the seven-branched candlestick and Moses and Aaron, a crown below and semicircular front with eight burners and tray. Dutch. XVII. Cent.

1744. HANUCA LAMP. *Henry Solomon.*
Silver filigree on the back, a crown and two pillars, a chain and implements; on a stage in front eight burners in form of lions. XVII. Cent.

1745. HANUCA LAMP. *Miss Solomon.*
Brass. Dutch work.

1746. HANUCA LAMP. *I. Spielman.*
Pricket candlestick with pillar and eight branches. Dutch. XVIII. Cent.

1747. HANUCA LAMP. *Mrs. Strauss.*
Silver *repoussé* on the back, with the seven-branched candlestick and crown supported by lions, and master wick on the side; in front eight burners resting on four claws. German. *Circa* 1700.

1748. HANUCA LAMP. *Mrs. Strauss.*
Silver, in form of a tent, open in front, with eight projecting burners and master wick, *repoussé* all over with cherubs and drapery; inside is a representation of the seven-branched candlestick. XVII. Cent.

1749. HANUCA LAMP. *Hambro' Synagogue.*
Brass; six feet high; master nozzle on twisted stem.

1750. HANUCA LAMP. *Great Synagogue.*
Branches of brass on wood pedestal; height, 5 feet.

1751. HANUCA LAMP. *Dalston Synagogue.*
Brass.

1752. HANUCA LAMP. *Bevis Marks Synagogue.*
Silver; with pillar and eight branches for lamps, green enamelled trees at back, and eight bells suspended, surmounted by a crown and pine, set with coloured stones. German. XVII. Cent.

1753. HANUCA LAMP. *Bevis Marks Synagogue.*
Silver; back bordered with scrolls, inscribed, with presentation and date, and usual lamps. Hall Mark 1750.

1754. HANUCA LAMP. *W. Holman Hunt.*

1755. PURIM DISH. *Rev. J. T. Fowler.*
Pewter; has a representation of Mordecai riding on horseback, Shushan the palace, &c. and inscriptions.

1756. PURIM PLATE.   *Emanuel Emanuel, J.P.*
An antique Persian shekel plate, for collecting. Engraved
Hebrew inscription.

1757. MEGILLA.   *Rev. D. H. Adler.*
Illuminated in papier maché.

1758. MEGILLA.   *B. L. Benas, J.P.*
Scroll of Esther; said to have belonged to Saul Wahl.

1759. MEGILLA.   *Rev. B. Berliner.*
Roll of Esther, illuminated.

1760. MEGILLA.   *Mrs. D. Castello.*
Scroll of Esther, mounted with pearl.

1761. MEGILLA.   *J. de Castro.*
In silver case.

1762. MEGILLA.   *L. Cohen.*
Scroll of Esther, written by a celebrated scribe of Wilna.

1763. MEGILLA.   *L. Cohen.*
Scroll of Esther, date about xv. Cent., in ivory case.

1764. MEGILLA.   *Lewis Emanuel.*
Roll of the Book of Esther, with coloured illustrations.

1765. MEGILLA.   *Lewis Emanuel.*
Roll of the Book of Esther, mounted on ivory. From
Bagdad.

1766. MEGILLA.   *E. A. Franklin.*
Scroll of Esther, as read on the Feast of Purim; mounted
in closed antique silver-gilt case; margin elaborately
illustrated.

1777. MEGILLA.   *Theodore Fry, M.P.*
Scroll of the Book of Esther. Parchment; illuminated
borders. Spanish Work.

1778. MEGILLA.   *Mrs. E. Keyser.*
Scroll of Esther, as used on the Feast of Purim. Written
on parchment in 1836 by the late Mr. M. S. Keyzer.
Mounted in a richly carved ivory case.

1779. MEGILLA.   *Augustus Samuel Levy.*
Scroll of Esther. Silver-gilt case.

1780. MEGILLA.   *G. L. Lyon.*
Written on leather.

1781. MEGILLA.   *E. A. Lindo.*
Scroll of Esther. Illuminated.

1782. MEGILLA.   *A. E. Franklin.*
Scroll of Esther. In silver case, shaped like a fish.

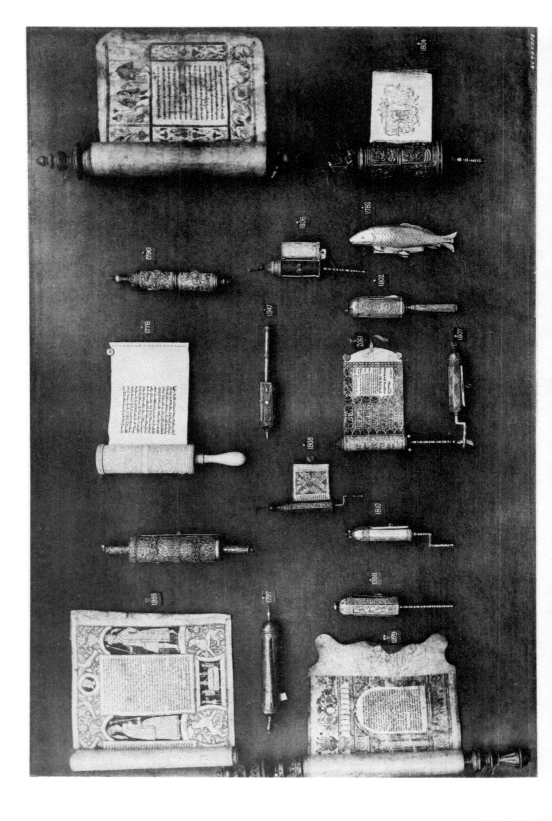

1783. MEGILLA.   *Major A. Goldsmid.*
Scroll of Esther from Jerusalem. In carved olive wood box.

1784. MEGILLA.   *Major A. Goldsmid.*
Scroll of Esther from Jerusalem. Filigree silver case.

1785. MEGILLA.   *Rev. S. M. Gollancz.*
Illuminated.

1786. MEGILLA.   *H. Groenervond.*

1787. MEGILLA.   *A. H. Jessel.*
Scroll of Esther. With illustrations, in carved oak case.

1788. MEGILLA.   *E. Joseph.*
Scroll of Esther. Silver case with blue enamel

1789. MEGILLA.   *E. Joseph.*
Scroll of Esther. Silver case.

1790. MEGILLA.   *E. Joseph.*
Scroll of Esther. Silver filigree case.

1791. MEGILLA.   *Lambert & Co.*
Illuminated in colours.

1792. MEGILLA.   *Lambert & Co.*
Decorated with etchings.

1793. MEGILLA.   *Lambert & Co.*
Scroll of Esther. In silver case.

1794. MEGILLA.   *Kate Levy.*
Scroll of Esther.

1795. MEGILLA.   *Rev. Prof. Marks.*
Miniature. Written on silk. Pressburg, 1302 (?). Silver case (plain).

1796. MEGILLA.   *F. D. Mocatta.*

1797. MEGILLA.   *F. D. Mocatta.*

1798. MEGILLA.   *Hyman Montagu.*
Illuminated.

1799. MEGILLA.   *S. Montagu, M.P.*
Scroll of Esther. Oak case.

1800. MEGILLA.   *S. Montagu, M.P.*
Scroll of Esther. Silver case. English workmanship.

1801. MEGILLA.   *Mrs. Neumegen.*

1802. MEGILLA.   *Mrs. Michael de Pass.*
In silver case.

1803. MEGILLA.   *D. N. Sanson.*
Scroll of Esther. Ivory roller.

I

1804. MEGILLA.   *S. M. Samuel.*
Scroll of Esther. Illuminated and in silver case, with
figures in bas-relief illustrating history of Esther.

1805. MEGILLA.   *S. M. Samuel.*
Moorish illuminations in colour.

1806. MEGILLA.   *J. S. Sassoon.*
In silver-gilt case, chased, an emerald cabochon at top. XVII.
Cent.

1807. MEGILLA.   *J. S. Sassoon.*
In engraved silver-gilt case, surmounted by a bird, and with
a winder. XVII. Cent.

1808. MEGILLA.   *J. S. Sassoon.*
In engraved silver-gilt case, coral at end. XVII. Cent.

1809. MEGILLA.   *H. Solomon.*

1810. MEGILLA.   *P. Solomon.*
Scroll of Esther. From Bagdad. In silver case.

1811. MEGILLA.   *S. Trenner.*

1912. MEGILLA.   *J. L. Hart.*
Engraved silver case.

1813. MEGILLA.   *J. Vallentine.*
On leather.

j.—SHECHITA.

[The special Jewish method of slaughtering cattle is principally intended to
remove the blood quickly and completely. For this purpose the sharp-
ness of the knives has to be considered. Various improvements have
been made of recent years in order to lessen the pain of the animals.]

1815. SHECHITA LAWS.   *M. Van Thal.*
A Code of Hebrew Laws, with plates relating to the killing
of animals for Jewish food.

1816. SHECHITA KNIVES.   *M. Van Thal.*
Set of knives used in the Jewish mode of killing oxen,
sheep and poultry.

1817. SHECHITA KNIFE.   *G. di R. Moro.*
For killing poultry according to Jewish custom.

1817a. LEADEN SEALS.
Marked כשר Affixed to meat killed according to Jewish
custom.

1818. ILLUSTRATION OF SHECHITA.
Director of Jewish Meat Market, Vienna.
Drawing. Method of killing cattle. Intended to make the
Jewish method of slaughtering cattle (*shechita*) as swift
and painless as possible.

PERSONAL.

k.—WEDDING.

[Jewish betrothals used to be equally formal and binding as marriages, and **Betrothal Rings** were made equally elaborate as **Wedding Rings,** which often contain the names of the wedded pair, with the addition of מזל טוב ("Good Luck"). The former in early times were used to surround a sprig of myrtle, whence their large size. At the wedding ceremony it is customary for the bridegroom to break the **glass** out of which the bride and he have drank the wine of sanctification. The ceremony is recorded in Hebrew in the marriage certificate (**Chetubah**). Divorce is only made known by a letter of divorce (גט), which are pierced and cut curiously.]

1822. BETROTHAL RING.   *Miss L. Cohen.*
 Gold; with five filigree bosses and enamel scrolls between; with small rings and Hebrew inscription. XVI. Cent.

1823. BETROTHAL RINGS.   *John Evans, F.R.S.*
 Three, gold. מזל טוב. German.

1824. BETROTHAL RING.   *J. Evans, F.R.S.*
 Gold; with five filigree bosses and enamel forget-me-nots between. XVI. Cent.

1825. BETROTHAL RING.   *E. Joseph.*
 Green enamel on gold; usual inscription. In centre triangular box with five bosses, scrolls between. Hebrew inscription. XVI. Cent.

1826. BETROTHAL RING.   *S. Montagu, M.P.*
 Gold and enamel; triangular box and five bosses, scrolls between. XVI. Cent.

1827. BETROTHAL RING.   *H. R. Soden Smith.*
 Gold filigree and coloured enamel; in centre triangular covered box surrounded by five bosses, flowers and scrolls between. Hebrew inscription. XVI. Cent.

1828. WEDDING RING.   *John Evans, F.R.S.*
 Inscription שקעין ושרה משיח רער

1829. WEDDING RING.   *E. Joseph.*
 Gold. Inscription מזל טוב. In centre model of synagogue surrounded by raised enamel. XVI. Cent.

1830. WEDDING RING.   *J. S. Sassoon.*

1831. WEDDING RING.   *J. S. Sassoon.*
 Gold; in centre a synagogue, the stark *repoussé* with flowers. Hebrew inscription. XVI. Cent.

1832. WEDDING WINE GLASS.

1833. WINE GLASSES.   *N. Rheinberg.*
 Two. With inscriptions, used at weddings. German.

1834. Wedding Girdle.   *Mrs. R. Strauss.*
Silver. Used at marriage by German Jewesses.

1835. Bridal Canopy.   *Chatham Synagogue.*
Embroidered velvet.

1836. Canopy for Marriage Ceremony.   *Great Synagogue.*
Red velvet with gilt stars and "Shield of David," ✡ in
which "good luck" in Hebrew מזל טוב.

1837. Marriage Certificates.   *N. I. Berlin.*
Nine.

1838. Chetuboth.   *G. di R. Moro.*

1839. Marriage Contract.   *I. Solomons.*

1840. Marriage Contract (Chetubah).   *I. Spielman.*
Illuminated.

1841. Marriage Contract   *Miss Bromley.*
Of Maurice Ximenes 5546=1786.

1842. Marriage Contracts.   *S. Levy.*

1842a. Marriage Contract.   *Cecil Sebag Montefiore.*
Illuminated.

1843. Letters of Divorce.   *N. I. Berlin.*
Nine.

1844. Bridal Ornaments.   *J. Sassoon.*
Worn in hair of Jewish brides in Turkey.

l.—CIRCUMCISION.

[The rite of Abraham, enjoined on all Jews: Gen. xvii. 7. The operation is
performed at the age of eight days.]

1845. Circumcision Armamentarium.   *Dr. M. Blok.*

1846. Circumcision Armamentarium.   *G. di R. Moro.*
Tortoise-shell and silver.

1847. Wrapper used in Synagogue to wrap Children in Circumcision Ceremony.   *I. Solomons.*
About 120 years old. Blue satin, lined with white silk.

1848. Knife used in Circumcision.   *E. Joseph.*
With agate handle set in turquoise and garnets.

1849. Two German Beakers.   *L. de Rothschild.*
Used for ceremonial purposes. Inscribed with devices of
successive (official) owners. The oldest date is 1690, and
it is recorded that the cups were renovated in 1716 by
the then treasurer, Herr Oppenheim. xvii. Cent.

m.—TEPHILLIN AND TALITH.

[In literal obedience to the command "they shall be for a sign on thy hands and as frontlets between thine eyes" (Deut. vi. 8), Jews wear at times of prayer *Tephillin* (תפלין, phylacteries), or cases including the following passages—Ex. xiii. 2–16; Deut. vi. 4–9, xi. 13–21. These are bound with intricate interlacing of the bands on the left arm and on the forehead between the eyes. Also in carrying out Numbers xv. 38, 39, garments are worn with fringes (ציצית), which are arranged to give the Ineffable Name by the alphabetical value of the number of threads in the fringes.]

1849a. TEPHILLIN FOR HEAD.   *W. Holman Hunt.*
Very large, 1½ in. each way.

1850. TEPHILLIN CASES.   *W. H. Cohen.*
Pair of large phylactery sheaths in silver, engraved with the device of the *Cohanim*, two hands with divided fingers.

1851. TEPHILLIN CASES.   *Messrs. M. & S. Lyon.*
Silver; chased flower pattern.   XVII. Cent.

1852. TEPHILLIN CASES.   *Hyman Montagu.*
Silver sheaths for Tephillin.

1853. TEPHILLIN CASE.   *S. J. Phillips.*
For holding phylacteries.   Silver.

1854. PHYLACTERIES.   *J. S. Sassoon.*
Set of Tephillin with heads in gold cases, set with diamonds.
XVII. Cent.

1855. TEPHILLIN BAG.   *M. N. Adler, M.A.*
For containing the phylacteries when not in use.

1856. TEPHILLIN BAG.   *Miss S. Goldstein.*
Bag for phylacteries, embroidered with Tables of Law, supported by two lions rampant and the shield of David.

1857. TEPHILLIN BAG.   *E. Joseph.*
Embroidery silk with scenes from Holy Writ, used as receptacle for prayer-books, phylacteries, &c.

1858. TEPHILLIN BAG.   *J. Nahon.*
Embroidered.   Tunis work.

1859. TALITH AND TEPHILLIN BAGS.   *L. Schaap.*
Gold embroidered velvet.

1860. TEPHILLIN BAG.   *I. Spielman.*
Embroidered in silver.

1861. ARBA' KANFOTH.
Small praying scarf worn under dress.

1862. TALITH.   *E. L. Franklin.*
Praying scarf; embroidered.   Modern.

1863. TALITH.   *Major A. Goldsmid.*
Praying mantle; embroidered net. As used by Bombay
Jews.

1864. TALITH.   *D. Jones.*
Praying scarf; satin, blue and white, damasked with
flower pattern.

1865. CORNERS AND COLLARS FOR TALITH.   *L. Schaap.*

1866. TALITH.   *Rev. S. J. Roco.*
An old Italian Synagogue scarf; cream-coloured silk, with
insertions of Venetian lace; corners embroidered.

n.—CHARMS.

[Mediæval Jews adopted much of the folk-lore and many of the superstitions
of their neighbours. Among the latter was the habit of wearing
charms, most of which had the name "Almighty" engraved upon them.
They are still in use as personal ornaments.]

1867. AMULETS.   *N. I. Berlin.*
Fourteen, two in cases as worn.

1868. CHARM.   *Joseph de Castro.*
Filigree gold; shape of heart with crown above.

1869. CHARM.   *Frederick Davis.*
Venetian. Silver-gilt, ornamented. Period, Louis XV.

1870. CHARM.   *Frederick Davis.*
Venetian. Silver-gilt ornament. Later than Louis XIV.

1871. CHARM.   *Frederick Davis.*
Venetian. Silver-gilt ornament. Period, Louis XIV.

1872. CHEMIAH.   *C. J. Ellis.*
Silver, *repoussé*, with scrolls, a hand above. XVIII. Cent.

1873. CHARM.   *Dr. John Evans, F.R.S.*
Algiers. Five-pronged; Hebrew inscription.

1874. CHARM RING.   *Dr. John Evans, F.R.S.*
Silver. Inscription צמרכד (last letters of five first verses of
Genesis). Algiers.

1875. TALISMAN.   *Rev. J. T. Fowler.*
Pewter. See *Notes and Queries*, 6th Ser., I., 354, and
explanation by Mr. Platt, p. 482. A similar object in
silver is in the Museum at York.

1876. TALISMAN.   *E. A. Franklin.*
In form of a hand, in red cornelian.

1877. TALISMAN.   *E. A. Franklin.*
In amber, with inscribed parchment.

1878. Chemiah.   *Mrs. G. Jacobs.*
Gold; shape of the Tablets of the Law. Inscribed with initials of the Ten Commandments.

1879. Chemiah.   *Miss Kate Levy.*
A silver hand.

1880. Chemiah.   *G. di R. Moro.*
Amulet, gold, cylindrical, with ring to attach to watch-chain.

1881. Amulets.   *G. di R. Moro.*
Four amulets for each side of room.

1882. Chemiah.   *J. Nahon.*
Worn by Jewish children in Morocco to ward off the evil eye. In form of an arm and hand in jade with gold rim.

1883. Chemiah.   *J. Nahon.*
Gold, in shape of Bible, with shield of David and name of Almighty. xvii. Cent.

1884. Chemiah.   *J. Nahon.*
Metal, enclosing parchment with writing.

1885. Chemiah.   *S. J. Phillips.*
Silver amulet, square, with Hebrew inscription.

1886. Chemiah.   *J. Pyke.*
Silver amulet. Dutch manufacture, with tree, and Hebrew inscription.

1887. Chemiah.   *E. J. Samuels.*
Amulet. Sixpence, with the Hebrew letter ה engraved upon it (abbreviation of the Tetragrammaton).

1888. Chemiah.   *J. S. Sassoon.*
Amulet mounted as a brooch, gold, bordered with turquoises. xvii. Cent.

1889. Chemiah.   *I. Spielman.*
Gold; oval, with miniature painting of Moses, and Hebrew inscription.

1890. Chemiah.   *Lionel D. Walford.*
Silver, *repoussé.* xviii. Cent.

1891. Chemiah.   *A. Wertheimer.*
Amulet. Spanish design, beginning of xviii. Cent. Silver-gilt, *repoussé.*

1892. Three Charms.   *Rev. S. Nahon.*
Written on grains of wheat in Hebrew; one dedicated to Mr. F. D. Mocatta.

1892a. Charm.   *Miss Bromley.*
Parchment. Dated 1783.

1893. Charms.   *J. Sassoon.*
Parchment, and medal.

1894. Pair of Chemiahs.   *Rev. M. Joseph.*

o.—MISCELLANEOUS.

1895. SABBATH KEY.   *Emanuel Lion.*
Silver key and chain, used by orthodox Jews to lock up
property previous to the Sabbath.

1896. PEG BOOK.   *Great Synagogue.*
For registering offerings on festivals without writing.

1897. CASE OF HEBREW PRAYER AND OTHER BOOKS, SYNAGOGUE
EMBROIDERIES, &C.   *L. Cohen.*

1898. CASE OF BOOKS AND EMBROIDERIES.   *P. Vallentine.*

1899. COSTUME OF TETUAN JEWESS.   *J. Nahon.*
Model: the clothes are those used on festivals, and are made
by Jewish workmen.

1900. COSTUME OF YOUNG TETUAN JEWESS (MARRIED).   *S. Levy.*

p.—THE STRAUSS COLLECTION OF HEBREW ECCLESIASTICAL ART.

Exhibited by M. STRAUSS.

N.B.—A descriptive catalogue of this collection was privately printed by M. Strauss
in 1878. (4to. Poissy: Legay & Cie, 16 Rue des Dames.)

1901. ARK FOR SCROLL OF THE LAW.
From the synagogue at Modena; walnut wood. Italian
Renaissance. Dated A.M. 5265 = 1505 C.E. Inscriptions:—
קדש לה' ("Dedicated to the Eternal"); שלם תורת' ה
תמימה' משיבת נפש עדות ה' נמפפהי מלם ("Peace. The
law of God is just; it saves souls"); לאלפי חמשה שבת
ברכי נפשי את ה' הללויה ("Made in the year 5000. May
my soul praise the Eternal, Hallelujah").

1902. SYNAGOGUE READING-DESK.
Surmounted by a bronze eight-branched candlestick. Date
and style of the preceding work. In the centre of each of
the two top panels a shield with leopard passant reversed.

1903. ARK FOR SCROLL OF THE LAW.
For domestic use. Chased and *repoussé* silver. Contains a
roll of the Law in which all the columns, with the
exception of six, commence with the same letter (ג).
German workmanship. XVII. Cent.

1904. TWO CANDLESTICKS.
Carved wood.

1905. HANUCAH LAMP.
Silver; each sconce is surmounted by an emblematical
design, and the movable burner in the centre is ornamented with a crown, and a figure of Judas Maccabeus
holding a sword in one hand and the head of Lysias
in the other. The base is supported by four lions.
XVIII. Cent.

1906. HANUCAH LAMP.
Repoussé silver. Inscription : כי נר מצוה ותורה אור " For the Commandment is a Lamp and the Law is light" (Prov. vi. 23). XVII. Cent.

1907. HANUCAH OIL LAMP.
Silver. XVII. Cent.

1908. HANUCAH LAMP.
Ornamented with figures of Moses and Aaron. Copper. XVIII. Cent.

1909, 1910. HANUCAH LAMPS.
Copper; ornamented in the style of the Italian Renaissance.

1911, 1912. HANUCAH LAMPS.
Similar in design. The ornamentation is non-Jewish, apparently inspired by the taste of the Italian Renaissance, especially the workmanship of Mantegna. Two dolphins and the head of Medusa are prominent in the design.

1913. HANUCAH LAMP.
Copper. Inscription : כי נר מצוה ותורה אור " For the Commandment is a lamp, and the Law is light" (Prov. vi. 23).

1914. HANUCAH LAMP.
Bronze. Found buried in the ancient Jewish quarter at Lyons. XII. or XIII. Cent.

1915. SPICE BOX.
Silver filigree work, ornamented with coloured stones and enamels representing Biblical scenes. Italian workmanship. XVII. Cent.

1916. SPICE BOX.
Silver filigree. Italian workmanship of a very delicate order. The design resembles a church steeple with a miniature belfry and vane.

1917. SPICE BOX.
Mauresque design.

1918. SPICE BOX.
Repoussé silver. XVI. Cent.

1919. SPICE BOX.
Silver-gilt. XVI. Cent.

1920. SPICE BOX.
Silver. The workmanship is very fine. The design includes a statuette of child resting its foot on a dolphin. XVI. Cent.

1921. Spice Box.

1922. Spice Box.
Chased silver.

1923. Spice Box.
Repoussé silver-gilt.

1924. Spice Box.
Bronze, chased and ornamented with mother-o'-pearl and
rock crystal. An heraldic lion on a lozenge. xvi. Cent.

1925. Crown for Scroll of the Law.
Silver-gilt. Has the following inscription in Hebrew:
"This object was offered to the Synagogue by Rabbi
Abraham and Sarah Kahn in the year 1780."

1926. Breastplate for Scroll of the Law.
Silver. The centre, inscribed with the name of the festival
on which it is used, is movable. The workmanship is
very remarkable. Cherubin, angels and lions. xvii. Cent.

1927. Breastplate for Scroll of the Law.
Silver-gilt. A miniature Tabernacle appears in the centre;
lions supporting a crown; between two stags is a plate
inscribed שבת "Sabbath," and below appears the admoni-
tion רץ דצבי "Be quick as a stag [to obey the divine
commands"]. xvii. Cent.

1928. Breastplate for Scroll of the Law.
Inscribed with the Ten Commandments. xviii. Cent.

1929. Breastplate for Scroll of the Law.
Repoussé silver.

1930. Breastplate for Scroll of the Law.
Similar in style to No. 27. Filigree silver, inlaid with
large coloured stones. xvi. Cent.

1931. Breastplate for Scroll of the Law.
Repoussé silver; oval shape, tasteful design.

1932. Pointer for the Scroll of the Law.
Chased silver. The design is very elaborate. A lion at
the top holds a representation of the tables of the Law,
on which the initials of the Ten Commandments in
Hebrew are inscribed. xvii. Cent.

1933. Pointer for Scroll of the Law.
xvii. Cent.

1934. Pointer for Scroll of the Law.
The Hebrew inscription states that it was presented to the
synagogue of Magdebourg by Rabbi Eleazar Ahlfeld and
his wife Rebecca, daughter of Samuel Hirsch, in 1713.

1935. POINTER FOR SCROLL OF THE LAW.
Bears an inscription from which it appears to have belonged to the learned Rabbi, Jacob of Bouchin, in 1710.

1936. POINTER FOR SCROLL OF THE LAW.
Resembles the preceding number.

1937. POINTER FOR SCROLL OF THE LAW.

1938. CITRON CASE.
Silver-gilt and *repoussé.* Inscription: בא סכות בא שמחה
"When the feast of Tabernacles comes joy comes."

1939. CITRON CASE.
Resembles the preceding number in shape and ornamentation.

1940. "TREE OF LIFE."
Silver-gilt. Ornaments for Scrolls of the Law. They are fixed on the lower extremities of the wooden rollers, whence their name. (*See* p. 87.)

1941. "TREE OF LIFE."
Silver.

1942. KIDDUSH CUP.
Silver-gilt, chased and *repoussé* in rather a primitive style. Two inscriptions being the two variants of the Fourth Commandment.

1943. KIDDUSH CUP.
Silver-gilt, chased. Inscription: וידבר משה את מועדי יי
אל בני ישראל ("Moses explained the festivals of the Lord to the children of Israel").

1944. KIDDUSH CUP.
Silver-gilt. Inscription: כוס של ברכה ("Cup of Blessing").

1945. CIRCUMCISION BASIN.
Silver-gilt. Renaissance. The design of the interior represents the ceremony of Circumcision. Inscription on the border Genesis x. XVI. Cent.

1946. KNIFE FOR CIRCUMCISION.
The handle (silver) is chased, on one side the design representing the circumcision ceremony, and on the other the operator returning home. The blade is very worn.

1947. CASE FOR ROLL OF ESTHER.
Silver, enamelled and richly jewelled. Cases of this description were formerly much used by Jewish women for divine service on the Feast of Purim. XVI. Cent.

1948. SCENT CASE.

Silver-gilt. Used by women in the Synagogue during the Fast of Atonement. The design represents a trophy of Jewish symbols with the Holy Name שׁדי inscribed in the centre. The shape and incidental ornamentation are heraldic. XVI. Cent.

1949. BETROTHAL RING.

Gold. Filigree and enamel ornamentation, very elaborate. Inscription : מזל טוב ("Good Luck"). The Louvre possesses a similar ring. XVI. Cent.

1950. BETROTHAL RING.

Gold. Ornamentation in relief. The collet is in the shape of a two-storied pavilion, with the roof inscribed on each side מ״ט (initials of the Hebrew for "Good Luck"). In design and workmanship the specimen is of extreme rarity. Renaissance.

1951. BETROTHAL RING.

Gold. Simple design with the usual inscription (*vide* No. 49) on the collet. XIII. Cent.

1952. BETROTHAL RING.

Exceptionally wide and elaborately chased with heads of lions. Instead of the collet there is a lid, ornamented with the figures of two lions in high relief, on opening which are disclosed two small sheets of gold, one inscribed with the usual felicitation, and the other with a legend, half effaced, which appears to have consisted of the name of the bride and bridegroom. Renaissance.

1953. BETROTHAL RING.

Gold. Usual inscription (*see* No. 1249). Renaissance.

1954. BETROTHAL RING.

Gold. Chased and enamelled ornamention.. XVI. Cent.

1955. BETROTHAL RING.

Similar in design to the preceding number. XVI. Cent.

1956, 1957. BETROTHAL RINGS.

Gold. Double rings. Filigree ornamentation.

1958, 1959. BETROTHAL RINGS.

Gold. Resemble No. 53, but are not so fine. Renaissance.

1960. BETROTHAL RING.

A simple band of gold, with the six letters of the traditional felicitation (*vide* No. 49) in relief, alternating with an ornament also in relief.

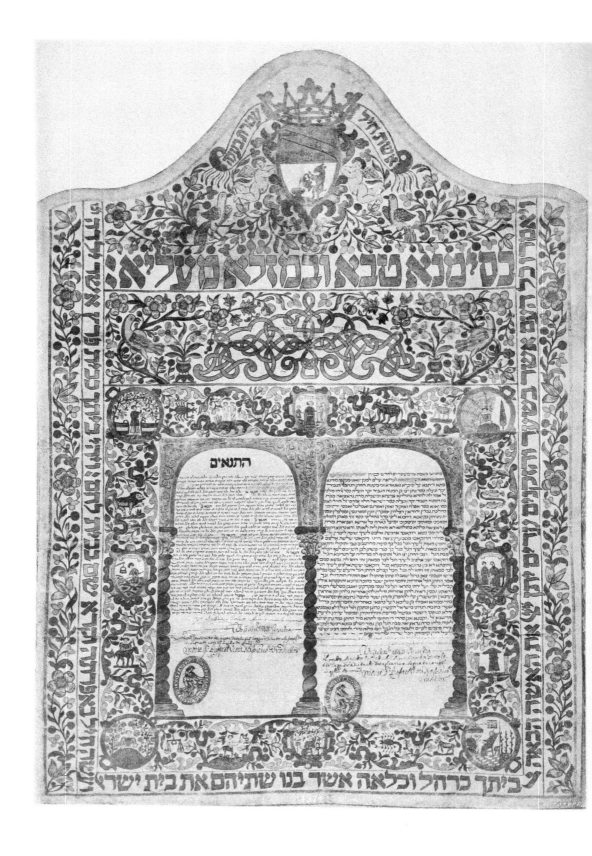

1961–1963. BETROTHAL RINGS.
Gilt bronze. In other respects they resemble the preceding numbers.

1964. RING.
Gold. The oval collet holds an onyx, on which is cut in relief the following inscription: יראת אלהם קדמון לכל דבר ("The fear of God before all things").

1965–1969. RINGS.
Copper. The collets engraved with the names of the owners, and family symbols, among them the hands of the Cohanim (Priests) with distended fingers and zodiacal signs.

1970. MANUSCRIPT FESTIVAL PRAYERS.
On parchment, illuminated.

1971. PRAYER-BOOK.
Bound in silver with clasps. Arabesque and *repoussé* design. A shield in the centre inscribed " W. D.," gilt and embossed back.

1972. PRAYER-BOOK.
Bound in wood covered with vellum. Gilt ornamentation. Silver corners and clasp. Imprint: Amsterdam, 1768.

1973. BOOK.
Pentateuch in Spanish, printed at Amsterdam, 1655, by Menasseh ben Israel. Bound in tortoise-shell, with silver corners and clasps and gilt and embossed back.

1974. MARRIAGE CONTRACT.
Of Baron Sina, written on parchment and richly illuminated. Among other ornaments is the Coat of Arms of the Sina family. Dated Venice, 1756.

1975. MARRIAGE CONTRACT.
Written on parchment, and signed at Ancona in 1776.

1976–80. ROLLS OF THE BOOK OF ESTHER.
Ornamented with miniatures and paintings, &c.

1981. CURTAIN FOR THE ARK.
Red velvet, ornamented with gold and silver embroidery. In the centre are the Tables of the Law inscribed with the Ten Commandments, and surmounted by the traditional crown.

1982. COVERING FOR THE READING-DESK.
Similar in design and workmanship to the preceding number.

1983. HEBREW ALPHABET.
On stone, possibly used in Jewish School.

1984. ORIENTAL AGATE.
Hebrew inscription at back.

1985. TEPHILLIN BAG.
Rose-coloured silk, with Hebrew inscription embroidered in
silver.

1986. HANUCAH LAMP.
Bronze, Roman.

1987. RING.
Bronze.   Hebrew inscription.

1988. SEAL.
Bronze.

1989. BAS-RELIEF.
Ivory figures of Moses and Aaron.

1990. CHAIN.
Copper, silvered.

1991. AMULET.
Gold; ornamented with Hebrew characters in brilliants.

1992. SCROLL OF THE LAW.
Small, mounted with silver, with crown, pointer, &c.

1993. ROLL OF ESTER.
XVI. Cent.

1994. PERFUME BOX.
Copper-gilt, Byzantine.

1995. RING.
Filigree-gilt.

1996. RING.
Filigree-gilt in three rows.

1997. GOBLET.
Serpentine, with Hebrew inscription.

1998. BELLS FOR THE SCROLL OF THE LAW.
Oriental workmanship.

1999. SABBATH LAMP.
Copper.

2000. HEBREW POEM ON SATIN.
Embroidered with Hebrew characters.   1479 A.D.

2001. MEDALLION.
Gold.   *Rev.* Temple of Jerusalem.

2002. ALMS BOX.

2003. Mezuzah.
Carved wood case.

2004. Spice Box.
Silver-gilt.

2005. Spice Box.
Silver filigree, turreted.

2006. Seal.

2007. Water-colour Drawing.
Representing a notable Dutch Jew carrying Scroll of the Law. xvii. Cent.

2008. Sabbath Candelabrum.

2009. Circumcision Knife.

2010. Band for Scroll of the Law.
Red velvet, embroidered in Hebrew characters.

2011. Band for Scroll of the Law.
Linen, embroidered with Hebrew characters.

2012. Circumcision Knife.

2013. Enamel.
Representing the Passover.

2014. Spice Box.
Filigree silver, ornamented with enamel. Period, Louis XIV.

2015. Statuette.
Bronze.

2016. Circumcision Knife.

2017. Alms Box.
Silver.

2018. Censer.
Silver.

2019. Case for Scrolls of the Law.
A carved wood figure of shape of Archangel; white and gold, enclosing four scrolls of the Law.

2020. Bronze Medallion.
Representing the famous Gracia Mendesia Nasi, mother-in-law of Juan Miquez the (Jewish) Duke of Naxos and Prince of the Cyclades, 1554.

2021. Bronze Medal.
King of Israel.

2022. POINTER FOR SCROLL OF THE LAW.
   Gold, ornamented with brilliants, hand of Jasper, covered
   with Hebrew inscriptions.   Dated 1734.

2023. STATUETTE OF MOSES.
   Bronze-gilt.   XVI. Cent.

2024, 2025. BANDS FOR SCROLLS OF THE LAW.
   Silk, with Hebrew inscriptions.

2026. SILK BANNERS.
   Four, embroidered, with Hebrew inscriptions.

2027. SILK CAP AND ROBE.
   Embroidered with gold.   Used by the person presiding at
   the Seder table on Passover night.

2028. COVER FOR READING-DESK.
   Crimson velvet fringed with gold.

2029. SABBATH LAMP.

2030. ALMS BOX.

q.—THE SASSOON COLLECTION OF HEBREW ECCLESIASTICAL ART.

Exhibited by REUBEN D. SASSOON, ESQ.

[The bulk of this Collection was made by the late PHILIP SALOMONS, ESQ.]

2031. ARK FOR SCROLL OF THE LAW.
   Silver, 2 ft. 6 in. high, *repoussé* and engraved with flowers,
   of square form with two wings; resting on a bell-shaped
   pedestal; surmounted by the Ten Commandments and
   supported by two lions, a crown above.   Date about 1650.

2032. EWER.
   For Cohanin or Priests.   Inscription relating to its use.
   Dutch.

2033. EWER AND LAVER.
   Silver-gilt, *repoussé* and chased with flowers and leaves,
   with medallions of two hands in benediction.   French.
   XVIII. Cent.

2034. EWER AND LAVER.
   Silver-gilt, engraved and chased, each with four medallions
   of Biblical subjects and *appliqué* terminal figures on the
   foot of Ewer.   French manufacture.   Modern.

2035. SCROLL OF THE LAW.
   With mantle of dark blue velvet and gold, embroidered
   crown and fringe; a pair of silver-gilt bells of three tiers
   enclosing small bells, *repoussé* with flowers, and a crown

XVIII. Cent.; a silver-gilt breastplate with the Commandments and crown enclosed by two columns, the ground ornamented with *appliqué* scrolls. The reverse engraved with the Sacrifice of Isaac and ground plan of the Temple, and a silver gilt pointer and chain.

2036. SCROLL OF THE LAW.

With ivory handles and ends, and a blue velvet mantle embroidered in gold with the Commandments, supported by lions and crown; a large silver gilt crown ornamented with filigree lions and *appliqué* work, set with coloured gems and six bells suspended; a silver-gilt breastplate, with two columns enclosing the Commandments, supported by lions and crown, and a silver-gilt pointer, with two diamond rings on the hand and chain. *Temp.* Louis XIV.

2037. SCROLL OF THE LAW.

With gold-embroidered red-silk mantle. A pair of silver-gilt bells of three tiers with small bells, *repoussé* and chased all over, surmounted by crowns. A silver-gilt breastplate, *repoussé* with elaborate ornamentations of *appliqué* animals, birds and scrolls. *Temp.* Louis XIV., and a pointer, with silver-gilt filigree handle set with garnets and turquoise.

2038. SCROLL OF THE LAW.

With white satin mantle. A pair of silver-gilt bells, hexagonal, of three tiers hung with small bells. A silver-gilt breastplate, with the Decalogue crowned and two pillars and *appliqué* scrolls, pointer and chain. Cf. 2035.

2039. SCROLL OF THE LAW.

With mantle of ruby velvet and gold-embroidered crown and scroll border. A pair of silver bells in form of vases, chased with leaves and bells hanging on brackets surmounted by a crown. English, 1784. A silver-gilt breastplate in two parts connected by chains, *repoussé* with scrolls and a silver-gilt pointer, three diamond rings on the hands.

2040. SCROLL OF THE LAW.

With mantle of green velvet, red fringe. A pair of silver-gilt bells of three stages of filigree, set with coloured stones, a crown above. A silver-gilt breastplate, with the Commandments, crowned. Moses and Aaron, and *appliqué* scrolls, silver pointer and chain. Inscription: David Lopez Pereira, 5520.

2041. SCROLL OF THE LAW.

With white satin mantle. A pair of silver-gilt filigree bells of three tiers hung with small bells surmounted by a crown, a gilt breastplate with crowned Decalogue, and border of coloured stones, silver pointer and chain.

2042. SCROLL OF THE LAW.
With blue velvet mantle and gold-embroidered cipher. A pair of silver bells, with *repoussé* flowers and three rows of bells. Silver breastplate with *appliqué* lions and bells, gilt pointer and chain.

2043. SCROLL OF THE LAW.
In red plush case. Writing of great beauty. Fitted with curious silver bells and pointer (Indian workmanship). Hebrew inscription: "Presented by David Sassoon in memory of his brother, Sassoon David Sassoon, 5628."

2044. SCROLL OF THE LAW.
With mantle. A pair of small silver-gilt bells with small brackets and fir cones, and a gilt scroll-shaped pointer.

2045. SCROLL OF THE LAW.
Small. With ivory handles, ruby velvet mantle in gold embroidery. A silver-gilt pointer and chain.

2046. SCROLL OF THE LAW.
Very small. With silver mounts and a pair of gilt bells, gold embroidered mantle, gilt breastplate with the crowned Decalogue and pillars and a small pointer in a case.

2047. SCROLL OF THE LAW.
Small; with ivory handles, blue silk mantle and small gilt pointer.

2048. SCROLL OF THE LAW.
Blue damask mantle, silver handles.

2049. BELLS FOR SCROLL OF THE LAW.
Pair of; silver; of three tiers of arcades of hexagonal shape enclosing bells surmounted by a crown. XVIII. Cent.

2050. BELLS FOR SCROLL OF THE LAW.
Pair of; silver gilt; filigree bells of three tiers; four rows of bells surmounted by a crown. XVIII. Cent.

2051. BELLS FOR SCROLL OF THE LAW.
Pair of; silver gilt; of three bulbs and crown, surmounted by an eagle; chased in scrolls, and three circlets of bells on dragon brackets. XVIII. Cent.

2052. SMALL CROWN FOR SCROLLS OF THE LAW.
Two; silver gilt; closed; one studded with coloured stones.

2053. PASSOVER DISH.
Silver gilt; border chased with flowers. Inscription relating to the Passover. XVII. Cent.

2054. CITRON BOX.
Silver gilt; wavy pattern. Inscription relating to Feast of Tabernacles. German. XVIII. Cent.

2055. HANUCAH LAMP.
Bronze; pierced and engraved with statuettes. German XVII. Cent.

2056. ROLL OF ESTHER.
In silver gilt case, the latter having scenes from the Book of Esther in relief.

2057. ROLL OF ESTHER.
Illuminated sketches of the events in the Book of Esther 6 in. Probably German.

2058. ROLL OF ESTHER.
24 in.; mounted on ivory; very finely written. German-English mounting.

2059. ROLL OF ESTHER.
On a silver stele and niello borders. Italian. XVI. Cent.

2060. ROLL OF ESTHER.
Illustrated with pen and ink sketches. 10 in. Probably Italian.

2061. ROLL OF ESTHER.
Mounted on silver. Illuminated. Very curious. Bagdad.

2062. PRAYER-BOOK.
Silver covers; *repoussé* in bold scrolls and medallions of lions and birds. *Temp.* Louis XV.

2063. AMULET.
Silver-gilt. Design includes representations of the Tablets of the Law, priest's mitre, incense-burner, and candlestick. Inscribed in Hebrew, " Almighty." XVIII. Cent.

2064. READING DESK COVER.
Brocade.

2065. READING DESK COVER.
Brocade.

III. ANTIQUITIES.

ANY complete collection of Jewish antiquities would range over the whole field of historic archæology. Scattered through all the nations of the civilized world, the Jews have had points of contact with every nation that has had a history. The few specimens drawn from this wide field shown in the present Exhibition cannot profess to represent in any degree the whole field of Jewish antiquities, and only afford a glimpse of the much broader basis on which Anglo-Jewish history itself rests. The collection is miscellaneous in character, and only admits of rough classification under the headings of MSS., Books, Inscriptions, the Temple, Holy Land, and Assyria, and lastly, Seals and Rings, on each of which a few remarks may here be made.

Almost all the Hebrew MSS. offered have been shown and catalogued as it is in inedited MSS. that ever fresh light is to be expected in the various departments of Jewish literature. Some rare liturgies, translations of the Arabic philosophers into Hebrew, will be found amongst them. But the chief attraction of our collection is formed by two collections, one of general range, exhibited by Sir Julian Goldsmid, Bart., M.P., and the Samaritan MSS. shown by the Earl of Crawford and Balcarres, the finest private collection of this class of MSS. in existence; no list of these has hitherto appeared in print, though an elaborate catalogue has been drawn up by the Rev. A. Löwy, and is exhibited with the MSS., to which it forms an indispensable guide. Turning from the sublime to the other extreme, attention may be drawn to the notorious "Shapira MS." which created such a sensation while the question of its authenticity was still *sub lite.*

The *Books* shown have been chiefly selected for the extrinsic merits of their binding, as the British Museum offered to exhibit a selection of its magnificent collection, with which we could not hope to cope. Besides this the Trustees are also displaying some sixty of their Hebrew MSS. selected from their collection of over one thousand codices. Scholars will be glad of even this small instalment of a catalogue of these treasures.

Under *Inscriptions* we may notice the collection of photographs found by M. Isidore Loeb, and kindly placed at our disposal; inscriptions from France, Spain, Germany, Arabia, and the Holy Land, are included under this head. Material is thus offered to the student for a study of Hebrew necrographic inscriptions.

The intimate connection of Jewish history and feeling with the Holy Land would justify the exhibits dealing with Palestine, even if there were no section of antiquities. Both in their own thoughts and in the views of others, the relation of Jews with the Holy Land is so close that no lapse of time can dissever their connection, if only imaginative, with the past glories of the

Holy Land. And of these the memory looks back with especial affection to the glories of the Temple. These are represented in the present Exhibition by a remarkable model reconstruction of Solomon's time, the result of the life study of Mr. Thomas Newberry, and of three years' labour of Messrs. Bartlett. Scholars will doubtless dispute as to the amount of the success with which the ancient building has been reconstructed from the scanty mentions in the Biblical records, but all will admire the industry and ingenuity with which the mechanical difficulties of such a conception have been approached and surmounted.

The Palestine Exploration Fund exhibit the choicest of their treasures, chief among which may be mentioned their own map, the most important contribution to Biblical study that has been made in England for many years. The other objects they exhibit have attracted such wide interest among Bible students that detailed descriptions would be an impertinence towards these, and in another sense impertinent to the wants of the general public. The Moabite Stone and the Siloam Inscription have been the subject of numbers of monographs which have not yet exhausted the instruction to be drawn from these earliest specimens of Semitic palæography. Students will have these at hand, others will be content to do without more explicit description.

Next to the Holy Land, the Land of the Captivity, where the Jewish exiles refused to sing their songs in a strange land, has chief interest to the student of Jewish history, not to speak of the many-coloured light that the cuneiform inscriptions have thrown upon Biblical archæology in general. A carefully selected collection of Assyrian objects discovered by Mr. H. Rassam, and exhibited by Mrs. G. E. Sandeman, will give the visitor some idea of the range of Assyrian archæology.

Lastly, a number of Seals and Rings offer some addition to the scanty materials of Jewish sigillography, a subject on which a complete monograph has been promised for some time past from the learned pen of M. Saige. In this department, as in others, the compilers regret that the hurry-scurry with which work such as theirs must be conducted, has prevented the full inscriptions and descriptions from being given. Their entries cannot profess to do more than record in the briefest possible way the nature of the exhibits and the source whence fuller accounts may be obtained.

---

a.—MANUSCRIPTS.

[*See* also British Museum Exhibits.]

2070. BIBLE WITH RASHI.   *Sir Julian Goldsmid, Bart., M.P.*
     Pentateuch, has Targum and small Massora. Owners, Moses
          ben Isaac, Kalonymus ben Gershom Bosham (Venice,
          1473), Joseppo Morpurgo and his son Abraham. Baruch,
          Augsburg. From Library of Duke of Sussex. Probably
          of XIV. Cent.

2071. BIBLE, WITH SHORT MASSORA. *Sir Julian Goldsmid, Bart.. M.P.*
Vellum; two vols. Written at Avignon, 1419. From the
Library of the Duke of Sussex.

2072. PSALMS.   *Sir Julian Goldsmid, Bart., M.P.*
Psalter, with points and German translation (in Rabbinic
characters) in the margin. Vienna, 5497 = 1737.

2073. HEBREW MS.   *Sir Julian Goldsmid, Bart., M.P.*
Commentary on the Psalms, by Rabbi David Kimchi
(commentary on the first twelve Psalms, deficient), on the
Book of Job, by Rabbi Levi ben Gerson, and on the
Proverbs of Solomon by Rabbi Zarachijah [damaged at
beginning and end], 5200 = 1440.

2074. MACHZOR (FESTIVAL PRAYERS).
                                       Sir Julian Goldsmid, Bart., M.P.
German rite, with commentary. Two vols. with illuminated
titles. Written at Ratisbon, 1525. From the Library of
the Duke of Sussex.

2075. DAILY PRAYERS.   *Sir J. Goldsmid, Bart., M.P.*
German rite at Amsterdam. Leaves 197 fol. with gilt titles.
Pointed. Dated 1727.

2076. HAGADA.   *Sir Julian Goldsmid, Bart., M.P.*
With commentary of Abarbanel and Cabbalistic comments.
From Duke of Sussex's Library. Richly illuminated.

2077. SHELOSHA SARIGIM.   *Sir Julian Goldsmid, Bart., M.P.*
On the beauties of the written and oral laws, compiled by
Joseph the son of Jacob the son of Moses, of Belgrade.
London 5477 = 1717.

2078. MORE NEBUCHIM.   *Sir Julian Goldsmid, Bart., M.P.*
By Moses Maimonides. S. Ibn Tibbon's Hebrew translation
from the Arabic. Paper and vellum. From the Library
of the Duke of Sussex. XVI. Cent.

2079. AVERROES' COMMENTARIES ON ARISTOTLE.
                                       Sir Julian Goldsmid, Bart., M.P.
Translated into Hebrew. Vellum, two vols. Spanish
writing. The works translated are: "De Generatione"
(Kalonymos), "De Anima" (Mose ibn Tibbon, three
copies), "Historia Animalum" (two copies), "Auscul-
tationes Physicae," "De Coelo et Mundo," "Meteorologica,"
XIV. Cent. From the Library of the Duke of Sussex.

2080. LIBNATH HASAPIR (THE SAPPHIRE PAVEMENT).
                                       Sir J. Goldsmid, Bart., M.P.
Hebrew Grammar, by R. Judah Aryeh of Modena. 4to.
leaves 9 (preface and poems) and 112. From Library of
Duke of Sussex.

2082. THE BIBLE.   *Balliol Coll., Oxford.*
Beautifully written and decorated, in handsome binding
with clasp.   Date 1491.

2083. BIBLE.   *Messrs. Goldschmidt.*
Illuminated and bound in velvet.

2084. BIBLE WITH MASSORA.   *B. Quaritch.*
Manuscript on vellum, small 4to. With illuminated ornament
at the headings of the sections; bound in blue morocco, gilt
edges, with the arms of Theodore Williams in gold on
sides.

2085. BIBLE WITH MASSORA.   *B. Quaritch.*
Manuscript on vellum, small fol.   With illuminated ornaments in a delicate style of penmanship, in treble columns,
entirely written in the square character, without any
intermixture of the modern Rabbinical, even in the
masoretic notes, bound in old calf. Spain, *circa* A.D. 1300.

2086. ECCLESIASTES.   *Rev. Dr. H. Adler.*

2087. PENTATEUCH.   *Dr. H. Adler, Delegate Chief Rabbi.*
Written by Jew of Senaa (Yemen, Arabia), with Targum of
Onkelos, translation into Arabic (in Hebrew letters), and
Commentary of Rashi.

2088. PENTATEUCH WITH HAPHTAROTH.   *Balliol College, Oxford.*
First few chapters of Genesis missing.

2089. BIBLE.   *S. Montagu, M.P.*
XIV. Cent. (?).

2090. BIBLE.   *Society of Biblical Archæology.*
Probably from South Arabia.   Said to be of XII. Cent.

2091. THE SHAPIRA MS.   *B. Quaritch.*
Fifteen fragments, supposed to be the original MS. of Deuteronomy.   Discovered by the late Mr. Shapira, and valued
at £1,000,000.   These MSS. were, on examination by
experts, declared to be forgeries; but for a time they
created a great sensation.

2091a. PSALMS.   *J. Nahon.*
Illuminated.

2092. COMMENTARY ON DANIEL, EZRA AND CHRONICLES.   *H. Guedalla.*
By R. Levi ben Gershom.   Dated 1338.

2093. MACHZOR.   *Dr. H. Adler, Delegate Chief Rabbi.*
Festival Prayer-book.   Roman rite.

2094. MACHZOR.   *Dr. H. Adler, Delegate Chief Rabbi.*
Festival Prayer-book.   Old German rite.

2095. MACHZOR. *Dr. H. Adler.*
Festival Prayer-book of Jews of Corfu.

2096. MACHZOR. *Dr. H. Adler, Delegate Chief Rabbi.*
Prayer-book of Jews in Senaa (Yemen, Arabia). Copy.

2097. PRAYER-BOOK. *Great Synagogue.*
כל בו. Fol. XVIII. Cent.

2098. MACHZOR. *B. Quaritch.*
The Jewish Ritual according to the Roman rite, folio, MS.,
vellum, with painted ornaments at the section-headings,
in the original stamped binding. XV. Cent.

2099. MACHZOR. *B. Quaritch.*
Roman rite, or Collection of Prayers, Hymns, and Lessons,
for the year, in Hebrew; small 4to., MS. on vellum, with
several initial words in gold, half bound. Italy, about
A.D. 1400.

One of the early possessors who have recorded their ownership of this
volume, was "Itzhaq Levi, who dwells at Casale of Monferrato." Another
possessor dates his inscription 5229=1469.

2100. MACHZOR. *J. Sassoon.*
Spanish rite. XV. Cent.

2101. BOOK OF PRAYERS. *E. Joseph.*
Illuminated and bound in silver.

2102. MACHZOR. *E. Joseph.*
Festival Prayer-book. Roman rite. XIV. Cent.

2103. PRAYER-BOOK. *F. D. Mocatta.*
Illuminated. XVII. Cent.

2104. MACHZOR. *F. D. Mocatta.*
Avignon rite.

2105. PRAYER-BOOK FOR HOSANNA RABBA. *H. Guedalla.*
Vellum. Spanish rite. Dated 1396.

2106. SELICHOTH. *H. Guedalla.*
XVI. Cent.

2107. MACHZOR. *Dr. N. M. Adler, Chief Rabbi.*
Prayers for Festival of Pentecost. Rite of Avignon.

2108. MINHAGOTH AND MIDRASHIM. *Dr. N. M. Adler, Chief Rabbi.*
Including Masseceth Sopherim.

2109. HAGADA. *J. Sassoon.*
Illuminated, with coloured initials.

2110. HAGADA. *L. Isaacs.*
Illustrated.

2111. HAGADA.   *B. Quaritch.*
  Liturgy for the Passover Service, in Hebrew, small folio,
    illuminated MS. on vellum, with numerous miniatures
    representing the ceremonial and domestic phases of the
    Passover service, and scriptural incidents connected with
    it, every page enclosed within architectural columns or
    floral decorations, all the large initials in gold and
    historiated ; old Dutch calf.   Sec. XVII.
  The inscriptions under the miniatures are German, in Hebrew characters.

2112. HAGADA.   *F. D. Mocatta.*
  Illuminated Levantine.   XVII. Cent.

2113. HAGADA.   *Lewis Lewis.*
  Illuminated.   Vellum.   Pictures by hand.

2114. HAGADA.   *Rev. S. M. Gollancz.*
  Illuminated.

2115. HAGADA.   *Benjamin L. Cohen.*
  Manuscript.   A.M. 5515.

2116. HAGADAH.   *Dr. N. M. Adler, Chief Rabbi.*
  Written and illuminated on vellum.

2116a. MS. PRAYER BOOK AND HAGADA.   *H. P. Moseley.*

2117. TWO LITURGIES.   *F. D. Mocatta.*
  Arabic.

2118. TWO LITURGIES.   *F. D. Mocatta.*
  Samaritan.

2119–2121. THREE HEBREW MSS.   *Rev. C. D. Ginsburg.*

2122. ROMANCE OF KING ARTHUR.   *Rev. C. D. Ginsburg.*
  In Jewish German, written in Hebrew characters.

2123. KABBALISTIC WORK.   *Rev. C. D. Ginsburg.*
  Including very early plan of Jerusalem, the earliest by a
    Jewish hand.

2124. PTOLEMY'S ALMAGEST.   *J. Sassoon.*
  The book entitled אלפרגני *al-Fargānī*, an abridgment of *al-
    Majisti*, translated from the Arabic of al-Fargānī into
    Hebrew by R. Jacob Anatolio. Copy in Brit. Mus.
    MS. Add. 27, 107, f. 135a ff.

2125. צורת הארץ   *J. Sassoon.*
  By Abraham bar Chiya.   Edited by Filipowski, also frag-
    ment of astronomical tables by Immanuel b. Jacob.

2126. ALGHAZZALI " VIEWS OF THE PHILOSOPHERS."   *H. Guedalla.*
  Translated into Hebrew, also Aristotle's ' De Poetica,' ·with
    Averroes' commentary.

2127. PHILOSOPHICAL TREATISE.   *Beth Hamidrash.*
  Of Averroes, Alfarabi, &c.   (*See* Neubauer, No. 42.)

2128. GAZZALI " VIEWS OF PHILOSOPHERS" *Beth Hamidrash.*
Also Petrus Hispanus " Trittalo." (*See* Dr. Neubauer's
Catalogue, No. 38.)

2129. M. C. LUZZATO " LOGIC." *Rev. J. Kohn Zedek.*
Hebrew. Dated 1742.

2130. לשׁוֹן הזהב *J. Sassoon.*
Treatise on the measures in the Bible, by R. Isaac ben
Solomon ben Tsaddik al-Achdab. [Wolf, B. H., i. p. 648].

2131. " SEDER HAYOM." *J. Sassoon.*

2132. " TRACTATUS SUPER TALMUD." *Lord Zouch.*
Jacob ben Asher's *Arba' Turim.* XIV. Cent.

2133. MANUSCRIPT. *Breslau Rabbinic Seminary.*
Written by a Jewess named Paula. 1228. fol.

2134. COMMENTARY. *Breslau Rabbinic Seminary*
By Joseph Kara.

2135. שׁערי דורא, &c. *Dr. N. M. Adler, Chief Rabbi.*

2136. MEDICAL WORK. DATED A.M. 5226 = A.D. 1466. *H. Guedalla.*
Canon of Avicenna.

2137. AVERROES. *S. Pariente.*
Translated into Hebrew. Spanish handwriting, 1327.

2138. LIBER DE MORBIS ET REMEDIIS. *H. Guedalla.*
Hebrew. Dated 1432.

2139. MANUSCRIPT. *S. Levy.*
From Algiers Dated 1694.

2139*a.* " DIALOGHI D'AMORI." *H. Guedalla.*
By Leo Hebræus. Italian, in Hebrew characters.

2139*b.* POLISH TALE. *Mrs. David Lewis.*
Manuscript of a Polish Legend as told by a wandering
Jewish *raconteur* in Judeo-German dialect.

2140. LA DIVINA LEY DE MOYSE. *F. D. Mocatta.*
By L. de Morteira.

2141. SPANISH MS. *Miss C. Cortissos.*
Prevenciones Divinas contra la Idolatria por Michael Lopez,
5473 = 1713.

2142. " THE EXCELLENCIES OF THE HEBREWS." *Miss Lindo.*
By Isaac Cardozo. Translated from the Spanish by the late
E. H. Lindo.

2143. " NOMOLOGY " OF ISAAC ABOAB. *Miss Lindo.*
Translated from Spanish by the late E. H. Lindo.

2144. "THE WORDS OF A BELIEVING ISRAELITE."   *Miss Lindo.*
Translated from the French by the late E. H. Lindo.

2145. "MENORAH HAMAOR" OF ISAAC ABOAB.   *Miss Lindo.*
Translated by the late E. H. Lindo.

2146–8. THREE TRANSLATIONS.   *Jews' College.*
By E. H. Lindo.

2149. SAMARITAN BIBLE.   *B. Quaritch.*
Leviticus and Numbers (Lev. x. 15 to Num. v. 5), in the
Samaritan character, roy. 4°., MS., on vellum, 16 leaves,
bound in half morocco gilt, bound for Mr. Henry Duck-
worth, who had brought it from Nablús.   Sec. XVI.

2150. SAMARITAN PENTATEUCH.   *Laurence Oliphant.*
Fragment of the XV. Cent.

THE CRAWFORD COLLECTION.

Exhibited by the EARL OF CRAWFORD AND BALCARRES.

2155. CATALOGUE OF THE CRAWFORD COLLECTION OF SAMARITAN MSS.
Drawn up by Rev. A. Löwy, with minute details of all the
points of interest in each MS.   The short accounts in the
following list have been abstracted from these.   MS.
pp. 168.

2156. SAMARITAN PENTATEUCH.
Written 1211 (only three older ones are known in Europe).
Colophon: "I Abi Berachhathah, son of Ab-Sason, son of
Ab-Nefushah, son of Abraham Zeraftnaah, wrote this
Holy Law for the two brothers Tabiah and Yasaph, the
sons of So'adah, the son of Yitzchak, in the year 608 of
the dominion of Ishmael."   Epitaphs giving the further
history of the scroll.

2157. SAMARITAN PENTATEUCH.
Parchment, 220 pp.   Written 1328.   Accompanied by
Arabic version (unedited).   Epigraphs giving the succes-
sive purchasers of the codex.

2158. SAMARITAN PENTATEUCH.
Paper, 358 pp.   Probably Egyptian.   With Arabic version
similar to preceding number.

2159. SAMARITAN GENESIS.
Fragments.   Vellum, 72 pp. 4to.   Gen. xxv. 30 to Exodus
i. 15.   Epigraph giving history of the MS.   Earlier than
XV. Cent.

2160 SAMARITAN PENTATEUCH.
Fragments.   From various codices.

2161. SAMARITAN GENESIS.
Fragments   Octavo, 31 leaves.

2162. SAMARITAN PENTATEUCH.
Fragments.   12mo.   From various codices.

2163. THEOLOGICAL ESSAYS (SAMARITAN).
Paper. 4to., 55 pp. By the Shikeh Ghazâl ben Ad-Davaiek in 1748.

2164. THEOLOGICAL AND HISTORICAL TREATISES (SAMARITAN).
Fol. 1 to 229, on Laws of Killing Animals by Abu'l Hassan Az-zuri; 230 to 259, History of Israelites.

2165. THEOLOGICAL AND HISTORICAL TREATISES (SAMARITAN).
Fol. 1 to 229, various points of interest; 230 to end, History of Israelites.   In Arabic.

2166. LIFE OF MOSES (SAMARITAN).
Paper. Fol., 60 leaves. Floral ornaments in red. This work is frequently referred to by Samaritans in their communications with European scholars.   Dated 1748.

2167. SABBATH AND FESTIVAL PRAYERS (SAMARITAN).
Paper. 4to., 317 pp. Written 1209. With Arabic version (in Samaritan letters) of the prayers.

2168. PRAYERS FOR NEW MOON (SAMARITAN).
Paper. 2 sheets. Dated 1277.

2169. PASSOVER PRAYERS (SAMARITAN).
Paper. 4to., 57 pp.

2170. PILGRIMAGE PRAYERS (SAMARITAN).
Paper. 4to., pp. 186. Prayers for pilgrimage to Mt. Gerizim.   Some of the poems are Arabic.

2171. LITURGY (SAMARITAN).
Paper. 4to., pp. 55. Written 1757.

2172. PRAYERS IN TIME OF DROUGHT (SAMARITAN).
Paper. 4to. Written 1724.

2173. LITURGY (SAMARITAN).
Paper. 4to., pp. 276. Miscellaneous poems and prose. Dated 1869.

2174. LITURGY (SAMARITAN).
Paper. 8vo., pp. 160. Written 1762.

2175. PRAYERS FOR BIRTH AND MARRIAGE (SAMARITAN).
By Abd Alah ben Shelamah and Sa'd Alah ben Zedakah the Cathari. Paper. XIX. Cent.

2176. PASSOVER RITUAL (SAMARITAN).
Written by Amran the priest in Shechem, 1822. Paper. Small 8vo., pp. 125.

2177. Treatise on Astrology (Samaritan).
Paper. Fol., 52 leaves. Written 1842.

2178. Calendar (Samaritan).
Paper. Fol., 155. Calendar from 1689 to 1785, with full
astronomical directions. Also record of tradition that
England is the home of the *Bene Mushe* (children of
Moses), kinsmen of the Samaritans.

2179. Calendar (Samaritan).
Fol., pp. 18. Written in 1750.

2180. Calendar (Samaritan).
Paper, pp. 16. Bound in original covers.

2181. Calendar (Samaritan).
Paper, pp. 18. Written in 1724.

2182. Astronomical Table (Samaritan).

2183. Koheleth (Ecclesiastes).
Vellum, 12 inches. At end chapter in Hebrew: This
Koheleth I David son of Israel wrote in Jerusalem, A.M.
5314 = A.D. 1554.

2184. Hagada (Service for Passover).
Folio, 52 pp., profusely illuminated from fol. 36 onwards
with tinted arabesques intertwined with Hebrew texts.
Poems by Berachya Halevi, Jehuda Habir, and others,
the titles enclosed in illuminated squares, Italian,
xv. Cent. Bound Italian in dark brown calf with
green calf inlaid in centre.

2185. Hagada (Service for Passover).
Small quarto, richly illuminated. Commentary at side
enclosed in grotesques of men, beasts, birds and fishes.
Bound in embossed leather. German. xiii. Cent.

2186. Migillah (Scroll of Esther).
Sheepskin, 10 inches. Silver handle with crown at top.

2187. Megillah (Scroll of Esther).
Sheepskin, 20 inches.

2188. Megillah (Scroll of Esther).
Sheepskin, 8 inches.

2189. Megillah (Scroll of Esther).
Parchment, with coronets, 10 inches high.

2190. Megillah (Scroll of Esther).
Illuminated with vignettes characteristic of the columns
over which they are placed. Arabesques between each
column. Written 1511, in Italy, where it formed an
heirloom of a Jewish family, at first in Ferrara, then in
Bologne; 11 inches, parchment.

b.—**BOOKS.**

2191. PRAYER BOOK. *M. N. Adler, M.A.*
Bound in silver.

2192. PENTATEUCH, SPANISH, 1691. *Miss Brandon.*
Bound in tortoiseshell and silver.

2193. SPANISH PRAYER BOOK, 1692. *Miss Brandon.*
Bound in tortoiseshell and silver.

2194. HEBREW PRAYER BOOK, 1728. *Miss Brandon.*
Bound in tortoiseshell and silver.

2195. DAILY AND FESTIVAL PRAYERS, AND FIVE BOOKS OF MOSES,
5387 = 1627. *J. de Castro.*
Bound in tortoiseshell, gold edges, and silver clasps.

2196. PSALMS. *Benjamin L. Cohen.*
A.M. 5486. Bound in tortoiseshell.

2197. PENTATEUCH AND HAPHTAROTH. *Benjamin L. Cohen.*
A.M. 5506. Bound in tortoiseshell.

2198. PRAYER BOOK. *H. Guedalla.*
Bound in tortoiseshell and gold. Spanish, A.M. 5429 =
1668.

2199. SPANISH TRANSLATION OF PENTATEUCH. *F. D. Mocatta.*
Bound in tortoiseshell and gold.

2200. PRAYER BOOK. *F. D. Mocatta.*
Bound in tortoiseshell and gold.

2201. DAILY AND FESTIVAL PRAYER BOOKS. *G. di R. Moro.*
Two vols. Bound in silver. Italian *Minhag.*

2202. PRAYER BOOK. *S. J. Phillips.*
Mounted in silver. Amsterdam, 1735.

2203. PRAYER BOOKS. *L. de Rothschild.*
In silver covers.

2204. CHINESE HEBREW PENTATEUCH. *M. N. Adler, M.A.*
Facsimile on rice paper of a portion of the Pentateuch, used
by the Chinese Jews at Kae fung foo.

2205. נתינה לגר *Dr. N. M. Adler, Chief Rabbi.*
Commentary on Onkelos' Chaldaic Paraphrase of the Pentateuch. 5 vols. Wilna, 1872.

2206. BIBLIA HEBRAICA. *Robert Browning.*
Four vols. Formerly belonging to Bishop Berkeley, whose
signature, with the motto "non sibi sed toli," together
with the date June 20, 1750, is prefixed to each volume.
Formerly in constant use by Elizabeth Barrett Browning.

2207. BIBLIA HEBRAICA. *Robert Browning.*
Two vols. 4to., without points, belonging to and annotated by Elizabeth Barrett Browning.

2208. PASSOVER HAGADA. *J. de Castro.*
With Map of Palestine in Hebrew, and coloured plates. Amsterdam, 1695.

2209. BIBLE. *Philip Falk.*
English. In original binding. Translation of the Psalms versified with music according to the old notation. Imprinted at London, 1598.

2210. MACHZOR. *Rev. S. M. Gollancz.*
London, 5532.

2211. PENTATEUCH. *H. Guedalla.*
Originally from Royal Library, Paris. Arms of Duke of Sussex, from whose library it was bought. A.M. 5506 = A.D. 1745. 8 vol.

2212. "THE WAY OF FAITH." *Prof. R. Meldola, F.R.S.*
Translated from the Hebrew of Raphael Meldola by David Meldola. 1848.

2213. HAGADA. *B. Quaritch.*
Passover Service, printed for the use of German and Italian Jews in Hebrew characters, folio, with a profusion of pictorial woodcuts and many elegant woodcut borders in olive morocco, super extra, gilt edges. Mantua, 5328 = 1568.

The instructions in the margin are in the German language, although in Hebrew characters. In one of the woodcuts is depicted the massacre of the Jewish children in order to prepare a bath of children's blood for Pharaoh, for whom this had been prescribed as a cure for the leprosy under which he suffered.

2214. MACHZOR. *B. Quaritch.*
In Hebrew. 12mo. Printed in black and gold upon vellum, blue morocco. Boloniia, 1537.

2215. MASHAL HA-KADMONI. *B. Quaritch.*
By Isaac ben Salomon ben Sahula, edited by Meir ben Jacob Franzoni: a work consisting of proverbial phrases in rhyme, illustrated by prose fables in Hebrew, small 4to., numerous woodcuts of talking animals and other facetious designs, somewhat in the style of Æsop and the Septem Sapientes, bound in hogskin, stamped with portraits and arabesques in compartments, and the arms of Saxony, from the Sunderland library. Venice, about 1560.

Bound along with three other rare Hebrew pieces: Shevil Amunah, Trent 1559; Shaar ha-Shamayim (the Cabbalistic *Porta Coelorum*), *Venet*, 1547, Evronoth, a Hebrew Calendar, Trent, 1561.

2216. SCHUDT'S " JÜDISCHE MERKWURDIGKEITEN." *H. M. Schiff.*

c.—INSCRIPTIONS, ETC.

2217. TOMBSTONE INSCRIPTION. *I. Loeb.*
At Vienne, in Dauphiné. Photograph. Chwolson, *Corp.* 179.

2218. TOMBSTONE INSCRIPTION. *I. Loeb.*
At Greffeuille, near Arles. Photograph. *Ibid.* 180.

2219. TOMBSTONE INSCRIPTION. *I. Loeb.*
Of Arles. Photograph.

2220. TOMBSTONE. *I. Loeb.*
At Leon. Photograph. Dated 1100. *Revue* iii. 139.

2221. TOMBSTONE INSCRIPTIONS. *I. Loeb.*
Two, at Corunna. Photographs. *Revue* vi. 118.

2222. RECEIPT. *I. Loeb.*
Given at Donge (Loire inférieure). Photograph. *Revue,*
No. 27.

2223. HEBREW LEDGER. *I. Loeb.*
From Vesoul. Facsimile page. Original records, transac-
tions of Jewish merchants of XIV. Cent. See *Revue des
Études juives,* No. 16.

2224. DOCUMENT. *I. Loeb.*
From Montorio in Leon. Photograph. *Revue,* No. 8, p. 227.

2225. DOCUMENT. *I. Loeb.*
From Leon. Photograph. *Ibid.* 230.

2226. SPANISH DOCUMENTS, 1296–1392. *I. Loeb.*
Six. Photographs. *Revue,* tome x.

2227. PORTRAIT OF ROVEN SALAMO. *I. Loeb.*
A Spanish Jew. About 1420. See *Revue des Études juives,*
No. 12, p. 268.

2228. HEBREW SIGNATURES. *I. Loeb.*
Affixed to a Spanish document. Photograph.

2229. VALENCE JEWRY. *I. Loeb.*
Two manuscript plans. *Revue,* No. 28.

2230. VIEWS OF CARPENTRAS. *I. Loeb.*
Carpentras Synagogue. Plan. Two photographs.

2231. JEWRY GATE. *I. Loeb.*
Carpentras. Photograph. *Revue,* tome xii.

2232. MAP OF CARPENTRAS. *I. Loeb.*
Showing situation of Jewry, 1276. Photograph.

2233. DECREE OF CARPENTRAS MUNICIPALITY. *I. Loeb.*
Relating to Jews. Photograph.

L

2234. JEWRY GATE.   *I. Loeb.*
Malaucene.   (Vaucluse.)   Two photographs.   *Revue* xii.
164.

2235. GERMAN CHARTER.   *I. Loeb.*
Two photographs.

2236. DOCUMENT FROM PISEK, 1693.   *I. Loeb.*
Original, with Jewish seals.

2237. SHOPHAR, SKETCH OF.   *I. Loeb.*
From Strasburg Museum.   Photo.

2238. INSCRIPTION FROM HAGENAU SYNAGOGUE.   *I. Loeb.*

2239. MOSAIC OF HAMAM LIF.   *I. Loeb.*
In Jewish Synagogue.   See *Revue des Études juives.*

2240. CHURCH OF EL TRANSITU, TOLEDO.   *Rev. Dr. H. Adler.*
Formerly a Synagogue.   Photograph.

2241. CHURCH OF SANTA MARIA LA BLANCA AT TOLEDO.
Rev. Dr. H. Adler.
Formerly a Synagogue.   Photograph.

2242. HEBREW INSCRIPTION.   *A. Phillips.*
From the Old Synagogue of the Transitu, Toledo.

2243. A PIECE OF STUCCO FROM EL TRANSITU, TOLEDO.
Albert Phillips.

2244. GRAVE STONES.   *Rev. J. T. Fowler.*
Rubbings and facsimiles of Hebrew gravestone inscriptions
from Worms and Aden.

2245. GRAVE STONES.   *Rev. J. T. Fowler.*
Four rubbings from Worms, some from the Rashi Synagogue
in that city.

2246. GRAVE STONES.   *Rev. J. T. Fowler.*
Six paper squeezes from Jerusalem.

2247. GRAVE STONES.   *Rev. J. T. Fowler.*
Paper squeezes from Jerusalem.

2248. MAP OF THE HOLY LAND.   *Samuel Funkenstein.*
Printed on white satin, with names of places in Hebrew,
English and French.   A similar map is in the possession
of H.R.H. the Prince of Wales.

d.—TEMPLE.

2249. MODEL OF TEMPLE OF SOLOMON.   *J. W. McKinnon.*
Designed from descriptions in Ezekiel and Kings on a scale
of 1 in. to 5 ft. and modelled by Messrs. Bartlett, showing
section of the Courts of the Separate Place, of the Great
Altar, of the Priests, and the outer or Great Court.   The
Temple itself is composed of Porch, Holy Place, and Holy
of Holies; side chambers and galleries.   The plan only
exhibits the north-west quarter of the Temple precincts.

2250. VESSELS FOR MODEL.   *J. W. McKinnon.*
Including Altar of Burnt Offerings, the Brazen Sea, ten
Lavers, Golden Altar of Incense, ten Lamp Stands, ten
Tables for Shew Bread, Ark of the Covenant, two Great
Cherubims, two pillars of brass (called " Jachin and
Boas "). The arrangement of the Holy Place and Holy
of Holies is shown separately, as also the priests' chambers
at back of the latter on the west side.

2251. BIRD'S-EYE VIEW OF TEMPLE.   *Messrs. Bartlett.*

2252. PLANS OF MODEL OF TEMPLE.   *Messrs. Bartlett.*
Four sheets of working drawings for figures and vessels
shown in Mr. McKinnon's model of Temple.

2253. VEIL OF HOLY OF HOLIES.   *Messrs. Bartlett.*
Design from which the veil in the model was made.

2254. INSTRUMENTS USED IN THE TEMPLE.   *W. McKinnon.*
Nine coloured drawings of instruments supposed to be used
in Temple.

2255. INCENSE BURNERS.   *L. de Rothschild.*
Three models of Temple incense burners by Bartlett.

e.—PALESTINE EXPLORATION FUND.

2256. WESTERN PALESTINE.   *Palestine Exploration Fund.*
Map, with the water basins.

2257. WESTERN PALESTINE.   *Palestine Exploration Fund.*
Map. Scale of 1 in. to a mile. Ordnance Survey.

2258. HEAD OF STATUE OF HADRIAN. *Palestine Exploration Fund.*
Supposed to have been the one that caused the last revolt
under Bar-Cochab.

2259. CASE OF SMALL ANTIQUITIES, ANCIENT LAMPS, &c.
                                        Palestine Exploration Fund.

2260. CASE OF POTTERY.   *Palestine Exploration Fund.*

2261-2263. SARCOPHAGI.   *Palestine Exploration Fund.*
Three.

2264. SLAB.   *Palestine Exploration Fund.*
From Jewish cemetery at Joppa.

2265. MOABITE STONE.   *Palestine Exploration Fund.*
Cast. The celebrated inscription of King Mesha of Moab.
The earliest long inscription in the " Phœnician " alpha-
bet, the parent of all the alphabets of Europe.

2266. SILOAM INSCRIPTION.   *Palestine Exploration Fund.*
 Cast. Found in 1881. Describes the process by which
 two bands of workmen contrived to make the mines meet
 in which the waters of Siloam were conveyed inside the
 walls of Jerusalem.

2267. BOUNDARY STONE OF GEZER.   *Palestine Exploration Fund.*
 Discovered by M. Clermont-Ganneau. Determined the
 boundary within which homicides were protected by the
 law of sanctuary. One of the few Biblical relics in
 existence.

2268. SKETCHES.   *Palestine Exploration Fund.*
 By Captain Conder.

2269. DRAWINGS.   *Palestine Exploration Fund.*

2270. VASE.   *Palestine Exploration Fund.*
 Of Herodian period, found near Jerusalem, supposed to be
 work of a prentice hand.

f.—SANDEMAN COLLECTION.

2271. IVORY PEN.   *Mrs. G. G. Sandeman.*
 For cuneiform writing (?).

2272. FRAGMENT OF STONE.   *Mrs. G. G. Sandeman.*
 From hanging gardens of Babylon.

2273. FRAGMENT.   *Mrs. G. G. Sandeman.*
 From Temple of Belus (Babel). Cardamon wood.

2274. NINEVITE SCULPTURE.   *Mrs. G. G. Sandeman.*
 A prisoner (Jewish?) seized by the throat.

2275. NINEVITE SCULPTURE.   *Mrs. G. G. Sandeman.*
 Male and female figures facing to right.

2276. CUNEIFORM INSCRIPTION.   *Mrs. G. G. Sandeman.*
 Framed in wood.

2277. BRICK.   *Mrs. G. G. Sandeman.*
 From Tower of Babylon.

2278. BRICK.   *Mrs. G. G. Sandeman.*
 Vitrified, from Birs Nimroud. Inscription, "Nebuchad-
 nezzar, eldest son of Nebupnlasar, King of Babylon."

2279. ENAMELLED BRICKS.   *Mrs. G. G. Sandeman.*
 One blue and yellow, from ruined palace of Belshazzar,
 where he is supposed to have held his last banquet.

2280. ENAMELLED TILE.   *Mrs. G. G. Sandeman.*
 Fragment from Temple of Ossar.

2281. DIVINING BOWL.   *Mrs. G. G. Sandeman.*
 Earthenware bowl from the time of Captivity. Probably
 used by Jews for the cure of disease. Dug out of ruins
 of Babylon.

2282. DIVINING BOWL. *H. Rassam.*
Earthenware, much chipped. Chaldee inscription, probably intended for medicinal charm.

2283. DIVINING BOWL. *H. Rassam.*
Earthenware, from Babylon, used for cure of disease. Letters very faint, but can be brought out by slight wetting.

g.—SEALS AND RINGS.

2284. SEAL. *W. H. Cohen.*
Oval, silver, with inscription.

2285. SEAL. *W. H. Cohen.*
Oval, cornelian, with man's head and initial I. C.

2286. SEAL. *W. H. Cohen.*
Round, brass, with Hebrew inscription. Believed to be cut by Joseph Cohen of Bielefeld, Charleston, S.C., and London at end of XVIII. Cent.

2287. SEAL. *Dr. John Evans, F.R.S.*
Hebrew inscription משה ארי בר מרדכי כ"ץ with representation of hands of the Cohamin, a crown and figures.

2288. SEAL. *Dr. John Evans, F.R.S.*
Brass. Inscription : משה כהרכ מדורו אליעזר זצ"ל.

2289. SEAL. *G. L. Lyon*
Bronze. Inscription יוכבד בת דוד around the figure of a horse.

2290. SEAL. *S. A. Samson.*
With white cornelian handle, the signet engraved in Jerusalem, with Hebrew inscription.

2291. SAPPHIRE RING. *Dr. H. Adler, Delegate Chief Rabbi.*
Inscription שמע ישראל "Hear, O Israel" (Deut. vi. 4).

2292. RING. *M. Linzburg.*
Silver, with Hebrew inscription.

2293. LADY'S GOLD SIGNET RING. *Leopold Loewenthal.*
Cornelian; three diamonds each side. Engraved with Hebrew inscription and representation of Sabbath lamp.

2294. RING. *S. Newman.*
Gold, set with a cluster of carbuncles; filigree ornament on the shank. Found while excavating at Jerusalem. XVI. Cent.

2295. SIGNET RING. *S. J. Phillips.*
Sapphire and gold; stone engraved with a stag, bird, grapes, &c. XVII. Cent.

IV.—COINS AND MEDALS.

THERE are, of course, no Anglo-Jewish coins; but it seemed natural that in our Exhibition some of the pieces referring to the History of the Jews in the Holy Land should find a place, and the result has been that a very creditable selection of Jewish coins has, by the kindness of the respective owners, been obtained from some of the best collections, and is being displayed within these walls.

It had been suggested that in connection with our own Loan Collection a short resumé should be given by me on the subject of the Jewish Coinage in general; and while, on the one hand, admitting the difficulty of compressing much elaborate detail into the few pages allowed to me for that purpose, I must, on the other hand, acknowledge the obligations under which I am to the authors of the various works and papers from which so much of my material is necessarily derived.

Mr. Frederic W. Madden, in his *History of the Jewish Coinage* (B. Quaritch, 1864), of which virtually a Second Edition is contained in the *International Numismata Orientalia*, vol. ii. (Trübner & Co., 1881), has made the subject peculiarly his own, and I am also indebted to him for some hints concerning this short paper. Other authors who have been and may be consulted with advantage are the Abbé Cavedoni (*Numismatica Biblica*, Modena, 1849 and 1850); Monsieur F. de Saulcy (*Recherches sur la Numismatique Judaïque*, Paris, 1854, and *Numismatique de la Terre Sainte*, Paris, 1874); Dr. Levy, of Breslau (*Geschichte der Jüdischen Münzen*, Breslau, 1862); Dr. Eugen Merzbacher ("Die Zeitrechnung der Sekel," in the *Zeitschrift der Numismatik*, 1878, vol. v., &c. &c.); Mr. Reginald S. Poole (article on "Money" in Dr. Smith's *Dictionary of the Bible*); and Dr. John Evans, a leading member of our Council, who not only has skilfully criticised Monsieur Saulcy's work, but has as ably dealt with other questions connected with the Jewish Coinage in the pages of the *Numismatic Chronicle*, and in which are also to be found scattered papers by the Revs. H. C. Reichardt (one of our most enterprising collectors), Churchill Babington, S. S. Lewis and H. J. Rose.

Among so many authors it may be assumed that there has not been a want of controversial discussion, but the limits assigned to me do not enable me to enlarge upon any disputed points, and I will now give a brief outline of the subject, leaving those whom it may interest to consult for fuller information and instruction the various authorities to whom I have referred.

The earliest medium of exchange in use among the Jews was uncoined silver, which passed by weight and not by tale. The word "shekel" (שקל),

which signifies " weight," is an evidence of this, and all the passages in the Pentateuch in which shekels or silver pieces are mentioned, refer to pieces weighed out, probably in the shape of ingots, and not to coined money or pieces struck under authority. It was an age of barter, and the currency question had not yet arisen.

After the return from Babylon gold talents and drams were also in use, as will be seen by reference to Ezra (viii. 25–27), but these again were divisions of weight and not of coined money.

The famous edict of Cyrus, King of Persia, authorizing the return to Jerusalem, was dated A.M. 3224 (B.C. 536), but our first record of actual coined money of the Jews dates only from the first year of Simon Maccabaeus (A.M. 3617, B.C. 143), or, according to Dr. Eugen Merzbacher, two years later, when the official era of the Government of Simon commenced.

The authority to the Jews to coin money was conferred upon them by Antiochus VII, Sidetes, in his grant of privileges addressed to Simon, containing the words, "I give thee leave also to coin money for thy country with thine own stamp;" but seeing that this edict was probably issued when the Syrian king was staying at Rhodes, Simon appears to have coined money in his first official year without authority.

The following is a synopsis of the periods during which were struck such pieces as can fairly be treated as coining within the scope of our Exhibition and of this paper :—

(I.) Maccabaean or Asmonaean family, A.M. 3617–3723 (B.C. 143–37).

(II.) Idumaean or Herodian Princes, A.M. 3723 to perhaps 3860 (B.C. 37–A.D. 100 ?).

(III.) Roman Procurators of Judaea, who governed it as a Roman Province during the ostensible reigns of some of the last-mentioned princes, A.M. 3766–3826 (A.D. 6–66).

(IV.) First revolt of the Jews under the leadership of Eleazar, son of Ananias; Eleazar, son of Simon; John of Gischala; Simon, son of Gamaliel; and Simon, son of Gioras, A.M. 3826–3830 (A.D. 66–70).

(V.) Coins struck in Palestine and at Rome, commemorating the capture of Jerusalem, A.M. 3830 (A.D. 70), and

(VI.) Second revolt of the Jews under Simon Barcochab, A.M. 3892–3895 (A.D. 132–135).

Of the money coined at these different periods I will now treat seriatim.

(I.) Maccabaean or Asmonaean family. The princes of this family who struck pieces for current use were Simon Maccabaeus (son of Mattathias), his son John Hyrcanus, Judas Aristobulus and Alexander Jannaeus (sons of John Hyrcanus), and Alexander II. and Antigonus (sons of Alexander Jannaeus and his wife Alexandra). In addition to these some very rare small copper coins are ascribed to Alexandra, the wife of Alexander Jannaeus, on the strength of the occurrence of ΒΑΣΙΛΙΣ (for ΒΑΣΙΛΙΣΣΑΣ, which in pure Attic would be ΒΑΣΙΛΕΙΑΣ) upon these pieces. One rare piece is also attributed to her son John Hyrcanus II.

Simon Maccabaeus coined shekels of his 1st, 2nd, 3rd, 4th, and 5th years, and probably also half-shekels of the same years; at present no half-shekel of the year 5 has made its appearance. The shekel of the 5th year was until lately unique in the collection of the Rev. S. S. Lewis, who exhibits it; but another was recently purchased in Paris by Mr. W. Talbot Ready, of 55 Rathbone Place, W., to whom I am much indebted for labelling and arranging, under my direction, the coins exhibited. This piece is now in the National Collection. Shekels of the 4th year were very rare indeed, until a recent find of some hundreds of shekels and half-shekels near Jerusalem, succeeding the previous but much smaller trouvaille near Jericho, materially diminished their rarity, but the half-shekel of that year (of which a specimen is also in the cabinet of Rev. S. S. Lewis), still continues to be excessively rare.

All known authentic Jewish coins bear inscriptions in old Hebrew (Hebreu archaique) or Samaritan characters; the later Syro-Chaldaean or square Hebrew letters are positively unknown on them, and any piece or coin, therefore, so inscribed may be at once determined to be a forgery or concoction. I find it convenient, however, to refer to inscriptions in the modern characters, owing partly to the difficulty in obtaining the necessary type, and partly to my desire to make the subject more intelligible to the general student.

The shekel has on the obverse a cup or chalice, with the inscription שקל ישראל (Shekel of Israel) above the number of the year, א for 1, ב for 2, &c., with (except in the case of the first year) a ש (for שנת, year) preceding it. On the reverse is a triple lily or hyacinth, or, according to some, the budding rod of Aaron,* with the legend ירושלם קדשה (Holy Jerusalem). After the first year, the name of the city, on both the shekels and half-shekels, is spelt ירושלים. The standard weight of the shekel is 220 grains, and the value in English money about 2s. 8d.

The half-shekel is similar, except that the inscription on the obverse is חצי השקל (half-shekel). Copper pieces, but only of the 4th year and including a copper shekel of that year, are also known. The copper shekel resembles those in silver; the other pieces bear the number of the year, together with designs of the palm-branch (Lulab) and citrons (Ethrogim), both sacred to the Feast of Tabernacles, and the legend לגאלת ציון (The redemption of Zion).

Of John Hyrcanus only copper pieces are known. His name is written יהוכן or יהוחן (Jehochanan) and יהונן (Jehonan), and the coins purport on the face of them to be issued by יהוחנן הכהן הגדול ראש החבר היהידים (Jehochanan, the High Priest and Prince of the Confederation of the Jews) with some slight variations.

Judas Aristobulus, whose name on his coins is יהודה (Judah), struck somewhat similar pieces in copper only, but these, owing to the shortness of his reign, are of extreme rarity.

Alexander Jannaeus was the first prince who adopted Greek inscriptions, as well as Hebrew legends, and on some of his pieces these are bi-lingual. In Hebrew, he is styled יהינתן המלך (the king Jehonathan); in Greek, ΑΛΕΞΑΝΔΡΟΥ ΒΑΣΙΛΕΩΣ (of the king Alexander). Flowers, anchors, palm-branches, &c., ornament his coins, which are known in copper only.

---

* "And behold the rod of Aaron for the house of Levi was budded and brought forth buds and bloomed blossoms and yielded almonds." Numbers xvii. 8.

The rare pieces ascribed to Alexandra, his widow, I have before referred to. There are several types of copper coins resembling those of Alexander Jannaeus, among which one unique piece may be ascribed to John Hyrcanus II., his son, and others, according to some numismatists, belong to Alexander II.; but, according to others, should await some more certain and final determination, the only consensus in opinion being that they were at all events struck before the reign of Antigonus.

This monarch was the last reigning prince of his race, and was probably the first king whom the Romans ever subjected to the disgrace of being executed with the axe. One series of copper coins of his reign is known, on which the inscription is bi-lingual. That in Greek reads ΒΑCΙΛΕΩC ΑΝΤΙΓΟΝΟΥ (of the king Antigonus), and that in Hebrew adds to his Hebrew name (מתתיה, Mattathias), the formula as before of "The High Priest and the Confederation of the Jews." One very rare type of his reign also bears the design of the seven-branched candlestick, which was taken by Titus, Emperor of Rome, from the Temple of Herod, and was borne in his triumph before him, as represented on the arch of Titus.

(II.) Idumaean or Herodian Princes. The founder of this race was Antipater, but the first of its members who bore regal power was the notorious Herod the Great, who had (among his ten wives) married Mariamne, the daughter of the Asmonaean Alexander II. Having regard to Herod's phil-Hellenic tendencies, it is not surprising to find that on his coins are Greek inscriptions only. During his reign and thenceforth, with the exceptions of the periods during the two Jewish revolts, only copper pieces were coined by Jewish princes. It is clear, however, that probably Roman denarii and Greek gold staters and silver pieces from time to time formed a portion of the currency of the land.

The devices on Herod's coins consist of vessels and tripods, probably in the nature of incense-burners, the pomegranate, the anchor, double cornu-copiae, helmets and other ornamental designs. The inscription is ΒΑΣΙΛΕΩΣ ΗΡΟΔΟΥ (of the King Herod), and on one rare piece is the monogram ☧ (for Τριχαλκων), which is another instance in addition to those already known in which the Christian monogram had, in a different signification, a pre-Christian origin.

The other Herodian princes who coined money were his sons Archelaus Antipas and Philip II. and the kings Agrippa I. and Agrippa II., the son and grandson respectively of Aristobulus, another son of Herod. Of Aristo-bulus we do not appear to have any numismatic record, and of all the others mentioned, the coins have Greek inscriptions and Greek characters only.

Herod Archelaus, son and successor of Herod the Great, is on the few coins existing which can be attributed to him, denominated ΗΡ or ѠΗΡ, clearly showing that he bore the same name as his father. He is the only Herodian prince, also, who and whose coins bear the title of Ethnarch (ΕΘΝΑΡΧΟΥ). His brother Antipas was in like manner styled on his coins ΤΕΤΡΑΡΧΟΣ (Tetrárch), and on these also his name appears as Herod. Many of these pieces were struck by the last-named prince at Tiberias, a city which had been built by him in honour of the Emperor Tiberius. Philip II., another brother, also coined as Tetrarch, and his pieces bear the heads of the

Emperors Augustus and Tiberius successively. A very rare piece of this reign is among the coins exhibited by Rev. Dr. Wright. It bears on the reverse the design of a Tetra-style temple, with the date L. IB. (year 12). Herod Agrippa I. coined as king (ΒΑΣΙΛΕΥΣ), with and without the busts and titles of the Roman Emperors Caligula and Claudius, under whose auspices he exercised his sway. Agrippa II., also, coined under the same title, with and without the busts and titles of the Emperors, who in his time were Nero, Vespasian, Titus, and Domitian.

(III.) Coins of the Roman Procurators of Judaea. These were struck in copper only, and always with Greek inscriptions and letters. The devices are the ear of corn, palm-tree, cornu-copiae diota or amphora (a two-handled vessel for wine, &c.), triple lily, lituus, or other ornamental designs. No representation was used which could be in any way offensive to Jewish ideas or customs, and therefore no images or symbols of living things occur as emblems, and in fact this forbearance on the part of the Procurators was carried further than by the later Herodian princes, as no coin is known of the former on which even the head of the reigning Emperor of Rome appears. The difference on this point between the two sets of rulers may be well explained by the studious servility of the princes in question on the one hand, and the no doubt stringent instructions on the other hand given from head quarters to the Procurators to avoid anything which might wound the susceptibilities of the people over whom they had so much difficulty otherwise in peaceably establishing their rule. This rule, however, became in other respects of so tyrannical a character as to have ultimately led to the active revolt of the Jews.

The following is a list of the Procurators dating from A.M. 3766–3826 (A.D. 6–66), i.e. during the reigns of the Emperors Augustus, Tiberius, Claudius and Nero.

(1.) Coponius.
(2.) Marcus Ambivius.
(3.) Annius Rufus.
(4.) Valerius Gratus.
(5.) Pontius Pilate.
(6.) Marcellus.
(7.) Marullus.
(8.) Cuspius Fadus.
(9.) Tiberius Alexander.
(10.) Ventidius Cumanus.
(11.) Claudius or Antonius Felix.
(12.) Porcius Festus.
(13.) Albinus, and
(14.) Gessius Florus.

Coins (all in copper) are known only of the first five of these, and of Claudius Felix. Of the last-mentioned Procurator there is one coin which is somewhat peculiar as bearing the name of the Emperor Nero on the obverse and of his brother Britannicus on the reverse, as Caesars, i.e. heirs presumptive to the purple. There is one copper coin also which may be attributed, though with some doubt, to the Procurator Marcus Ambivius.

(IV.) Coins struck under the First revolt of the Jews. Notwithstanding my expressed intention not to introduce matters of controversy into these few pages, it is well to admit that there is more contention as to what coins are to be referred to the First Revolt under Eleazar and others, and which to the Second Revolt under Simon Barcochab, than, perhaps, on any other subject connected with Jewish numismatics. Although there are many points of agreement, yet as to others there may never be any certain mode of final determination where, as Mr. Madden rightly observes, "there is so little to guide, so much to guess."

The First Revolt lasted four years, and I prefer on the whole to adopt the attributions of Dr. Levy and of Mr. Madden in respect of this period. On this basis, coins are known of Eleazar the Priest, son of Simon, in silver, which bear the device of a vase and a bunch of grapes, and on which he is styled אלעזר הכוהן (Eleazar the Priest), and the reverse inscription of which is שנת אחת לגאלת ישראל (First year of the redemption of Israel). Copper coins also occur with a bunch of grapes, as also the palm-tree, and with legends similar to those on the silver pieces. One rare silver coin, the authenticity of which was at one time under some suspicion, has the name of Eleazar on one side and that of Simon on the other.

Simon Nasi (נשיא, prince) the son of Gamaliel, also coined money, and bore the title referred to, with the authority of the Sanhedrin, on his coins, which occur only in copper, and are similarly inscribed to those of his predecessor. The devices are those of the vase, the palm-tree, vine-leaf, lyre, and other ornamental designs. The inscriptions on the coins of both Eleazar and Simon are in old Hebrew characters, but slightly varying in formation from those on the pieces of the Asmonaean princes. There is one fine and rare silver shekel, probably belonging to this period, which has on the obverse a representation of the Beautiful Gate of the Temple, with the inscription ירושלם and on the reverse the Ethrog and Lulab (citron and palm-branch), and the same inscription as on Eleazar's silver pieces.

(V.) The coins struck in Rome commemorating the capture of Jerusalem are those with the well-known legends of IVDÆA, IVDÆA CAPTA, IVDÆA DEVICTA, &c., and more properly belong to the province of Roman numismatics. It will suffice to state that they were struck in gold, silver, and brass, under Vespasian, Titus, and Domitian, and have the head of the Emperor on the obverse, and generally Judaea, mourning, seated under a palm-tree, on the reverse. Trophies and other accompaniments sometimes vary the design. Those struck in Palestine by the Roman Emperors to commemorate the same event mostly bear Greek inscriptions, and have generally on the reverse the legend ΙΟΥΔΑΙΑΣ ΕΑΛⲰΚΥΙΑΣ (Judaea Captured). Some, however, coined by Domitian, have Latin legends in the more usual Roman style.

(VI.) Coins struck during the Second Revolt of the Jews under the Roman Emperor Nerva, great indulgence was shown to the Jews, and the abuses connected with the collection of the special tax levied upon them were abolished. In commemoration of this concession, a large brass Roman coin has on the reverse a palm-tree and the legend FISCI IVDAICI CALVMNIA SVBLATA. During the reign of his successor Trajan, however, the chosen people again revolted, and the insurrection was quelled with great difficulty and only after much bloodshed on both sides. On Hadrian's accession he meditated rebuilding Jerusalem under the name of Aelia, and of dedicating the temple to Jupiter Capitolinus. He also promulgated stricter laws against the Jews, who once more burst into revolt under the leadership of Simon Barcochab (i.e. son of a star). It was during this revolt that the famous Rabbi Akiba, a zealous advocate of Simon, perished at the hands of the Romans, exclaiming while being torn into pieces with red-hot pincers, " Hear, O Israel, the Lord is our God, the Lord is One."

Simon issued coins with the old Hebrew characters, both in silver and copper. His silver shekels of the 1st and 2nd year are very rare, and both have the name of שמעון (Simon) on the obverse, with a representation, somewhat conventional in its form, of the Beautiful Gate of the Temple, and on the reverse an Ethrog and Lulab and לחרות ירושלם (The Deliverance of Jerusalem). A rare shekel of the 2nd year exhibited in the collection of the Rev. Churchill Babington has on the obverse a much more elaborate representation of the Beautiful Gate with the inscription ירושלם.

Simon's smaller silver coins are of numerous types, and were most often struck over denarii of Trajan and other Emperors. They have his name sometimes with and sometimes without a bunch of grapes on the obverse, and the design of a vase, lyre, palm-branch or two trumpets, with the usual legend " The Deliverance of Jerusalem" on the reverse. His copper pieces are of various sizes; the larger ones with the palm-tree and his name on the obverse, and a vine-leaf and " The Deliverance, &c.," on the reverse, the smaller with the same or similar inscriptions, and with varied designs of the palm-tree or branch, lyre, bunch of grapes, vase, &c.

After Simon's death, which took place on the capture of Bethar, Hadrian carried out his design of building a new city on the site of Jerusalem, and which thenceforth was called Aelia Capitolina, and became a Roman Colony. The Jews were practically excluded from the City, which issued its coins in the way usual among the Roman Colonies of the period.

The record of Jewish numismatics, pure and simple, may therefore be said to end here, and it will be perceived that the series of coins described is not a very long one. It may be added that, however interesting they may be from an historical point of view, the Jewish coins are, with one or two exceptions, far from being of artistic worth, and are generally (particularly in the case of the copper pieces) in an inferior state of preservation. The want of artistic design may with justice be attributed to the national objection against any representation of living forms or symbols, and which extended even to the representation of the head or bust of the reigning prince, a rule which was infringed only by the later Herodian Princes. A similar objection to the bust of the reigning authority appearing on the coins, but founded upon very different grounds, existed among all the ancient Greek nations until after Alexander's time, but the heads of divinities supplied instead in their case ample material for the artistic talents of Greek die—engravers whose skill at the highest period of their art has never been surpassed, or even equalled to this day.

In conclusion, I will only warn my readers against the numerous counterfeits of Jewish coins which exist, and on most of which the legends are, as

before stated, in square Hebrew characters, which never occur on genuine
pieces, and which afford most certain proof of forgery. One specimen of
such a forgery is among the pieces exhibited by myself, and is of such a
nature as hardly to be capable of deceiving the merest tyro in numismatic
science.

H. MONTAGU, F.S.A.,
Vice-President of the Numismatic Society of London.

Exhibited by LEOPOLD HAMBURGER, Esq. (Frankfurt-am-Main).
(Per H. MONTAGU, Esq., F.S.A.

SERIES A.—*Coins of* ASMONAEAN *and* IDUMAEAN *princes, of the* ROMAN
PROCURATORS, *and leaders of the* FIRST *and* SECOND REVOLTS, *&c.*

2301–4. COINS OF SIMON MACCABAEUS, 3617–3625.
2301. Half-shekel of the First Year. *Obv.* "Chatzi-ha-shekel"
(half-shekel) in early Hebrew characters around a cup.
Rev. "Jerusalem Kedoshah" around a triple-flowered
lily-stem.
2302. Shekel of the Third Year. *Obv.* "Shekel of Israel"
around a cup, above which date letter Gimel (year 3).
Rev. "Jerusalem-ha-Kedoshah" (Jerusalem the Holy)
around a triple-flowered lily stem.
2303. Quarter-shekel of the Fourth Year (bronze). *Obv.* "In
the Fourth Year, one quarter," round a lulab. *Rev.* "Redemption of Zion" around an ethrog.
2304. One-sixth of a shekel of the Fourth Year. *Obv.* "Redemption of Zion' around a cup. *Rev.* "Shenath Arba"
(year 4) around an ethrog, placed between two lulabs.

2305–9. EXAMPLES OF COUNTERFEITS OF SHEKELS OF SIMON MACCABAEUS.

2310, 11. BRONZE COINS OF ANTIOCHUS IV. (EPIPHANES).
Struck in Egypt about 3590. *Obv.* Laureate head. *Rev.*
ΒΑΣΙΛΕΩΣ . ΑΝΤΙΟΧΟΥ . ΘΕΟΥ . ΕΠΙΦΑΝΟΥΣ · around
an eagle.

2312, 13. BRONZE COINS OF JOHN HYRCANUS, 3625–3654.
Obv. "Cornucopiae." *Rev.* "Jehochanan Hakkohen Haggadol. Vecheber Hajehudim" (Johanan the High Priest
and the Confederation of the Jews). (No. 13 is similar,
but the reverse legend reads, ". . . Rash Vecheber Hajehudim" (Chief of the confederation of the Jews).)

2314. BRONZE COIN OF ANTIOCHUS VII. (SIDETES), 3622–3631.
Probably struck in Jerusalem. *Obv.* Flower. *Rev.* ΒΑΣΙ-
ΛΕΩΣ . ΑΝΤΙΟΧΟΥ . ΕΥΕΡΓΕΤΟΥ . and an anchor, the
Seleucid badge.

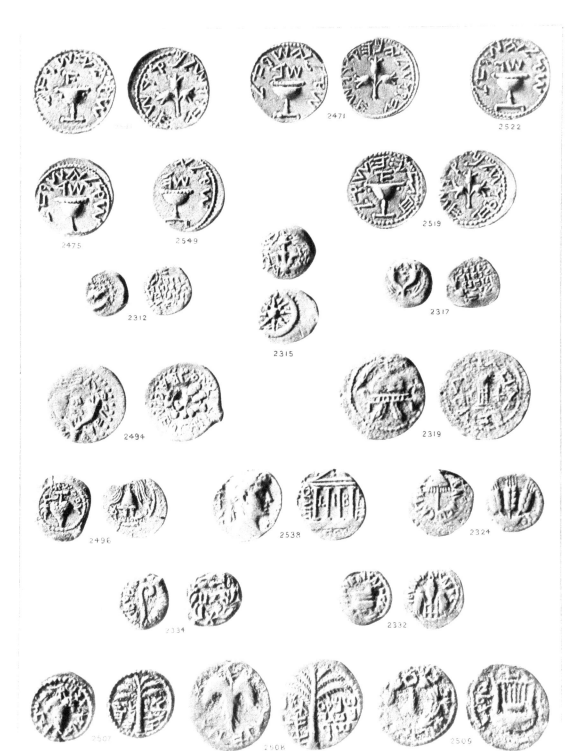

2315–17. BRONZE COINS OF ALEXANDER JANNAEUS, 3655–3682.
2315–16. *Obv.* "Jehonathan Hammelek" (Jonathan the King). *Rev.* ΒΑΣΙΛΕΩΣ . ΑΛΕΞΑΝΔΡΟΥ . around an anchor.
2317. Minted after his reconciliation with the Pharisees. *Obv.* cornucopiae and poppy-head. *Rev.* "Jehonathan Hakkohen Haggadol Vecheber Hajehudim" (Jonathan High Priest and the confederation of the Jews).

2318. BRONZE COIN ATTRIBUTED TO ALEXANDER I. OR II.
Obv. ΒΑCΙΛΕΩΣ . (ΑΛΕΞΑΝΔΡΟΥ) . around an anchor. *Rev.* Star of eight points, between which traces of letters.

2319, 20. BRONZE COINS OF HEROD THE GREAT.
2319. *Obv.* Helmet (?) *Rev.* ΒΑΣΙΛΕΩΣ . ΗΡΩΔΟΥ . around a tripod placed between the date letter L . Γ . (year 3), and *crux ansata.*
2320. *Obv.* Two cornucopiae. *Rev.* ΗΡΩ . ΒΑCΙ . (Herod the King) around an anchor.

2321–23. BRONZE COIN OF HEROD ARCHELAUS, 3756–3766.
2321–22. *Obv.* ΗΡΩΔΟΥ and bunch of grapes. *Rev.* ΕΘΝΑΡΧΟΥ below a crested helmet.
2323. *Obv.* ΗΡ. (Herod) and prow of ship. *Rev.* ΕΘΝ within a wreath.

2324, 25. BRONZE COINS OF HEROD AGRIPPA I., 3797–3804.
Obv. ΒΑCΙΛΕΩS . ΑΓΡΙΠΑ around an umbrella. *Rev.* The date letters L . S (year 6) and three ears of corn.

2326. BRONZE COINS OF HEROD, KING OF CHALCIS, 3801–3808.
The brother of Herod Agrippa I. *Obv.* ΒΑCΙΛ . ΗΡΩΔ . (The King Herod) and cornucopia. *Rev.* An eagle.

2327. BRONZE COIN OF HEROD AGRIPPA II., 3808–3860.
Struck under Nero. *Obv.* Name, title, and bust of Nero. *Rev.* ΕΠΙ . ΒΑCΙΛΕ . ΑΓΡΙΠΠ . ΝΕΡΩΝΙΕ within wreath.

2328. BRONZE COIN OF HEROD AGRIPPA II., 3808–3860.
Struck under Domitian. *Obs.* Name, title, and bust of Emperor. *Rev.* ΕΤ.ΚS . ΒΑCΙ . ΑΓΡΙΠΠΑ (year 26 of the King Agrippa).

COINS STRUCK BY THE PROCURATORS.

2329. BRONZE COIN STRUCK BY COPONIUS, PROCURATOR UNDER AUGUSTUS. 3766–3770.
Obv. Palm branch between ΚΑΙCΑΡΟC . *Rev.* Palm and date letters.

2330. BRONZE COIN STRUCK IN 3776 BY VALERIUS GRATUS, PROCURATOR UNDER TIBERIUS.
Obv. L . Γ . (year 3). *Rev.* ΙΟΥΛΙΑ (Jul a, mother of Tiberius) within a wreath.

2331. BRONZE COIN STRUCK IN 3776 BY VALERIUS GRATUS, PROCURATOR UNDER TIBERIUS.
Obv. TIBEPIOY . L . Γ . (year 3), cornucopiae. *Rev.* KAICAP within a wreath.

2332–35. BRONZE COINS STRUCK IN 3789–90 BY PONTIUS PILATE, PROCURATOR UNDER TIBERIUS.
2332, 33. *Obv.* TIBEPIOY . KAICAPOC . L . IS. (year 16). A covered vessel. *Rev.* IOYΛIA . KAICAPOC · around three ears of corn bound together.
2334, 35. *Obv.* TIBEPIOY . KAICAP around augural staff. *Rev.* L . IZ . (year 17) within wreath.

2336–38. BRONZE COINS STRUCK IN 3814 AND 3818 BY CLAUDIUS FELIX, PROCURATOR UNDER THE EMPERORS CLAUDIUS AND NERO.
2336. *Obv.* TI . KΛAYΔIOC . KAICAP . ΓEPM . L . IΔ . (year 14). Two palm branches, crosswise. *Rev.* IOYΛIA AΓPIΠΠINA within wreath.
2337. With names of the Caesars Nero Claudius and Britannicus. *Obv.* NEPω . KΛAY . KAICAP . around two shields placed crosswise over two spears. *Rev.* BPIT . KAI . L . IΔ (year 14) above and beneath a palm.
2338. *Obv.* L . Є . KAICAPOC . around palm. *Rev.* NEPωNOC . within wreath.

FIRST REVOLT OF THE JEWS, 3826–3830.

2339. BRONZE COIN STRUCK BY ELEAZAR THE HIGH PRIEST.
Obv. "Eleazar Hakkohen" beneath palm. *Rev.* "First year of the Redemption of Israel," cluster of grapes.

2339a. BRONZE COIN, PROBABLY ISSUED BY SIMON SON OF GIORAS.
Obv. "Jerusalem" below palm. *Rev.* "Lacheruth Jerusalem" around cluster of grapes.

2340. BRONZE COIN OF SIMON NASI, CHIEF OF THE SANHEDRIM.
Obv. Simon . . . . &c., around wreath enclosing palm. *Rev.* Lyre and inscription.

2341–43. BRONZE COINS STRUCK BY AUTHORITY OF THE SANHEDRIM.
Obv. "Shenath Shetaim" (year 2) around vase. *Rev.* "Cheruth Zion" (Deliverance of Zion) around vine-leaf. (*Obv.* of No. 2343 reads "Shenath Shelosh," and vase with cover.)

COINS STRUCK IN ROME WITH TYPES REFERRING TO JUDAEA.

2344. DENARIUS OF VESPASIAN.
Referring to the defeat of the First Revolt, 3830. *Obv.* Name, title, and bust of Emperor. *Rev.* IVDAEA . Judaea seated under trophy.

2345. ANOTHER DENARIUS.
Recording the same event. *Rev.* Judaea seated under palm.

2346. BRONZE COIN.
Referring to same. *Rev.* IVDAEA CAPTA . Judaea seated beneath trophy.

2347. BRONZE COIN BY THE EMPEROR TITUS.
Recording the same event as preceding. Struck in Judaea. *Obv.* Names, titles and bust. *Rev.* ΙΟΥΔΑΙΑΣ . ΕΑΛΥΚΥΙΑΣ. (Judea captured); Victory writing ΑΥΤ . ΚΑΙC . on shield.

2348. BRONZE COIN.
Recording the abolition of the Jewish tribute, by the Emperor Nerva in 3856. *Obv.* Names, titles and bust of Emperor. *Rev.* FISCI . IVDAICI . CALVMNIA . SVBLATA . Palm between S. C. (By consent of the Senate.)

2349. BRONZE COIN.
Recording the reduction of Armenia, &c., by Trajan in 3876. *Obv.* Names, titles and bust of Emperor. *Rev.* ARMENIA . ET . MESOPOTAMIA . IN . POTESTATEM . P . R . REDACTAE . Emperor and captives.

SECOND REVOLT OF THE JEWS, 3892–3895.

2350. SHEKEL OF SIMON BAR-COCHAB.
Struck in 3893. *Obv.* " Simon " around a tetrastyle temple with arched portal in the centre. *Rev.* " Year 2 of the Deliverance of Israel ;" ethrog and lulab.

2351. SILVER COIN.
Struck over a Roman Denarius. *Obv.* " Simon." *Rev.* " Deliverance of Israel, Year 2."

2352. BRONZE COINS OF SIMON BAR-COCHAB.
Obv. " Simon " below palm. *Rev.* " Deliverance of Jerusalem " and date letters around a vine leaf.

2353–2468. SERIES OF COINS.
Struck at local mints in Palestine and adjoining countries— Acca, Cæsarea, Nicopolis, Beth-Djiboin, Samaria (bronze coin of Domitian, 3846, with countermark of the X Legion, the Legion occupying Jerusalem), Jerusalem (*Rev.* Temple with figure of Astarte, also two dinars struck by caliphs in Jerusalem), Sichem, Samaria, Beth-Shen, Sepphoris, Baal-Gad, Tiberias, Gadava, Dium, Gaba, Hippus, Kennoth, Bostra, Ascalon, Gaza, Anthedon, Berytus, Heliopolis, Damascus, Rabbath-Ammon, Petra, Nabathean kings.

Exhibited by JOHN EVANS, ESQ., D.C.L., P.S.A., Treas. R. S.

SHEKELS AND HALF SHEKELS *struck during the government of* SIMON MACCABAEUS, 3617–3625.

2469. SHEKEL OF THE FIRST YEAR.
Obv. "Shekel of Israel," in early Hebrew characters around a cup, above which is the date-letter, an Aleph (year 1). *Rev.* "Jerusalem Kedoshah" (Jerusalem the Holy) around a triple-flowered lily stem.

2470. HALF-SHEKEL OF THE SAME YEAR.
The design is similar to that of the shekel, but the obverse legend reads, "Chatzi Ha-shekel" (half-shekel).

2471–76. SHEKELS AND HALF-SHEKELS OF THE SECOND, THIRD, AND FOURTH YEARS. ELECTROTYPE OF SHEKEL OF FIFTH YEAR.
The designs and legends are similar to the preceding pieces, excepting that the reverse legends read "Jerusalem-*ha*-Kedoshah," and that the date-letters are preceded by the initial letter of the word Shenath (year).

2477. QUARTER-SHEKEL OF THE FOURTH YEAR (COPPER).
Obv. "Shenath arba Raba" (in the Fourth Year—one quarter); two lulabs. *Rev.* "Ligullath Zion" (The Redemption of Zion) around an ethrog.

2478. SIXTH OF SHEKEL (?) OF THE FOURTH YEAR (COPPER).
Obv. Lulab between two ethrogs. Above, "Shenath arba" (in the Fourth Year). *Rev.* Cup, around which "Ligullath Zion" (Redemption of Zion).

2479. SIMILAR TO No. 2478.
⁎ The attribution of these copper coins to Simon Maccabaeus is not positively certain, but in the form of the letters and general treatment they approach nearer to those of his time than to any other period, The division of them into sixths is somewhat doubtful, on account of the great variance of weight found in the various specimens. sixths is somewhat doubtful,

COINS OF THE LATER MACCABAEAN PRINCES, &c.

2480–81. BRONZE COINS OF JOHN HYRCANUS, 3625–3654.
Obv. Two cornucopiae and poppy-head. *Rev.* "Jehochanan Hakohen Hagadol Vecheber Hajehudim" (John, High Priest, and the Community of the Jews).

2482–83. BRONZE COINS STRUCK IN JERUSALEM (?) BY ANTIOCHUS VII. (SIDETES) OF SYRIA, 3627, 3628.
Obv. A lily flower. *Rev.* ΒΑΣΙΛΕΩΣ . ΑΝΤΙΟΧΟΥ . ΕΥΕΡΓΕΤΟΥ · and dates ΑΠΡ . (181), or ΒΠΡ . (182). An anchor, the badge of the Seleucidae.

2484. BRONZE COIN OF ALEXANDER JANNAEUS, 3655–3682 (First coinage).
Obv. A flower, and "Jehonathan Hammelek" (Jonathan the King) in early Hebrew characters. *Rev.* ΒΑΣΙΛΕΩΣ ΑΛΕΞΑΝΔΡΟΥ around a circle enclosing an anchor.

2485–89. BRONZE COINS OF ALEXANDER JANNAEUS, 3655–3682 (Second coinage).
Struck after the reconciliation of the King with the Pharisees. *Obv.* Two cornucopiae and poppy-head. *Rev.* A wreath within |which "Jehonathan hakohen Hagadol Vecheber Hajehudim" (Jonathan Priest, and the Community (or Senate) of the Jews).

2490–93. BRONZE COINS STRUCK BY ALEXANDER JANNAEUS, 3655–3682, OR HIS GRANDSON ALEXANDER II., 3695–3711.
Obv. A star, between the rays of which, in early Hebrew characters, "Jehonathan Hammelek" (Jonathan the King). *Rev.* ΒΑΣΙΛΕΩΣ ΑΛΕΞΑΝΔΡΟΥ around an anchor.

2494. BRONZE COIN, ANTIGONUS (MATTATHIAS), BROTHER OF ALEXANDER II., 3720–3723.
Obv. Two cornucopiae, encircling which is the legend "Mattathiah Hakohen Hagadol Vecheber Hajchudim" (Mattathias the High Priest, and the Confederation of the Jews). *Rev.* ΒΑΣΙΛΕΩϹ ΑΝΤΙΓΟΝΟΥ around a wreath.

COINS OF THE HERODIAN OR IDUMÆAN PRINCES.

2495. BRONZE COIN OF HEROD THE GREAT, 3723–3756.
Obv. Two cornucopiae and a caduceus. *Rev.* ΒΑϹΙ . ΗΡΩ . around an anchor.

2496–97. BRONZE COINS OF HEROD ARCHELAUS, 3756–3766.
2496. *Obv.* Bunch of grapes, vine leaf, and stalk; above which ΗΡΩΔΟΥ . *Rev.* Plumed helmet, with cheek-pieces; below, a caduceus and ΕΘΝΑΡΧΟ[.Υ] .
2497. *Obv.* ΗΡ around the prow of a galley. *Rev.* ΕΘΝ in a wreath of laurel.

2498–99. BRONZE COINS OF HEROD AGRIPPA I., 3797–3804.
Obv. ΒΑϹΙΛΕωϹ . ΑΓΡΙΠΑ around a fringed umbrella. *Rev.* Three ears of corn and date-letters Ⳑ . Ϲ. (Year 6 = 3803).

COINS ISSUED BY THE ROMAN PROCURATORS OF JUDÆA.

2500–1. COINS STRUCK BY ANNIUS RUFUS, PROCURATOR UNDER AUGUSTUS, 3773, 3774.
Obv. ΚΑΙϹΑΡΟϹ by the sides of an ear of corn. *Rev.* Palm tree and date letters Ⳑ . Λ Θ (39), or Ⳑ . Μ . (40).

2502 Coin Struck by Pontius Pilate, Procurator under Tiberius, 3786–3796.
Obv. TIBEPIOC KAICAPOC . L . IS . (year 16). In the centre is a covered vessel, or simpulum. *Rev.* IOYΛIA KAICAPOC around three ears of corn bound together.

2503–6. Coins Struck by Claudius Felix, Procurator under Claudius and Nero, 3812–3820.
2503. *Obv.* TI . KΛAYΔIOC . KAICAP . ΓEPM . L . IΔ . around two crossed branches of palm. *Rev.* IOYΛIA · AΓPIΠΠINA . within a wreath.
2504. With names of the Caesars Claudius Nero, and Britannicus. *Obv.* NEPW KΛAY . KAICAP around two shields placed crosswise above two spears. *Rev.* BPIT . KAIC . L . IΔ . (year 14) written above and below a palm tree.
2505–6. Under Nero. (Struck 3819.) *Obv.* KAICAPOC . around a branch. *Rev.* NEPWNOC within a wreath.

FIRST REVOLT OF THE JEWS, 3826–3830.

2507. Bronze Coin issued by Eleazar, the High Priest, 3826–3827.
Obv. "Shenath Achath Ligullath Israel" (year 1 of the Redemption of Israel), in early Hebrew characters, around a cluster of grapes. *Rev.* "Eleazar ha-cohen" (Eleazar the Priest), in similar characters placed below a palm.

2508. Bronze Coin issued by Simon Nasi, Chief of the Sanhedrim.
Obv. "Shenath Achath Ligullath Israel" around a vine leaf. *Rev.* "Shimoun Nasi Israel" (Simon, Prince of Israel) in similar characters placed below a palm.

2509. Bronze Coin issued by Simon Nasi.
Obv. "Simon Nasi . . . Israel" around a wreath enclosing a palm branch. *Rev.* ". . . Israel" around a five-stringed lyre.

2510–12. Coins issued by the Sanhedrim.
2510. Bronze coin dated in the Second Year. *Obv.* "Shenath Shetaim" (year 2) around a two-handled vase. *Rev.* "Cheruth Zion" (Deliverance of Zion) around a vine leaf.
2511–12. Bronze coins dated in the Third Year. *Obv.* "Shenath Shelosh" (year 3) around a two-handled vase with cover. *Rev.* Similar to No. 2510.

SECOND REVOLT OF THE JEWS, 3892–3895.

2513. Silver Coin issued by Simon Bar-Cochab.
Obv. "Lacheruth Jerusalem" (Deliverance of Jerusalem) around a three-stringed lyre. *Rev.* "Simon" around a cluster of grapes.

2514. BRONZE COIN ISSUED BY SIMON BAR-COCHAB.
Obv. "Lacheruth Jerusalem" around a vine leaf. *Rev.* "Simon" in field below a palm.

2515–17. BRONZE COINS.
With devices and inscriptions similar to No. 46.

Coins and Medals exhibited by H. MONTAGU, ESQ., F.S.A.

SHEKELS AND HALF-SHEKELS *struck during the government of* SIMON MACCABAEUS, 3617–3625.

2518. SHEKEL OF THE FIRST YEAR.
Obv. "Shekel of Israel," in early Hebrew letters, around a cup, above which is the date-letter, an Aleph (or 1). *Rev.* "Jerusalem Kedoshah" (Jerusalem the Holy) around a triple-flowered lily stem.

2519. HALF-SHEKEL OF THE SAME YEAR.
The design is similar to that of the shekel, but the obverse legend reads "Chatzi-ha-Shekel" (half the shekel).

2520–5. SHEKELS AND HALF-SHEKELS OF THE SECOND THIRD AND FOURTH YEARS.
The designs and legends are similar to the preceding pieces, excepting that the reverse legend reads "Jerusalem *ha*-Kedoshah," and that the date-letters are preceded by the initial letter of the word Shenath (year).

2526. BRONZE COIN STRUCK BY JUDAS ARISTOBULUS, 3654–3655.
Obv. Two cornucopiae and a poppy-head. *Rev.* "Jehudah," &c., in early Hebrew letters within a wreath.

2527. BRONZE COINS OF ALEXANDER II. (GRANDSON OF ALEXANDER JANNAEUS), 3695–3711.
Obv. ΒΑΣΙΛΕΩΣ. ΑΛΕΞΑΝΔΡΟΥ. around an anchor, the badge of the Selucidae. *Rev.* A star of eight points.

COINS STRUCK BY THE PROCURATORS OF JUDÆA.

2528. BRONZE COIN STRUCK IN 3789 BY PONTIUS PILATE, PROCURATOR UNDER TIBERIUS, 3786–3796.
Obv. ΤΙΒΕΡΙΟΥ. ΚΑΙϹΑΡΟϹ. L. IϹ. (year 16). A simpulum, or covered vase. *Rev.* ΙΟΥΛΙΑ. ΚΑΙϹΑΡΟϹ three ears of corn bound together.

2529–31. BRONZE COINS STRUCK IN 3814 AND 3819 BY CLAUDIUS FELIX, PROCURATOR UNDER CLAUDIUS AND NERO, 3812–3820.
2529. *Obv.* ΤΙ. ΚΛΑΥΔΙΟϹ. ΚΑΙϹΑΡ. ΓΕΡΜ.. L. ΙΔ. (year 14); two palm branches. *Rev.* ΙΟΥΛΙΑ. ΑΓΡΙΠΠΙΝΑ. written within a wreath.

2530. With names of the Caesars Nero Claudius and Britannicus. *Obv.* NEPѠ. ΚΛΑΥ. ΚΑΙCAP around two shields placed crosswise over two spears. *Rev.* ΒΡΙΤ . ΚΑΙC L . ΙΔ . (year 14); above and below a palm tree with fruits.

2531. With name of Nero, struck 3819. *Obv.* ΝΕΡѠΝΟC within a wreath. *Rev.* ΚΑΙCAPOC . . L . Є . (year 5) by the sides of a palm branch.

FIRST REVOLT, 3826–3830.

2532. Bronze Coin issued by authority of the Sanhedrim, 3828. *Obv.* "Shenath Shetaim" (year 2) in early Hebrew characters around a two-handled vase. *Rev.* "Cheruth Zion" (Deliverance of Zion) around a vine leaf.

2533. Counterfeit of a Shekel of Simon Maccabaeus. *Obv.* Vase, and "Shekel of Israel" in modern characters. *Rev.* Flowering rod, and "Jerusalem the Holy."

2534. Medal Commemorative of Asher Lemlein. Asher Lemlein, a fanatical German Jew living about 1500, professing to be gifted with inspiration, prophesied the advent of the Messiah in 1503. Becoming aware of his having prefixed too short a time for his prophecies, he stated in excuse that the people's sins had retarded the appearance of the Deliverer. He had many ardent supporters, and to one of these — of the family *dei Piatelli*—the production of this medal is attributed. The medal has a portrait, presumed to be that of the pretender himself, and is surrounded by a long Hebrew inscription, in which the initial letters of the words give, in the form of an acrostic, the name of "Benjamin, the son of Eli Beer," the particular member of the dei Piatelli to whom the production of this medal is ascribed. The reverse has an inscription in Latin of similar import to that on the obverse, and the date D . III . M . (1503).

2535. Broker's Medal of the City of London. This one was issued to the late Sir Moses Montefiore, Bart., after whose death it came into the possession of the exhibitor.

Exhibited by the Rev. Dr. W. Wright.

2536. Bronze Coin of Antiochus VII. (Sidetes) of Syria, struck in Jerusalem (?) between 3622–3631. *Obv.* Flower. *Rev.* ΒΑΣΙΛΕΩΣ . ΑΝΤΙΟΧΟΥ ΕΥΕΡΓΕΤΟΥ. an anchor, the badge of the Seleucidae.

2537. BRONZE COIN OF HEROD I. (THE GREAT), 3723–3756.
Obv. Macedonian buckler. *Rev.* ΒΑΣΙΛΕΩΣ . ΗΡΟΔΟΥ
Helmet with cheek-pieces; in field, *crux ansata*, and date
L . Γ. (year 3 = 3726).

2538. BRONZE COIN OF HEROD PHILIP II. UNDER AUGUSTUS.
Struck in 3768. *Obv.* ΚΑΙΣΑΡΙ . ΣΕΒΑΣΤΟΥ . head of
Augustus. *Rev.* ΦΙΛΙΠΠΟΥ . ΤΕΤ[ΡΑΡΧΟΥ]. around a
tetrastyle temple, between the columns of which the date
letters, L . ΙΒ. (year 12).

2539. BRONZE COIN OF HEROD AGRIPPA I.
Struck in 4003. *Obv.* Three ears of corn, and date S.L.
(year 6). *Rev.* ΒΑΣΙΛΕΩΣ ΑΓΡΙΠΑ . written around an
umbrella.

2540. BRONZE COIN OF ELEAZAR THE HIGH PRIEST.
Struck in 3826, during the First Revolt. *Obv.* Bunch of
grapes, and the legend "Shenath Achath Ligullath
Israel" (First Year of the Redemption of Israel), in
old Hebrew characters. *Rev.* Palm-tree, below which
"Eleazar Hak-kohen" (Eleazar the High Priest) in old
Hebrew characters.

Exhibited by the REV. S. S. LEWIS, M.A.

2541. SHEKEL.
Struck in the First Year of the government of Simon Maccabaeus, 3619. *Obv.* "Shekel of Israel" in early Hebrew
letters. The design, a cup, is supposed to represent the
vessel in which the manna was preserved in the Temple.
Rev. "Jerushalem kedoshah" (Jerusalem the Holy)
written in early Hebrew letters around a conventional
design representing the flowering rod of Aaron; above
is the date letter, an Aleph (or 1).

2542. HALF-SHEKEL.
Also of the First Year of Simon Maccabaeus. The design is
similar to the preceding coin, but the legend on the
obverse is " Chatzi-ha-Shekel " (half-shekel).

2543. SHEKEL OF THE SECOND YEAR OF SIMON MACCABAEUS. 3620.
As No. 1, but reading " Jerushalem ha-kedoshah " (Jerusalem the Holy); the date letter, Beth, is here preceded
by Schin, and is to be read as " Shenath Shetâim
(year 2).

2544. HALF-SHEKEL OF THE SECOND YEAR.
The types and legends as No. 2542, with the variations
given under No. 2543.

2545–48. SHEKELS AND HALF-SHEKELS OF THE THIRD AND FOURTH
YEARS OF SIMON MACCABAEUS, 3621, 3622.
The designs as Nos. 2543–44, differing only in the date letters.
The half-shekel of the Fourth Year is extremely rare.

2549. SHEKEL OF THE FIFTH YEAR OF SIMON MACCABAEUS, 3623.
The design, &c., is similar to the preceding coins, and differs
only in the date letter.
₊ This piece is of excessive rarity, only one other of this
year being known. No half-shekels with this date have
been found.

2550–51. SHEKELS OF SIMON BAR-COCHAB.
Struck between 3892–3895. *Obv.* "Lacheruth Jerushalem"
(Deliverance of Jerusalem) in early Hebrew characters;
in the centre is an ethrog and lulab. *Rev.* "Simon" in
early Hebrew characters. The design is a conventional
representation of the Temple, showing a tetrastyle
building, with an arched portal in the centre; above
is a star, supposed to refer to the name of *Bar-Cochab*
(son of a star).
₊ One of these coins is struck upon a tetradrachm of
Titus minted in Antioch, similar to No. 2552, and the
letters T. ΦΛΑVΙ (ΟΥΕΣΠΑΙΑΝΟΥ) are easily traced.
This is an important help in the attribution of these
coins to Bar-Cochab, as they have often been ascribed to
Simon ben Gioras, one of the leaders of the First Revolt.

2552. TETRADRACHM OF VESPASIAN AND TITUS, MINTED AT ANTIOCH
ABOUT 3840.
Obv. ΑΥΤΟΚΡΑΤ ΚΑΙΣΑ . ΟΥΕΣΠΑΖΙΑΝΟΥ. laureate head
of Vespasian to l. *Rev.* T . ΦΛΑVΙ . ΟΥΕΣΠ . ΚΑΙΣ .
ΕΤΟΥΣ . ΝΕΟΥ . ΙΕΡΟΥ . laureate head of Titus to r.;
in field, date letter B. (year 2).

2553. AUREUS OF VESPASIAN, COMMEMORATING THE CAPTURE OF
JERUSALEM in 3830.
Obv. Name, titles, and laureate bust of Emperor. *Rev.*
IVDAEA . (Judaea) disconsolate, seated on ground by the
side of a trophy of arms.

2554–55. TWO OTHER AUREI REFERRING TO THE SAME EVENT.
Obv. Similar. *Rev.* (14) Captive Jew, or (15) Captive
Jewess seated on ground beside palm.

Exhibited by the REV. C. C. BABINGTON, M.A.

2556. SHEKEL OF THE FIRST YEAR OF SIMON MACCABAEUS, 3617–3625.
Obv. "Shekel of Israel" in early Hebrew characters around
a cup, above which is the date letter A (year 1). *Rev.*
"Jerusalem Kedoshah" (Jerusalem the Holy) in similar
characters placed around a triple-flowered lily stem.

2557. SHEKEL OF THE FOURTH YEAR.

The design and legend similar to the preceding piece, but the reverse legend reads "Jerusalem-*ha*-kedoshah," and the date letter is preceded by the initial letter of the word Shenath (Year).

2558-59. SIXTH OF SHEKEL OF THE FOURTH YEAR (COPPER).

Obv. Lulab between two ethrogs; above, "Shenath arba" (in the Fourth Year). *Rev.* Cup, around which "Ligullath Zion" (Redemption of Zion).

COINS OF THE LATER ASMONAEAN PRINCES.

2560. BRONZE COIN OF ALEXANDER JANNAEUS, 3655–3682.

Obv. A flower and "Jehonathan Hammelek" (Jonathan the King). *Rev.* ΒΑΣΙΛΕΩΣ ΑΛΕΞΑΝΔΡΟΥ. around a circle enclosing an anchor.

2561-62. BRONZE COINS OF ALEXANDER JANNAEUS.

Obv. Two cornucopiae and poppy-head. *Rev.* "Jehonathan Hakkohen Haggadol Vecheber Hajehudim" (Jonathan the High Priest, and the confederation of the Jews).

2563. BRONZE COIN OF ALEXANDER JANNAEUS; OR HIS GRANDSON ALEXANDER II.

Obv. Star, between the rays of which "Jehonathan Hammelek." *Rev.* ΒΑΣΙΛΕΩΣ ΑΛΕΞΑΝΔΡΟΥ around an anchor.

2564. BRONZE COIN OF ANTIGONUS (MATTATHIAS), 3720–3723.

Obv. Two cornucopiae, encircled by the following legend in early Hebrew letters, "Mattathias the High Priest, and the confederation of the Jews." *Rev.* Palm, within a wreath, around which is ΒΑΣΙΛΕΩΣ. ΑΝΤΙΓΟΝΟΥ.

COINS OF THE IDUMÆAN PRINCES.

2565. BRONZE COIN OF HEROD THE GREAT, 3723–3756.

Obv. Helmet (?) between two palm branches. *Rev.* ΒΑΣΙΛΕΩΣ ΗΡΩΔΟΥ. around a tripod, between which are the date letters . L . Γ (year 3), and the *crux ansata*.

2566-67. BRONZE COINS OF HEROD ARCHELAUS, 3756–3766.

11. *Obv.* ΗΡѠΔΟΥ., cluster of grapes, &c. *Rev.* Plumed helmet, below which ΕΘΝΑΡΧΟΥ.

12. *Obv.* Η . Ρ. and prow of galley. *Rev.* ΕΘΝ. in a wreath.

COINS ISSUED BY THE ROMAN PROCURATORS.

2568. BRONZE COIN STRUCK BY PONTIUS PILATE, PROCURATOR UNDER TIBERIUS, 3786–3796.
Obv. TIBEPIOY . KAICAPOC . and augural staff.   *Rev.* L . IZ . (year 17) within a wreath.

2569. BRONZE COIN STRUCK BY CLAUDIUS FELIX, PROCURATOR UNDER CLAUDIUS, 3812–3820.
Obv. TI . KΛAYΔIOC . KAICAP . ΓEPM . . L . IΔ . (year 14), two palm branches placed crosswise.   *Rev.* IOYΛIA . AΓPIΠΠINA in a wreath.

COINS STRUCK DURING THE FIRST REVOLT, 3826–3830.

2570. SILVER COIN.
Obv. "Shenath] Achath. (year 1) Ligullath Israel." Bunch of grapes. *Rev.* S(henath) Beth (year 2). [La] cheruth Israel. Lyre. This coin appears to be perfectly genuine, but the use of two reverse dies, with different dates, is remarkable.

2571. BRONZE COIN ISSUED BY AUTHORITY OF THE SANHEDRIN.
Obv. "Shenath Shetaim" (year 2), vase. *Rev.* "Cheruth Zion" (Deliverance of Zion) round a vine leaf.

SECOND REVOLT OF THE JEWS, 3892–3895.

2572. SHEKEL OF THE SECOND YEAR OF SIMON BAR-COCHAB.
Obv. A tetrastyle temple, with an arched portal in the centre; at the sides "Jerusalem;" above, a star, referring to the name of Bar-Cochab. *Rev.* S(henath) Beth (year 2); Lacheruth Israel around lulab and ethrog.

2573. SILVER COIN ISSUED BY SIMON BAR-COCHAB.
Obv. "Simon," cluster of grapes. *Rev.* "Lacheruth Jerusalem," vase and palm branch.

2574. BRONZE COIN ISSUED BY SIMON BAR-COCHAB.
Obv. "Simon" below a palm. *Rev.* "S(henath) Beth Lacheruth Israel?" vine leaf.

COINS STRUCK IN ROME REFERRING TO THE CAPTURE OF JERUSALEM, 3830.

2575. AUREUS OF VESPASIAN.
Obv. Name, titles and bust. *Rev.* DE . IVDAEIS . trophy of arms.

2576. DENARIUS OF VESPASIAN.
Obv. Name, titles and bust of Emperor. *Rev.* IVDAEA. Judaea, desolate, sitting beside trophy.

2577. DENARIUS OF VESPASIAN.
Obv. Name, titles and bust of Emperor. *Rev.* Palm to r., captive Jew; to l., the Emperor holding spear and parazonium.

2578. LARGE BRASS COIN OF VESPASIAN.
Obv. Name, titles and bust of Emperor. *Rev.* IVDAEA. CAPTA. palm tree, beneath which Judaea sitting disconsolate; to the l. the Emperor holding spear and parazonium.

2579. LARGE BRASS COIN OF VESPASIAN.
Obv. Name, titles and bust of Emperor. *Rev.* IVDAEA. CAPTA. palm tree; to the r. a captive Jew; to the l. Judaea sitting upon trophy of arms.

2580–97. SERIES OF COINS OF SYRIAN KINGS, &c.
Struck at Lebania, Damascus, Baalbek, Aradus, Berytus, Byblus, Sidon, Tyre, Tripolis.

2598. BRONZE COIN OF ANTONINUS PIUS.
Struck at Jerusalem. *Obv.* Name, titles and bust of Emperor. *Rev.* COL . AE . CA.

Exhibited by B. L. BENAS, ESQ., J.P.

2599. VESPASIAN DENARIUS.
Obv. Bust to right IMP . CÆSAR VESPASIANVS AVG *Rev.* Judaea seated beneath trophy " IVDÆA." Æ

2600. FORGED SHEKEL OF SIMON MACCABAEUS, SECOND YEAR.
Cleverly struck from concocted dies.

Exhibited by MARCUS N. ADLER, ESQ., M.A.

2601. SIMON MACCABAEUS. ONE-SIXTH SHEKEL.
Obv. Chalice, " Redemption of Zion." *Rev.* Palm-branches, " In the fourth year." Æ

2602. VESPASIAN. DENARIUS COMMEMORATING THE CAPTURE OF JERUSALEM.
Obv. Emperor's bust and titles. *Rev.* Victory and Judaea seated. TR . POT, &c. Æ

2603. VESPASIAN.
Similar, but with EX . SC . on reverse.

2604. VESPASIAN.
Large brass. *Obv.* Bust of Emperor IMP . CÆS . VESPASIAN . AVG . PM TR . PPP . COS III . *Rev.* Judaea under palm-tree. Victory inscribing VIC . AVG . *Leg.* VICTORIA AVGVSTI. Unpublished in Cohen.

2605. MODERN FORGERY OF SHEKEL.
   With square Hebrew inscriptions. *Obv.* " Shekel of Israel."
   Rev. " Holy Jerusalem."

Exhibited by REV. J. L. STRACHAN-DAVIDSON, M.A., *Balliol College,*
   Oxford.

2606. FIRST REVOLT OF THE JEWS. SIMON NASI.
   Obv. Diota שנת שתים " Year Two." *Rev.* Vine-leaf חרות
   ציון " Deliverance of Zion." Æ

2607. VESPASIAN.
   On the capture of Jerusalem, A.D. 71. Large brass. *Obv.*
   Head of Emperor IMP . CÆS . VESPASIAN , &c. *Rev.*
   Judaea under palm-tree, and captive Jew to the left,
   IVDÆA CAPTA . S . C .

2608. VESPASIAN.
   A similar piece with similar inscriptions.

Exhibited by B. HEYMANN, ESQ., *Hamburg House, Clifton.*

2609. HAMBURG GILT MEDAL.
   Struck by Gebrüder Nathan in 1841, to commemorate the
   return of Sir Moses and Lady Montefiore from Egypt.
   Obv. Arms and Hebrew inscriptions. *Rev.* Inscriptions
   in German.

Exhibited by DR. L. LOEWE, *Oscar Villas, Broadstairs.*

2610. SIMON MACCABAEUS. SHEKEL OF THIRD YEAR.
   Obv. Chalice " Shekel of Israel " שׁ. *Rev.* Triple lily " Holy
   Jerusalem." Æ

2611. JOHN HYRCANUS I.
   Obv. " Jonathan, the High Priest, and the Senate of the
   Jews." *Rev.* Two cornucopiae and poppy-head. Æ

2612. ALEXANDER JANNAEUS.
   Obv. Anchor, ΒΑCΙΛΕΩC ΑΛΕΞΑΝΔΡΟΥ " King Alexander."
   Rev. Sun with eight rays. Æ

2613. HEROD ARCHELAUS.
   Obv. ΗΡΩΔΟΥ " Herod," bunch of grapes. *Rev.* ΕΘΝΑΡΧΟΥ
   " Ethnarch," helmet, &c. Æ

2614. HEROD AGRIPPA I.
   Obv. Tabernaculum ΒΑCΙΛΕΩC ΑΓΡΙΠΑ " King Agrippa."
   Rev. Three ears of corn, L.S. " Year 6." Æ

2615. ANNIUS RUFUS, PROCURATOR OF JUDAEA.
   Obv. An ear of corn ΚΑΙCΑΡΟC " Cæsar." *Rev.* Palm-tree,
   LMA " Year 41," i.e. of the reign of Augustus. Æ

2616. Second Revolt. Simon Bar-Cochab.
Obv. שמעון "Simon." *Rev.* Pitcher and palm-branch, "The deliverance of Jerusalem." Struck over a Roman denarius. Æ

2617. Same Period.
Obv. Bunch of grapes שמעון "Simon." *Rev.* Two trumpets, "The deliverance of Jerusalem," also struck over a denarius." Æ

2618. Same Period.
Obv. Palm-tree, שמעון "Simon." *Rev.* לחרות ירושלם "Deliverance of Jerusalem." Æ

Exhibited by James L. Hart, Esq.

2619. Medal.
Silver-gilt, formed of two cast plaques soldered together. Dutch work, probably of XVII. Cent. *Obv.* Anointment of King David (1 Samuel xii.). *Rev.* King David playing before the Ark (2 Samuel xvi.).

Exhibited by Sydney Myer, Esq.

2620. Modern Forgery of Shekel.
With square Hebrew letters. *Obv.* "Shekel of Israel." *Rev.* "Holy Jerusalem."

Exhibited by Lucien Wolf, Esq.

2621. Bronze Medal.
Sir Moses Montefiore, Italian, on his Centenary. *Obv.* His bust. *Rev.* A MOSE MONTEFIORE SINTESI PERFETTA DEL GIVDAISMO NEL SVO CENTENARIO VIII KESVAN. 5645.

2622. Medal on same event.
Obv. Bust. &c., אשרי כל. *Rev.* A UNIVERSAL TRIBUTE, &c. Issued by Loewenstark & Sons.

Exhibited by Samuel Montagu, Esq., M.P.

2623. Simon Maccabeus—Half-shekel of Fourth Year.

2623a. Second Revolt. Simon Bar-Cochab. Shekel of Second Year.
Obv. שמעון "Simon;" tetrastyle temple with representation of the Beautiful Gate. *Rev.* שב לחר(ות) ישראל "The Second Year of the Deliverance of Israel;" ethrog and lulab. Æ

Exhibited by Rev. J. T. Fowler, M.A.

2624. Pewter Amulet.
With magic square of Jupiter and Hebrew words according to the rules of H. C. Agrippa and the old magicians.

Exhibited by Mrs. Almosnino.

2625. Modern Forgery of Shekel.
  With square Hebrew letters. *Obv.* " The Shekel of Israel."
  Rev. "Holy Jerusalem."

Exhibited by Joseph Goldstone, Esq.

2626. Mediaeval Bronze Medal.
  Probably of xvi. Cent. *Obv.* Bust, with horn, as on head
  of Jupiter Ammon, intended for Moses. *Rev.* " לא יהיה
  לך אלהים אחרים על פני "

EXHIBITION OF DOCUMENTS, &c.,

ILLUSTRATING

ANGLO-JEWISH HISTORY,

HELD AT

THE PUBLIC RECORD OFFICE,

BY KIND PERMISSION OF THE DEPUTY KEEPER.

[The following List was drawn up by Mr. CHARLES TRICE MARTIN, F.S.A.]

1. Pipe Roll, or Great Roll of the Exchequer, 31 Hen. I., containing an entry of sums of money paid to the king by Rubi Gotsce, Jacob, Manasser, and Abram, Jews of London, and notice of a fine of £2000 exacted from the Jews of London for killing a sick man (*pro infirmo quem interfecerunt*). Printed by Hunter, pp. 148, 149. (Rubi Gotsce is the first Rabbi mentioned in the records.)

2. Charter Roll. 2 John, m. 5. Enrolment of a charter confirming to the Jews in England the liberties enjoyed by them in the reign of Henry III., and settling the procedure in cases of disputes between Christians and Jews. Dated 10 April, 2 John, 1201. (Original of the photograph. No. 17.)

3. Miscellanea of the Exchequer. Queen's Remembrancer Department. Jews. Account of money received from Jews in various counties and places throughout England, in the fifth year of Richard I. Contains a list of over 300 names of Jews. $\frac{556}{2}$).

    This series consists of documents relating to the taxation and monetary affairs of the Jews in England from the reign of Henry II. to the Expulsion.

4. Roll containing an account of the tallages and fines paid by
Jews, Hilary term, 17 Hen. III. 1233. At the top is
a drawing, of which the photograph is exhibited at
Albert Hall. (No. 15). (Exch. of Receipt Jews' Roll,
No. 87.)

5. Roll of Pleas of the Forest for 5 Edward I., containing an
account of the killing of a doe at Colchester by certain
Jews, and on the margin a caricature portrait of one of
them. (*See* No. 14.) Chapter House. County Bags,
Essex. (Placita Forestæ, No. 1. 5 Edw. I.

6–8. Exchequer tallies on a card; the third is a memorandum of a
debt of 20*s.* to Joscy of Kent. It is the original of the
facsimile exhibited at the Albert Hall.

---

9. The account of the whole tallage of the Jews paid at the New
Temple, London, 2 Edw. I. (Exch. Q. R. Misc. $\frac{557}{2}$)

10. Roll containing an account of sums received in the Exchequer
from divers counties as fines for Jews, Easter term, 14
John to Mich. 15 John, 1213. (Exch. of Receipt Jews
Rolls, No. 86A.)

11. Writs addressed to various bailiffs touching enquiry to be made
of the debts, &c., of Jews in their bailiwicks, with some
inquisitions taken thereon, temp. Hen. III. (Exch. Q.R.
Misc. $\frac{556}{13}$). Among these is the original of the facsimile
exhibited at Albert Hall (No. 514).

12–17. A writ and inquisition, touching agreements for payments
of money entered into between John de Gurnay and
certain Jews, with five Shetaroth. (Exch. Q. R. Misc. $\frac{557}{6}$)

18–21. Four Shetaroth. Chapter House. (London and Middlesex
Bag, No. 14.)

22. Shetaroth and bonds to Jews, before the Expulsion.
(Chapter House. Jews' Bonds Box 43.)

---

23. Roll containing pleadings in cases between Jews. and
Christians and Jews before the Justices of the Jews,

for the years 3 and 4 Hen. III., 28 Oct., 1218, to June,
1220. Forty-seven of these rolls exist, of which this
is the earliest. Printed in "Selections from the Miscellaneous Rolls of the Exchequer," p. 285. (Exchequer of
Pleas, Jews' Rolls, No. 1.)

24. The last roll in the same series. Conta:ning pleas, essoins,
recognisances in the Exchequer of the Jews, etc.
Trinity term, 14 Edw. I., 1286. (Exch. of Pleas, Jews'
Rolls, No. 47.)

---

25. Roll containing particulars of the account of Ric. de Ayrmynne,
Warden of the House of Converts, of his receipts, expenses and liveries, from Mich. 5 Edw. III. to 10 Dec.
7 Edw. III. The number of Converts mentioned, nine
men and thirteen women, is greater than at any sub-
sequent time. In some accounts there is no convert
mentioned.

26. Account of John Yong, LL.D., Master of the Rolls and of
the Hospital for the second and third year of Henry VIII.,
with three receipts of converts. Dr. Yong's tomb is in the
Rolls Chapel.

27. Acquittances from four converts, Arthur Antoe, Jas. Wolfgang,
Nathaniel Menda and Eliz. Fardinando, during the
wardenship of Edward Lord Bruce, Commendator of
Kinloss, Master of the Rolls, whose tomb is in the Chapel.
Lord Bruce's accounts have not been preserved.

Nos. 25 to 27 are specimens of the accounts of the Wardens
of the House for Converted Jews, which stood on the
site of Roll's House, from 5 Edw. III. to 6 James I.
See also No. 50.

---

28. Trial of Jacob of Norwich and other Jews for the abduction
and circumcision of Odardus, son of Wychardus Physicus,
a boy of five years old. This case is referred to by
Matthew Paris in his Historia Anglorum, vol. i. p. 375,
and also in the Chronice Majora, vol. iv. p. 30. (Tower
Coram Rege Roll. 18 Hen. III. m. 21.)

29. Inquisition as to the property held in London by Jacob
Crespin, a Jew, consisting of houses in Wudestrate and
Ismongerelane. The writ is dated 6 May, 34 Hen. III.
1250. With Hebrew endorsement. (Inq. P.M. 34 Hen. III.
No. 50.)

N

30. Inventory of the goods and chattels of Abraham de Berke-
    hamstede, including his debts deposited in the "Archa"
    of London, 24 May, 34 Hen. III. 1250. (Exchequer, Q. R.
    Misc. Jews. $\frac{556}{6}$)

31. Roll containing an account of the sale of the houses of Jews
    forfeited to King Edward I. by their condemnation for
    various offences.   (Tower Miscellaneous Rolls, No. 144.)

32. Writs to the Sheriffs of various counties commanding them to
    cause the "Archæ" containing the chirographs of the
    Jews to be carried to Westminster; to summon Christians
    to produce bonds with Jews; to discover and seize all
    houses and tenements held by Jews at the Expulsion; and
    to proclaim that all persons having goods and chattels of
    the Jews are to deliver them to the treasurer and barons.
    4 and 5 Oct.   18 Edw. [I.]   Inquisitions taken in pur-
    suance of the above writ.   (Exch. Q. R. Misc. $\frac{557}{9}$)

33. Roll containing a list of the grantees of houses which escheated
    to the king at the Expulsion of the Jews.   19 Edw. I.
    1291.   (Tower Miscellaneous Roll, No. 74.)

34. List of bonds and deeds in the old *Archa* at Exeter, which
    came to the king's hands after the abjuration of the Jews
    from England.   20 Edw. I.   ($\frac{557}{13}$)

35. Roll showing the profits and fines still accruing from the
    debts of Jews at Easter.   22 Edw. I. 1294, *i.e.* after the
    Expulsion.   (Exch. of Receipt Jews' Roll, 113 A.)

36. Appointment of a Committee by the Council of State, to
    answer the letter of Manasseh Ben Israel, 10 Oct. 1651.
    (Council of State Order Book, vol. xxiii., pp. 25–28.)

37. Pass for Manasseh Ben Israel to come from Holland to
    England, 22 Nov. 1652. (Council of State Order Book,
    vol. xxxv., p. 101.)

38. Pass for Manasseh Ben Israel to come from Amsterdam to
    England, 17 Dec. 1652. (Council of State Order Book,
    vol. lxviii., p. 117.)

39. Pass for Manasseh Ben Israel to come to England, 16 Sept.
    1653.   (Council of State Order Book, vol. lxx., p. 380.)

40. Order of Council, on hearing that Manasseh Ben Israel is attending at the door with books which he wishes to present to the Council, that Mr. Jessop receive them and bring them in, 31 Oct. 1655. (Council of State Order Book, vol. lxvi., p. 353.)

41. Pass for Abraham de Mercado, M.D. Hebrew, and David Raphael de Mercado his son, to Barbadoes, to exercise his profession, 20 April, 1655. (Council of State Order Book, vol. lxxvi., p. 49.)

42. Petition of Manasseh Ben Israel to Cromwell, for the Jews to be allowed to live in England, with liberty to exercise their religion and to trade, 13 Nov. 1655, and report of the President of the Council, Major Lambert, and others thereupon. (Domestic State Papers, vol. ci., 115.)

42a. Appointment of a Committee to consult with the Committee to whom the above petition was referred. (*Ibid.* No. 133.)

43. Petition of Manasseh Ben Israel and other Jews in London for license in writing to meet in their houses for worship, and to bury their dead outside the city, 24 March, 1656. (Domestic State Papers, Commonwealth, vol. cxxv., No. 58.)

44. Petition of Manasseh Ben Israel to Cromwell for assistance, 19 Feb., 1657. (Dom. State Papers, Commonwealth, vol. cliii., No. 122.)

45. Order in Council advising Cromwell to grant Manasseh Ben Israel a pension of £100 a year, 19 Feb., 1657. (Council of State Order Book, vol lxxvii., p. 726.)

46. Petition of Manasseh Ben Israel to Cromwell, asking for £300 in lieu of his pension, as he wishes to carry his son's corpse back to Holland, 17 Sept., 1657. (Dom. State Papers, vol. clvi., No. 89.)

47. Order in Council for payment of £200 to him in discharge of his pension, 17 Sept., 1657. (Council of State Order Book, vol. lxxviii., p. 153.)

48. Petition of John Sadler to Richard Cromwell for the payment to Manasseh Ben Israel's widow of the sums granted to him by Oliver Cromwell, 4 Jan., 1659. (Dom. State Papers, vol. cc., 8.) Note of the Reading thereof in Council. (Council of State Order Book, vol. lxxxiv., col. 37.)

49. Remonstrance against the permission to the Jews to reside in England, and proposing the imposition of heavy taxes and the seizure of their personal property. The writer

N 2

suggests that they offered to buy St. Paul's for a synagogue in Cromwell's time. [30 Nov.], 1660. (Dom. State Papers, Chas. II., vol. xxi., 140.)

50. Petition of Peter Samuel and Paul Jacob, converted Jews, for a share in the benefits of the Domus Conversorum. (Dom. State Papers, Chas. II., vol. ix., No. 171.)

51. Enrolment of the patent appointing Sir George Jessel, Master of the Rolls, 30 Aug. 37 Vict., 1873. (Patent Roll, 37 Victoria, p. 1, No. 17.)

EXHIBITION OF OBJECTS

ILLUSTRATING

JEWISH ECCLESIASTICAL ART

AT THE

SOUTH KENSINGTON MUSEUM.

Corridor.   *Case.*

1. SCROLL OF LAW.

Deerskin. Used in the Maghreb synagogues. Incomplete.

2. MANTLE FOR SCROLL OF LAW.

Crimson velvet and silver tissue embroidered in gold thread, representing Ark of Sephardic Congregation at Amsterdam for which it was made. Gold fringe and silver tassels. Spanish. XVII. Cent.

3. BELLS FOR SCROLL.

Silver filigree openwork; a sphere resting on leaves, crowned and surmounted with fleur-de-lys, with silver-gilt bells attached. Spanish. XVII. Cent.

4. YAD (POINTER).

Carved ivory with silver chain attached. Chinese workmanship.

5. MEGILLAH (ROLL OF ESTHER).

Vellum; illuminated with incidents in medallions. Roller silver gilt *repoussé* with foliage, crowned, and with figures of Mordecai and Esther. Spanish. XVII. Cent.

6. WEDDING RING.

Gold; with relief of Temple on bezel. Usual Hebrew inscription "Good luck." Venetian. XVI. Cent.

7. WEDDING RING.

Gold; with Temple on bezel with movable vines at top. Usual Hebrew inscription enamelled in colours. German. XVI. Cent. From Waterton Collection.

8. WEDDING RING.

Brass gilt; bezel opening on hinge, revealing "Good luck" in Hebrew, eight solid bosses round the hoop. German. XVI. Cent.

9. WEDDING RING.
   Gold filigree with blue enamel. "Good luck" in Hebrew inscribed within. Venetian. XVII. Cent.

10. WEDDING RING.
    Gold hoop joined with small plate, with Hebrew inscription, the rest enriched with six openwork bosses. Venetian. XVI. Cent.

11 WEDDING RING.
   Bronze gilt; broad hoop, edged with rope ornament, engraved with "good luck" in Hebrew, and having three openwork projections. German. XVII. Cent.

12. WEDDING RING.
    Gold; with high projecting bezel, openings on each side of boss, the shoulders angular and boldly chased, the hoop ribbed. Italian. XVI. Cent.

13. WEDDING RING.
    Gold; with high projecting bezel in form of tower with four entrances, finished with scroll ornaments. Italian.

14. WEDDING RING.
    Gold; with filigree bosses: the Hebrew inscription inside. German. XVII. Cent.

15. WEDDING RING.
    Gilt metal; broad hoop, with spiral edgings and four openwork projections: "Good luck" in Hebrew. German. XVII. Cent.

16. WEDDING RING.
    Broad gold hoop, with row of raised dots along middle and ridged edges: bezel representing Tabernacle, and engraved with initials of the usual Hebrew inscription. German. XVII. Cent.

17. WEDDING RING.
    Broad gold hoop, with five bosses of filigree, small flourish in blue enamel, with edgings of cable pattern: Hebrew inscription within and without. German, late XVI. Cent.

18. WEDDING RING.
    Gold; with Hebrew inscription, raised and enamelled, a turret with triangular gables and movable vanes affixed. German. XVI. Cent.

19. CHEMIAH (AMULET).
    Square, silver gilt, to be suspended on wall. Coral columns at side and garnets set in collets on the front, with "Almighty" in Hebrew inserted on a coral heart. Italian workmanship. XVII. Cent.

ANGLO-JEWISH HISTORICAL EXHIBITION.

SUPPLEMENTARY EXHIBITION OF

MSS.,ENGRAVINGS, AND PRINTED BOOKS,

HELD IN THE

KING'S LIBRARY, BRITISH MUSEUM.

BY KIND PERMISSION OF THE TRUSTEES.

I.—DEPARTMENT OF MSS.

The descriptions have been provided by the kindness of Mr. E. MAUNDE THOMPSON, Keeper of the Department, and Dr. RIEU, Keeper of the Oriental MSS.

a.—CHARTERS.

1. Acquittance by Aaron, Jew of Lincoln, and Benedict Grossus, son of Pucella, to the men of Barton [Barton-upon-Humber, co. Linc.], for ten pounds and ten shillings paid at Michaelmas after the death of Roger [de Pont l'Evêque], Archbishop of York [*ob.* 26 Nov. A.D. 1181]. *Latin.* On the back is the *Hebrew* attestation under signature of Baruchias son of Eliahu [Berachjah, son of Eliah.] [Add. Ch. 1250.]

2. Acquittance by Salomon of Paris to Richard de Malebis for four pounds due to his lord Aaron, paid on Monday after Martinmas following the death of Geoffrey [Kirtling], High-Dean of Lincoln, in part payment of "the great debt which he owes to my Lord Aaron, whereof I have appointed him a day [for settlement]." *Latin.* On the back is the *Hebrew* form, dated 2 Dec. A.D. 1183 (?) [Add. Ch. 1251.]

3. Covenant by which William filius Gregorii assigns to Biddlesdon Abbey, co. Bucks, the rent of a mill, with certain lands in his Manor of Finmere, co. Oxon; which lands he had pledged to Belasez the Jewess of Oxford, for £32; on

condition that the Abbey should hold the lands and pay the interest, till he should have repaid the debt. Witnesses: William, Prior Sancti Augustini de Bruston [Bristol], Geoffrey de Larder, Will. fil. Helis, Will. de Ghend, Nic. de Scaldeswelle, and others. [*Temp.* Ric. I.?] *Latin.* [Harl. Ch. 84 D. 15.]

4. Chirograph bond by Peter de Eclisfold to Margaret, daughter of Jurnet [of Norwich], to pay five silver marks on the second Midsummer day after the death of Gerard, Prior of Norwich [*ob.* A.D. 1201]. *Latin.* On the back is the acquittance of the aforesaid Margaret to Peter de Eclisfeld, partly obliterated. *Hebrew.* [Harl. Ch. 43 A. 54.]

5. Sale by Abraham, son of Muriel of London, to Geoffrey de Mandeville, Earl of Essex and Gloucester, of a house late belonging to Abraham son of Raby, in Westcheap, London, in St. Mary Colechurch parish, for 35 silver marks. Among the witnesses are Serlo Mercer, Mayor of London; Ralph Eswi, Alderman of the Market; Stephen and Fermin, goldsmiths; Garsya son of Sanson; and Mosses son of Jacob. *Latin.* Signed in Hebrew characters by Abraham ben R. Samson and Yehoshâya ben R. Yehuda; attested by Abraham son of Joseph, son of Miryam daughter of R. Isaac. [A.D. 1214–1222.] [Harl. Ch. 43 A. 56.]

6. Precepts of Henry III. to the Jew-bailiffs of Gloucester, to enquire for all old charters, etc., held by the Jews of Gloucester and executed "ante communem capturam Judeorum," and to cause them to be produced, under heavy penalties, at Westminster before the Justices "ad custodiam Judeorum"; also to collect arrears of the late talliage imposed at Bristol, from certain Jews, some being mentioned by name. Witness: E[ustace] de Facunbr[idge], Treasurer, [afterwards Bishop of London]. Westminster, 16 Nov., [1220?] *Latin.* [Add. Ch. 7178, 7179.]

7. Sale by William, son of William de Silvedune, to Newhouse Abbey [co. Linc.], of land in Kelby [co. Linc.], for 12 silver marks. Dat. Floridum Pascha [Palm-Sunday], A.D. 1230. *Latin.* With it is the release of the land by Jose ben Elias of Nicol [Lincoln]. *Hebrew.* [Harl. Ch. 43 A. 63 A.B.]

8. Sale by William, son of William de Silveduna, to Newhouse Abbey [co. Linc.], of a messuage, land, and rent of 3*d.* yearly, in Kelby [co. Linc.], for 50 silver marks. Among the witnesses is Robert de Rowelle, Dean [of Newhouse]. *Latin.* With it is the release of the land by Jose ben Elias of Nicol [Lincoln]. *Hebrew.* [Harl. Ch. 43 A. 63, A.B.]

9. Grant by William, son of Roger de Castre, to Newhouse Abbey [co. Linc.] of a messuage late belonging to Arn Thol in the town of Castre [Caistor, co. Linc.], at a yearly rent of 8*d.*; the Abbey acquitting the grantor of £10 due by him to the Jews. A.D. 1232. Among the witnesses are: Ralph de Rowelle, Dean of Newhouse, and William de Silvedune. *Latin.* With it is the acquittance by Jose ben Alis, Jose ben Mose, and Jehuda the Frenchman (has-Sarăfăti) to the grantor of debts, and release of the messuage. *Hebrew.* [Harl. Ch. 43 A. 60 A.B.]

10. Lease made in presence of Hugh de Battonia and William Brito, "Justiciarii Judeorum," from Ralph de la Newe-lond to Hugh of London, of "Ailwinesfeld" and other lands lying in [the manor of] Newland in Roxwell, co. Essex. The lessee to discharge the lessor of his debts to the Jews, on condition that he do not again encumber the property. Witnesses: Roger de Bocland and Alexander de Tilleberi, chaplains, William de la Newelond, knight, and John his brother, and others. [A.D. 1235.] On the back are: (i.) Memorandum that Hugh of London is debtor to Benedict Crespin, the Jew, to the amount of three marks; dat. 25 July, 1235. *Latin.* (ii.) Release to Hugh of London, from Benedict Crespin, Jacob Cohen and Solomon Cohen, of all claims on the lands mentioned in the charter. *Hebrew.* (iii) Notification to William le Briton, from the same three Jews, of the receipt of three "zuzim" [? marks] from Master Hugh, the Archdeacon (?) of London, and of their release of the charter between Ralph de la Niulonda and the said Hugh. *Hebrew.* [Lansd. Ch. 30.]

11. Release by Ivo, son of Robert de Wicham, to Newhouse Abbey [co. Linc.], of land at Pinkenhou in Netelton [co. Linc.], in consideration of a payment of 20 silver marks by the Abbey to the Jews on his behalf. Among the witnesses are Gilbert, Abbot of Beauchief [co. Derby]; and Clement, Abbot of Barlings [co. Linc.]. A.D. 1236. *Latin.* With it is the acquittance of Garsie son of Juda; Josceus son of Abraham of Bungai [Bungay. co. Suff.]; Deiae son of Elias; Vives and Benedict sons of Mosses; and Josceus son of Samuel, Jews of Lincoln. Signed in Hebrew and attested by the following :—Gerson bar Yehuda hak-Kohen; Jose son of Elias; Phoebus son of Moses; Bendit ben Mose; Manser ben Davi (who signs on behalf of his father-in-law Jose]: Joseph son of Samuel. *Latin* and *Hebrew.* [Harl. Ch. 43 A. 61 A.B.]

12. Acquittance by Garsia Zakin (?), Jew of Lincoln, to New-house Abbey, co. Lincoln, of claim to land purchased by the abbey from Ivo de Wicham. *Hebrew.* With seal of Ivo de Wicham. [Cotton Ch. xxvi. 29.]

13. General release by Mosse son of Jacob, and Josce son of Mosse, to Peter de Bending. [A.D. 1236–7.] *Hebrew.* [Add. Ch. 16,384.]

14. Grant by Johanna de Bramtona, widow of Ralph de Vermels, to Newhouse Abbey, of land in Brampton [co. Linc.]. To this are attached acquittances: (i.) by Mossy de Colton, Jew, signed by Moses of Colton; and (ii.) by Manser de Broddeswrd, signed by Eliyah Kohen and Mansēr Ribrargursa, for debts on the land. St. Valentine's Day, 41 Hen. III. [A.D. 1257.] *Latin.* [Harl. Ch. 43 A. 66 A.B.C.]

15. Release by Reginald, son of Margery of Lincoln, to Hamo Scotte of Lincoln, of a wall measuring 18¼ ells in the parish of Holy Trinity in Wikeford [Wigford, Lincoln city]. Among the witnesses are William de Holgate, Mayor; and Andrew Cause and Andrew de Horkestowe, Bailiffs of Lincoln. *Latin.* To this is attached the release by Abraham, son of Jacob, Jew of Lincoln, to Bullington Priory of land in the parish of "Holy Trinity Lincoln in Wyckford," formerly belonging to Alan Tixtor, or the Weaver, free from claim for debt due by the said Alan to him or his father Jacob "nomine Judaismi." Dat. the Morrow of St. Katherine, 49 Hen. III. [A.D. 1264]. *Latin.* At the foot is the Jewish contract, signed by Abraham son of Jacob. *Hebrew.* [Harl. Ch. 43 A. 67 A.B.]

16. "Starrum" or Contract of Isaac de Suthwerke with Sir Adam de Stratone, relating to a seal. *Hebrew.* At the foot is a certificate of the enrolment of this "starrum" among those of Michaelmas Term, 50–1 Hen. III. [A.D. 1266], before Sir William de Ordlavestone, and Sir Robert de Foleham, "Justices of the Jews." *Latin.* [Harl. Ch. 43 A. 68.]

17. Release by William Pycot to Walkeline de Rosey of land in Melebury Osmund [co. Dorset], for £50. To this is attached the acquittance of Isaac of Shugirk (? Suthwerke) to the above William for all debts. 52 Hen. III. [A.D. 1267–8]. [Add. Ch. 16,174.]

18. Order from Edward I. to Roger de Seyton, to hold an inquisition concerning the tenure by the Abbot of Pipewell, co. Northampton, of lands in Newbold-on-Avon and Cosford, co. Warw.; the Abbot claiming exemption from debts to the Jews incurred by Burga de Bendeng, the late tenant of the lands. Dat. 15 May, 1278. *Latin.* [Add. Ch. 21,484.]

19–21. Grant by Ursel [ben Jacob] "le Eveske" and . . . his wife to William . . . ham, Draper of Norwich, of land in the parish of St. Peter de Manncroft, Norwich, near the messuages of Isaac of Yarmouth, the Jew, for 18 silver marks, and a yearly rent of 10*d.* to the lords of the fee, and to the grantor a clove of garlic. Among the witnesses are: Adam de Toftes, John Bate, and others, Bailiffs of Norwich; Hubert de Morlee, chirographer; Abraham of York, Ysaac son of Deulecres, Ysaac son of Samuel, and Mosseus of Cunesford. *Latin,* with *Hebrew* signatures. [A.D. 1280.] With two Hebrew deeds. [Lansd. Ch. 666, 667, 669.]

22. Enrolment before Hamo Hauteyn and Robert de Ludham, Justices "ad custodiam Judeorum," of a release by Bateman filius Cressi, a Jew, to Adam de Stratton, "clericus," of lands in "Westerle" [lying in Pitstone, co. Bucks?], acquired from John Taylleboys, debtor to the said Bateman. Dat. 21 June, 1286. *Latin.* With a duplicate in *Hebrew.* [Cott. Ch. Aug. II. 107 a. b.]

23. Grant by Hugh Painel of Lincoln to Newhouse Abbey [co. Linc.], of land in the parish of St. Michael on the Mount, Lincoln, paying yearly 1*d.* to the King. To it is attached the acquittance of Leo son of Salaman and Muriel (?), of Lincoln, to the Abbey, signed in Hebrew and attested by Baruch ben Shelmi. *Latin.* Early XIII. Cent. [Harl. Ch. 43 A. 59 A.B.]

24. Grant by Ralph, son of William de Barkeworde, to Kirkstead Abbey [co. Linc.], of land in Stretton Magna [co. Leic.]. To it is annexed a release by Ursellus the Jew to the Abbot of Kirkstead of the debts of Ralph son of Yvo de Barkeworde, signed by Ursel ben Fanzel [Wenzel?] attesting the payment. Middle XIII. Cent. *Latin.* [Harl. Ch. 43 A. 58.]

25. Release by Isaac Gabois [Gabbai], son of Benedict, Jew of Lincoln, to Bullington Priory [co. Linc.], of land in Hacthorne [co. Linc.], held of Peter de Vendoure. Signed in Hebrew by Isaac ben Benait. Middle XIII. Cent. *Latin.* [Harl. Ch. 43 A. 57.]

26. Grant by William, son of Ranulf de Flamhang, to Roger de Stowe of land in Totestoke [co. Suff.], charged with the yearly payment of $\frac{1}{2}$*d.* to the king for the [Castle] Ward of Norwich. *Latin.* To this is attached the release by Isaac son of Elu (Elivah) Rob (*sic*), of the land. Middle XIII. Cent. [Harl. Ch. 43 A. 64 A.B.]

27. Grant by Geoffrey Berner of Haburg [Habrough, co. Linc.], to Newhouse Abbey, of land in Haburg. With it is the release by Leo, son of Salomon, Jew of Lincoln, to Newhouse Abbey, of the land; signed, in Hebrew, on behalf of his father Leon, by Jakufa ben Leon, who affirms the truth of the statements contained in the document. Middle XIII. Cent. [Harl. Ch. 43 A. 65 A.B.]

28. Release by Jacob, son of Sampson Levy, Jew of Lincoln, to Greenfield Priory, co. Lincoln, of land in Grenefend [Greenfield], given to it by Roger son of Henry de Askeby, free of any debt to a jew or jewess. *Latin*, with Hebrew signature of Jacob son of Samson Levi. *Temp.* Edw. I. [Harl. Ch. 43 A. 69.]

b.—MSS. ILLUSTRATING ANGLO-JEWISH HISTORY.

29. The Psalter, in *Latin* and *French*, with a series of miniatures of Bible History. Vellum. Executed, probably at St. Swithun's Priory, Winchester, in the 12th century; and afterwards belonging to Shaftesbury Abbey, co. Dorset. The volume is opened at the miniature representing the Presentation in the Temple and Christ among the Doctors. [Cotton MS. Nero, C. iv.] The face of the High Priest and another in the lower part of the page are clearly intended for Jewish types.

30. Theological and other collections from various authors, arranged in alphabetical order of subjects, by Jacobus "Omne Bonum." In two volumes. Vellum. XIV. Cent. The volume exhibited is opened at the heading "Judei," which has an ornamental initial letter, in which are painted three figures, two of them intended to represent Jews. [Royal MS. 6 E. vii.]

31. "Disputatio Judei et Christiani": a dialogue on the Christian faith written by Gilbert Crispin, Abbot of Westminster [A.D. 1082–1114.] Preceded by a letter to Anselm, Archbishop of Canterbury, submitting the work for approval and stating that it represents an actual discussion between the author himself and a learned Jewish friend educated at Mainz. This MS. belonged to the Abbey of St. Albans and bears the inscription: "Hic est liber sancti Albani, quem qui ei abstulerit aut titulum deleverit anathema sit. Amen." Vellum. Late XII. Cent. [Cotton. MS. Titus. D. xvi.]

33. "Les Establissemenz le Rey Eadward le fiz le Rei Henri, a sun primer parlement general apres sun coronement a Westminster a la cluse Pasche, le an de sun regne tierz," [A.D. 1275], including enactments against usury practised by the Jews. Vellum. Late XIII. Cent. [Add. MS. 15,667.]

34. Statutes of the Realm; including "Chapitles tuchaunz la Gywerie," or statutes on the Jews, usury, etc.; and a precept of Edward I. entitled: "Statutum de Judeis exiundis (*sic*) regnum Angliæ," whereby he orders the Treasurer and Barons of the Exchequer to recover only the capital loans from Jews to Christians, without usury, dat. 5 Nov. 18 Edw. I. [1290]. Vellum. Late XIII. Cent. [Add. MS. 32,085.]

35. Lists of the first Jews who settled in London about 1658. From Emanuel Mendes da Costa's papers. [Add. MS. 29,868, ff. 15, 16.]

36. Memorandum of a Commission of King Charles II., when in exile at Bruges, to Lieut.-General Middleton, to treat with the Jews of Amsterdam, who had declared that the application lately made to Cromwell on their behalf by some persons of their nation was absolutely without their consent, and to promise that, if they should be ready to assist his Restoration by any contribution of money, arms, or ammunition, he would extend to them that protection which they could reasonably expect; dat. 24 Sept. 1656. [Add. MS. 4106, f. 253.]

37. " Previlleges granted to the People of the Hebrew Nation that are to goe [from Holland ?] to the Wilde Cust " [of Brazil ?]. Late XVII. Cent. [Egerton MS. 2395, f. 46.]

38. Minutes of the Royal Society, and Minutes of the Society of Antiquaries of London, taken by Emanuel Mendes da Costa, F.R.S., F.S.A.; 1757-1762. [Egerton MS. 2381.]

39. Arguments for the removal f Jewish disabilities by Basil Montagu : a transcript, with autograph corrections. [Add. MS. 20,041.]

40. Hebrew Contract of Marriage. Written and illuminated in Gibraltar, A.D. 1786. [Add. Roll. 1998.]

41. Grant of privileges by Airvi Brahmin, a native Rajah, to the Jews at Cochin; without date. A Hebrew translation, with an English version by Rev. C. Buchanan. [Add. MS. 26,581.]

> The celebrated Tamil inscription of Cranganor translated into Hebrew by some of the Beni Israel. Printed in Benjamin II.'s " Eight Years in Asia and Africa," p. 187. The date attributed to the document is 490 A.D.

c.—SEALS.

42. Sampson, son of Sampson. Red sealing wax. $\frac{7}{8}$ in. XIII. Cent. [L. 9.] Round ; a lion passant *contourné.* שמשון בן שמשון The matrix was found at Westminster.

43. Solomon ben Isaac. Red sealing wax. $1\frac{1}{16}$ in. XIII. Cent. [L. 8.] Round seal : a head in profile to the left, wearing a fillet with tasselled ends, the neck draped. Field replenished with foliage. Borders beaded. שלמה בן יצחק See *Proceedings of the Soc. of Antiquaries of Scotland,* vol. i., pp. 39, 50 ; H. Laing, *Supplementary Catalogue of*

Scottish Seals, No. 1294, from which it appears that the brass matrix of this seal was found on the east side of Arthur Seat near Duddingston, and is now in the Museum of the Soc. of Ant. of Scotland.

44. Todros Hallevi or Ha-Levi, son of Samuel Hallevi, son of Al-Levi, of Toledo. Red sealing-wax. 1⅜ in. XIV. Cent. [L. 7.] Shape of a pointed quatrefoil : a triple-towered castle with battlements, in a square, containing the inscription :— טדרום הלוי בן שמואל הלוי נא בן אללוי־ In each of the cusped spaces a fleur-de-lis. Borders beaded.

45. The Jewish Congregation of the City of Seville. ed sealing-wax. 1⅜ in. XVII. Cent.? [L. 10.] Round : a triple towered castle. חקהל הקדוש קהל אשביליה יאאו

d.—HEBREW MSS.

(Selected from over 1000 in the Museum.)

47. Commentary on the Talmudical Tract Baba Metsi'a by Solomon Yitschaki (Rashi). A.D. 1190. Paper. 4°. [Or. 73.]

48. The Historical Books of the Old Testament and the Prophets. Vellum. XII. or XIII. Cent. Folio. [Add. 21,161.]

49. The Pentateuch : Text and Targum in alternate verses, both provided with the super-linear punctuation. Massora Magna and Parva. Imperfect at the beginning. XII. or XIII. Cent. Vellum. Folio. [Or. 2363.]

50. Commentary of Soloman Itschaki (Rashi) on the Pentateuch. A.D. 1273.—Tikkun Middoth han Nephesh of Solomon lbn Gabirol. (Imperf.) Early XIV. Cent. Vellum. 4°. [Add. 26,917.]

51. Machzor according to the Roman rite. Part II. A.D. 1297. Vellum. 4°. [Add. 26,998.]

52. Machzor according to the German rite (imperf.); with additions. A.D. 1308. Vellum. 4°. [Add. 26,970.]

53. Cheshbon ha-'Ibbur, a treatise on the Calendar by Abraham ben Chiyya.—Abridgment of the Choboth hal-lebaboth, or Moral Philosophy of Bechai (or Bachye).—Tikkun Middoth han-Nephesh, an ethical treatise of Solomon ibn Gabiral, translated by Jehudah ibn Tibbon. Vellum. A.D. 1317. Small folio. [Add. 26,899.]

54. Treatise on things lawful and unlawful, by Zedekiah Anav ben Abraham ha Rophé. XIV. Cent. (Before A.D. 1341.) Vellum. 4°. [Add. 26,918.]

55. Ruach Chen, an introduction to the Moreh Nebuchim, on philosophical terminology, etc. A.D. 1341. Vellum. 4°. [Add. 27,179.]

56. The Pesakim, or decisions of Asher ben Jechiel on the Talmudic tracts Baba Kamma, Baba Metsiá, and Baba Bathra. Imperfect. A.D. 1355. Paper. 4°. [Add. 27,557.]

57. The books of Joshua, Judges, Samuel, Kings, Jeremiah, Ezekiel, Isaiah, and the twelve minor prophets, with the Massora, the Targum of Jonathan (partially printed), and the commentary of Solomon Yitschaki (Rashi). Imperfect. (Before A.D. 1359.) Vellum. [Add. 26,879.]

58. Piske ha-Rosh, or "the decisions of Rabbi Asher ben Jechiel," on the Seder Móed. Imperfect. A.D. 1366. Paper. [Add. 27,293.]

59. Chiddūshīm of Solomon (ben Abraham) ibn Addereth on the Talmudical tract Giṭṭīn. A.D. 1368. Paper. 4°. [Or. 851.]

60. Commentary on passages of the Commentary of Abraham ibn 'Ezra on the Pentateuch. A.D. 1382. Paper. Small 4°. [Add. 27,561.]

61. 'Ôthôth hash-Shamayim, the Meteorologica of Aristotle, translated by Samuel ibn Tibbon.—Hegyôn han-Nephesh, or "the Meditation of the Soul," a moral treatise by Abraham ben Chiya. — Sepher hab-Bahir, ascribed to Rabbi Necuniah ben hak-Kanah, etc. A.D. 1384. Paper. 8°. [Or. 832.]

62. Sepher Midrashim, a series of discourses on the pericopes of the Pentateuch, A.D. 1384.—'Arugath hab-Bosem, or "the Bed of Spices," a similar series of discourses. XIV. Cent. Vellum. 4°. [Add. 27,292.]

63. The Helacboth of R. Isaac ben Jacob Alfasi, being an epitome of the Talmud, with the commentary of R. Salomon ben Isaac and the glosses of R. Mordechai. A.M. 5146 = A.D. 1386. Vellum. Folio. [Add. 17,050.]

64. Sepher Mitsvôth Gādōl of Moses of Coucy. A. M. 5150 = A.D. 1390. Vellum and Paper. Folio. [Or. 1081.]

65. Sepher Mitsvoth Katon, or Lesser Book of Precepts, by Isaac of Corbeil, with additions of Joseph of Zurich (impf.). A.D. 1391. Vellum. 4°. [Add. 26,982.]

66. Mordechai, the Pesakim, or Decisions of Mordechai ben Hillel on 26 Talmudical tracts. A.D. 1393. Vellum. 4°. [Add. 19,972.]

67. The fifteen books of the Elements of Euclid, translated from
    Arabic into Hebrew, by Moses ben Samuel ben Jehudah
    ibn Tibbon, A.D. 1270.   Written early in the xv. Cent.
    Vellum and Paper.   4°.   [Add. 20,746.]

68. The Commentary of Abraham ibn 'Ezra on the Pentateuch.
    A.D 1401.   Vellum.   Folio.   [Add. 26,880.]

69. Works of Isaac ben Abraham Ibn al-Latif: viz. Zākhūth hā-
    Ādām; extracts from the Sha'ar Hash Shāmayim; Ginzē
    ham-Melech;   Tsurath' Olām;   Tserōr Ham - Mor.
    A.M. 5163 = A.D. 1403.   Paper.   4°.   [Or. 1084.]

70. Zikkaron Tob, a Commentary on the Pentateuch by Nathan
    ben Samuel (ibn Tibbon).   A.D. 1426.   Vellum.   4°
    [Add. 19,777.]

71. Tseri hag-Guph, a treatise on the art of Medicine, in four
    books, by Nathan ben Joseph Palquera: imperfect at the
    beginning.   A.D. 1447.   Vellum.   Folio.   [Add. 19,943.]

72. The latter Prophets, with the Commentary of David Kimchi
    in the margin.   A.D. 1448.   Vellum.   Folio.   [Add.
    27,046.]

73. The Hagiographa (Kethubīm), provided with vowel-points and
    accents, and accompanied by an Arabic version, partly
    (the five Megilloth) also by the Targum with the
    superlinear punctuation.   Massora Magna and Parva.
    To it is appended a treatise on the accents, in Arabic,
    written in Hebrew characters.   xv. Cent.   Paper.   Folio.
    [Or. 2375.]

74. Meshib Nephesh, a treatise on penitence, by Menachem Meiri:
    imperfect at the beginning.   A.D. 1459.   Paper.   Small 4°.
    [Add. 19779.]

75. The Decisions (Pesakim) of Isaiah (the Elder) of Trani, on
    the Talmudical tracts Yebamoth, Kethuboth, Nedarim,
    Gittin, Kiddushim, and Niddah.   (Before A.D. 1462.)
    Vellum.   Small folio.   [Add. 26,893.]

76. Chobath hal-Lebaboth of Bechai ben Joseph, translated into
    Hebrew by Jehudah ibn Tibbon (imperfect).   A.D. 1463.
    Vellum.   Small 4°.   [Add. 26,952.]

77. Iggereth hav-Vikkuach, or Disputation between Theology
    and Science, and other tracts.   A.D. 1463.   Paper.   Small
    folio.   [Add. 26,925.]

78. Commentary on the Pentateuch by Rabbi Meynchas bar
    Elijah.   Written at Nicopolis, A.D. 1469.   Vellum and
    paper.   4°   [Add. 19,970.]

79. The former Prophets (Joshua, Judges, &c.). Hebrew Text with Targum and Massora. The Targum has the super-linear punctuation. Shtaroth 1780 = A.D. 1469. Paper. Folio. [Or. 2210.]

80. Sepher ham-Michtam, a Commentary on the Talmudical tracts Sukkah, Betsah, Moéd Ḳaton, Megillah, and Pesachim, by David ben Levi. A.D. 1476. Paper. Small folio. [Add. 19,778.]

81. The Commentary of Ibn Rushd, or Averroes, on Aristotle's eight books of Physics, translated from the Arabic into Hebrew by Kalonymus ben Kalonymus ben Meir. A.D. 1481. Paper. 4°. [Add. 25,879.]

82. Siddur, or Prayer-book, according to the Roman use, com-prising the Pirké Aboth, the Perek Rabbi Meir, &c. Written by Abraham Farissol, A.D. 1482. Vellum. Small 4°. [Add. 27,072.]

83. Haphṭaroth with Targum. The latter has the superlinear punctuation. Massora. Shtaroth 1795 = A.D. 1484. Vellum. Folio. [Or. 1470.]

84. The Michlol or Hebrew Grammar of David Kimchi.—'Et Sopher, a grammatical and Massoretic treatise by the same. A.D. 1487. Vellum. Folio. [Or. 1045.]

85. Eben Ezra's Commentary on the Pentateuch. A.D. 1488. 4°. [Or. 1088.]

86. Medical works of Joannes Messuae (Yahya ibn Másawaih), viz. De Simplicibus and the Antidotarium. To these is appended a treatise de Unguentis (Seder ham Merkachoth) by another author. A.D. 1491. Paper. Small 4°. [Or. 46.]

87. Diné Mamonoth, a treatise on Arithmetic by Gad Astruc ben Jacob :—Likkutim, or extracts from the work of Lucas Paciolus, entitled Summa Arithmeticæ et Geometriæ, etc. Venice, A.D. 1494. Paper. 4°. [Add. 27,039.]

88. Midrash hag gadol on Deuteronomy. Dated A. Contr. 1807 = A.D. 1496. Paper. Large 4°. [Or. 1483.]

— — —

89. The Samaritan Pentateuch. XIII. Cent. Vellum. Folio. [Or. 1443.]

90. Fragment of the Samaritan Pentateuch, containing the Hebrew text with the Arabic and Samaritan versions. XIII. Cent. Vellum. Folio. [Or. 1441.]

o

91. The Hebrew Pentateuch, written in Samaritan characters, by Nathaniel ben Ishmael. A.H. 838 = A.D. 1434–5. Vellum. Large Quarto. [Add. 21,581.]

92. The Samaritan Pentateuch. A.H. 901 = A.D. 1495. Paper. Large folio. [Or. 1444.]

93. The Hebrew Bible (without the Pentateuch), with the Massora and grotesque initials. xiv. Cent. Vellum. [Or. 2091.]

94. Exodus, ch. i. 1–viii. 5 : Hebrew text, written in the Arabic characters and provided with the Hebrew vowel points (in red) and the accents (in green). Ornamental designs in gold and colours. x. Cent. Paper. 4°. [Or. 2540.]

95. Genesis, ch. xxx. 35–xxxii. 40, and a large portion of Exodus : Hebrew text, written in the Arabic character, and provided with the Hebrew vowel-points and accents in red. x. Cent. Paper. Small 4°. [Or. 2541.]

96. Fragments of Genesis, the whole of Exodus, Leviticus and Numbers, and the greater portion of Deuteronomy : Hebrew text, written in Arabic character, and provided with the Hebrew vowel-points and accents in red. xi. Cent. Paper. 4°. [Or. 2542.]

97. The Pentateuch ; Haftaroth ; list of the Parshiyyoth Pethuchoth and Sethumoth ; Megilloth ; Sederham-Ma'aracha, by Eliyya bar Menachem ; Haggadah for the Easter Festival, Prayers, &c. Written on vellum and ornamented with numerous miniatures and illuminated titles of French art. xiii. Cent. [Add. 11,639.]

98. The Haggadah shel Pesach, accompanied by Azharoth of Zerachiah hal-Levi, and various Piyutim and other liturgical pieces, relating to the Feast of the Passover ; with miniatures. xiv. Cent. Vellum. 4°. [Add. 27,210.]

99. Haggadah Pesach, or Liturgy of the Passover : with illuminated headings and miniatures in Italian style. xiv. Cent. 4°. Vellum. [Or. 1404.]

100. Machzor for Pentecost and the Feast of Tabernacles, according to the German use, including the books of Ruth and Ecclesiastes with the commentary of Joseph Kara ; with miniatures. xiv. Cent. Vellum. Folio. [Add. 22,413.]

101. The Pentateuch: Text and Targum in alternate verses; the five Megilloth, and the Haftaroth provided with vowel-points and accents, and accompanied by the Massora Magna and Parva; with illuminations. xiv. Cent. Vellum. Large 8°. [Add. 15,282.]

102. The Pentateuch, with the five Megilloth and the Haphtaroth for the Sabbaths, &c.—'En hak-Koreh, a treatise on the vowel-points and accents, by Zalman han-Nakdan :— Simane hak-Keriah. Written at Coburg, A.D. 1395. Vellum. 4°. [Add. 19,776.]

103. Haggadah Pesach, or Liturgy of the Passover: with illuminated headings. xiv. Cent. 4°. Vellum. [Or. 1424.]

104. The Books of the Hebrew Canon, handsomely written on vellum with illuminated titles and borders. Dated Lisbon, A.D. 1483. Three volumes. In Oriental binding. Large 4°. [Or. 2626–2628.]

105. Machzor or Ritual, according to the Roman use. Written at Florence, A.D. 1441. Vellum. Folio. [Add. 19,944.]

106. Machzor, or Festival Prayers, according to the Roman rite. Illuminated initials and arabesques of Italian art. xv. cent. Vellum. Folio. [Add. 16,577.]

106a. Commentary of Aben Ezra on the Pentateuch: with ornamental headings. xv. Cent. Small 4°. Vellum. [Or. 1487.]

106b. The Pentateuch, with a grammatical introduction (Machbereth hat-Tīgān) and a copious Massora. Written in Yemen towards the end of the 15th or the beginning of the 16th cent. Paper. 4°. [Or. 1379.]

II. DEPARTMENT OF ENGRAVINGS.

a.—CARICATURES ISSUED DURING THE AGITATION OF 1753.

[An Act was then passed naturalising the Jews, but a great popular clamour was raised against it with the cry "No Jews, no wooden shoes," and the Act was accordingly repealed in the following year (see Nos. 162–165).]

107. Vox Populi, Vox Dei, or the Jew Act Repealed. Showing Sampson Gideon, the great Jewish financier of the time, a Bishop, Lord Bolingbroke, &c. [3202.]

108. The Grand Conference, or the Jew Parliament. Printed for Israel de Coster in Bevis Marks near the Synagogue (3203). A number of Jews seated round a table.

109. A Prospect of the New Jerusalem.

110. The Circumcised Gentiles, or a Journey to Jerusalem, Issachar Barebones, jun^r., inv^t. et sculp^t. Sold by Moses in Cheapside (3205). Bishop on donkey with Talmud under his arm. Placard with "Jews 96, Christians, 55," number of votes recorded for and against the Bill.

111. The Jews showing the Parl.m.t or the Know^s ones taken in. Published according to Act of Parliament by Tim Barber at the Dexterous Trimmer over the Water (3208). Inscription "Long live Solomon II."

112. Four Prints of an Election, Plate I. by W. Hogarth 1754 (3285). Through open window is seen procession with effigy of Jew carried on a chair and placard inscribed "No Jews." "A label'd Jew up-lifted high."

b.—PORTRAITS.

(In addition to those at the Royal Albert Hall.)

113. Menasseh ben Israel. Etching by Rembrandt. The chief instrument in bringing back the Jews to this country. Voluminous author (*see* Nos. 126–55).

114. Lord George Gordon with hat and beard. R. Polock pinxit engraver's name erased. Taken in Newgate, 1783, after Lord Gordon had become a Jew and had persisted in wearing his hat in court as a sign of his persuasion. His family bought up these engravings, only two of which are known to be in existence.

115. Richard Brothers, Prince of the Hebrews. "Fully believing this to be the Man whom God hath appointed, I engrave his likeness, William Sharp." R. B. was a fanatic who prophesied that he would lead back the Jews to Jerusalem in 1798. He attracted little interest in the Jewish community, but had a large Gentile following 1758–1824.

III. DEPARTMENT OF PRINTED BOOKS.

a.—BOOKS
CONTAINING ENGRAVINGS AND INSCRIPTIONS ILLUSTRATING THE PRE-EXPULSION PERIOD.

116. Anglia Judaica; by D'Bloissiers Tovey, LL.D.   Oxford, 1734. Standard history of the Jews before 1290.   The volume is opened at the page containing an engraving of the bronze ewer now in the Bodleian.   The arms of the ewer are not figured.

117. Hugues de Lincoln.   Recueil de ballades anglo-normande et ecossoises relatives au meurtre de cet enfant commis par les Juifs en MCCLV, &c.   Par Francisque Michel.   Paris, 1834.   8°.

118. The ancient sculptures in the roof of Norwich Cathedral.   By E. M. Goulburn and E. Hailstone.   London, 1876.   4°. Contains copies of pictures of St. William of Norwich, and of his crucifixion by the Jews.

119. Records of York Castle, by A. W. Twyford and A. Griffiths. London, 1880.   Gives view of Clifford's Tower, the scene of the massacre of Jews at York, 1189.

121. Leicestershire Archæological Society's Transactions.   Vol. I. Contains view of the Jewry Wall at Leicester.

122. Devon (Frederick).   Issues of the Exchequer, being a collection of payments made out of his Majesty's revenue, from King Henry III. to King Henry VI. inclusive.   London, 1837.   4°.   The volume contains a caricature of the Jews.

124. Some account of domestic architecture in England, from the Conquest to the end of the thirteenth century.   By T. Hudson Turner.   Oxford, 1851.   8°.   Contain plates representing the Jews' House at Lincoln, and windows in Moyses' Hall, Bury St. Edmunds.

125. De jure naturali juxta disciplinam ebræorum, by J. Selden. Lond. 1640. fol.   Contains (p. 195) a Hebrew inscription found at Winchester mentioning the expulsion of the Jews from England.

b.—WORKS BY MENASSEH BEN ISRAEL.

126. מקוה ישראל   Esto es, Esperança de Israel, &c.   Span.   Amsterdam, 5410 (1650).   8°.

127. ספר מקוה ישראל   Lemberg, 1847.   8°.

128. ספר נישמת חיים   Liber quatuor de immortalitate animae. Amstelodami, 1651.   4°.

129. פירוש מלות זרות בכל המשניות   Amsterdam, 1646.   8°.

130. ספר פני רבה והוא מפתח במדרש רבה [Re-arranged and edited by Manasseh Ben Israel.] Amsterdam, 1628.   4°.

131 תשועת ישראל   Wien, 1813.   8°.

132. Argumentum operis de animæ immortalitate. [Amsterdam? 1651?]   4°.

133. [El Conciliador, o de la conviniencia de los lugares de la S. Escriptura, que repugnantes entre si parecen.]   4 pt. [Francofurti] Amsterdam, 1632–51.   4°.

134. Conciliator, sive, de Convenientia Locorum S. Scripturæ quæ pugnare inter se videntur, *etc.*   Francofurti, 1633.   4°.

135. The Conciliator, a reconcilement of the apparent contradictions in Holy Scripture.   2 vol.   London, 1842.   8°.

136. מקוה ישראל Esto es, Esperança de Israel. (Relacion de Aharon Levi, alias, A. de Montezinos [concerning a tribe of Jewish descent, said to be discovered by him in South America.])   Amsterdam, Año. 5410 [1649?].   8°.

137. Origen de los Americanos. מקוה ישראל esto es Esperanza de Israel Reimpression á plana y renglon . . . Madrid, 1881.   8°.

138. The hope of Israel . . . translated into English . . . The . . . relation of . . . A. Montezines, &c.   London, 1650.   8°.

139. The Hope of Israel . . . Whereunto are added some Discourses upon the point of the conversion of the Jewes by Moses Wall. 2nd edition, corrected and amended (the Relation of A. Montezinus).   London, [December 2], 1651.   4°.

140. De Hoop van Israël . . . Met een Verantwoordingh voor de eedele volcken der Jooden [by E. Nicolas], *etc.*   Amsterdam, 1666.   12°.

141. M. ben J. de la fragilidad humana y inclinacion del hombre al peccado.   Amsterdam, 5402 [1642].   4°.

142. M Ben Israel Dissertatio de Fragilitate humana ex Lapsu Adami, de quo divino in bono opere auxilio, &c.   Amsielodami, 1642.   8°.

143. M. Ben Israel De Creatione, Problemata xxx.   Amstelodami, 1635.   8°.

144. M. ben I. de termino vitæ, libri III.   Quibus veterum Rabbinorum ac recentium doctorum, de hac controversiâ sententia explicatur.   Amstelodami, 1639.   12°.

145. M. Ben I. de resurrectione Mortuorum libri III.   Quibus animæ, immortalitas & corporis resurrectio contra Zaducæos comprobatur.   Amstelodami, 1636.   8°.

146. Manasseh ben I. de la resurreccion de los muertos, libros III. En los quales contra los Zaduceos, se prueva la immortalidad del ama, y Resurreccion, &c. Amsterdam, Año. 5396. de la criacion del mundo. [1636.] 12°.

147. M. Ben Israel Rettung der Juden, aus dem Englischen übersetzt. Nebst einer Vorrede von M. Mendelssohn, &c Berlin und Stettin, 1782. 8°.

148. Gegen die Verleumder! Eine Stimme aus dem 17. Jahrhundert. Rabbi M. Ben Israel "Rettung den Juden" ... übersetz [from the Hebrew] von M. Mendelssohn. Bamberg, 1882, &c. 8°.

149. אבן יקרה Piedra gloriosa o de la Estatu de Nebuchadnesar, &c. Amsterdam, 5415 [1655]. 12°.

150. Thesouro dos Dinim que o povo de Israel, he obrigado saber, e observar, 5 pts. [Amsterdam] 5405–7 [1645–47]. 8°.

151. To His Highnesse the Lord Protector of the Commonwealth of England, Scotland, and Ireland, the humble addresses of M. Ben I ... in behalfe of the Jewish Nation. [London, 1655]. 4°.

152. To his Highnesse the Lord Protector, etc. [Edited, with an Introduction, by A. F. O.]. Reprinted, Melbourne, 1868. 4°.

153. Vindiciæ Judæorum, or a letter ... touching the reproaches cast on the nation of the Jewes ... &c. [London, May 15.] 1656. 4°.

154. Obrona Izraelitów przez Rabbi Manasse ben Izrael, ... [translated into Polish] w przez J. Tugendholda. w Warszawie, 1831. 12°.

155. Bijdrage tot de Levengeschiedenis van M. Ben I. [s'Gravenhage? 1858.] 12°.

c.—ACTS AND DOCUMENTS RELATING TO THE POLITICAL HISTORY OF THE JEWS.

156. An apology for the honorable nation of the Jews, and for all the Sons of Israel. Written by Edward Nicholas. London, 1648. 4°.

157. A narrative of the late proceeds at White-Hall concerning Jews: who had desired by R. Manasses an agent for them : that they might return into England. [By Hen. Jesse.] London, 1656. 4°.

158. Anglo-Judaeus, or the history of the Jews whilst here in England .... caused by a book written to the Lord Protector by Menasseh ben Israel by W. H. London, 1556.

159. Petition from the Jews of London to the House of Commons against a clause in the Act for preventing frauds and regulating abuses in the Plantation-Trade against alien merchants and factors. [1696.] s. sh. fol.

160. The Case of Mr. Anthony da Costa with the Russia Company. 1727. s. sh. fol. A claim for admission to the Company, which was refused on the ground of his being a Jew.

161. An Act for naturalizing such foreign Protestants and others therein mentioned [including Jews] as are settled or shall settle in any of His Majesty's colonies in America. [1740.] 13 Geo. II. c. 7.

162. An Act to permit persons professing the Jewish religion to be naturalized by Parliament, &c. 26 Geo. II. c. 26. [1753.]

163. Volume of Tracts relating to the Naturalisation Bill of 1753. Including " The Prancing Jew, or Solomon catch'd in a Bridle," also " Esther sent to King Ahasuerus on behalf of the Jews."

164. The Popular Clamour against the Jews indefensible. A Sermon preached at Huntingdon, Oct. 28th, 1753, by P. Peckard.

165. An Act to repeal an Act of the Twenty-sixth year of His Majesty's reign, intituled, An Act to permit persons professing the Jewish religion to be naturalized by Parliament, &c. 27 Geo. II. c. 1. [1753.]

166. Copy of a letter from the Right Honourable Lord George Gordon to E. Lindo, Esq., and the Portuguese; and Nathan Salomon, Esq., and the German Jews. [Against the English Ministry.] London, 1783. fol.

167. House of Commons.—Debates. Debates in the House of Commons on a resolution preparatory to the introduction, and in the House of Lords of the motion for the second reading, of the Bill for removing the Civil Disabilities of the Jews, &c. London, 1834. 8°.

168. An Act for the Relief of persons of the Jewish Religion elected to Municipal Office. 8 & 9 Vict. cap. 52. [1845.]

169. An Act to substitute one oath for the oaths of allegiance, supremacy and abjuration, and for the relief of Her Majesty's subjects professing the Jewish Religion. 21 & 22 Vict. cap. 48. [1858.]

170. An Act to amend the Act of the Twenty-first and Twenty-second years of Victoria, Chapter Forty-nine, to provide for the Relief of Her Majesty's subjects professing the Jewish Religion. 23 & 24 Vict. cap. 63. 1860.

d.—INTERESTING CONTRIBUTIONS TO ENGLISH LITERATURE BY EARLY ENGLISH JEWS MOSTLY OUTSIDE THEOLOGY.

171. Abraham Aben Hassan, the Levite. Præcepta in Monte Sinai data Judæis sunt 613, ... collecta per ... Abrahamum filium Kattani ... translata in linguam Latinam per Philippum Ferdinandum Polonum. Cantabrigiæ, 1597. 4°.
P. Ferdinandus was a converted Jew, teacher of Hebrew at Cambridge.

172. Ferdinandus Mendez. Stadium Apollinare sive Progymnasmata Medica, &c., Lugduni, 1668. 4°.
Mendez was Court physician to Queen Catharine of Braganza.

173. A relation of the most memorable thinges in the Tabernacle of Moses and the Temple of Salomon, according to text of Scripture. By Jacob Jehudah Leon [or Aryeh]. Amsterdam, 1675. 4°. The writer exhibited his model of the Temple before Charles II.

174. Pascalogia overo discorso della Pasca, in cui si assegnano le ragioni delle discrepanze vertenti, circa il tempo di celebrar la Pasca, trà la Chiesa Latina, Greca, *etc.* Da David Nieto. Colonia, 1702. 12°.

175. Volume of Spanish Tracts, written by Jews in England about 1704. Chiefly with reference to the orthodoxy of D. Nieto.

175*a.* Catalogue of 216 Hebrew books, presented to the British Museum by S. da Costa. (*See* Nos. 216, 241, 244.)

176. Do uso e abusa das minhas agoas de Inglaterra, *etc.* Pello inventor das mesmas agoas, J. de Castro Sarmento. Londres, 1756. 8°.

177. Mendes da Costa (Emanuel). A natural history of Fossils. Vol. I. pt. 1. London, 1757. 4°.

178. Lyons (Israel). A treatise of Fluxions. London, 1758. 8°.

178*a.* Mendez (Moses). The Double Disappointment ; a farce, etc. London, 1760. 8°.

179. Lyons (Israel). Fasciculus Plantarum circa Cantabrigiam nascentium, quæ post Rajum observatæ fuere. Londini, 1763. 8°.

179*a.* Nieto (Isaac). A sermon preached in the Synagogue on Friday, February 6, 1756; Being the day appointed for a general Fast, etc. London, 1756. 4°.

181. Mendes da Costa (Emanuel). Elements of Conchology ; or, an introduction to the knowledge of Shells. London, 1796.

182. Mendes da Costa (Emanuel). Historia Naturalis Testaceorum Britanniæ, or the British Conchology. Engl. & Fr. London, 1778. 4⁰.

184. Curiosities of Literature, by Isaac D'Israeli. London, 1791. First edition of this well-known work.

185. An authentic account of the late expedition to Bulam on the Coast of Africa, &c. By J. Montefiore. London, 1794. 8⁰.

186. Disraeli (Isaac). Romances. London, 1799. 8⁰.

187. Goldsmith (Lewis). The Crimes of Cabinets; or a review of their plans and aggressions for the annihilation of the liberties of France, &c. London, 1801. 8⁰.

188. Vallentine (Nathan Isaac). משברי ים The discourse of the three sisters, respecting the fall and murder of Admiral Nelson, &c. London, 1806. 8⁰.

189. Lyon (Emma). Miscellaneous poems. Oxford, 1812. 8⁰.

190. Gompertz (J.) The Modern Antique: or the Muse in the Costume of Queen Anne. London, 1813. 8⁰.

191. Memoirs of the life of Daniel Mendoza [the Jewish pugilist]. London, 1816. 8⁰.

191a. On the Principles of Political Economy and Taxation; by David Ricardo. London, 1817.

193. Hurwitz (Hyman) קינת ישרון A Hebrew Dirge, chaunted in the Great Synagogue on the Day of the funeral of the Princess Charlotte, &c. London, 1817. 8⁰.

194. Hurwitz (Hyman). The Knell, an elegy on George the Third. From the Hebrew of H. Hurwitz by the Rev. W. Smith. With the Hebrew in English characters. Thurso, 1827. 8⁰.

195. Gompertz (Lewis). Moral Inquiries on the situation of Man and Brutes. London, 1824. 8⁰.
    The founder of the Animals' Friend Society.

196. Isaacs (Nathaniel). Travels and adventures in Eastern Africa, descriptive of the Zoolus, their manners, customs, etc. 2 vols. London, 1836. 8⁰.

198. Blumenfeld (J. C.). The New Ecce Homo, at issue with King and Priest; or, the Self-redemption of Man, etc. London, 1839. 8⁰.

e.—JEWISH MUSIC.

201. Baer (A.) Baal t'fillah, oder der Practische Vorbeter. Vollständige Sammlung der gottesdienstlichen Gesänge und Recitative der Israeliten nach polnischen, deutschen (asch-k'nasischen) und portugiesischen (sephardischen) Weisen, *etc.* Zweite Auflage. Frankfurt a. M., 1883. fol.

202. Biblia Hebraica, cum notis Hebraicis . . . ex recensione Danielis Ernesti Jablonski. Berolini, 1699. 4°.

At fol. e 2, of the Introduction, is the earliest transcription of the Spanish Jews' Version of the Cantillation of the Law, written by Dr. David Pinna, of Amsterdam.

203 Braham (T.) and Nathan (T.). A Selection of Hebrew Melodies, Ancient and Modern ... the poetry by Lord Byron. London, 1815. fol.

203a. Hamerik (A.). Jüdische Trilogie, für Orchester. Op. 19. [Full Score.] Leipzig, 1869. 8°.

204. Karpenko (D.) Васильковскій Соловей Кіевской Украины ... Альбомъ ... составленный изъ 115 Малороссійскихъ ... пѣсенъ ... съ присовокупленіемъ Малороссійсскихъ и Еврейскихъ танцевъ. St. Petersburg, 1864. fol.

On p. 169 is a Russo-Jewish Dance-tune.

205. Kircher (A.) Musurgia Universalis. Romae, 1650. fol.

p. 67 of Tom. I. contains the cantillation for the Pentateuch.

206. Marcello (B.) The first fifty Psalms set to Music...adapted to English words by John Garth. Vols. II. and IV. London, 1757. fol.

207. Margoliouth (M.) Sacred Minstrelsy: a Lecture on Biblical and Post-Biblical Hebrew Music. 2nd ed. London, 1863. 8°.

On p. 34 is an example of the midnight songs.

208. Nathan (I.) An Essay on the History and Theory of Music, &c. London, 1823. 4°.

pp. 45 and 46 contain specimens of Anglo-Jewish Music.

209. Naumbourg (S.) זמירת ישראל Chants religieux des Israélites, contenant la Liturgie complète de la Synagogue, des temps les plus reculés jusqu'à nos jours. Paris, 1847. fol.

210. Offenbach (J.) Hagadah, oder Erzählung von Israels Auszug aus Egypten ... Neu bearbeitet ... mit Musik-Beilagen der alten, durch Tradition auf uns gekommenen und einigen neu komponirten Melodien. Cöln, 1838. 8°.

211. Reuchlin (J.). De Accentibus et orthographia Linguae Hebraicae. Hagenoæ, 1517. 8°.

At the end of Book III. is the earliest known printed transcription of Jewish music, comprising the accents for the ordinary cantillation of the Pentateuch, according to the German Jews, harmonized for four voices, by Christophorus Sillingus.

212. Rittangel (J. S.) Liber Rituum Paschalium, mit was für Ceremonien und Gebräuchen die Juden das Osterlamb gegessen haben. Regiomonti, 1644. 4°.

On fol. R. 3 is the old form of hymns still thus sung at table on the first evenings of the Passover festival.

213. Solomon meha Adumim (Salomo de' Rossi), קוינטו השירים אשר לשלמה. 1623.

    The earliest known Hebrew music by a trained musician.

214. Speidel (J. C.) Unverwerffliche Spuren von der Alten Davidischen Sing-Kunst ... mit e nem exempel zur Prob, &c. Stuttgardt, 1740. 4º.

215. Vecchi (O.) L'Amfiparnaso, Comedia Harmonica. Venetia, 1597. 4º.

    In Act III. is a chorus of Jews.

*f.—*HEBREW BOOKS.

216. Abraham ben Judah Almalic. לקוטי שכחה ופאה [Explanations of Talmudical passages.] Ferrara, 1566. 4º. One of the Collection presented by S. Da Costa, in the original binding as ordered for Charles II., and as described by Da C. in his catalogue.

217. Amadis de Gaula. The 1st book, translated into Hebrew by Jacob ben Moses de Algaba. Printed by E. Soncino. Constantinople, 1540. 4º.

218. Amsterdam. German Jews' Congregation. Rules of Benevolent Society. On vellum. Amsterdam, 1776. 8º.

219. Bible. Biblia, etc. On vellum. Christ. Plantin: Antverpiæ, 1569–72. fol. This copy has at the beginning a printed leaf dated 1571, showing that it was presented by B. Arias Montanus at the command of Philip II., King of Spain, to the Duke of Alva, in recognition of his services in the Netherlands.

220. Bible. Biblia sacra, &c. [Known commonly as " Walton's Polyglott Bible."] Londini, 1657. fol.

221. Bible.—Old Testament. Joshua, Psalms, Proverbs, Job, Daniel, Ezra, Nehemiah and Chronicles, accompanied by a Latin Translation in MS. The greater part of it apparently in the handwriting of Thomas Cranmer, Archbishop of Canterbury. Ed. Prin. Soncino, 1488. fol.

222. Bible.—Old Testament. The first Biblia Rabbinica, &c. Printed by D. Bomberg: Venice, 1517. fol.

223. Bible.—Old Testament. תנ"ך [Crimean Turkish, or Tatar printed in Hebrew characters.] Eupatoria, 1841. 4º.

224. Bible.—Pentateuch. On vellum. Fara, 1487. fol.

225. Bible.—Pentateuch. Constantinople, 1516. 16º. Unique.

226 Bible.—Pentateuch. Facsimiles of the Hebrew manuscripts obtained at the Synagogue in K'Ae-Fung-Foo. Shanghae, 1851. 4º

227. Bible.—Prophets. Former prophets and later Prophets, with the commentary of David Kimchi. Ed. Pr. Soncino, 1485? fol.

228. Bible.—Psalms. De Rossi, Ann. Sec. xv. p. 14. "Primi Sacri Textus editio." Bologna? 1477. fol.

230. Daily Prayers. Roman Rite. On vellum. Soncino. 1486. 8°.

231. Daily Prayers. Roman Rite. On vellum. Thalmai or Ptolomei: Bologna, 1537. 8°.

232. Festival Prayers. Roman Rite. מחזור On vellum. Ed. Pr. Soncinati; Soncino, &c. 1485. 8°.

233. Festival Prayers. מחזור On vellum. Augsburg, 1536. 4°.

234. Ḥusain (Abū 'Alī) called Ibn Sīnā, or more commonly Avicenna. Avicenna's Great Canon of Medicine, with Hebrew corrections in MS. by W. Heidenheim. Printed by Azriel ben Joseph: Naples, 1491–92. fol.

236. Jacob ben Asher. Jacob ben Asher's Code. [ארבעה טורים] Ed. Pr. Printed by Meshullam Kozi Pieve di Sacco. 1475. fol. The second or perhaps the first Hebrew book printed.

237. Jacob ben Asher. Jacob ben Asher's Code. [ארבעה טורים] Mantua and Ferrara, 1476–79. fol.

238. Joseph ben Gorion. History. Ed. Pr. Conath: Mantua, 1480? fol.

239. Joseph ben Gorion. [Josippon.] The wonderful and most deplorable history of the latter times of the Jews, etc. London, 1652. 8°. The following words are impressed in gold on the cover: "The Gift of George III."

240. Joseph ben Gorion. Josippon. Calcutta, 1841. 4°. Presented to the British Museum by Sir D. Sassoon.

241. Joseph Nasi, Duke of Naxos. בן פרת יוסף Constantinople, 1577. 4°. In the original binding as ordered for Charles II., and as described by S. Da Costa in his catalogue.

242. Isaac ben Joseph Caro. תולדות יצחק Mantua, 1558. fol. One of the collections presented by S. Da Costa, by the original binding as ordered to be bound for Charles II., and as described by Da Costa in his catalogue.

243. Isaac ben Solomon Sahula. משל הקדמוני [Fables.] Ed. Princ. G. Soncino Brescia? 1491? 4°. The only complete copy known.

244. Judah ben Abraham Zarko. ספר לחם ודה Constantinople 1560. 4°. No other copy known. In the original binding as ordered for Charles II., and as described by S. Da Costa.

245. Levi ben Gershon. Commentary on Job. Abraham b. Chayim de' Tintori. Ferrara, 1477. 4º.

245a. Mishnah on vellum. Riva di Trento, 1559. fol.

246. Mishnah. Two vols., bound in three parts. Either edited or corrected by Manasseh Ben Israel. Amsterdam, 1644.

247. Mishnah.—Pirke Aboth. The Ethics, with commentary by Moses ben Maimon. With the introduction, translated by Samuel ben Judah Aben Thibbon. Soncino, 1484. 4º.

248. Moses ben Maimon. More Nebuchim [Guide of the perplexed]. About 1480. fol.

249. Moses ben Maimon. Code [משנה תורה]. Ed. Pr. [Printed in Italy before 1480.] fol.

250. Moses ben Maimon. Tractatus de regimine Santitatis, &c. Printed in the convent of " S. Jacobus de Ripolis," at Florence, 1477. Extremely rare. 4º.

251. Moses ben Nachman. Nachmanides' Commentary on the Pentateuch. Ed. Princ. *circa* 1480. fol.

252. Nathan ben Jehiel. הערוך Talmudical Dictionary. Ed. Pr. About 1480. fol.

253. Samuel ben Isaac Yafeh. יפה עינים [Sermons.] Venice, 1631. fol. One of the collection presented by S. da Costa in the original binding as ordered for Charles II. and as described by Da C. in his catalogue.

254. Shem Tob, Ben Shem Tob. Sermons. Salonica, 1525. fol. Unique.

255. Talmud. The first complete edition ever printed. [Daniel Bomberg, Venice, 1520–23.] fol.

256. Talmud. Vienna, 1860-72. fol.

257. Talmud-betsah מסכת יום טוב Printed by Joshua Solomon. Soncino, 1483. fol.

258. Talmud of Jerusalem. Venice, 1523. fol. Ed. Princ.

REPORT

Members of the General Committee

OF THE

ANGLO-JEWISH HISTORICAL EXHIBITION.

———•———

GENTLEMEN,

We submit herewith a report of the work connected with the Anglo-Jewish Historical Exhibition dealing with the history of the movement itself, and summarising its results. It is, perhaps, needless to observe that, while every effort was made to ensure economy, there was from the beginning no hope of making the Exhibition a lucrative undertaking, and very little expectation of its meeting its expenses. Exhibitions which chiefly subserve antiquarian or scientific interests cannot be expected to pay their way, and any subventions they need must be regarded as aiding the spread of historical or scientific knowledge.

In the present instance it was desired on the part of the promoters of the Exhibition to revive, we might almost say to create, interest in the history of the Jewish race in England. The extent of the materials was unknown, the sources whence they could be derived awaited investigation, and, generally speaking, the aids to a scientific and impartial study of Anglo-Jewish history, especially in its earlier and more romantic phases, were beyond the reach either of the ordinary reader or the special student. The Exhibition was designed to alter this state of things, and it will be seen in the sequel how successful have been the efforts of the various Committees in bringing to light what was hitherto unknown, and arranging systematically the information that was already before the world. Besides the main objects of the Exhibition, a subsidiary one soon presented itself in the collection of interesting articles of Jewish ecclesiastical art, which formed one of the main attractions of the Exhibition, and added the charm of artistic beauty, which could not be secured by the display of objects interesting only for their historical associations.

The means by which these aims were secured may now be briefly recounted. The idea of holding the Exhibition originated with Mr. I. Spielman, who, from its inception to its end, was the leading spirit of the undertaking, at which he worked with indefatigable energy. He consulted several gentlemen who were likely to promote it by their influence or their special knowledge, most of whom consented to lend their hearty

P

co-operation. Mr. F. D. Mocatta undertook the Presidentship of the proposed Exhibition, and the Rev. Morris Joseph and Mr. Spielman acted as joint Honorary Secretaries, and a preliminary meeting was held at Mr. Mocatta's house on Sunday, May 16th, 1886.

The meeting expressed a lively sympathy with the objects of the Exhibition, and it was decided that an influential Committee should be formed to give practical effect to the movement. Accordingly the leading members of the Jewish community, and many important personages in the kingdom, were asked to promote the undertaking by their interest and influence. Among them were included many dignitaries of the Church, the Presidents of the Society of Antiquaries, the Archæological Institute, the Anthropological Institute, the Palestine Exploration Fund, of the Society of Biblical Archæology, and the Royal Historical Society. Dr. John Evans, P.S.A., kindly consented to take the post of Vice-Chairman, Mr. C. Trice Martin, F.S.A., was good enough to act as Chairman of the Literary and Art Sub-Committee, to the deliberations of which he contributed most valuable assistance, and Mr. J. N. Castello rendered most efficient services as Treasurer. On the many legal points which arose during the course of the Exhibition, Mr. H. Montagu was kind enough to advise as Honorary Solicitor.

The Committee having been formed, a selection was made from it to constitute the Executive Committee, who decided on holding the Exhibition at the Royal Albert Hall. This Committee also determined the classes of objects which would be acceptable. (See Appendix A.) Circulars were addressed to all persons or bodies likely to possess such objects, the Presidents and Secretaries of the Provincial Jewish congregations, all the members of the Metropolitan Synagogues, the Mayors and Corporations throughout the kingdom, as well as the leading members of the principal literary and scientific societies. Correspondence was also entered into with many centres abroad where valuable objects were known to exist. As a result a large number of suggestions and offers were sent in on the forms issued for that purpose. These were carefully considered, and a final selection from them was made by the Literary and Art Sub-Committee, which did good work by suggesting further lines of inquiry as well as by imitating new spheres of activity.

Mr. Joseph Jacobs, B.A., kindly undertook the important office of Honorary Secretary of the Literary and Art Sub-Committee, and for the very arduous duties which this involved from the commencement till the finish of the Exhibition, and for the able and generous manner in which those duties were fulfilled, the Executive Committee tender him their sincere thanks. The Committee wish to record their appreciation also of the kind services rendered by Mr. Lucien Wolf, and to both gentlemen for the Catalogue which they so successfully compiled.

About six weeks previous to the date announced for the opening of the Exhibition, circulars were issued to those who had been kind enough to offer exhibits, giving a list of the objects selected by the Sub-Committee, and fixing the day when they would be called for. The collection was made in due course, and without any hitch the exhibits arrived at the

Albert Hall. Here they were submitted to a further process of elimination by a small Committee of experts. This was rendered necessary by want of space, the three crush-rooms (each 60 feet by 20 feet) which had first been hired, and a fourth room subsequently engaged, proving utterly inadequate to contain the very numerous exhibits, so that many had necessarily to be excluded. Suitable glass cases and other receptacles were erected in these rooms, and the work of arrangement occupied the attention of a small number of gentlemen who worked assiduously to get the exhibits arranged in good time, so that everything, without exception, was in its place by the date previously fixed for the opening. Mr. B. S. Marks kindly undertook to arrange the pictures; Mr. H. Montagu, F.S.A., the coins; Messrs. Chas. Davis and W. Chaffers, F.S.A., the works of art; Rev. F. L. Cohen, the music; Mr. M. D. Davis, the Hebrew documents; and Mr. Lucien Wolf, the engravings; and the Committee tender them their best thanks for their valuable services.

Besides the large number of exhibits collected at the Albert Hall, there exist many others in the public institutions of the Metropolis which illustrate Anglo-Jewish History or Jewish Ecclesiastical Art, but these could not be shown at the Albert Hall owing to the stringent conditions which prevent the authorities at the British Museum, the Record Office, and South Kensington Museum from letting any of their treasures pass beyond their immediate control. The Committee felt it eminently desirable that the many objects of Jewish interest at these institutions should be exhibited concurrently with this Exhibition, and they were enabled to effect this owing to the ready kindness with which their suggestion was met by the authorities in each case. Mr. Bond, the Principal Librarian of the British Museum, and Mr. H. M. Lyte, Deputy-keeper of the Public Records, gave every facility in their power for selecting and arranging the charters, deeds, books and prints at the one institution, and the extremely valuable and interesting records at the other. In the work of arrangement at the British Museum, Mr. E. Maunde Thompson gave effectual assistance, while at the Record Office, Mr. C. Trice Martin arranged and catalogued the most interesting of the large number of records preserved at the Rolls House.

All the exhibits, as they were received, were described by Messrs. J. Jacobs and L. Wolf, who then arranged the descriptions according to subjects, prefixed general introductions, and were enabled to have the Catalogue ready by the day of opening. It was intended that the Catalogue should contain a list of all the objects which illustrate Anglo-Jewish History or Jewish Ecclesiastical Art in this country, and considering the shortness of time at the disposal of the compilers, the aim has been most creditably accomplished, and the Catalogue will remain of permanent value for the historical student and for all interested in the Jews of England. The Catalogue in itself forms no unimportant contribution towards the ends which the Exhibition was intended to promote.

Rooms, exhibits, and Catalogue were ready for the date originally appointed for the opening of the Exhibition, Monday, April 4th. The President, Mr. F. D. Mocatta, desired to give special distinction to its opening, and for that purpose invited on the preceding Saturday a large number of those likely to be interested to a *soirée* in the Albert Hall, during which the Exhibition rooms were thrown open for inspection. The gathering was a brilliant one and achieved its purpose of in-augurating the Exhibition, over 1,250 visitors being present.

The contents of the Exhibition rooms will be sufficiently remembered without any long recital. But reference may be made to the chief collections that formed the attractions of the display. Among the historic records of the pre-expulsion period, the bronze Ewer, lent by the Curators of the Bodleian library, still remains the puzzle of antiquaries. The unique collection of deeds from Westminster Abbey contained a large number of *Shetaroth*, or Hebrew contracts, perhaps the earliest of their kind in existence. The gallery of portraits, the many relics of recent Jewish celebrities, and the Synagogue archives, illustrated the more modern history of the Jews, as did also a large collection of rare works throwing light on the subject, which were frequently consulted by the visitors. Reference, too, may be made to the Newman collection of engravings illustrating all sides of Anglo-Jewish life during the past century. The curious and interesting exhibits sent from India by Messrs. J. Ezekiel and S. Solomon, threw considerable light on the history of the Beni Israel community. In the region of Ecclesiastical Art, the Committee were fortunate enough to obtain the collections of M. Strauss, of Paris, and of Mr. R. D. Sassoon, of London, the most important of their kind in existence, and these were supplemented by the more modern examples lent by the chief Synagogues and many private individuals. In the department of Antiquities there were the objects lent by the Palestine Exploration Fund, the elaborate model of the Temple, designed by Mr. T. Newbury, and the collection of ancient Jewish coins, the largest and one of the most interesting ever brought together. The collections of rare MSS. lent by Lord Crawford and Sir Julian Goldsmid also deserve notice. Mr. J. Sebag-Montefiore was good enough to place at the disposal of the Committee the heirlooms of the late Sir Moses Montefiore. The Exhibition was thus sufficiently diversified in its contents to attract visitors of various tastes who might become acquainted with its existence and attractions. The thanks of the Committee are due to the above-mentioned gentlemen and to the Exhibitors in general, for their kindness in lending such valuable and interesting articles. It is needless to add that all the objects lent were insured against loss or damage, and were ultimately returned without injury.

Various other means were taken to make the Exhibition known, though it was impossible to spend as much money on this as would, perhaps, have been desirable if it had been merely a commercial undertaking. The notices in the press were uniformly favourable, and brought the existence of the Exhibition to the knowledge of all those likely to be interested. Altogether, during the twelve weeks the exhibits were on view, they were inspected by upwards of twelve thousand visitors. Large numbers of clergymen of all denominations, testifying to the general interest felt in Jewish matters, visited the Exhibition. Throughout, the

Exhibition was open on Saturdays, and during the month of June entrance was free on those days, so as to render the Exhibition accessible to those Jewish visitors who were only disengaged on their Sabbath. Catalogues were also provided for these visitors by the kindness of some friends of the movement, who purchased a sufficient number for presentation. This course of action may have caused some slight pecuniary loss to the Exhibition, but it contributed greatly in spreading its influence over as large a field as possible.

Mr. Frank Haes, one of the Executive Committee, was unremitting in rendering every possible assistance; he was constant in his attendance, and ever ready to give information. The Committee tender him their best thanks for his exertions, which contributed so greatly to the success of the undertaking. Dr. Friedlander also gave great help in literary matters, and Mr. A. I. Myers assisted the Committee in all matters requiring business skill. Thanks are also due to Mr. A. Weil, who kindly volunteered to give organ recitals of Jewish music during the afternoons. Mr. P. Ornstein gave efficient assistance as assistant secretary, and Mr. Phillips also performed the various duties entrusted to him in a most efficient manner.

The educational objects of the Exhibition were not lost sight of during its progress. By the kindness of several friends of the movement, children from most of the Jewish Schools of London were enabled to visit the Exhibition and become acquainted with the chief records of the history of their race in this country. It had also been determined from the first to hold conferences during the Exhibition, at which Papers bearing on Anglo-Jewish history might be read by competent scholars. The Committee were fortunate enough to secure the services of a number of gentlemen fully capable of expounding what was known and of revealing much that was unknown of Anglo-Jewish history. The interest taken in the Exhibition was widespread enough to induce Prof. Graetz, of Breslau, the most illustrious of living Jewish scholars, to pay a visit to this country and honour the Exhibition with a discourse which was delivered before a brilliant audience on June 16th. Lectures were delivered successively as follows :—

1. May 5th. JOSEPH JACOBS, ESQ., B.A.
   " The London Jewry, 1290."

2. May 12th. LUCIEN WOLF, ESQ.
   " The Middle Age of Anglo-Jewish History, 1290—1656."

3. May 16th. REV. FRANCIS L. COHEN.
   " Rise and Development of Synagogue Music" (with Musical Illustrations).

4. May 26th. WALTER RYE, ESQ.
   " The Persecution of the Jews."

5. June 2nd. REV. A. LOWY.
   " Hebrew Literature in England."

6. June 9th. DR. C. GROSS.
   " The Exchequer of the Jews of England in the Middle Ages."

7. June 16th. DR. GRAETZ.
     "Historic Parallels in Anglo-Jewish History."

8. June 23rd. REV. DR. GASTER.
     "Jewish Sources of the Arthur and Merlin Legends."

9. June 30th. REV. DR. H. ADLER, Delegate Chief Rabbi.
     "The Chief Rabbis of England."

Special mention should be made of the paper on the " Exchequer of the Jews," by Dr. Gross, which was a contribution not only to Anglo-Jewish, but to English history, and of the paper by Mr. Walter Rye, who undertook to detail the persecutions of the Jews in Early England, a subject which unfortunately fills so large a space in pre-expulsion annals. A choral and instrumental recital, in illustration of Jewish music, was organised by the Rev. F. L. Cohen and proved a great success, towards which the singing of Mrs. F. L. Cohen and Miss Albu and the choir of the West London Synagogue as well as the organ accompaniment of Dr. Verrinde1 largely contributed. So successful was the recital, that a repetition before a larger audience at Princes' Hall was arranged for at the close of the Exhibition, but had, unfortunately, to be abandoned in consequence of the lamented death of Sir Barrow H. Ellis and Mr. L. L. Cohen, M.P., both members of the Committee.

It will be seen that even during the progress of the Exhibition much was done to promote the objects for which it had been instituted—to ascertain the materials for Anglo-Jewish history and to promote a knowledge of it. The Exhibition and its catalogue did much for the former object; the conferences promoted the latter aim. The Committee desired that these results should not cease with the Exhibition, and arrangements were early made for printing the Papers read at the Conferences. In addition to this, Messrs. Joseph Jacobs and Lucien Wolf, the compilers of the catalogue, have been good enough to prepare a bibliography of Anglo-Jewish history, detailing the printed materials and indicating the manuscript sources available for the history of the Jews in England. Among these manuscript materials the most important were undoubtedly the Hebrew *Shetaroth* preserved at Westminster Abbey and at various public institutions : they are among the earliest deeds of the kind of any European Jews, and throw a curious side-light on English history. As they had been copied and studied by Mr. M. D. Davis, the Committee commissioned that gentleman to prepare them for publication with English abstracts, thus making them available to English antiquaries and historians. These three volumes—the Exhibition Papers, the *Shetaroth*, and the Bibliography—are now ready for publication, and will form, when published, a valuable addition to our knowledge of Anglo-Jewish history. By the issue of these volumes and of the catalogue, to which previous reference has been made, the Committee may claim to have done all that was possible for organised effect towards the accomplishment of the two main objects of the Exhibition. The rest must be left to individual research, the ground for which has been paved by the general interest in Anglo-Jewish history aroused by the Exhibition.

Another result emanating from the movement may be referred to in conclusion. The display of so many articles in which artistic skill had been applied to objects connected with Jewish ceremonies cannot fail to have raised the taste for the beautifying of Jewish domestic worship. A permanent record of the most beautiful of these objects, and of the most important of the historical exhibits, has been made in the form of an illustrated edition of the catalogue prepared by the kindness of Mr. F. Haes. Owing to the general interest in these matters produced by the movement, sufficient subscribers' names have been received to enable all the above works to be produced at practically small cost to the Committee It may therefore be fairly hoped that the Exhibition has accomplished the purpose for which it was designed—the promotion of Anglo-Jewish history; and has, in addition, furthered another subsidiary aim—the advancement of Jewish ecclesiastical art. These have been the results of the Anglo-Jewish Historical Exhibition, of which the Committee have here offered a short record.

Signed on behalf of the Committee,

F. D. MOCATTA, *President.*

September 29th, 1887.

APPENDIX A.

OBJECTS ADMISSIBLE FOR EXHIBITION.

CLASS I.—HISTORIC RELICS.

A. Relics and Records (or Photographs and Descriptions of them) of the Pre-Expulsion Period.
B. Title-deeds of Earliest Land and Property holders; Charters and Shetaroth.
C. Historical Records.
D. MSS.—General; Synagogue Archives.
E. Letters and Autographs of Distinguished Persons.
F. Lists and Mementoes of Jews celebrated in Anglo-Jewish History.
G. Records of Jews (not now living) who have received Honours in the British Empire.

CLASS II.—PORTRAITS AND PRINTS.

H. Portraits and Prints of Anglo-Jewish Rabbis, &c.
I.   ,,   ,,   of Members of Representative Jewish Families.
J.   ,,   ,,   of distinguished Foreign Jews temporarily visiting England.
K. Pictures illustrating Jewish Family Life, Ceremonies, &c.
L. Photographs, &c., of Ancient Anglo-Jewish Graves.
M. Pictures, Photographs, Models and Drawings of Places of Interest in Anglo-Jewish History, Ancient and Modern.
N. Pictures, Prints, &c.

CLASS III.—BOOKS, &c.

O. Mementoes of Jewish Rabbis and Teachers, Ancient and Modern.
P. Pamphlets and Books bearing upon Anglo-Jewish History; Jewish Works written in England; Periodicals; Illuminated and other Curious Books, &c.
Q. Map of United Kingdom, indicating Congregations past and present.
R. Map of British Empire, showing distribution of Jewish Population.
S. History of Jewish Congregations of the British Empire.

CLASS IV.—ECCLESIASTICAL ART.

T. Scrolls of the Law, Megilloth, Mezuzoth, &c.
U. Embroideries, Curtains, Vestments, Bells, Sabbath and Hanuca Lamps, Cups, Pointers, Passover Requisites, Plate, &c., for Synagogue Use and Domestic Rites.
V. Jewish Seals, Medals, Tokens, Rings, Coins, &c.
W. Ancient and Modern Hebrew Music.

LONDON: PRINTED BY WM. CLOWES AND SONS, LIMITED, STAMFORD STREET AND CHARING CROSS.

For EU product safety concerns, contact us at Calle de José Abascal, 56–1°, 28003 Madrid, Spain or eugpsr@cambridge.org.

www.ingramcontent.com/pod-product-compliance
Ingram Content Group UK Ltd.
Pitfield, Milton Keynes, MK11 3LW, UK
UKHW030859150625
459647UK00021B/2722